My Way

My Way

Speeches
and
Poems

Charles Bernstein

The University of Chicago Press

Chicago & London

CHARLES BERNSTEIN is David Gray Professor of Poetry and
Letters at the State University of New York, Buffalo. He is the
author of two collections of essays, *Content's Dream* and *A Poet-
ics*, and twenty books of poetry, including *Dark City, Rough
Trades* and, with Susan Bee, *Log Rhythms*.

The University of Chicago Press, Chicago 60637
The University of Chicago Press, Ltd., London
© 1999 by Charles Bernstein
All rights reserved. Published 1999
08 07 06 05 04 03 02 01 00 99   1 2 3 4 5

ISBN: 0-226-04409-2 (cloth)
ISBN: 0-226-04410-6 (paper)

Library of Congress Cataloging-in-Publication Data

Bernstein, Charles, 1950–
    My way: speeches and poems / Charles Bernstein.
        p. cm.
        ISBN 0-226-04409-2 (alk. paper). —ISBN 0-226-04410-6
    (pbk. : alk. paper)
        1. Bernstein, Charles, 1950– —Aesthetics. 2. Poetics.
    I. Title.
    PS3552.E7327M9 1999
    818'.5408—dc21   98-30345
                                                           CIP

♾ The paper used in this publication meets the minimum re-
quirements of the American National Standard for Informa-
tion Sciences—Permanence of Paper for Printed Library Ma-
terials, ANSI Z39.48-1992.

for Felix

I come to guard the city *in that* somewhere I am
uttered.

Cantares Mexicanas, tr. John Bierhorst

"And what is the use of a book," thought Alice,
"without pictures or conversations?"

Lewis Carroll

Contents

xi   Preface

1   A Defense of Poetry

3   The Revenge of the Poet-Critic, or The Parts Are Greater Than the Sum of the Whole

18   Thelonious Monk and the Performance of Poetry

25   An Interview with Manuel Brito

33   Solidarity Is the Name We Give to What We Cannot Hold

36   What's Art Got to Do with It?: The Status of the Subject of the Humanities in an Age of Cultural Studies

52   A Test of Poetry

56   The Book as Architecture

58   Dear Mr. Fanelli

63   An Interview with Hannah Möckel-Rieke

73   I Don't Take Voice Mail: The Object of Art in the Age of Electronic Technology

81   Weak Links (on Hannah Weiner)

83   Claire-in-the-Building

86   Again Eigner

90   Frame Lock

100   "Passed by Examination": Paragraphs for Susan Howe

104   The Value of *Sulfur*

108   Shaker Show

109   Gertrude and Ludwig's Bogus Adventure

110   Introjective Verse

113   Poetics of the Americas

138   Unzip Bleed

140   Lachrymose Encaustic / Abrasive Tear

141   Stein's Identity

145   Provisional Institutions: Alternative Presses and
       Poetic Innovation

155   Pound and the Poetry of Today   √

166   Inappropriate Touching

168   Robin on His Own (on Robin Blaser)

175   Water Images of *The New Yorker*

178   The Response as Such: Words in Visibility

186   From an Ongoing Interview with Tom Beckett

191   Explicit Version Number Required

192   Hinge Picture (on George Oppen)

197   Reznikoff's Nearness

229   An Autobiographical Interview

253   Beyond Emaciation

255   Riding's Reason   √

268   Whose He Kidding

270   Unrepresentative Verse (on Ginsberg and Eliot)

273   Poetry and [Male?] Sex

279   Close Listening: Poetry and the Performed Word

302   Taps [In memoriam Eric Mottram]

304   Warning—Poetry Area: Publics under Construction

312   The Republic of Reality

317   Notes and Acknowledgments

Preface

I'm incorrect: the learnèd say
That I write well, but not their way . . .
Nor with their stupid rules control
The sacred pulse that beats within my soul.
"The Amorous Lady" (1734)

What is the difference between poetry and prose, verse and essays? Is it possible that a poem can extend the argument of an essay or that an essay can extend the prosody of a poem? Whose on first, or aren't you the kind that tells?

Theory is never more than an extension of practice, but then again practice is always informed by theory, like the cuckoo clock that won't make whoopee unless the lights are on. Maybe the relation of theory to practice is like the relation of strategy to tactics; or, come to think of it, maybe theory's tactical and poems strategic. Or perhaps it's like the relation of body to mind: the best picture of an aesthetic is a work of art, and vice versa.

Or as my wife says to me most mornings: "Don't give me another one of your theories."

My Way: Speeches and Poems includes essays, conversations, addresses, and verses. The book is arranged so as to put at play formal and thematic relations that cut across the selections. There are essays in poetic lines and prose that incorporates poetic motifs, there are interviews that mime speech and speeches that veer into song. The idea is to put a wide, yet decisive, range of styles into conversation with one another. The point is not to break down generic distinctions as much as to bring genres and styles into rhetorical play with one another.

My Way addresses the limits and possibilities both for poetry in the society and for literary studies in the university, which are treated as intertwined topics. It repeatedly comes back to the (often perverse) relation of public space to art that is aversive to cultural and linguistic norms but nonetheless remains committed to exchange, interaction, communication, and community.

What I would like is for the reader seeking critical prose to find herself humming the tunes of a poem. What I would like is for the listener to a poetry performance to end up in the middle of a critical practice that can't quite be assimilated as verse or idea.

The various pieces in this book mostly make their own acknowledgments, but not to Susan Bee, whose editorial advice has been consistently useful, if not always heeded. Consult the notes at the end of this volume for details about each of these works, including information on the original context. Once again, I've chosen to do the punctuation, and much else, my way; I realize this has meant departing often from the style of the press and its *Manual*, which nonetheless remains one of my primary sources. I take personal responsibility for the discrepancies and inconsistencies that weave this work together.

A Defence of Poetry

for Brian McHale

My problem with deploying a term liek
nonelen
in these cases is acutally similar to
your
cirtique of the term ideopigical
unamlsing as a too-broad unanuajce
interprestive proacdeure.
You say too musch lie a steamroller when
we need dental (I¡d say jeweller's)
tools.
(I thin youy misinterpret the natuer of
some of the poltical claims go¡ not
themaic
interpretatiomn of evey
evey detail in every peim
but an oeitnetation towatd a kind of
texutal practice
that you prefer to call "nknsense" but
for *poltical* purpses I prepfer to call
ideological!
, say Hupty Dumpty)
Taht is, nonesene see¡msm to reduce a
vareity of fieefernt
prosdodic, thematic and discusrive
enactcemnts into a zeroo degree of
sense. What we have is a vareity of
valences. Nin-sene.sense is too binary
andoppostioin, too much oall or nithing
account with ninesense seeming by its
very meaing to equl no sense at all. We
have preshpas a blurrig of sense, whih
means not relying on convnetionally

1

methods of *conveying* sense but whih may
aloow for dar greater sense-smakinh than
specisi9usforms of doinat disoucrse that
makes no sense at all by irute of thier
hyperconventionality (Bush's speeches,
calssically). Indeed you say that
nonsenese shed leds on its "antithesis"
sense making: but teally the antithsisi
of these poems you call nonselnse is not
sense-making itslef but perhps, in some
cases, the simulation of sense-making:
decitfullness, manifpulation, the
media-ization of language, etc.
I don't agree with Stewart that "the
more exptreme the disontinuities . . . the
more nonsisincial" : I hear sense
beginning to made in this sinstances.
Te probelm though is the definaitonof
sense. What you mean by nomsense is
soething like a-rational, but ratio (and
this goes back to Blake not to meanion
the pre-Socaratics) DOES NOT EQUAL
sense! This realtioes to the sort of
oscillation udnertood as rhytmic or
prosidci, that I disusccio in Artiofice.
Crucialy, the duck/rabitt exmaple is one
of the ambiguity of *aspects* and clearly
not a bprobelm of noneselnse: tjere are
two competing, completely sensible,
readings, not even any blurring; the
issue is context-depednece)otr
apsrevcyt blindness as Witegenstein
Nonesesen is too static. Deosnt't
Prdunne even say int e eoem "sense occurs
"at the contre-coup:: in the process of
oscillatio itself.
b6y the waylines 9–10 are based on an
aphorism by Karl Kraus: *the closer we
look at a word the greater the distance
from which it stares back.*

The Revenge of the Poet-Critic, or The Parts Are Greater Than the Sum of the Whole

The men on the hill, they say, "learn the rules, *then* break them."

I like to "think the reverse" whenever possible and even if not:

break 'em enough times you won't have to learn 'em, or the rules will have changed, or you will change them, or make up your own rules and don't follow those either; anyway whose rules are they?, I didn't see the signs, musta missed them in the duststorm; or as we say in Medias Res (Medias Res, Nevada)—rope 'em and then learn 'em, shoot 'em and then cook 'em (chop up fine before marinating indefinitely), float jerkily and carry a Bic pen at all times, where aim I?, is this my fear / or did I just step into the public sphere?, are you there Mordred?; Give me your tired tuxes, your tattered nabobs of oligarchy yearning to Keep that Smut Off the Net, Thank you Senator Exxon the open spaces around here were scaring me, how many syllables can you fit on the head of a pin cushion? what's that spell, Mario? who are you calling a verse? That's not what I meant y'all, not what I meant at all.

Up High Down Low Too Slow

Values like the butter on the table melting
before the memory of the butter on the table
melting: a ring around the four o'clock
shadow made with a horseless bark
and liltless sigh by an organ grinder
peering over the leaning tower formally known
as Pisa. Get a rocking chair and put
her sequence in it, tie it with the sting
of soot & smoke & kerosene, then
sucker punch all those blundered trusts
cuffed to the caboose of unreturnable
rebukes. A penny for a
paradise, a nickel for a ride, a

3

> quarter for a roll of tens, a dollar
> for the slides . . .

If I speak of a "politics of poetry", it is to address the politics of poetic form not the efficacy of poetic content. Poetry can interrogate how language constitutes, rather than simply reflects, social meaning and values. You can't fully critique the dominant culture if you are confined to the forms through which it reproduces itself, not because hegemonic forms are compromised "in themselves" but because their criticality has been commandeered. There is no wholly intrinsic meaning to any form, nor are there a priori superior forms. Devices and techniques—the tools and styles of the past—shift in their meaning and value over time, requiring continuing reassessment. Yet forms do have extrinsic, social meanings that are forged through a contestation of values from which it is impossible to withhold judgment.

Forms, like words, can never be separated from their meanings, which come into being in a social and historical process that is never finished.

A politics of poetic form recognizes that poetry's social and collaborative—material—dimensions frame our ability to read poems as solitary personal expression. It acknowledges the semantic contribution of the visual dimension of language, of the means of production and distribution, and of the context of publication. Such a politics insists that poems are partial and particular not universalizable expressions of humanity.

To speak of politics in this context is to contrast the politics in and of the rhetorical with the poetics of truth, authority, and sincerity in order to insist that politics is always at play—never to put that play to rest, nor banish or repress it.

When a poem enters into the world it enters into a political, in the sense of ideological and historical, space. By refusing the criteria of efficacy for determining the political value of the poem, we confer political value on the odd, eccentric, different, opaque, maladjusted—the nonconforming. We also insist that politics demands complex thinking and that poetry is an arena for such thinking: a place to explore the constitution of meaning, of self, of groups, of nations,—of value. The politics of poetry for which I speak is open-ended; the results of its interrogations are not assumed but discovered in the process and available to reformulation. Its complexity and adversity to conformity puts such a poetic practice well outside the stadium of dominant culture. It is this refusal of efficacy, call it a refusal of submission, that marks its political character.

For the destination is always staring just out-of-view and all the signs are flashing "access denied." I make meaning of the failure to arrive, for so often it is a breaking down of the chain of sense that lets me find my way. A way away from the scanning over and over what went wrong—the failure of community that may, in flits and faults, give way to conversation. I start with the senselessness of the world and try to make some sense with it, as if words were visceral and thoughts could be tolls. It's the loss, I want to say, I don't know *of what*—but not to find either (neither voice nor truth: voicings, trusts).

Don't Be So Sure
(Don't Be Saussure)

My cup is my cap
& my cap is my cup
When the coffee is hot
It ruins my hat
We clap and we slap
Have sup with our pap
But won't someone please
Get me a drink

What is a poet-critic, or critic-poet, or professor-poet-critic?; which comes first and how can you tell?; do the administrative and adjudicative roles of a professor mark the sell-out of the poet?; does critical thinking mar creativity, as so many of the articles in the Associated Writing Program newsletter insist? Can poets and scholars share responsibilities for teaching literature and cultural studies or must poets continue to be relegated to, or is it protected by, creative writing workshops, where, alone in the postmodern university, the expressive self survives?

Of course I must agree, I confide to the prize-winning poet, all this stuff about poetry groups and movements is a publicity stunt for poets without the imaginative capacity to assert their unique individuality in forms and voices utterly indistinguishable from the other prize-winning poets who vote these awards to each other on panels and juries that systematically rule out any trace of individuality expressed by particularity of tone, diction, syntax, or form. Indeed, you force me to concede the point, I tell the politically committed academic, this poetry excludes most of the people in the world (who haven't yet learned English!); it's turned its back on the ordinary reader by making no effort to reach out to him or her. And, yes, indeed, Professor, I also must admit, even though it seems to go against your last point, that all this poetics stuff is just an attempt to attract readers, making the work just one more commodity being peddled. Of course you're right, I tell the few friends I have left, now that I am poet-professor

at the University at Buffalo, I have retreated to an Ivory Tower, removed
from the daily contact I used to have, as a poet–office worker in Manhat-
tan, with the broad masses of the American people . . . the ones that I used
to meet at downtown poetry readings and art openings.

And surely it is a scandal, I tell my students, how Americans are afflicted
with attention-deficit disorder, just like they say in *Time* magazine, which
after all should know, being one of the major sites of infection for the dis-
ease it laments, with its "you can never simplify too much" approach to
prose and its relentless promotion of exclusively predigested cultural prod-
uct. And since we all know students can't follow a linear and symbolic ar-
gument of a conventional poem, how can you possibly expect them to
read the even-more-difficult poems you seem bent on promoting, inter-
jects a concerned younger member of the faculty, eager, in his own classes,
to present the ideological cracks in the surface of popular culture? You
want to take things that appear accessible and linear, I reply, and show how
they are complex and inaccessibly nonlinear; I want to take things that ap-
pear complex and nonlinear and show how this complexity is what makes
them accessible in the sense of audible (auditable). And, I continue, wav-
ing my arms and upping the tempo as my colleague's eyes begin to spin in
orbits, isn't the nonlinearity of much so-called disjunctive poetry indeed
a point of contact with the everyday cultural experiences of most North
Americans, where overlays of competing discourses is an inevitable prod-
uct of the radio dial, cable television, the telephone, advertising, or in-
deed, at a different level of spatialization, cities? But isn't advertising and
the commercialization of culture a bad thing, interrupts the future public
intellectual, isn't that what poetry should be trying to resist; and isn't the
sort of poetry you promote just a capitulation to the alienated, fragmented
discourse of postmodern capitalism? If you say so, I reply in the manner
of Eeyore, as if I had found myself caught in a Gap ad (Robert Frost Wore
Khakis: "the gaps I mean"). But you can't quite have it both ways: the form
of much of the most innovative modernist and postwar poetry may not
be the obstacle you imagine it to be, so don't use that fact as a way of dis-
missing the activity as esoteric. Neither hypotaxis nor parataxis has an in-
trinsic relation to poetry, cultural resistance, or accessibility: the mistake
is to demonize radically paratactic approaches as both the unreflected
product of the worst of the culture and at the same time as esoteric, though
I would suggest this particular double bind is a very effective tool for the
stringent enforcement of cultural hegemony within a multicultural envi-
ronment. And do beware the role of public intellectual, my friend, for
when *The New York Times* starts talking about either the death or rebirth of
public intellectuals, it can only remind us that intellectuality as a form of
linguistically investigative activity has been banned for a long time from

its pages and that public intellectuals unwilling to clip their tongues the better to induce in readers thinking-deficit disorder have not gone away, they have been barred from this and other standard bearers of the culture.

So a guy comes over to me, very agitated—we're just a block from Lincoln Center, across the street from the new Sony Imax theater—and he says, "How d'ya get to Carnegie Hall?"
    —"Theory."

One thing I am proposing is a modular essay form that allows for big jumps from paragraph to paragraph and section to section. In such essays, it becomes possible to recombine the paragraphs to get another version of the essay—since the "argument" is not dependent on the linear sequence.

    Juxtaposing disparate, if related, material, forms an array or constellation or environment.

    Equally, I think of paragraphs as a series of extended remarks or improvisations on aphoristic cores. So you have these series of paragraphs that are semi-autonomous making up sections that are themselves serial. (I like that idea of semi-autonomy as opposed to disjuncture. The paragraphs can't really stand alone. They're dependent on what comes before and after. But, still, they have some qualities of autonomy or completeness. A bit like you and me, after all.) The idea is that the order of the paragraphs could be shifted, and, more importantly, that space is left for new paragraphs to be inserted, something like leaving room for (more) thought.

    In some of my essays, the jump between paragraphs is greater than the jump between sentences, so you get a shift or a torquing of perspectives. *möbius* I am particularly interested in a möbius or twisting paragraph seriality. So that you can see the same thing from multiple points of view or different angles. Like radar or sonar scanning a three-dimensional object. As the angles torque, you almost can't recognize the scene; or maybe what's being switched is the mode of scanning, the scanning technology. So the essays consist in a series of scans, shifting from paragraph to paragraph. It's not a matter of inconsistency, of the romance of the non sequitur. It's a method.

    Of course, I'm not scanning a single discrete object or scene. But the idea of torquing or twisting or permuting or turning or curving of angles or points of view gives you some idea of the prose prosody I'm proposing.

    Now a turn or curve—that's not disjuncture. The elements are related. It's not collage.—You're driving down the street and you take a right turn. You feel the turning, the contingency of the connection as you switch directions. Or you could drive into a traffic circle and come back to where you were. You're going down the road and hit a traffic circle and loop back around to the road you were just on, except, looking at it from the other direction, it doesn't seem the same, as if it ever could. I retrace my steps to where I started, and then I realize that the essay must be over.

So that's different from the rupture of radical or extrinsic parataxis, which provides a different kind of modulation, contour, and discontinuity. The relation between paragraphs is more about continuity than discontinuity but it allows a shift in its path while still continuing on, still relating to what happened before.

I'm on a train but keep missing my stop but then it comes up again, every so often, but never in the same way. The drunk man never steps into the same argument twice before falling off the stool.

Other essays, other rhetorics.

So part of it is that I want to have different textures and different moods not only from paragraph to paragraph but from essay to essay.

The constructing of grammatical space through various forms of sequencing pervades all levels of writing, from the ordering of syllables, words, phrases, lines, and stanzas within a poem to the overall arrangement of poems or essays in a book. Poetic composition consists of a series of displacements constantly opening up upon new emplacements; or, to speak literally of metaphors, composition consists of measuring or registering a series of dislocations that produces the poem's or essay's motion or kinesis.

Shaked but Not Mixed
after Baudelaire

The mumblers have the air of verse
The tumblers are tipsy with time
The old tunes are bust-up now
Make a picture of rime

I do not say there is nothing outside the text but that there is text outside the nothing.

In the 1990s, the problems of group affiliation (the neolyric "we") pose as much a problem for poetry as do assertions of the Individual Voice (the lyric "I"). If poems can't speak directly for an author, neither can they speak directly for a group. Just as a poetry may wish to question the authorial voice, it also may wish to question all forms of group affiliation—national, state, linguistic, ethnic, and, indeed, aesthetic. Each poem speaks not only many voices but also many groups and poetry can investigate the construction of these provisional entities in and through and by language.

If individual identity is a false front, group identity is false fort.

But saying that, I also want to acknowledge that the suspicion of many kinds of collective action or identification in poetry, that is the stigmatization of groups, does torque the equation, so that active exchange, shared interests, and concerted activities that run counter to the BIG GROUP consciousness of rugged individuality will get targeted as a sinister and anti-poetic "party" (in the bad sense) organization. I'm for a poetry that neither sheds its identities nor uses them as shields against the poem in the-making nor, for that matter, selves-in-the-making nor society-in-the-making. But also that does not hide behind bland assurances of human or national generality in refusing the necessity of partiality or highly particularized commitments that acknowledge the manner and matter of allegiances, affiliations, identifications, markings, separations, shivers, splinters, remnants, fragmentations. The parts are greater than the sum of the whole.

The social grounding of poetry cannot be evaded by recourse to a purely intellectual idea of the materiality of language since the materiality of language is in the first instance a social materiality and, at the same time, a materiality not of selves and identities but of bodies, including gendered bodies. Materiality, that is, is not just an idea but also a responsibility. Here I very much agree with the Italian poet Nanni Cagnone's insistence that poetics not be pre-scriptive but, if to make the distinction at all, post-scriptive: ('Poetry is action above and beyond what a person is able to think.) So that my own poetic ethics, again to echo Cagnone, is to enact language's refusal to abandon the world but also to articulate the way the world cleaves to language.

A poem should make its own experience, Uncle Hodgepodge used to say. I tend to dislike readings where the poet defines every detail and reference of the work so that by the time you get to the poem it's been reduced to an illustration of the anecdotes and explanations that preceded it. I figure if a reader or listener can't make out a particular reference or train of thought, that's okay—it's very much the way I experience things in everyday life. If the poem is at times puzzling or open-ended or merely suggestive, rather than explicit, maybe it gives readers or listeners more space for their own interpretations and imaginations. Different readers pick up different things and for any reader certain allusions are bound to be striking while others will seem opaque, but which is which changes from

Poetry is action above and beyond what a person is able to think.

reader to reader. What I like in poems is encountering the unexpected and I enjoy not knowing where I am or what comes next.

Flotsam in My Jetsam

There's flotsam in my jetsam
Barnacles in the stew
I got a letter from my lawyer
Says he's gonna sue
Wheels of gold on fire
Sirens slouching in the rain
If five'll get you ten at 9 o'clock
I'd still want to stay in bed

Sometimes I wonder how "mainstream" the idea of the transparency of language really is. It may operate as the conventional wisdom, at least since the Enlightenment, but there has been a consistently powerful counter-hegemonic stream, and not only among poets. Yet this history, the heterodoxy of our poetic traditions, is constantly being erased or tamed. The lyric tradition, with its emphasis on the enunciative, on sound, and on subjectivity remains extremely valuable to my poetic concerns. But lyric poetry needs to be viewed in its specific historical contexts and read for its specific rhetorical forms; that is, away from the Romantic ideology that makes the lyric a generalized, even universal, expression of human sentiment. This would be to emphasize the concrete particulars of sound and form over and against the dematerializing idea of voice or purity of expression, and also to privilege poets who particularly insist on this double hearing, say Ossian or Swinburne, Poe or Dunbar, Skelton or Hopkins. Surely I use more of the tones and those high, swooning sounds from this tradition than many of my contemporaries and I have even suggested a name for this movement of verse, "The Nude Formalism" (the form stripped bare by her bachelors, maybe), an ideolectical counter to a "New Formalism" that claims a continuity with conventional lyric prosody but disdains its sonic excesses. Over the past few years, I have actively solicited members for my new movement, but few have wished to join me on this often rather giddy, though potentially hilarious, course.

Um, hm. My thesis is coming around again, like that recurring train stop for Charlie and the MTA. So much scholarly and philosophical prose—like so much lyric poetry—is locked into a single emotional tone. And this "tone lock", this rigid holding to a particular temperament, restricts what you can say. Part of what you find in Emerson—and certainly what I'm

New Formalism

interested in in my own writing—is strong, abrupt changes in emotion. So something that's somber turns into something that's like a Borscht Belt comedy routine which turns into something that's perhaps elegiac— because all those emotions can be relevant to a given topic or series of topics. You can be very gloomy, you can be very sanguine, distant, rigorous (as a mood); I want to shift between those different emotional, or let's say philosophical, tones. *prosody-making argument*

Verse is born free but everywhere in chains. It has been my project to rattle the chains. That's one way to approach my prosody, or perhaps not prosody but prosody-making arguments.

I don't teach writing workshops but reading workshops. The reading workshop is less concerned with analysis or explanation of individual poems than with finding ways to intensify the experience of poetry, of the poetic, through a consideration of how the different styles and structures and forms of contemporary poetry can affect the way we see and understand the world. No previous experience with poetry is necessary. More important is a willingness to consider the implausible, to try out alternative ways of thinking, to listen to the way language sounds before trying to figure out what it means, to lose yourself in a flurry of syllables and regain your bearings in dimensions otherwise imagined as out-of-reach, to hear how poems work to delight, inform, redress, lament, extol, oppose, renew, rhapsodize, imagine, foment . . .

Poetry is tranquillity recollected in emotion, commotion projected in tranquillity, recollection unsettled by turbulence.

If I am making an argument for the aesthetic, I hope it will be apparent that I use "aesthetic" not to suggest an ideal of beauty but rather to invoke a contested arena of judgment, perception, and value where artworks and essays operate not as adjudicators of fixed principles but as probes for meaning, prods for thought. To investigate the conditions that make value possible is not to abandon value to historical contingency but rather to insist that values be argued for, demonstrated, and enacted. I am in every way a partisan but I do not hold that the values of that to which I am partial are self-evident or obligatory. Yet I do hold out for a realm of value that is determined by judgments made without recourse to rationalizable justification and claim that this realm of aesthetic judgment is the basis for reason.

Not unstructured essays but differently structured: not structurally challenged, structurally challenging.

Poetry continues to make active *methodological* interventions into critical and philosophical discourse so that any serious consideration of the long-standing "discrepant engagement"—to use Nathaniel Mackey's great term—between criticism and poetry needs to look closely at the work of contemporary poets fully as much as the work of contemporary theorists.

My point of departure is poetry that is aversive to conventions of literary or expository or spoken language. To what degree are these conventions necessary for sense and what approaches have poets, working in aversive traditions, taken to issues of sense and, to use Khlebnikov's word, transense (*zaum*)? I am arguing that a number of poets working in English today are mounting a sustained critique of the norms of description and argument and that this critique has important implications for the forms not only of poetic discourse but also for the forms of critical and philosophical discourse. For contemporary poetry's active questioning of the relation of form and style to content shows also that there can be no neutral form of philosophical or critical argument. Thus criticism's blindness to the meaning of its forms is a denial of reason in the name of rationality.

Salute

after Mallarmé

Nothing, this cum, verging verse
Only to design the cut
Such loins know a troupe
Of sirens married in environs

Loose navigations, O my diverse
Amis, moi just on the poop
You who want faster coups
The float of fools and shivers

An ivoried bell men gage
Sand's cranes maim son's tonnage
Then portend debut this salute

Solitude, retreat, tolls
To no importance that value
The blank sail of our soul
    The blank toil of our sail
        The blank soul of our toil

The question of who is the audience for poetry is different than the question who is the audience for a poem: the first is sociological, the second ontological. At the same time, critical advocacy through essays and talks does make a call for new readers and listeners, even as it provides something other than poetry for them to attend. Yet I count on the measurable audience for what I write to be small, for my work constantly invokes the necessity of the small-scale act, the complex gesture, the incontrovertible insinuation, the refractory insouciance of the intractable. Which is to say poetry is (or can be) about measure but it counts differently.

The poetry audience has become atomized; Balkanized is the more ominous phrase. Insofar as this represents the downfall of Poets as Universal Voice of Humanity, broadcasting on the Official Verse Cultural Network, this is a necessary development. Not that no one is claiming the mantle for such Generalized Address, just that the emptiness of the address is more readily apparent. Poetry is no match for advertising and the mass culture industry if reaching the broadest public is what you have in mind (irrespective of the message). This is not to say that the address of poetry is not crucial for the public but that as a culture we are bloated with Public Voices (most of them pathogenic); poetry has other voices to offer (even if most poetry revels in its phobia of its own possibilities). Yet, insofar as Balkanization has meant that poetry is framed by identity politics, where identity is something that is assumed prior to the poem and not discovered in the process of writing the poem, poetry risks losing one of its most resonant formal features: its radical genericness. (Such a risk may sometimes be worth taking.) There is nothing new in dividing poetry into types: nature poetry or narrative poetry or love poetry or war poetry; but these are merely pretexts for poetry; identity is no more. Language is poetry's vocation, which is not to say poetry is about language but that it locates itself as language, in language.

Language poetry

Which leads me to say that there is no audience for the poem, only readers. Or better, no readers for the poem, only readings. Or then again, no readings, only audiences.

Nobody out there but us. And I can never figure out who that was or will be, much less is.

Or put it this way: The poem is like a heat-seeking missile that finds its target but refuses to detonate. Often the target is not aware it has been hit. This is the secret life of poetry.

Who knows what shadows lurk in the hearts of readers? The poet knows but prefers to tell it on her own terms. S/he is an intellectual without portfolio.

—"Ceil, what is he saying now? What does it mean?"

I am a product of the U.S. and an example of it; this is a source of considerable discomfort to me but this discomfort is perhaps the basis of my work. For my themes, to call them that, have pretty consistently been awkwardness, loss, and misrecognition.

But when I say that, I want to go on by remarking on the shrunken representation of U.S. literary, art, and intellectual culture within the major national intellectual and cultural journals and on the public broadcasting channels. I would call this development the rise of the mediocracy; that is, the triumph of the mediocre in the dominant institutions of intellectual and literary culture. The vitality of North American (not just U.S.) cultural production at this time is all but elided by the selection and commentary in so-called leading journals of opinion such as *The New York Review of Books, The Times Book Review, The New Yorker, The Nation,* and *New Republic*, the news weeklies, the cultural sections of the major newspapers, etc. These venues have dismally failed to account for most of the significant intellectual and cultural work of the past decade, choosing instead an insular repetition of the same names, issues, and explanations that gives the impression that the culture suffers from the same terminal anemia and mediocrity as afflicts the publishers and editors and frequent contributors to these journals. (A striking example of this is James Atlas's piece "Why 'Literature' Bores Me", which appeared in *The New York Times Magazine* [March 16, 1997]. This is not just an idiosyncratic attack on the innovative literary arts of the past hundred years; Atlas, an editor of the magazine, should be taken as representing, at least in part, the newspaper's cultural politics.)

What is striking today is the refusal to recognize that it is a degraded cultural agenda of the major print and electronic media, and not the state of culture, that has given rise to mediocracy.

Consider the problem of public broadcasting, a paradigm case of mediocracy as official policy. With the deplorable decline of government support for public radio and television, NPR, PBS, and their affiliates have moved their focus from singularity of program content to homogenization of audience. Within the context of public radio, this has meant sending out a cadre of consultants to every local public station, urging station managers to make their programs as uniform as possible. Any diversion is considered a dangerous refusal to focus on maximizing the audience and increasing contributions. In practice, this means that all public radio is being reduced to wallpaper middle-of-the road jazz or noncontemporary classical, with the usual complement of NPR news. Nothing else is allowed, with the possible exception of some odds and ends on the weekend or very off-peak hours. The consultants who promote this policy attack dissenters as "elitists" and characterize independent programming on poetry, gay issues, books, history, as well as new music, "other" music, popular music of the past, as "special interest" programming. In other words, these consultants stigmatize as elitist anything that would provide a contrast to the bland and uniform programming their market research supposedly mandates. This is what Leslie Fiedler calls the "tyranny of the normal" but might just as well be called the tyranny of the familiar. "Elitism" is the code word for a process of cultural lobotomization that offers the same prospect for the cultural life of the nation as lobotomies offer for the creative potential of the individual.

There is no alternative for public funding as a means of supporting small-scale public projects. The dismantling of the NEA and NEH, despite the problems with both agencies, is a major setback. At the same time, too many foundations that support the arts or public broadcasting are convinced that to present art (or ideas) to the public risks turning the public off to art and ideas. They prefer to support projects that translate art and ideas into administrative and presentation packages most similar to what is already available, generally reducing art to personal narrative and ideas to feelings about these personal narratives. Such "dumbed down" programming is counterproductive because it reinforces the common conception that unpopular art just offers bad versions of what you get in popular art and entertainment, and if that's true, why give it government handouts, much less the time of day. What was useful about the NEA was its commitment to provide direct support for artists based on peer-review of the merits of the work and its support of presses and magazines largely without reference to large-scale audiences.

For artists and intellectuals, the problem is not that their work does not speak to the public but that few public spaces will permit them entry to make their pitch. In place of public parks of ideas we have private malls of predigested cultural packages. The small press, some scholarly journals, and the internet certainly offer an alternative but these are the infrastructure, the research and development, sectors; they are necessary but barely sufficient.

Typically, intellectual and cultural work is not *readily* familiar. At its best it resists endless repetitions of the already known. But this does not mean it is inaccessible. While diet and exercise have become a national obsession, the idea of exercising the mind is treated with increasing contempt. The problem isn't that Sally and Dick can't read anything more difficult than the Op Ed pages, the problem is that the Op Ed pages reinforce this ignorance.

I believe that artists and intellectuals have a commitment to try to make their work and the work they support available in public spaces, not in the watered down forms that only capitulate to the mediocracy, but in forms that challenge, confront, exhilarate, provoke, disturb, question, flail, and even fail.

It is the continued fate of the new to be misunderstood by some in exact proportion to the intensified comprehensibility it provides to others.

What I am talking about here is the production of ignorance that is enforced by restraints on complexity of thought; political, social, and aesthetic content; and form.

Universities can be a crucial base of opposition to the construction of ignorance, but not if they view their role as merely ameliorative. Indeed the production of ignorance is aided by the passivity of the scholarly community in accepting narrow definitions of disciplinarity and specialization that enforce irrational constraints on the nature of research and writing, supposedly in the name of professionalization but actually in the service of containment and control. Insofar as professors choose to see their work as only scholarship and so hardly writing, they evade the possibility that their work can have social force. In judging the value of writing or research, the criteria should not be whether a work meets with the current norms in the field as currently defined, but rather whether each of its sentences and paragraphs is necessary to say. Otherwise one is only aiding and abetting those inside and outside universities who are all too willing to capitulate to the idea that public discourse can only be written in "simple" sentences; or that compound-complex sentences, or long paragraphs, are not "clear".

The idea that complex or unfamiliar ideas, indeed that compound-complex sentences, are "elitist" must be countered as demagogic populism and quasi-totalitarianism. It is not that writers and artists and intellectuals, any more than listeners or readers, are ignorant; but the constraints enforced in public spaces produce, protect, and defend ignorance. With the instigation of media consultants and large foundations, the noncommercial sector has too often copied the worst features of the commercial sector (though usually stripped of the dynamism of the market that makes commercial culture so vibrant). It is commendable for noncommercial venues to try to get the largest possible audience for the programming they produce. However, it is destructive to determine your programming primarily on the audience it is able to get.

So what I am advocating, then, is the production of public cultural work in unpopular modes and on unfamiliar subjects.

Distance Learning

caught at where the
peripalpitations
detain, as in a blender
bursts upon persons
unhinged by refraction
where going goes atumbling
fells
buckling bows
your tidal mill
o'ertains ensconced
tethers
at lilting ends
of frowning cuts
brokered at such
mumbling tirades

Words so often fail us. They do so little and they are so disappointing, leading us down blind alleys and up in smoke. But they are what we have, what we are given, and we can make them do what we want. Every poem is a model of some other world, a practice of some other reality: but it always leads back to this one; for if words give a way to envision possible worlds they don't provide the way to inhabit them. Words are what I work with and through which I am made. They are the means of our mourning and of our morning but also of our mooring. There is no place words cannot take us if we don't take them as authorities, with fixed codes hardwired into the language, but as springs to jump with, or as trampolines to hurl ourselves, inward and outward, upward and downward, aslant and agog, round and unrounded.

I open the door and it shuts after me. That is, the more I venture out into the open the more I find it is behind me and I am moving not toward some uninhabited space but deeper into a maelstrom of criss-crossing inscriptions. The open is a vanishing point—the closer I get to it the greater the distance from which it beckons. And I begin the journey again.

Thelonious Monk and the Performance of Poetry

What is the status of performance
in poetry? This statically
worded question will not likely lead me
to a discussion of Thelonious Monk.
But you start where you can,
where mood flings you, like an old dish
towel drying in the rain.

Of course, there are still those who don't read
their poems, insisting that the page is sufficient,
the rest gets in the way. I used to feel more
that way myself, that is I thought my work existed
in some primary way as words
on a page & that in doing
a reading I was *adding* a performance
element, suggesting one way that a work might be
read. Reading
poems required a number of performance decisions
not obvious from the texts &
a reader might well make
other decisions in reading to her-
or himself than I had
done. My insistence on the primacy
of the
poem as written was partly a reaction against
the popular notion of poems as merely
scores to be performed, something deficient
without infusion of theatrical or
musical overlays, as if
poems were like lyrics on the back of a record album.
A page, a book,
seemed to me—still does—an unexcellable site
for poetic activity.

Nonetheless, I've come to feel
that the idea of the written
document as primary makes for an unwarranted
or anyway unwanted
hierarchy; hearing
work performed is in no way inferior to
reading it to yourself. Rather, these are two competing
realizations of the work, each
with its own set of advantages &
limitations. Moreover
all reading is performative
& a reader has in some ways to supply the performative
element when reading—
not silently before a page but out
loud & with a beat.

(One advantage of hearing
work performed
is that it does
not allow opportunities to
reread or rehear; at least in my
work, it pretty much forces listeners
to get lost, to give up
any notion of following in detail, fore-
grounding tempo & sound,
association & texture
[making the experience
more like hearing music or watching
a movie]. Of course, the ability to read in
detail
is just what gives the written
its primacy—much of what
is happening pros-
odically, thematically, & structurally can't
really be grasped in performance.)

Paul Schmidt, lamenting
performance styles at many poetry
readings, has recently advocated
that poets memorize their work,
suggesting that a declamatory
style of reading would bring life
to an otherwise often deadly practice.

Strong medicine
& met more with a denial of disease
than a discussion of alternative
therapies. *Why spend time preparing*
for a performance when that
time could better be used
writing? —For many poets will make much
of the authenticity or naturalness of their reading
style—mumbling, stumb-
ling over words, fumbling through papers, virtual
inaudibility, sitting in a chair bent over page, no
discernible shape or rhythm in the pro-
jected sound of the work.
Yet this is just as much
a performance style as the most
declamatory reading: all readings
are performative, whether they appear
to deny the performative or flaunt
it.

My experience is that if I really care
about a poet's work, then I am interested
in hearing them read regardless
of their attitude to performance, & that
a good deal about the rhythm & acoustic
dimension of the work is made more explicit
(is exhibited). Indeed, there are some poets
who "overperform" their work to the detriment
of being able to hear it—kind of
like doing an electric guitar version, in triple
time, of "Misterioso"; or revving
your car engine while the gear is set to
neutral. Loud is not always better
which is one reason Monk
seems to suggest so much for poetry
performance. & for certain
works, the dreaded monotone style is not only
appropriate but
powerful & evocative; but then there is a difference
in holding to a single tone over a period
of time & just droning on
aimlessly.

To perform a poem is to make it a physically present
acoustic event, to give bodily dimension—beat—to what is
otherwise spatial & visual. Poems, no matter how short,
necessarily involve duration, & writing as much as performing
is an act of shaping this durational passage. In
performance, it becomes possible to lay down a rhythmic
beat, a pulse, that is otherwise more speculative or tenuous
in the scoring of words on a page. For me, this pulse is
constructed around "nodal" points of pauses or silences or
breaks—a *point* I want to put as technically as I can to
distinguish this from notions of breath or speech rhythms or
other notions of an unconstructed or unimposed reading style.

While I am skeptical
about the value of appropriating
musical terms to discuss
performance prosody, I am still tempted
to suggest that breaks or
silences can be a most active
musical device in poetry performance
in that they create musical phrases
that are then syncopated by the rhythmic pace
that precedes & follows them. In my
performances, I'm interested in employing
several different, shifting, tempos
& several different intonations (voices)
that pivot
& spin around these nodal
shifting
points. These blank spaces—
silences or
intervals—serve as ful-
crums for making audible
the rhythmic pulse & phrasing
being
played out, at the same
time scissoring
the syntax of the language (that is, cutting
against expected breaks of the
grammatical phrase or unit of
breath). Given these interests, the sound I am
laying down is

not simply that of a
person reading words
in any "straightforward" way
but playing
each
word
as if a
note or
chord on
the
piano, with slight
pauses creating unexpected
spaces between words, allowing phrases
to veer off into
unexpected sequences of wobbling
sound. I
no more take for
granted how to do this than I assume
the syntax
or prosody of a
poem I am
writing; it is a highly constructed, albeit
improvised, process, based on choosing
from a variety of different tonal,
rhythmic, & phrasal possibilities.

* * *

A number of years ago, I was asked to read in the International
Sound Poetry Festival in New York, despite the fact that my work
& style of reading would not normally be considered sound
poetry or performance poetry. I prefaced my reading by saying
that I thought there were only two types of poetry: sound
poetry & unsound poetry. But now I would change that to
sounded poetry & *unsounded* poetry.

It is perhaps a remnant of Romantic ideology that still
haunts that performance styles of poetry readings
are so often self-represented in terms of an authentic
voicing of "the" emotions or "the" unconscious, where
effacement of the performative is equated
with genuineness of the work, where
the acting style is to pretend that there is no

acting, where the performance style is to feign
that no performing is going on. This of course
is the story of our everyday life—where troubling
social acts are performed as if without
premeditation or self-conscious intent; it's
the sort of acting that resembles puppetry.
The best symbol of this phenomenon is a presidential
actor widely praised for his relaxed, natural—
I hear this as untheatrical & nonrhetorical—
style.

Every reading (whether one's own reading of a book or a
poet's reading to an audience) is an enactment, a
sounding, an
embodiment, which is to say a
reading that takes or makes
time, that enters into
the social, material, & historical space of
our lives. To deny the performative
aspect of poetry is to repress
its most literally political dimension, which is to
say, how it
enters into the world. To deny the rhetoricity
(rhetoricalness?)
& theatricality of a poem is to idealize a
literary space outside of ideology & history, a zone
timeless
& blank in which evasion substitutes for the friction
of interaction. Yet this
friction is the music of our lives. The
acknowledgment of the performative dimension
of poems is a
recognition of their political bearing
in the world, fully as
much as recognition of the theatricality of each
of our
social performances is a necessary prerequisite
for us to find
out how these ingrained
habits might be changed or reshaped. For
to sound is to give a hearing—
speeches not speech—

& without such forums
we are doomed to endless repetition of sounds
we have not ourselves
participated
in
making. The performative dimension
of poetry can
be understood
in Louis Zukofsky's sense
as its upper limit—
music. This would make
an attempt to understand the relation of
the work of Thelonious Monk to
contemporary poetry
an essentially political gesture.

An Interview with Manuel Brito

Manuel Brito: Could you be defined as a "demanding poet" looking for
  answers?
Charles Bernstein: I'm more looking for questions, constantly trying to
  upturn any set way of putting things, although, in the process, I do
  hover in proximity to something like answers, if responding, or
  being answerable to yourself, to your language, is an answer. I sup-
  pose I make a lot of presumptions in my work, in that the poems
  don't explain themselves. What interests me in a phrase or line is not
  always self-evident, it's only that it strikes me. I demand a lot from
  the materials (the words and the connections among them), but
  then, it seems like they demand a lot from me. Yet I'm never far from
  what's for me, anyhow, verbal pleasure, because if you demand a lot
  from words all of sudden they start to talk back to you in the most
  intimate and also engaging way, and that engagement has a lot to do
  with the intensified soundscape of the poem and also with the accel-
  eration of play (puns, rimes, misnomers, vowel and consonant repe-
  tition, and the dozens of other related devices of a trade in lan-
  guage).
    I figure if a reader or listener can't make out a particular reference
  or train of thought, that's okay—it's very much the way I experience
  things in everyday life. If the poem is at times puzzling or open-
  ended or merely suggestive, rather than explicit, maybe it gives
  readers or listeners more space for their own interpretations and
  imaginations. Different readers pick up different things and for any
  reader certain allusions are bound to be striking while others will
  seem opaque, but which is which changes from reader to reader.
  What I like in poems is encountering the unexpected and I enjoy
  not knowing where I am or what comes next.
    Which means I try to derail trains of thoughts as much as follow
  them; what you get is a mix of different types of language pieced
  together as in a mosaic—very "poetic" diction next to something
  that sounds overheard, intimate address next to philosophical imper-

atives, plus a mix of would-be proverbs, slogans, jingles, nursery rhymes, songs. I love to transform idioms as much as traditional metrics because I'm looking to say things I can only say in poems; I'm driven by that necessity. Sometimes there's a gap between sentences, sometimes the sound or sentiment carries over that gap: these shifting, modulated transitions express my philosophy as much as my prosody.

For me poetry and poetics are not so much a matter of how I can make words mean something I want to say but rather letting language find ways of meaning through me. Form is never more than an extension of sound and syntax: the music of poetry is the sound of sense coming to be in the world.

—I wouldn't know an answer if it stood on my head. A good joke, though . . . that's a different matter.

MB: You affirm in "Amblyopia" [in *The Sophist*] that we have to assume the spirit of balance, in which sense?

CB: That's the section about the "rate on purchase" and "the balance of every purchase". I loved the strains of Puritan sermon that run through this passage, lifted verbatim from the back of a credit card bill, and set in lines. One of the many "fine print" language types that are constantly at the periphery of consciousness, but which we rarely focus on. I only focussed on it myself because I was reading it aloud as part of a proofreading job. Is this the poetry of everyday life, a discrete particular?—well, only in my twisted (twisting) sense of these things. Or do things like our credit card contracts provide an allegory for a spiritual or religious contract we've entered into— as if, in a consume-on-credit society, we are, indeed, each judged by the balance of (and on) our purchases, and where our purchase is much more than a dinner or a couch, but a "purchase" in the figurative sense of that word, a position of advantage in the world, for which we may not be prepared to pay the bill, unaware of the hidden charges.

I've never been much for balance, but there's clear advantage to staying on your feet or not falling off the bed. I was a slow learner (which I suppose may be why I like to teach): I found it difficult to reproduce socially prized models of balance, symmetry, and grace; no doubt I grew to resent these things, more often conventions than the immutable principles they purported to be. It seemed to me I kept my balance in some mighty awkward ways: it may be my aesthetic now, but it was largely given to me by disadvantage. Disadvantage, that is, puts you in mind of your particular vantage and that enables some sort of eco-balance: balance within a complex, multilevel system—

where posture, say, or grammar, is not the only factor. Within a poem, the more active questions of eco-balance are ones of proportion and judgement. I think what may make my work seem difficult is that I am always testing my judgments, throwing them off-balance so that I can see where they land: and this testing, this interrogation, of judgment and senses of proportion constitute the aesthetic process for me.

On balance, I am reminded of a remark made by Wittgenstein to his sister, Hermine: "You remind me of somebody who is looking out through a closed window and cannot explain to himself the strange movements of a passerby. He cannot tell what sort of storm is raging out there or that this person might only be managing with difficulty to stay on his feet." When the reader is sealed off from the world of the poem, it may well seem strange and demanding; it is only when you get a sense for this world, and not just the words, that the poem can begin to make sense.

MB: Sometimes you seem to be really concerned about the arrangement of lines, a preoccupation you share with poets such as Pound and Olson. How does this aspect affect your mode of writing?

CB: Preoccupation is a good way to put, ever so much nicer than obsession, which is one way to look at a recurring interest that has no rhyme or reason. I'm attracted to the idea of lines being a primarily visual feature of the poem—it's a modest way of designing (or arranging) how the page looks, an overlay—one more dynamic of the poem's multilayered ecosystem.

Often I don't leave pauses for the line breaks when I perform a poem, which suggests that they are not principally related to the temporal soundtext (or phonotext). But then again, in performance, there are many more ways to cue different tones, voices, rhythms, beats, and phrasing than on the page, so that the line becomes a crucial device for setting such things in motion. If the line is relatively independent of the phonotext, then that's one of its great advantages, because you can play with the peculiarly visual space of the page, which is a particular feature of writing as opposed to spoken language or other nonverbal signifying practices. Given my interest in interruption (more than fragmentation), the line allows for a visual interruption of the phrase (or sentence) without necessarily requiring a temporal interruption, a pause: that's why I so often cut the line where you are least likely to pause (say between an article and a noun). When you break the line against the phrase, rather than at the end of a phrase, it's called syntactic scissoring; this preoccupies me because I can use it to set in motion a counter-measure that adds to the rhythmic richness of the poem—the main measure

in the phrasally forward movement of the phonotext, and the coun-
termeasure of the syntactic scissoring of the visual text.

I'm mindful of Dennis Tedlock's useful discussion of the line as a
device for registering oral dynamics of native American verbal art.
Tedlock's use of the line in his translations/transcriptions is as far
from traditional prosody as anything modernist poetry has come up
with. Tedlock roundly condemns the use of prose to convey the
hyperdynamic soundspace of oral literature, and has developed ways
to cue not just different lengths of pausing, but also pitch, loudness,
and other features of the phonotext. I'm very attracted to the
acoustic tactility both of the oral literature he is attending to and
also his ways of transforming it into a multitextured writing.

In creating an aural poetry, I think it's possible to have the reso-
nant presence of language without hypostatizing a single speaker as
the source of the language. Writing, that is, can become answerable
to itself in ways that do not advance upon orality but are co-present
with it. To do this, however, writing cannot revert to the conditions
of orality, nostalgically imagining itself as secondary, as transcript of
the voice, but rather must acknowledge its own materiality and
acoustic density/destiny, its visible aurality.

MB: Indeed, *Poetic Justice* and *Disfrutes* are characterized by the objectu-
al dimension of the word itself: you play with the typography,
sound, and a certain disorientation at the level of the content.
Would you explain more profoundly the purposes of your position?

CB: *Disfrutes*, my earliest published work, basically plays on slight shifts
in sound patterns and miniature word arrangements. The most mini-
mal is four one-word lines: "sand / and / sane / an" which follows the
an sound through to itself. I still find this kind of progression curi-
ously satisfying, even though I wouldn't isolate it the way I did in
Disfrutes: but it does typify the kind of detail I use in composing my
by now rococo works. In *Poetic Justice* I intErrUPT woRds by uSiNg
caPitAL lETTeRs tO cREaTe A kiNd of pulsInG eNergY: again with
the idea that interruption and disruption actually create intensity
and rhythm, by emphasizing the physical qualities both of the
sound and the visual representation of words.

MB: Can the films you realized with Henry Hills be seen under this
same perspective?

CB: What Henry's done is to create a soundtext—soundtrack—by
splicing together small bits of sync-sound film, often just a few sec-
onds each. It's an incredible mosaic, which exemplifies the sort of
constructed aurality I've been discussing.

One way I write poems is to assemble, create an order for, an increasingly wild variety of bits, units, bytes, hits, sections, units, phrases—segments. Hills shoots in sync sound then cuts the shoots into short "scenes". The soundtrack is made by physically splicing these scenes—bits of sync sound/image—together. Focussing just on the acoustic level, he is creating, by this process, a sound poem, or collage text.

Still, there are crucial differences between film and poetry. One of the main differences, retrievability, the ability to reread, review specified moments, is beginning to vanish. When Hills's films are seen in video, you'll be able to slow them up, stop them, a viewing situation that approaches, without ever intersecting, reading a book. In contrast, a screening of the film would more closely parallel hearing a poet perform a work. Two different performance modes are now available.

There's another aspect, however. Because it's in sync sound, meaning that all the sound was recorded live, whenever the sound is cut-up you also have the *picture*, and therefore a gesture, also cut-up. Accompanying the sound is always this outward picture—*a body*. When Henry's editing the particular sound or syllable or phrase— sequencing segments—you have in each segment, in addition to the sound, the movement, the gestures of the body. That's again the extraordinary thing about the films, that the sound is simultaneously registered as gestures of the body, the sound embodies even as it is cut-up, dislocated from its original context. In Hills's films, there is an elaborate scoring or choreography of these gestures.

MB: Is experimentation, as an active process, sufficient by itself?

CB: That would be true for some of the works of Jackson Mac Low or John Cage or William Burroughs—works that are a valuable resource for my writing. My own preoccupations, however, are not with experimentation as much as evocation, instantiation, arbitration, and reclamation.

Still, I don't want to abandon the experimental so quickly, at least not before acknowledging how the term is used to designate, but also to denigrate, much of the poetry I care most about. "Experimental" can sound like you don't know what you are doing, as if the poems were a rehearsal for some future product, or as if aesthetic intention were not at play. As a result, "experimental poetry" is often disparaged as mere "exercises", preliminary and incidental to the "actual work" of poetry. Indeed, both "exercise" and "experiment" are deployed, positively and negatively, against assumptions not only about intentionality and its others, but also that other barbed binary—process/product. You see, I'm still holding out for a poetry in which meaning is discovered rather than refined; where poetry is on trial, but where the trial is sufficient to itself, producing innovation and investigation not verdicts or conclusions.

Anyway, what is the difference between a sonnet or sestina and a poetry "experiment" (for example, producing a poem by erasing half the words in a source text or writing a poem each word of which begins with a different letter of the alphabet, or writing a poem in the form of an index)? Such experiments might just as well be called nontraditional, or new, poetic forms; they have the advantage of a less than fully authorized literary history.

I would say the most common, and empty, charges against non-conventional literary works is that they are *only* about their nonconventionality or antitraditionality or, so the refrain goes, only about "language"; as if one breaks forms or finds new ones for the sake of that activity rather than to be able to make articulations not otherwise possible (which itself may be pleasurable for writer and reader). Such comments (and they are just as frequent in the alternative poetry worlds as in the mainstreams) mask the fact that conventional and traditional literary writing reinscribe the meanings implicit in their forms but that poetry is not limited to this activity of reinscription (lovely or comforting or pleasurable as it sometimes may be). There may be no pure outside (chorus: "no pure outside" "no pure outside") but there isn't no pure inside either (chorus: "no inside ether, no inside ether").

MB: The quotidian, or elements related to our daily life, are present in many of your poems. What is your interest in this approach?

CB: Another preoccupation: the ordinary, a tradition more often associated with a plainer style than mine, but then what could be more everyday than words? It's a strange pull, since I often use arcane, rather than everyday, words. And my syntax, s/he isn't exactly ordinary either. But it's the texture of everyday experience I'm after, how language both constrains and engenders experience. And many of the particulars that litter my poems are indeed everyday sayings (sometimes inverted) and overheard comments. Moreover, the mix of elements, including the discontinuity and interruption, is part of the fabric of everyday life in the present. I suppose one thing I'm after is the sheer—nonsymbological—viscosity of experience. I want to intensify, not rarify or elevate or moralize about nor transcend or explain (away) everyday experience.

MB: *Veil* is introduced by a quotation from Hawthorne's "The Minister's Black Veil". How can we understand the metaphor of the veil as applied to your poetry? Is the veil counter to the "us"ness you write about in *Content's Dream?*

CB: *Veil* is my most visually oriented work. The visual emblem is produced by several layers of overtyping, so that much, but not all, of the freely composed writing is obliterated. One model I had was Morris Louis's "Veil" paintings, where successive stains of color occlude the inner layers, though at the edges the brightest of the suppressed underlayers of color shine through, ecstatically.

The sense of stain, as in soiling, and its associated sadness, is crucial; but also, as in biochemistry, the stain allowing you to identify otherwise invisible substances. In this sense, my poetry is an acoustic staining. That's why I'm inclined to dwell on (in) forms of damage, maladjustment, dislocation. This is not an aesthetic theory so much as an experiential dynamic—call it (to come back to it again) the ordinary: that we have our misalignments more in common than our adjustment to the socially correct norms. Normalcy is the enemy of poetry—my poetry, "our" poetry.

When today's *New York Times* (8/19/92) runs a piece on "out-of-sync" kids and how "we" can help them fit in, I see my poetics (and their debt to Hawthorne, Thoreau, and Emerson) spelled out in reverse. "We've all known children like this," Jane Brody begins, "they stand too close or they touch us in annoying ways; they laugh too loud or at the wrong times; they make 'stupid' or embarrassing remarks, . . . they mistake friendly actions for hostile ones, . . . they move too slowly, or too fast, for everyone else; their facial expressions don't jibe with what they or others are saying, or their experience is seriously out of step with current fashions." While I both identify with and try to attend to such differences, peculiarities, and idiosyncrasies of perception, the article predictably prescribes the psychological orthodontics of correction and behavioral modification to obliterate the dis-ease, which is given the high-fallutin' name of dyssemia (flawed signal reception), a suitable companion discipline to my own poetic preoccupation, dysraphism.

The veil acknowledges the stigma that is our common ground, our point of adjacency with one another, our "us"ness. Here, *Veil* is related to a short book of my poems called *Stigma,* based on the title of one of Erving Goffman's resonant books on this topic.

In the Hawthorne story, the minister who veils his face gives an explanation that I use as the epigraph for the book: "There is an hour to come when all of us shall cast aside our veils. Take it not amiss, beloved friend, if I wear this piece of crape till then." Our

bodies veil us from transparency (say, assimilation) and the veil
acknowledges that: that we can't communicate as if we had no veils
or bodies or histories separating us, that whatever communication
we can manage must be in terms of our opacities and particularities,
our resistances and impermeabilities—call it our mutual translucency
to each other. Our language is our veil, but one that too often is
made invisible. Yet, hiding the veil of language, its wordness, its tex-
tures, its obstinate physicality, only makes matters worse. Perhaps
such veils will be cast aside in the Messianic moment, that utopian
point in which history vanishes. On this side of the veil, which is
our life on earth, we live within and among the particulars of a here
(hear) and now (words that speak of and to our condition of every-
dayness).

Solidarity Is the Name We Give to What We Cannot Hold

I am a nude formalist poet, a sprung
syntax poet, a multitrack poet, a
wondering poet, a social expressionist
poet, a Baroque poet, a constructivist poet,
an ideolectical poet. I am a New York poet in
California, a San Francisco poet on
the Lower East Side, an Objectivist poet
in Royaumont, a surrealist poet in Jersey,
a Dada poet in Harvard Square,
a zaum poet in Brooklyn, a merz poet
in Iowa, a cubo-futurist poet in Central Park.
I am a Buffalo poet in Providence, a London
poet in Cambridge, a Kootenay School
of Writing poet in Montreal, a local poet
in Honolulu.
I am a leftist poet in my armchair
and an existential poet on the street;
an insider poet among my friends,
an outsider poet in midtown.
I am a serial poet, a paratactic poet, a
disjunctive poet, a discombobulating poet,
a montage poet, a collage poet, a hypertextual
poet, a nonlinear poet, an abstract poet,
a nonrepresentational poet, a process poet,
a polydiscourse poet, a conceptual poet.
I am a vernacular poet, a talk poet, a dialect
poet, a heteroglossic poet, a slang poet, a
demotic poet, a punning poet, a comic poet.
I am an iambic poet I am,
a dactylic poet, a tetrameter poet,
an anapestic poet.
I am a capitalist poet in Leningrad

and a socialist poet in St. Petersburg;
a bourgeois poet at Zabar's, a union poet
in Albany; an elitist poet on TV,
a political poet on the radio.
I am a fraudulent poet, an incomprehensible poet, a degenerate
poet, an incompetent poet, an indecorous poet, a crude poet,
an incoherent poet, a flat-footed poet, a disruptive poet, a
fragmenting poet, a contradictory poet, a self-imploding poet,
a conspiratorial poet, an ungainly poet, an anti-dogmatic poet,
an infantile poet, a theoretical poet, an awkward poet, a sissy
poet, an egghead poet, a perverse poet, a clumsy poet,
a cacophonous poet, a vulgar poet, a warped
poet, a silly poet, a queer poet, an
erratic poet, an erroneous poet, an anarchic poet,
a cerebral poet, an unruly poet,
an emotional poet, a (no) nonsense poet. I am a language
poet wherever people try to limit the modes of
expression or nonexpression. I am an experimental poet
to those who value craft over interrogation, an
avant-garde poet to those who see the future
in the present. I am a Jewish poet hiding in the shadow
of my great-grandfather and great-grandmother.
I am a difficult poet in Kent, a visual poet in
Cleveland, a sound poet in Cincinnati.
I am a modernist poet to postmodernists and a postmodern poet
to modernists. I am a book artist in Minneapolis
and a language artist in Del Mar.
I am a lyric poet in Spokane, an analytic
poet in South Bend, a narrative poet
in Yellow Knife, a realist
poet in Berkeley.
I am an antiabsorptive poet in the morning,
an absorptive poet in the afternoon,
and a sleepy poet at night.
I am a parent poet, a white poet, a man poet, an urban poet, an
    angered poet, a sad poet,
an elegiac poet, a raucous poet, a frivolous poet, a detached
    poet, a roller-coaster poet, a
volcanic poet, a dark poet, a skeptical poet, an eccentric poet, a
    misguided poet, a reflective

poet, a dialectical poet, a polyphonic poet, a hybrid poet, a
    wandering poet, an odd poet, a
lost poet, a disobedient poet, a bald poet, a virtual poet.
& I am none of these things,
nothing but the blank wall of my aversions
writ large in disappearing ink—

What's Art Got to Do with It?

*The Status of the Subject of the Humanities
in an Age of Cultural Studies*

The gradual shift from literary studies to cultural and multicultural studies is probably the most useful change to have occurred within the American academy in the past decade.

The literary studies approach to the humanities tended to make a clear-cut distinction between works of art and works of mass or popular culture. Works of art were the primary field of study for the critic, whose secondary role was to explicate or illuminate these art objects. Yet it is difficult to provide a rule for distinguishing great art from cultural artifact, and the ideological biases of much of the prevailing literary and art connoisseurship have served literary studies poorly.

In contrast, the cultural studies approach seems both more reasonable and more malleable. We start not with art and its others but with a variety of signifying practices. The field of possible attention is vast and might just as well include film comedies of the thirties as Dickens's novels, Kewpie dolls as much as Picassos; although, for practical purposes, the focus of any given study will be narrowed.

The shift to poststructuralist cultural studies has been precipitated by an intriguing variety of frames of interpretation—theoretical, historical, psychological, and sociological. I say interpretative frames rather than methods, for within each of these frames there are a number of distinct, and competing, methodologies. The present crisis of cultural studies results from the seeming autonomy of the frames of interpretation from what they are to interpret; we have less objects of study than what Stanley Fish calls "interpretive communities". What is to be interpreted is by no means secure, nor are the objects of interpretation necessarily of any determining significance. This is a somewhat awkward, even anxious situation. But it is not fundamentally different from the methodological approach of much modernist and contemporary art, where forms of interpretation constitute the subject.

In large measure, the controversy in the national media over the political crisis of higher education—whether characterized in terms of "political correctness", the canon, multiculturalism, or the ascent of theory—can be attributed to the shift from literary to cultural studies. While I am troubled by aspects of the cultural studies model, my own disagreements have little in common with the chorus of self-described liberals and conservatives who see in cultural studies the loss of "disinterested" scholarship and common cultural standards.

This is a disorienting debate to enter since cultural and new historical studies, as practiced in American universities, often extend many of the most conservative features of literary studies. If the naysayers better understood the issues, they might find they have little to fear from new developments in the literary academy and that, indeed, cultural and multicultural studies offer a revitalized version of the traditional humanities, which have suffered from near asphyxiation by means of the anti-democratic arguments for the received authority of a narrow band of cultural arbiters.

Far from challenging the legitimating process of the university, the cultural studies movement actually extends this process in ways that are largely consonant with a tradition that comes to us in fits and starts from the Enlightenment's attack on Scholasticism. Indeed, cultural studies extends the principles of critical self-reflection and disinterested observation in ways that actively work to preserve existing cultural values. The exponents of cultural and multicultural studies represent mainstream American conceptions of value and practice. In this light, the abusive series of attacks in the media can be understood in the first instance as anti-intellectual and in the second, when carried out by scholars, as a form of intellectual self-hatred.

By speaking of intellectual self-hatred I mean to carry over Sander Gilman's arguments in *Jewish Self-Hatred*. The intellectual imagines that there is a hidden language of truth from which she or he is barred by reliance on the slippery and partial slopes of metaphoric language. In this fantasy, intellectuals, like Jews, are exiled from a deeper connection to the world and so denounce their own language, the only language that they know or can speak.

Self-hating intellectuals internalize the anti-intellectuals' conception of their co-workers as professional ciphers, unmoored from the values of the "larger" society. By internalizing the larger community's most negative stereotype of their activity, self-hating intellectuals become the most vocal critics of the relativism and social anarchy that they testify is the true message of "theory". For who could know better the dangers of theory than one who has witnessed its dark secret or its corrosive powers? For the self-hating intellectual, the hidden language of reason is nihilism.

The vehemence of the attacks on cultural and new historical studies has left too little room for a critique of the ways in which these approaches continue to perpetuate a deterministic or professional rather than rhetorical or poetic approach to its subjects. This left-libertarian or aesthetic critique of cultural studies becomes almost impossible to hear amidst the mischaracterizations of the goals of cultural studies that seem mischievously aimed at preventing any thoughtful discussion of the issues. As in national politics, the right has been able to define the terms of the debate.

What, for example, could be more disorienting than casting Stanley Fish as a radical? Fish's defense of professionalization is the model of an enlightened, pragmatic approach to the humanities. He is witty and ingenious in his critiques of any attempt to give special moral weight or ideological force to one theoretical position rather than another. While that may undercut the Romantic humanism that gives a self-righteous tone or hubris to so many traditional professors of English literature, Fish's antifoundationalism is rooted in the values of the profession of which he is a part. Moreover, he insists on politesse, against the authoritarian demagoguery that tends to undermine the values of consensus and reason in an academic setting.

Fish's position is aimed at preserving and respecting institutional memory; it assures continuities and the representation of a variety of viewpoints in any dispute. That is, Fish's antifoundationalism is a moderate and centrist position—no more radical than the democratic principles upon which it is based. It is a measure of the corrosiveness of racism and misogyny that his position favoring the inclusion of African Americans and women in determining curricular policy is so routinely caricatured as extreme.

My own misgivings about Fish's position take an entirely different direction since I find his professionalization of discourse undermines the possibility of any trenchant critique of canonical values or indeed of the institutionalized rationality that Fish enacts. Fish's system suffers from being a self-enclosed artifact, unable to confront its own, inevitable positionality. It represents the professionalization of professionalization and precludes the aestheticizing of its own values, insofar as such aestheticizing might ground judgments outside the context of a profession, holding one's judgments to a continual testing of and in the world.

Many of the welcome changes in the humanities curriculum reflect not revaluations of the role of high or canonical culture but shifts in the representation of various groups in determining what these canonical works should be. The Arnoldian criterion of touchstone works of a culture simply has been applied to a greater number of contexts, just as the Jeffersonian conception of democracy has at times been applied to a greater number of constituencies. The mechanism of discrimination between canonical and noncanonical works is not dismantled but rather extended to previously uncovered areas. Institutionalized multiculturalism represents the culmination of Arnoldian principles of distinction; its great failure lies in its tacit acceptance of the concept of touchstone or representative works. To be sure, institutionalized multiculturalism represents a necessary revision of the concept of representation. In this newer context, what is represented by a work is not, at least in the first place, the culture understood as a homogenous whole. But an initial recognition of ethnic origin often gives way to a supervening program of cultural recuperation, where works are chosen because they represent "ennobling" voices of their subculture, voices that enter into "the great conversation" of universal human values, as proponents of the Great Books used to put it. Houston Baker, in *Modernism and the Harlem Renaissance*, makes an eloquent case for something like this strategy when he argues for the mask of mastering form over the guerrilla tactic of deforming mastery. The uncertain success of this strategy is represented by the pride of place given, in such textbooks as the *Norton Anthology of Modern Poetry*, to the sonnets of Countee Cullen and Claude McKay and the exclusion in the same anthologies of the dialect and vernacular poems of Paul Laurence Dunbar, James Weldon Johnson, and Sterling Brown, which, however, can be found in the new multicultural *Heath Anthology of American Literature*.

Despite the fact that the Heath anthology does a better job of "representing" the touchstones of American culture than Norton, I see no radical conceptual difference between the two. Both have the primary effect of taking a very heterogeneous field and domesticating it. Both represent literature in measured doses, uniform typography, and levelling head- and footnotes—making the poetry the subject of its frame rather than presenting poetry itself as a contest—a conflict—of frames.

One thing the Norton modern poetry anthologies have never done is to represent white or European culture. Yet this point is too rarely acknowledged because of a confusion as to what constitutes "high" or canonical culture in America, a situation abetted by the fact that many of the defenders of a putative "high" culture imagine this culture to exist solely in the past—or as if it were in the past.

The cultural canon of the Norton anthology is as aggressively anti-"high" cultural as the Heath anthology. As a matter of policy, the Norton anthology systematically excludes the aesthetically radical innovations of European and American art in preference for a "middlebrow" or suburban poetry that tends to be anti-European and is often anti-aesthetic. Within this deaestheticizing ideology, it is far easier to include token ethnic representation, as the Norton *Modern* does in its most recent version, than to include works, including those written by historically underrepresented groups, that undermine the formally complacent, content-focussed biases of official verse culture.

Yet, it turns out that those most likely to defend the importance of great art are themselves the major perpetrators of a disastrous lowering of standards. Indeed, it's a wild irony to see *The New York Times* run article after article debunking the new university barbarians for abandoning the great works of our cultural heritage, when in its own book supplement it primarily promotes literary works that make no claims on the most resonant cultural traditions of Europe or America.

"High" "middle" "low"—there are no fixed meanings for these terms and I mean to use them against themselves. For example, I want to suggest that a collapsing of the low and the high against the middle is a feature not just of cultural studies but also of significant directions within 20th century philosophy and poetry.

In philosophy, this is most explicitly signalled by the "quest for the ordinary", in Stanley Cavell's phrase, a quest related to the preoccupation with the vernacular, dialect, the everyday, and the common in poetry. High and low are also literally collapsed when elements from popular or regional or "other" (for example, tribal) cultures are collaged into poems or paintings—a feature some have argued is a hallmark of postwar modernisms but whose roots go back much earlier and, indeed, suggest a model for cultural studies in modernist collage and appropriation. Finally, the insistence of many artists, contemporary and modern, on the taboo, the vulgar, and the mean also represents an alliance of the high and the low against a self-defining middle. It is this direction that has caused the greatest fury, with attacks on the National Endowment for the Arts being the most visible battleground. Those concerned with the fate of cultural, multicultural, and poststructuralist studies need to join artists in resisting these attacks—which have targeted gay and feminist performance artists—as passionately as they would attacks on academic freedom, which they closely resemble.

We're all middle class now, or it is as if the culture inscribes this allegiance to middle class values as a psychic tax on consumer purchases. As with all regressive taxes, this one hits those with less than middle incomes the hardest and is easily absorbed by the wealthy. Which is to say, it is the right to define the "middle" that is being contested by the left, right, and center. But earning this right requires the rejection of all the highs and lows—the obscure, the peripheral or marginal or minor, the avant-garde, the complex, the eccentric, the dark, the distasteful, the ugly, the unassimilable, the erotic, the repulsive, the formally unsettling. From the populist perspective, such work may be discounted as elitist or regressive or both; from the defenders of transcendental literary values, such work is attacked as corrosive. Moreover, the contest for the middle is less something that pits high culture against low culture than it is a struggle within "high" and "popular" culture: Kathy Acker vs James Merrill, Vanilla Ice vs Linton Kwesi Johnson, *The Cosby Show* vs *The Simpsons*.

Just because something is neglected is sufficient reason to consider it.

Is there a special status of high art that should be accorded our most respected poets and novelists and denied Paul Rubens or Peter Straub or Jackie Mason? Are these writers any more deserving of a place in the classroom than *Pee-Wee's Playhouse* or *Mystery* or *The World according to Jackie Mason*? On the contrary, these three works are more interesting and worthier of close reading than many of the recent winners of the Pulitzer Prize or National Book Award. If the prize winners are the contemporary case for high culture, then there can be no question that those who prefer to study cultural and social texts are probably right. There's more innovation and more cultural acumen in any episode of *Ren and Stimpy* than in any of the books of our last trio of national poet laureates.

Our worst examples, foisted on us by the cultural orthodontics of official literary culture, serve us badly. We keep thinking that what is canonized as high art is what art is all about—but this whitewash of our literary and aesthetic histories represses what indeed is the lasting legacy of even white, Eurocentric male artists, much less artists of different origins and, perhaps more useful to say, different destinations. In the great shell game of art in the university, the "art" has too often disappeared, replaced by administered culture. And administered art may be no better than no art, since it's the administration that is doing most of the signifying.

What, then, accounts for the complacently narrow range of styles and tone in the official verse culture of the postwar period? Perhaps this too can be understood as a manifestation of intellectual self-hatred. Professional anti-intellectualism plays itself out in a particularly uninhibited form in the promoting of works of poetry that espouse a distaste for the intellectual and rhetorical nature of writing—poems that insist on affiliation with innocuous abstractions like the "universal human spirit" while denying their implication in the material forms in which particular human spirits actually might appear. Ironically it is such nostalgic values, fundamentally aversive to a contemporary engagement with the poetic, that those who profess both literary and cultural studies too often ascribe to poetry as such.

The products of official verse culture are no more interesting or valuable than the products of Madison Avenue. (What would be the state of film studies if it were confined to Oscar nominees?) However, poetry can also be a form of cultural studies that incorporates reading the products of Madison Avenue; call it, Social Expressionism. Yet the university as a professional environment remains hostile to this type of approach both in its creative writing programs and in its normalizing writing practices.

There is no art, only signifying practices. Or rather, who's to say what's just a signifying practice and what a work of art? Once the fixed points of difference are undermined, there can be no rule to make such distinctions. But it doesn't follow from this that distinctions cannot be made in particular contexts.

Of course if poetry is above the fray of competing social discourses then its special status is secure. But there is no Poetry, only poetries. The patchwork quilt of works I have in mind insists on its reflectiveness as a means of refracting the pull of commodification or, to put it more historically, zeitgeistization. The works of social expressionism—whether by Bruce Andrews or Hannah Weiner, Ron Silliman or William Burroughs— are neither the unreflected products of their period nor the lyric expression of individual selves. Rather the social field itself is expressed, in the sense of brought into view, represented by means of interpretation and interpenetration.

The university environment is not just nonpoetic, which would be unexceptional, but antipoetic. And this situation has remained constant as we have moved from literary studies to the more sociologically and psychoanalytically deterministic approaches to cultural studies. At the same time, the university is perhaps the only one among many anti-poetic and anti-philosophic American institutions that will entertain its antipathy to the poetic and the philosophic as a significant problem, and it is this approach that I think becomes more possible in the age of cultural studies.

Within the academic environment, thought tends to be rationalized— subject to examination, paraphrase, repetition, mechanization, reduction. It is treated: contained and stabilized. And what is lost in this treatment is the irregular, the nonquantifiable, the nonstandard or nonstandardizable, the erratic, the inchoate. (Is it just a mood or sensibility I'm talking about, and if that's it, can mood be professionalized?)

Poetry is turbulent thought, at least that's what I want from it, what I want to say about it just here, just now (and maybe not in some other context). It leaves things unsettled, unresolved—leaves you knowing less than you did when you started.

Here, then, is my thesis: There is a fear of the inchoate processes of turbulent thought (poetic or philosophic) that takes the form of resistance and paranoia. A wall (part symbolic, part imaginary) is constructed against the sheer surplus of interpretable aspects of any subject. You fix upon one among many possible frames, screens, screams, and stay fixed on that mode monomaniacally. Such frame fixation is intensified by the fetishizing of dispassionate evaluation not as a critical method but as a marker of professional competence and a means of enforcing a system of ranking.

In theory, the proliferation of frames of interpretation (feminist, psychoanalytic, grammatologic, economic, sociologic, Romantic, historical materialist, new critical, reader-response, canonic, periodic) is a positive development. In practice, the incommensurability among these frames has led to a Balkanization of theory. The normalizing tendency, resisted by some of the most resourceful practitioners of cultural studies, is to elect one interpretive mode and to apply it, cookie-cutter-like, to any given phenomenon. On the one hand, this can be defended on scientific or religious grounds, and, on the other hand, as a form not of faith or positivism but of specialization.

Frame fixation bears a family resemblance to aspect blindness, as described by Wittgenstein in part 2 of *Philosophical Investigations*, where the single figure that can be interpreted as a duck and a rabbit is discussed. Different contexts may suggest the appropriateness of particular interpretive systems, some of which may then seem determining. That is, once viewed through a particular frame, it becomes difficult to recognize alternate readings. A gaze freezes into a stare; only one aspect of an ambiguous figure is visible. The projection overwhelms the text without exhausting the work.

To say that the literary academy is antipoetic is not to say poets or literary artists are the sole repository of the poetic. This would be to split the aesthetic and philosophic from other forms of cultural activity when it is just this splitting—splintering—that is the problem. The poetic is not confined to poetry but rather is embedded in all our activities as critics, teachers, researchers, and writers, not to mention citizens. When we use figurative language, which is just about whenever we use language at all, we are entangled in the poetic realm. Whenever we choose one metaphoric or trope-ic system of interpretation we make aesthetic choices, moral judgments. Poetry is too important to be left to poets, just in the way that politics is too important to be left to politicians or that education is too important to be left to educators; though poets, politicians, and educators may exercise a valuable function when they elucidate how poetry, politics, and learning can be hyperactivated in everyday life.

Our political and academic culture of imposed solutions at the expense of open-ended explorations, of fixed or schematic or uniform interpretive mechanisms and political platforms versus multiple, shifting, context-sensitive interventions, splits off the "bad" poetic from "good" rigor and critical distantiation. Such splitting eclipses reason in its uncontained denial. Out of fear of the Dark, we turn our back to the lights we have at hand, in hand.

With justification, we have removed poetry—the "literary"—from any privileged status as an object of study but have not enlisted the poetic as an allied interpretive activity. Because of the lingering hold of reductive rationalism, we have administered to art the one-two punch: neither valuing it, Romantically, for itself nor valuing it for its critical and cognitive function.

My point is not to relegate criticism or literary theory to secondary status. I agree with Fish and others that the new interpretive approaches change the objects of study. Rather, I am insisting that art not be reduced to secondary status, the "object" of critical projection, but understood as an irreplaceable method of interpreting culture, including other artworks—"poetry as discourse" in Antony Easthope's useful formulation.

The poetic—the aesthetic—the philosophic—the rhetorical: these intertwined figures dissolve into the art of everyday life, the multiple and particular decisions and revisions, recognitions and intuitions, that make up—constitute—our experiences of and in the world. The poetic is not simply another frame of interpretation to be laid down next to the psycholinguistic and sociohistorical. The poetic is both a hypoframe, inhering within each frame of interpretation, and a hyperframe, a practice of moving from frame to frame.

Such hypertextuality offers not a theory of frames—a supervening or hypotactic ordering principle—but an art of transition through and among frames. Call it the art of parataxis, where the elements set side by side are critical methods rather than images or ideas: an art of practice, which provides not answers but paths of reading and provisional connections among these paths. The alternative to frame fixation is context sensitivity; that is, allowing different contexts to suggest different interpretative approaches while at the same time flipping among several frames, or at the least, acknowledging the provisionality of any single-frame approach. The poetic is not a master frame, able to reconcile incommensurable approaches. Rather, poetry has its expertise in encompassing incommensurable elements without getting locked into any one of them; this, anyway, is a strain of poetry that goes back to Blake and Heraclitus and forward to many writers—poets and critics, scholars and theorists— in our own time.

It is not theory that has supplanted criticism or art but rather an axiometric solution-focussed theory that marks a continuity from literary to cultural studies, over and against the heterogeneous traditions of critical theory and aesthetic practice associated with such antipositivist writers as Barthes and Cavell, Goffman and Creeley, de Certeau and Mayer, Federman and Ashbery, Clifford and Irigaray, Debord and Hejinian, Mac Low and Feyerabend; *add your name here.*

Of course, it is possible for any writer's work to be turned from practice to doctrine and surely this is what has happened to the work of many of the governing Proper Names of structuralist and poststructuralist theory.

It is not surprising that literary professionals might prefer answers to questions, explications to evocations, doctrine to introspection, probity to pleasure. But this system of preferences and inclinations, this habitat (or habitus) of professionalism, in Pierre Bourdieu's sense, is untheorized, uncritical. The habitat of professionalism marks not a substantive position but a self-justifying apparatus of control.

While one of the defining axioms of cultural studies is the death of the author, the authors of cultural studies seem to exempt themselves from the full effect of this theory, much the way a queen might be exempted from her own decrees. The theory death of the author seems to apply to other people's authors.

If we are to understand, following Bourdieu, that the value of a work of art is determined by the same system of discriminations—class-based dispositions or tastes—that determines the differential value of styles of furniture or dresses or table manners, then why not apply this to Bourdieu's *Distinction: A Social Critique of the Judgment of Taste*? Why not demystify the social scientific claim for his theory and see his book as a commodity whose status is determined by its role in the professional habitat to which he belongs? On such a sociometric reading, on what basis do we make a distinction between Bourdieu's empirical analysis and that found in consumer surveys in *Elle* or *Ladies Home Journal*. Put another way, Is Fredric Jameson's writing on postmodernism a symptom of postindustrial capitalism?

For those who wish to model cultural and new historical and psychoanalytic studies on the social sciences, these questions will seem merely silly. It is literary authors who are the product of their period, while social scientists are able to maintain their authority and, not unimportantly, their status as authors and professors, because their methods immunize them from becoming subjects of the historical forces within which they operate.

My method immunizes me against nothing, accelerating my subjection to the multivectoral forces I am periodically digested by. My signifying behavior is eclipsed by the semiotic maelstrom I feel myself falling, slipping, tumbling, and twirling into. The only distance I know the one from *me* to *you*; yet it's enough to ground me in the runes of what I would otherwise imagine could be my possession. For there is nothing other than this grounding in "communities of discourse", a language play of hide and seek. & this makes me count my judgment, learn what making judgment is.

Signifying practices have only art from which to copy.

The idea that a statistical or objectifying orientation, or else a tone of disinterested probity, raises criticism or theory above the level of cultural artifact is profoundly ahistorical; nor is there any reason to suppose that this has changed in the age of cultural studies. Art and critical writing can be sites of social and aesthetic resistance. Yet both share the tendency to conformism and complacency. Typical professional criticism, like the dominant forms of verse and visual arts, reifies more than resists. Against its most advanced theory, such writing retains the illusions of voice and its authority, in blissless compliance with received standards. Its authors are not so much dead as operating on automatic pilot and it is as if cries to wake them are jammed by the control towers.

This is not an unregulated process. Norms are strictly enforced by a system of hazards and penalties for those who drift outside the narrow stylistic confines of official critical discourse. And what justifies this monologic, tone-jammed prose? Not the intrinsic virtues of the style since the threats of being unmarketable or unpublishable are internally enforced professional criteria, part of a system of self-regulation, in Foucault's sense, that gains its legitimacy by being able to enforce a distinction between acceptable and unacceptable discursive manners. The need for discipline preexists the particular distinction that gives content to the discipline. Thus the poetic as a negative space is necessary to give disciplinarity to disinterested scholarship or rigorous theory.

Research and analysis can exist independent of the forms in which they are represented but cannot, finally, remain unaffected by them. The governing principle of the plain style of much critical prose is that it should be as neutral as possible, that it should not call attention to itself. Untidy thoughts and facts must be made to conform to this "anti"rhetoric, if not by the author then by the interventionist editorial practices of professional journals that enforce mood and tone control as if a loose sentence were a case of intemperance or the conventions of grammar and style were hieratic laws not matters of agreement and disagreement.

It is always fair to ask of a mode of writing—what interests does it serve? Are there studies that demonstrate that the currently enforced dissertation styles make better teachers? Do they increase interest on the part of readers in their subjects? Are they the only way to encourage the depth of detailed knowledge of a particular subject or period that remains one of the overriding values of scholarship? Are they more a rite of initiation into a profession than a mark of an active engagement with a culture?

Is prose justified? Or aren't you the kind that tells? That's no prose that's my default. Default is in our sorrow not our swells.

I am writing this with a fountain pen on a yellow legal pad, lying down on a couch, the pad propped up by my knee. I resist sitting down at a machine on a desk; I want to write from a more comfortable position. I enjoy writing more this way.

Does not knowing the relevance of this factor argue that I should leave it out? What kind of writing results from suppressing all the elements that can't be justified? My most fruitful thoughts at first seem unfounded, foundering; if not elusive, then wildly speculative. I like to follow the course of such thoughts even as I am taken to more and more improbable conclusions. In my court of writing, I have loose rules of evidence. If a phrase occurs to me and I don't see the pertinence, I know better than to abandon course. Perhaps some useful turning is at hand. Rather than discount what may not at first appear to fit my theme, and risk losing a new and more resonant address, I hold a thought relevant until proven otherwise, give the benefit to what I doubt, pursuing a flicker in preference to reiterating what I already knew.

The shortest distance between two points is a digression. I hold for a wandering thought just that I may stumble upon something worthy of report.

Montaigne is the most typical writer in all of Western prose.

The idea is to put the shoe on the other foot—evaluate the evaluators, historicize the historicizers, decode the decoders, critique the critics, rebuke the rebukers, debunk the debunkers, categorize the categorizers, schmooze the schmoozers, level the levellers, revel with the revellers.

Put the shoe on the other foot and tear it.

"There's a lot of anger there, Charles. You really need to work it out."

"You've got a million crackpot theories, I only wish one of them would pan out." (As if writing were prospecting for the pleated gold at the end of the theory rainbow.)

I suppose the only thing I count as an absolute moral virtue is learning difficulties, disorientation, and lexical hindrances. When I hear people talking about scanning lines I assume they're referring to the security guards at grocery checkouts. Not that I don't admire scrupulous accuracy and competence, I just happen to prefer the company of small businesspersons.

But seriously, you can't go wrong if your attitude is bad from the start. You've got nowhere to go but up. Virtue is easier to strive for than to hold onto.

A friend of my daughter just got into the school for the gifted and talented, but she was confused and wanted me to tell her if she was gifted or talented. I always wanted to be gifted but evidently didn't have the talent for it. Anyway, my philosophy of education is—don't take gifts, but don't pay retail either.

Yet many of my friends in the university are conflicted—are they artists or scholars, teachers or writers, as if you aren't one by virtue of the other. That's what virtue is all about.

Or consider the professor who was always distracted at his seminars because, he said, they were taking him from his work. My teaching also keeps me from my work, which is teaching.

But while I love Art, I wouldn't want to marry her.

Or have you heard the one about the person who was half critic and half artist. What she can't objectify, she appropriates.

Behind every successful artist is a new historian who says it's all just a symptom. Behind every successful new historian is an artist who says you forgot to mention my work—and, boy, is it symptomatic!

I've never met an artist who felt she or he was getting enough attention. Prizes, books on the work, multiyear grants. "But still, did you see the fifth sentence of that review where it says 'possibly the greatest . . .'?" Or: "Did you see the index to that book on the 20th century?—no mention of my name." Scholars, in contrast, seem surprised if you've ever read a paragraph of theirs. "What? You saw that article? I didn't realize anybody read that journal." "What? You read my book? But it was just published eight years ago and I didn't realize your research took you so far afield to read about the decline of modern civilization."

One can learn as much about a profession by dwelling on what it frowns upon as on what it prizes. Our professionalism encourages us to act as administrators of culture rather than participants, collaborators, or partisans enthralled with our subjects. Yet this very professionalism can preclude perspective on our own absorption in the fictions of critical distance. The problem with the normalizing critical writing practices of the humanities is not that they are too theoretical but that they are not theoretical enough—they fail to theorize themselves or to keep pace with their own theories.

For models for the new writing the age demands, North American literary and cultural critics, essayists, and historians have turned to the radical literary arts of this century producing a startling range of prose forms, including (to mention just those from the last few years) the dialogues of Jerome McGann; the use of typographic and visual elements as integral to both the critical analysis and mode of argument in Trinh T. Minh-ha's *Woman, Native, Other*, Art Spiegelman's *Maus*, Avital Ronell's *The Telephone Book*, and Johanna Drucker's *Simulant Portrait*; the insistence on the autobiographical in the recent talk essays of David Antin, Samuel R. Delany's *Motion of Light in Water*, and Nancy Miller's *Getting Personal*; the politically and performatively charged essays of Kofi Natambu; the pataphysically playful, detail-centered 16th and 17th century textual criticism of Randall McLeod; the new historiography of Susan Howe's *The Birthmark: Unsettling the Wilderness in American Literary History*; the improvisatory prose of Amiri Baraka; the essays-in-film of Yvonne Rainier and Guy Debord; the exuberant championing of nonstandard poetries as part of a context of visual and popular culture in Cary Nelson's *Repression and Recovery* and Marjorie Perloff's *The Futurist Moment, Poetic License*, and *Radical Artifice*; the reworking of biography and autobiography as oral history in Quincy Troupe's rethinking of the vernacular in *Miles: The Autobigraphy* and Peter Brazeau's earlier book on Stevens, *Parts of a World*; Dennis Tedlock's continuing explorations of oral and performative modes of interpretation and translation; Larry McCaffery's championing of the interview and other metafictional critical forms; the glorious speculative flights of Nick Piombino in *Boundary of Blur* or Steve McCaffery in *North of Intention* and of McCaffery and bp Nichol in *Rational Geomancy* and in Christopher Dewdney's natural history as sci-fi; the intertwining of poetry and philosophy in Linda Reinfeld's *Language Poetry: Writing as Rescue*; the hypertextual investigations of Michael Joyce and Jay Boltner and the electronic format of the e-mail magazines *Postmodern Culture* and *Rif/t*; and such marvelous reworkings of the essay form as Larry Eigner's *Areas/Lights/Heights*, Nathaniel Mackey's *Bedouin Hornbook*, Madeline Gins's *Helen Keller or Arakawa*, James Sherry's *Our Nuclear Heritage*, Nicole Brossard's *Picture Theory*, and Leslie Scalapino's *How Phenomena Appear to Unfold* and *Objects in the Terrifying Tense / Longing from Taking Place*.

No doubt this collapses conventional distinctions among scholarly, popular, and general interest prose; but in an age of cultural studies such segmentation will not hold. The space of prose is an operating environment that embeds genres within genres. Nor does one have to choose between fiction and story: for there are the stories of our searches and researches. The art of the essay; but also, the essay as art.

For prose can sing. It can swim against the remorseless tide of axiomatizing and tone-lock. But that requires that as writers we listen to the sounds that we make with our words; that we own the shapes our paragraphs declare as they crash into one another or erode each other's edges; that we hear both the studied and the studying as always art, music, the movement of ideas through measures and measuring, shifted and shifting tempos and modulations. This is the promise of a writing-conscious cultural studies as much as of a proactive poetics.

The test of the new poststructuralists will be whether we will change the prevailing institutionalized infatuation with triumphalist specialization, neoscientific prose, and all shape and manner of standardization, from tests to course designs. Will we apply our theories of ambiguity, provisionality, and the nomadic not just to reinterpreting the power dynamics of centuries no doubt prematurely consigned to history, but also to our own workplace and its administrative and professional apparatuses?

Of course poetry and fiction are institutionalized in university creative writing programs. But for the most part such programs do little to further social expressionism in poetry or cultural activism in criticism. Too often creative writing programs lock themselves into counterproductive antagonism with English departments, especially with the new literary theory, fearing philosophy will compromise the intuitive and emotional capacity on which a poet must rely in fabricating her or his voice.

It doesn't have to be this way. Creative writing programs could be transformed into university centers for the art of writing, specializing in research and development into the social and aesthetic dimensions of writing. At the same time, literature classes could be transformed from a knowledge-acquisition approach to creative reading workshops, replacing tests with poetic response in the form of free-form journals, poems, and literary imitations.

I don't teach Literature I teach poetry-as-a-second-language, or PSL— People in Solidarity with Language. That means I try to immerse the workshop, formerly class, in poetic forms, poetic sounds, and poetic logics. Tapes of poets reading their own work are indispensable, since there is no way to fully explain sound values; it would be as if you tried to teach music only from scores. Poetry readings, along with regular visits by literary artists to graduate and undergraduate classes, can be catalytic, offering an entirely different context for poems than books and anthologies, one immensely more immediate and performative.

PSL isn't focussed on just the big nouns; its immersion is into the wide and varied syntax of poetic practice, from popular and folk and novelty to conventional to radically innovative (a project it shares with cultural and multicultural studies). There's nothing like juxtaposing Service's "The Shooting of Dan McGrew" with Eliot's "Prufrock", or Melvin Tolson with Lorine Neidecker, or Laura Riding with John Masefield. And the fact that no anthology represents this conflict and context of poetries is all the better, since it helps to dispel any notion that poetry is a single activity with a unified purpose. (Eliot is the only one of these six poets in either the Norton *Modern* or the Heath anthologies.)

PSL immersion need not be confined to 20th century literature, for one can read poems through other poems as much as through more traditional critical methodologies. I can't help but read the poems of the past with the benefit of the many new critical approaches of the present, but neither can I read these older poems without having my reading altered by the poetry of the present. I understand Wordsworth better because I've read *Flow Chart*. I'm convinced William Cowper read J. H. Prynne before writing *The Task*. And I'm more likely to give a Jabèsian reading of Heine than a Kristevan one.

Finally, let me turn to one of the most pressing issues facing the university in the 1990s: PC.

I believe that PC is crucial for a writer—personal cappuccino. Of the three types—the Italian hand-pump style, the German electric, and the American pump or press—all have much to offer.

A Test of Poetry

What do you mean by *rashes of ash*? Is *industry*
systematic work, assiduous activity, or ownership
of factories? Is *ripple* agitate lightly? Are
we *tossed in tune* when we write poems? And
what or who *emboss with gloss insignias of air*?

Is the *Fabric* about which you write in the epigraph
of your poem an edifice, a symbol of heaven?

Does *freight* refer to cargo or lading carried
for pay by water, land or air? Or does it mean
payment for such transportation? Or a freight
train? When you say a *commoded journey*,
do you mean a comfortable journey or a good train
with well-equipped commodities? But, then, why
do you drop the 'a' before *slumberous friend*? And
when you write, in "Why I Am Not a Christian"
*You always throw it down / But you never
pick it up*—what is *it*??

In "The Harbor of Illusion", does *vein*
refer to a person's vein under his skin or
is it a metaphor for a river? Does *lot*
mean one's fate or a piece of land?
And does *camphor* refer to camphor trees?
Moreover, who or what is *nearing*. Who or
what has *fell*? Or does *fell* refer to the
skin or hide of an animal? And who or what has
stalled? Then, is the *thoroughfare of
noon's atoll* an equivalent of *the template*?

In "Fear of Flipping" does *flipping* mean
crazy?

How about *strain*, does it mean
a severe trying or wearing pressure or
effect (such as a strain of hard work),
or a passage, as in piece of music?
Does *Mercury* refer to a brand of oil?

In the lines
shards of bucolic pastry anchored
against cactus cabinets, Nantucket buckets
could we take it as—pieces of pies
or tarts are placed in buckets (which
are made of wood from Nantucket)
anchored against cabinets (small
rooms or furniture?) with cactus?

What is *nutflack*?

I suppose the *caucus of caucasians*
refers to the white people's meeting
of a political party to nominate candidates.
But who is *Uncle Hodgepodge*?
And what does *familiar freight*
to the returning antelope mean?

You write, *the walls are our floors*.
How can the *walls* be floors if the floors
refer to the part of the room which forms
its enclosing surface and upon which one
walks? In *and the floors, like balls,*
repel all falls—does *balls* refer to
nonsense or to any ball like a basket ball
or to guys? Or to a social assembly for
dancing? *Falls* means to descend
from a higher to a lower
or to drop down wounded or dead?
But what is *the so-called overall*
mesh?

Is the *garbage heap* the garbage heap
in the ordinary sense? Why does
garbage heap exchange for *so-called*
overall mesh? Since a *faker* is
one who fakes, how can
arbitrary reduce to *faker*?

Who or what are disappointed
not to have been?

Does *frames* refer to form, constitution,
or structure in general? Or to a
particular state, as of the mind?

In the sentence,
If you don't like it
colored in, you can always xerox it
and see it all gray
—what is *it*? What does
colored in mean?

A few lines later you write,
You mean, image farm when you've got bratwurst—
Does *bratwurst* refer to sausage?
Does the line mean—the sausage
you saw reminded you of a farm which you imagined?

Does *fat-bottom boats* refer to boats with thick bottoms?
Is *humble then humped* used to describe the actions of one
who plays golf? In the phrase *a sideshow freak—*
the *freak* refers to a hippie? *Sideshow* refers to secondary
importance? Or an abnormal actor in the sideshow?
Then, who or what is *linked* with *steam of pink*. And
how about *the tongue-tied tightrope stalker—*
does the *stalker* refer to one who is pursuing
stealthily in the act of hunting game? The stalker
is a witness at first and then a witless witness?

You write *The husks are salted:*
what kind of nut husks can be salted for eating?
What does *bending* mean—to become curved,
crooked, or bent? Or to bow down in submission
or reverence, yield, submit? Does *bells*
refer to metallic sounding instruments or
a kind of trousers?

Just a few lines later you have the phrase
Felt very poured. Who felt poured? Toys?
Is *humming* in the sense of humming a song?
Stepped into where? *Not being part of* what?

In "No Pastrami" (*Walt! I'm with you in Sydney / Where*

the echoes of Mamaroneck howl / Down the outback's
pixilating corridors)—does the *pastrami* refer
to a highly seasoned shoulder cut of beef? Is
Mamaroneck a place in the U.S. where wild oxes howl?
I take it *corridors* refers to the passageway
in the supermarket? Could I read the poem as—
The speaker is doing shopping in a supermarket
in Sydney; he is walking along the eccentric
passageways among the shelves on which goods
are placed; he does not want to buy the pastrami
as he seems to have heard the echoes of wild oxes
howling in the U.S. while he addresses Walt Whitman?

In "No End to Envy", does the envy refer to admire or
in the bad sense?

The Book as Architecture

Architectural terms are more than just metaphors for reading, yet it's difficult to track the parallels without getting impossibly abstract or painfully elusive.

You can start with the idea of "grammatical space" and Louis Kahn's idea that material—and I would include verbal material—"is spent light". Something of the darkness of reading comes out in this phrase, a reminder of the opaque spaces of the interior that poetry can aspire toward just as easily as back away from: the sightless interrogative of writing, its blackening of the page a resistance to the oppressive insistence of visibility. Aldo Rossi's topology of fractures, contaminations, areas of waiting, and intermediate/non-determinate units are as much terms for a new prosody as a new architecture.

The constructing of grammatical space through various forms of sequencing pervades all levels of writing, from the ordering of syllables, words, phrases, lines, and stanzas within a poem to the overall arrangement of poems in a book. Poetic composition consists of a series of displacements constantly opening up upon new emplacements; or, to speak literally of metaphors, composition consists of measuring or registering a series of dislocations that produces the poem's motion or kinesis.

In organizing my books, including this one, I've tried to invent different ways of ordering the individual pieces, avoiding, where possible, both chronological and thematically developmental patterns. For example, borders between poems are occasionally confused: sometimes a stanza of a long poem may not be formally different from a discrete short poem in the same book, or a short poem in one book becomes part of a longer poem in another. Various sequencings of contrasting styles or rhetorics or shapes attracts me as a model. I've sometimes imagined my collections of poems to be something like those oversized books of samples that used to be in tailor's shops, with small swatches of different fabrics—one page with a dozen types of herringbone and another with different thicknesses. My father, who was in the textile business, used to have dozens of such books in his office, in fact it was probably the kind of book he knew best and took

56

the greatest interest in. Yet my own temptation is to allow for maximum contrast from one poem to another, that by means of this conflict of modes I can bring into greater audibility musical or aesthetic or emotional pre-occupations not otherwise articulable. Sometimes I think of a book as a "group" show; but I want the formal divergences among the poems to produce an "inner" space that seems impossible to evoke if there is too much uniformity among the elements.

Organizing a book is something like constructing a durational tunnel that a reader can ride through, like riding through a multichambered House of Horrors at an amusement park. The creation of durational spaces in a poem—great but empty halls, narrow corridors, closets, enclosed pools, formal picture galleries, off and on ramps, pulleys and trap doors between levels—produces an internal or negative (in the sense of inverted or inner) architecture.—You are entering a building through a dark and musty subbasement; proceeding a few steps, you trip onto an elevator platform and are whisked to what is something like the 23rd floor, where you are stepping out into an abandoned soundstage for a 1930 production of a Fenimore Cooper story; sighting a ladder, you climb up a flight onto a floor filled with hundreds of irregularly shaped cubicles populated by women dressed as Matadors . . .

Against the Romantic idea of poems as transport, I prefer to imagine poems as spatializations and interiorizations—blueprints of a world I live near to but have yet to occupy fully. Building impossible spaces in which to roam, unhinged from the contingent necessities of durability, poems and the books they make eclipse stasis in their insatiable desire to dwell inside the pleats and folds of language.

Dear Mr. Fanelli,

I saw your picture
in the 79th street
station. You said
you'd be interested
in any comments I
might have on the
condition of the
station. Mr. Fanelli,
there is a lot of
debris in the 79th street
station that makes it
unpleasant to wait in
for more than a few
minutes. The station
could use a paint
job and maybe
new speakers so you
could understand
the delay announcements
that are always being
broadcast. Mr.
Fanelli—there are
a lot of people sleeping
in the 79th street station
& it makes me sad
to think they have no
home to go to. Mr.
Fanelli, do you think
you could find a more
comfortable place for them
to rest? It's pretty noisy
in the subway, especially with

all those express trains
hurtling through every
few minutes, anyway when the
trains are in service.
I have to admit, Mr. Fanelli, I
think the 79th street station's
in pretty bad shape
& sometimes at night
as I toss in my bed
I think the world's
not doing too good
either, & I
wonder what's going
to happen, where we're
headed, if we're
headed anywhere, if
we even have heads. Mr.
Fanelli, do you think if
we could just start
with the 79th street
station & do what
we could with that
then maybe we could,
you know, I guess, move
on from there? Mr.
Fanelli, when I saw your
picture & the sign
asking for suggestions
I thought, if
you really wanted to
get to the bottom
of what's wrong then
maybe it was my job
to write you: Maybe
you've never been inside
the 79th street station
because you're so busy
managing the 72nd street
& 66th street stations,
maybe you don't know
the problems we have
at 79th—I mean the

dirt & frequent
delays & the feeling of
total misery that
pervades the place. Mr.
Fanelli, are you reading
this far in the letter
or do you get so
many letters every day
that you don't have
time to give each
one the close attention
it desires? Or am I
the only person who's
taken up your invitation
to get in touch &
you just don't have enough
experience to know how to
respond? I'm sorry
I can't get your attention
Mr. Fanelli because I really
believe if you ask
for comments than you
ought to be willing
to act on them—even
if *ought* is too
big a word to throw
around at this point.
Mr. Fanelli
I hope you won't
think I'm rude
if I ask you a
personal question. Do
you get out of the
office much?
Do you go to the movies
or do you prefer
sports—or maybe
quiet evenings at a
local restaurant? Do
you read much, Mr. Fanelli?
I don't mean just
Gibbons and like

that, but philosophy—
have you read much
Hannah Arendt or
do you prefer
a more ideological
perspective?
I think if I understood
where you're coming from,
Mr. Fanelli, I could
write to you more cogently,
more persuasively. Mr.
Fanelli, do you get out
of the city at all—I
mean like up to Bear
Mountain or out to
Montauk? I mean do you
notice how unpleasant
the air is in the 79th
street station—that we
could use some cooling
or air-filtering system
down there? Mr.
Fanelli, do you think
it's possible we
could get together
and talk about
these things in
person? There are
a few other points
I'd like to go over
with you if I could
get the chance. Things
I'd like to talk to
you about but that
I'd be reluctant to
put down on paper.
Mr. Fanelli, I haven't
been feeling very good
lately and I thought
meeting with you face
to face might change
my mood, might put

me into a new frame
of mind. Maybe we
could have lunch?
Or maybe after work?
Think about it, Mr.
Fanelli.

An Interview with Hannah Möckel-Rieke

Hannah Möckel-Rieke: Readers confronted with a new kind of writing always like to have a term which is not necessarily a label, but which may simply serve as a marker, triggering off a number of issues at stake. I think that "Language poetry" has been such a term, which is however much disliked among the poets concerned. Is there a term more adequate that you would use?

Charles Bernstein: The problem has more to do with the process of naming than with any specific names.

"Language poetry" is a term I prefer not to use, although I recognize how pervasive it has become both as a generic term and as an historically specific designation. In one sense, the term refers to an extremely diverse and even conflicting series of works that depart from conventional poetic practices. There isn't one kind of form, one kind of style, or one kind of approach that interested us in $L=A=N=G=U=A=G=E$—the magazine Bruce Andrews and I edited from 1978 to 1981. Just as now there is not a single form, style, or approach that can characterize the related tendencies in contemporary North American poetry that are sometimes labeled in this way. I suppose my resistance to "Language" Poetry as a group or school is related to not wanting to inscribe anyone's partialities, working biases, into inappropriate domains; not to transform pragmatic and provisional choices into the realm of "essentializing" descriptions.

HMR: Ron Silliman's anthology *In the American Tree* includes about 40 poets. It is obvious that the writing thus represented must be very heterogeneous. In my understanding, it is not so much "characteristics"—that is solutions—as questions, common concerns, which give the group contour. Would you agree with that? And if so, could you name some of the major concerns that most of these poets share?

CB: One thing some of us involved in $L=A=N=G=U=A=G=E$ did share was a dislike of aesthetic rigidity—the narrow focussing of putting forward one stylistic or procedural choice above all others (a rigidity that has plagued both avant-gardists and conventionalists). Not that a particular technique might not be valuable or that attention should not be called to it, but that specific techniques should not be idealized. What was interesting about the work associated with $L=A=N=G=U=A=G=E$ is precisely that it did not represent a school or a style or a single linear tradition with a starting point and a series of red letter dates; if anything, grouping together these approaches to writing exploded the idea of a single origin, a single school. We are talking about synthesizing or grafting approaches with very different agendas, styles, origins, and concerns but which, nonetheless, were being related in terms of specific frames provided.

I'm not suggesting that these scenes of writing were free from doctrinaire aesthetics—that is a utopian idea that bears little relation to the social exchanges of actually existing poets. But I do think that the many doctrines we sometimes debated and sometimes practiced did undercut the tendency among many clusters of poets toward social exclusivity. The issue and aesthetic orientation of $L=A=N=G=U=A=G=E$ tended to bring in a larger and more unpredictable assortment of interested parties than a more social (or scene) focus could possibly have allowed. You might say we met each other through the work and not the other way around. And the number of people involved has always been well beyond any easy count.

I would say that the interconnection among the poetic styles attended to in $L=A=N=G=U=A=G=E$ has to do with the rejection of certain traditionally accepted techniques for poem-making and an openness to alternative techniques, together with a distrust of the experimental as an end to itself—i.e., theatricalizing the processes of poem generation rather than making the poems (though this last point treads a narrow and arguable line). Surely, there was a deep distrust of the typical "workshop" poem of too easy personal epiphany—"Your glances, like lances / incise the blister / of my feelings // or am I just a mat / for you to rub off / the muck of your life-like life"—poems that assume a "voice" without making any effort to hear the voices and sounds in the language, in the materials—the poem's "actual word stuff", to use a phrase of Zukofsky's. But also, built in, was the distrust that any new style or technique or device was the gold pot at the end of the rainbow; that is, a commitment to the need for a multiplicity of stylistic approaches among a multiplicity of poets, and even for one poet. So a shared "opposition", a shared dissidence.

Or put it this way: a poem by Tina Darragh or David Melnick has less in common with a poem by Lyn Hejinian or Bruce Andrews, though all are in the *Tree* anthology, than any two poems by their contemporaries in any of the more conventional "aboveground" anthologies of contemporary American poetry. Which is to say, you got a far greater range of poetic explorations in anthologies like *In the American Tree* (1986) and *"Language" Poetries* (1987) than you find in the truly schoolish, dispiritingly conformist poetry pages of the mainstream. The reason for this is that official verse culture is quite uniformitarian in its approach to poetry, and quite averse to poetic exploration or innovation. In $L=A=N=G=U=A=G=E$ we focussed on "a spectrum of writing that places its attention primarily on language and ways of making meaning, that takes for granted neither vocabulary, grammar, process, syntax, program or subject matter"—indeed where all of these dynamics remain at issue. And we were committed to talking and writing about these issues, to conversation and interchange as crucial to the poetic process.

Much of the commentary of the work associated with such magazines as $L=A=N=G=U=A=G=E$ has emphasized the rejection of the unreflected reliance on the conceit of the sincerity of the personal voice of the poet, but perhaps now it would also be useful to emphasize the problems associated with poets read primarily as a representation of a group or subculture. Poetry, at its most active, can investigate the constitution of persons as much as groups: it explores identity rather than fixing it.

Certainly, some often overlooked tendencies in the American poetic tradition are an important shared influence. For one thing, there are the many innovations of the radical modernist poets of the early part of the century—Gertrude Stein, Charles Reznikoff, Louis Zukofsky, Langston Hughes, Mina Loy, Sterling Brown, William Carlos Williams, Melvin Tolson, Laura Riding, to name a few of many (and one might add, in Britain, Basil Bunting and Hugh Mac-Diarmid, and in Ireland Samuel Beckett, James Joyce). Then there are the "New American Poets" (to use the title of the famous Don Allen anthology), including Robert Creeley, David Antin, John Ashbery, Jack Spicer, Amiri Baraka, Allen Ginsberg, Larry Eigner, Jack Kerouac, Jackson Mac Low, Barbara Guest, &&&. Poets born in the late thirties to the early fifties—roughly the generation of $L=A=N=G=U=A=G=E$—had a very rich recent poetic history from which to draw. Two new anthologies chart this trajectory: *From the Other Side of the Century: A New American Poetry, 1960–1990*, ed. Douglas Messerli (1994), and *Postmodern American Poetry: A Norton Anthology*, ed. Paul Hoover (1994).

But shared influences outside either this specific poetic tradition or the tradition of English verse are equally, probably more, important. For one thing, many of us were active on the left as part of the anti–Vietnam War movement of the late 1960s. We saw our poetry (and essays and publishing and "arts" organizing) as growing out of that oppositional politics. This has meant a concentration on the nature of ideology, both as it pertains to political discourse, of course, but more importantly to "ordinary" language and to poetic discourse. I would point to the Frankfurt School and Walter Benjamin, Louis Althusser, and the sociologists Erving Goffman in the U.S. and Basil Bernstein in the U.K., as writers who suggest, at least for me, some of the issues I think these poets have addressed, though in ways that could not be anticipated from such "theory".

Another category of shared interests would be language philosophy; for me, the late writings of Ludwig Wittgenstein, in particular, along with the related work of the American philosopher Stanley Cavell. Russian formalist linguistics, for example the work of Roman Jakobson, should also be mentioned here, and Ferdinand de Saussure, although he has been of more use to some of my friends than he has been to me. Roland Barthes, Michel Foucault, Gilles Deleuze & Félix Guattari, and later Michel de Certeau and Jean-Jacques Lecercle, have also been important, and of course others would emphasize different writers and have less interest in these (but I can't speak for them).

Equally important has been the rethinking of the scope and purpose of the artistic domain. I would point to Jerome Rothenberg's several anthologies as the most useful example of this opening, including his first, *Technicians of the Sacred*, which presented quite radical transactions and transductions and performances of what are often mislabeled "tribal" or even "primitive" poetries from the Americas as well as Oceania and Africa. The implications of theses materials are profound, as suggested by James Clifford's recent *The Predicament of Culture*. Finally, the early century work of many Russian futurist (and formalist) poets, artists, bookmakers, and performers is surely the most inspiring, and ultimately unsettling, model for the sort of collective and collaborative activity of artists some few or many of us envisioned.

HMR: Talking about "traditions". How is your writing related to Objectivist poetry and Projective Verse?

CB: I recently wrote a long essay on Charles Reznikoff, one of the so-called "Objectivist" poets, and several people asked why I had written it, since Reznikoff's work seems so different than my own. In looking at the literary past, I am not interested in emphasizing how what I do is different than the poets whom I admire, but in the forms of continuity with the earlier work. Saying this, it is impossible to summarize my relations to so many different poets. But in Olson and Zukofsky and Niedecker and Oppen I continue to learn from the insistence on new forms and structures and also the social grounding of the poem. There are of course many ways that the contemporary moment mandates different approaches to form than practiced by these poets. Form is particular, historically contextual: one lesson I take from these poets is to make my own way.

Still, some features of "Objectivist" work, as well as Stein's, do stand out for me, especially as they worked to "materialize" the language by emphasizing compositional processes. In Zukofsky and Stein, one begins to hear a music of poetry that is acoustic rather than metrical: a poetry that foregrounds the sound shape of the poem. In all of these poets you also see the use of serial, or linked, forms, as ways of eliding closure. You find a resistance to the "high" diction or ornate rhetoric of symbolist poetry and a turn to a subject matter of the everyday, to what at the time seemed anti-poetic subject matter. You find extensive use of found or collaged material and the use of invented rather than received form. And, finally, perhaps philosophically most significant to my own work, a breaking down of the barrier between the observer and the observed, description and event, poetry and poetics.

HMR: In your essay on "The State of the Art" from your book *A Poetics* you write: " . . . we can't rely on the tools and forms of the past, even the recent past, but must invent new tools and forms that begin to meet the challenges of the ever-changing present." What does history mean to you, and why do you consider it as a useless burden?

CB: I certainly don't consider history as a useless burden! But I wonder which history—both in the sense of whose history and what account of history, histories. Poetry is a place to explore these methodological issues, so that history, in my own work anyway, is felt more in the forms of the poems than in the subject matter. What I want is a poetry that interrogates how language constitutes, rather than simply reflects, history; and not only history, but social meaning and values.

Devices and technique—the tools and forms of the past—shift in their meaning and value over time, requiring continual reassessment. I try to suggest this in my essay on postwar American poetry, "The Second War and Postmodern Memory", also in *A Poetics*, where I account for the shift in attitude toward authority, declarativeness, and cultural optimism—and indeed the aversion of representation, the realization that there are some things that cannot be represented in the wake of the Systematic Extermination Process. The sort of evasion of pride of group that is reflected in my answer to your first question. What I emphasize in that essay is not poems "about" the systematic extermination process, although that is discussed, but a shift in sensibility, form, and diction that is quite profound but almost never remarked on as being connected to this fundamental historical frame. In this context, a poetry's diffidence toward direct political statement as well as its asociality (its withdrawal from not only mass culture but also popular—folk, street, "counter", Beat— culture as well) has a social and historical meaning. Poetry becomes a necessary response to the Second War (and also, as in the return of the repressed, the Vietnam War), but in its unconsoled mutters and elegiac stutters, its hesitations and influidities, its intractabilities and distempers.

HMR: That reminds me of what Bertolt Brecht said about the impossibility to write about the beauty of trees. You mentioned that Brecht's writing is of particular interest to you. Which part of his work are you referring to, and why?

CB: Brecht figures prominently in my verse essay "Artifice of Absorption" because I am interested in the dynamic of both being absorbed in the textual "action" and at the same time remaining aware of the structures producing the effect. Like the Russian futurist's idea of *ostranenie* (making strange), Brecht's *Verfremdungseffekt* is a crucial model for breaking the empathic connection between reader and poem, where one reads through the words to get to the idea of content "on the other side." In contrast, I want to materialize the word, create a work in which the words remain audible, rather than unsounded and invisible.

HMR: I read your major poetological statement, "Artifice of Absorption"—among other things—as an attempt to blur the boundaries between poetry and theoretical discourse. As far as I know, the dissolution of this dividing line is also one of the issues you emphasize in the writing of Stein and other modernists and it is strongly supported in the Poetics Program at Buffalo, that is in the work of younger poets. What does this issue mean to you and/or these younger poets?

CB: Poetry is necessarily theoretical and it can evade this no more than it can evade its historicality. Blur poetry and poetics as I might, I do see them as distinct genres with specific traditions and I rely on the generic distinctions to perform my hermeneutic oscillations between the two. I'm not promoting an undifferentiated writing but, on the contrary, I am interested in increasing differentiation of writing forms. But that means we can't take our conventions for granted, else they become markers for distinctions no longer having any necessity. The writing style of most theoretical prose, like most non-theoretical poetry, is inert. I am looking for ways to keep the genres active, alive, aware of themselves. If I write an essay in verse it's not because I think there's no difference between poetry and prose but because I think it does make a difference to use the poetic form. And after all, in the history of Western writing, prose emerges from poetry, not the other way round; the verse essay calls to me of its historical precedence over the prose essay.

HMR: "The death of the subject" and "the death of the author" are concepts that are very common in academic discourse, which has quickly integrated and annihilated the powerful implications of these concepts. What do they actually mean for poets writing today, for their relation to their own texts, their circulation, their relationship to the book markets, etc.?

CB: In her introduction to *The Birth-mark,* Susan Howe makes the forceful point that, just as those who have been silenced in literary history have begun to speak, the author is said to have died. What has died, however, is not authors but an idea of the author as Representative Man. For me, this actually potentiates the poetic possibilities for individualities, for personal agencies, by removing the scaffolding and stilts that came with the Representative Verse Kit ($44.95, batteries not included). My own rather concerted effort to avert some of the hallmark conventions of verse and exposition, grammar and prosody; my insistence on doing it my way, even in the face of, even because of, being ostensibly wrong, can also be understood as a resurgence of willfulness, obstinacy, stubbornness, dissidence— themselves marks of a newly forming individuality, not displaced to narration of subjective "inner" space, but textually enacted in the "outer" space of the poem.

HMR: In the paradigm of "subjectivity"—even in the double sense of autonomy and being subjected to—the concept of "inspiration" always played a crucial role. I'm thinking of Denise Levertov, and of course all the romantic poets.

CB: I'm more drawn to speak of intuition than inspiration. Intuition is a crucial term to describe a working practice of poetry (as well as science, business, much else): it suggests an arena for judgment based on hunches, guesses, quick assessments. I love the fact of intuition not being defensible, at least on rational grounds, even if perfectly reasonable; and also that you can learn to use your intuition, that is learn when to go with it and how, but it's something you have to pretty much learn on your own, though perhaps being inspired by someone else's model. I guess I'd say sometimes my intuitions are inspired and sometimes not. Meanwhile Denise Levertov, whose early poetry I admire, uses "inspiration" as a cudgel to knock down instances of radically imaginative poetry that refuse to conform to the bland and conventional verse styles with which she has affiliated herself. I suppose that only proves that inspiration is being used as cover for a refusal to think.

HMR: Marjorie Perloff claims, that in language poetry—like in futurist poetry—the search for the "mot juste" is most important. My impression, however, is, that it is not the single word, but the "in between", what happens between the words, the friction that arises from new contexts, and very often the gaps, erasures what is interesting for many contemporary poets in the U.S. What is your view on that?

CB: Depending on what poet, and indeed what poem, I think all these things are going on. For myself, I am enthralled by the possibility of word substitution—using an unexpected word where a particular word is expected. For this to work with the torquing I want, it is necessary, ironically perhaps, to find the exact right word; that word is, from another angle, of course, exactly the wrong word, "le mot mauvais" (and as long as we are talking about Moe, let's not neglect Larry and Curly). Then again if words could actually bring about justice, we might need no poetry at all.

HMR: Is television, and other new visual media, important for your own poetry? TV aesthetics and language seem to play a major role in your writing, and in one essay you write about a competition between poetry and the mass media. What do you mean by that?

CB: The mass media is part of the environment in which I live and so my poems, to some degree, reflect on that environment, which is not to say simply reflect it. In a culture like the U.S., where value is usually equated with audience size or commercial potential, poetry has a virtue of providing an active "counter" culture which is intensely productive but quite small in scale. This smallness of scale is a value in itself. I am a part of the first generation to grow up on, or anyway with, TV. My work is as influenced by *Dragnet* as by Proust. Indeed, quite apart from the sorts of contexts and influences I was belaboring earlier, I would insist on the primary influence of the contemporary moment: on the forms and materials given to us in the specific time we are living. This makes for a poetry that engages the social world directly, by taking on its jargon and its technologies, its blather and its displacements, not only as subjects but as methods of organization, as environments, to be sounded and tested and thought through by and in the poem.

HMR: TV is by now of course a relatively old medium. The "new media" proper are computer networks, CD-ROMs, and various software systems. How do these new media affect the writing of poetry? Do the networks really offer the chance of a "free flowing of language", or are the networks just as subject to "discourse"-effects (exclusion mechanisms) as any other kind of language?

CB: Computers can often make reading and writing harder than previous technologies—but it's just the difficulties that make for poetic interest.

So it's not a question of poetry being enabled by new technology but of writers needing to come to terms with the present communication environment. The alphabet remains a still-underutilized technology, and perhaps not all that old as human history goes. The radio offered immense possibilities for poetry but access, in the U.S. at least, has been virtually denied to innovative sound works.

The practical question is how innovative forms of art will find even a small place within an "information superhighway" so that it will not become as homogenous and empty as the cable TV spectrum. Poetry publishing and distribution will always seek the least capital-intensive means of reproduction; that is what spurred the "mimeo revolution" of the 1960s and 70s, the great "xerox" and offset explosion of the 70s and on, the desktop wave of the 90s, and now the enormous activity on the internet, ranging from electronic magazines to "book" publishing and, perhaps most crucially, exchange of information on poetry events and the full range of print publications. It seems certain that the net will be a crucial site for the distribution of works of poetry, including what would otherwise be out-of-print works, as well as for information on obtaining books and magazines. Certainly these are the things that we—and I should point to an individual here, the EPC's virtual author, Loss Pequeño Glazier—have tried to put together at the Electronic Poetry Center (http://wings.buffalo.edu/epc).

But that description primarily registers those formats we have imported from previous print culture into this new medium. Electronic publishing is radically altering the material, specifically visual, presentation of text, making available the integration of visual and linguistic material anticipated by the great collage artists and visual poets of the century, but never before so easily fabricated or reproduced. (Texts with pictures can be transmitted as cheaply as text alone and, equally important, black and white need no longer be the dominant color scheme.) The advent of audio on the net promises to make available the sound of poetry in a way that has been previously stymied by the dearth of readily available audio recordings. And, finally, the possibilities for conversation and collaboration among poets nationally and internationally, through electronic discussion groups, promises to open up scene- and regionally based enclaves to greater participation and new modes of exchange.

HMR: Finally: Apparently there is a discussion going on whether the effects created by interactive media, computer networks, "hypertexts", etc., can serve as metaphor for what language-centered writing has been doing. What is your opinion on that?

CB: Hypertext as metaphor is for me a crucial way to discuss what interests me in linking up different textual and discursive environments in a nonhierarchic way. Certainly this relates to collage, which would make Schwitters a hypertext innovator, and it also relates to the nonlinear approaches to reading, invented by many modernists and contemporary poets. Equally important, hypertextual organization may finally help to break teaching, textbooks, and critical writing from their deadly boring fetishization of narrative and expository ordering of information, moving these activities away from outmoded forms of ideational mimesis and toward poetic methods of exploring associated fields of information or material.

I Don't Take Voice Mail

The Object of Art in the Age of
Electronic Technology

Before diagnosing the condition of the art object in an age of electronic technology, let me first address the question of the object of art in an age of global commodification. I won't be the last to note that capitalism transcends the technologies through which it operates. So just as today's art world is dominated by marketing, sales, and promotion, so the object of art in the age of electronic technology will continue to be profit; and the values most typically promoted by the art world will continue to be governed by market, rather than aesthetic, formal, philosophical, or ethical, values.

Within the art world, as in the corporate board rooms, the focus of discussion has been on how to exploit the emerging electronic media, as if cyberspace were a new wilderness from which to carve your niche—better get on board, er, on line, first before the prime sites are staked out. For if the object of art is to sell objects, then the new electronic environment presents many problems but also many opportunities.

But art, if it could speak, might well object to these assumptions. (If art could speak we could not understand it—that's one way to put it; perhaps it's more accurate to say if art could speak it would be poetry and poetry's got nothing to sell.) Art might speak not of its object but its objects; it might testily insist that one of its roles is to resist commodification, to use its materiality to push against the total absorption of meaning into the market system, and that's why it got one of the first e-mail accounts on the net—to talk about it. But you can't sell talk, or not for much, and that can make the net a vexing place for the purveyors of art.

Today's internet—a decentralized, largely text-based, linking of individual sites or constellations of users—will be superseded by what is aptly called the information superhighway. Just as the old dirt roads and smaller rural routes were abandoned by the megatraffic on the interstates, so much of the present informal, noncapital intensive exchanges on the net will become marginal back channels in a communications system owned and controlled by Time & Space, Inc., and other giant telecommunication conglomerates, providing new and continually recirculating versions of

USA Today with up-to-the-minute weather and sports information, sound files offering *Nirvana: The Classic Years* including alternate studio versions, hypertext tours with high resolution graphics of the British Museum collection, plus hundreds of other choices, available at the click of an icon, including items never before available in any media such as *In Her Home: The Barbra Streisand Collection;* a construct-it-yourself simulation of making a Shaker chair; and a color-it-yourself portfolio of the complete appropriations of Sherrie Levine, together with hypertextually linked case dossiers of all related legal suits. All with modest fees for each hour of viewing or receiving (the gaze finally quantified and sold) and downright bargain prices for your "own" personal copy, making available unlimited screenings (but remember, "it is a federal offense to make unauthorized copies of these copies", or, as we say in Buffalo: it's okay to copy an original but never copy a copy). Indeed, much of what is now the internet promises to become the largest shopping network on earth, and possibly in the universe (even exceeding the Mall of the Milky Way on Galactica B282); those old back roads will be the place to hang out if you are looking for something other than franchise FastImage.

One of the hallmarks of formalist art criticism as well as media theory has been an analysis of the effects of newer media on already existing media. So we talk about the effect of photography on painting, or movies on theater; or how movies provided the initial content for TV before it arrived at its own particular formats (just as the content of the net is now largely composed of formats taken from books, letters, and magazines). It is useful to remember that in the early days of TV, many observers predicted that such spectator sports as baseball would lose their stadium audiences once the games were broadcast "live". However, the opposite occurred; TV increased the interest in the live-and-in-person event. In a similar way, art on the net may actually increase interest in seeing art in nonelectronic spaces.

Formalist critics have wanted to emphasize how new technologies "free up" older media to explore their intrinsic qualities—to do what only they can do. But new media also have a corrosive effect, as forces in the older media try to shift their focus to compete for the market and the cultural capital of what they may see as their new competitors. Within the visual arts, many of the most celebrated new trends of the last decade—from simulationism to multimediamania to the transformation of *Artforum*—are symptoms of a fear of the specific and intractable materiality of painting and sculpture; such fear of materiality (and by extension face-to-face interaction) is far greater and long-lasting than the much more often discussed fear of technology—a fear so often discussed the better to trivialize and repress.

What are the conditions of visual art on the net, or art in computer space? We can expect that most visual art on the net will be reproductions of previously existing work, along the line of Bill Gates's plan to display in his home rotating CD-ROM images of the masterpieces of World Art, images for which, notably, he has purchased the CD-ROM reproduction rights. The Thing, a new visual arts online service, which has been immensely useful in imagining many possible formats for art on the net, already features an innovative, in the sense of anachronistic, pricing structure—selling over its BBS (bulletin board system) a numbered and "signed" diskette of an art work. (The idea of selling a disk is itself no more objectionable than selling a book, but numbering and signing a disk is an attempt to simulate scarcity and limit in a medium in which these conditions do not apply. I wouldn't be surprised, however, if this format was included on The Thing to call attention to the issue and also to poke fun at the net's prevailing ideology of utopian democracy, a.k.a. netiquette.) In any case, telecommunications systems promise to dominate the distribution of text and image in the near future at a price—though few are now willing to acknowledge it—of more controlled and more limited access (through high user fees, institutional restrictions, and technological skills barriers) and loss of privacy rights we now take for granted. But technological change—it's a mistake to call it progress—will not be reversed and artists run the risk of nostalgia if they refuse to recognize and respond, the better to resist, the communications environment within which, for better or worse, they find themselves.

I want, then, to focus not on how electronic space will actually be used, or how e-space will be exploited, but rather to think about the new media that have been created by technological developments combining computers and telecommunications, and how works of visual art can recognize and explore these new media—even if such works run the risk of being relegated to the net's backchannels, along with "new mimeo revolution" poetry magazines and psychic readings by electronic Tarot.

The most radical characteristic of the internet as a medium is its interconnectivity. At every point receivers are also transmitters. It is a medium defined by exchange rather than delivery; the medium is interactive and dialogic rather than unidirectional or monologic. At this moment, the most interesting format on the internet, apart from the basic electronic mail function, is the listserve: a series of individuals join a list—any post to the list address is immediately delivered to all list subscribers. Individuals can then post replies to the entire list or to the individual that sent the post. Lists may be open to anyone to join or may be private. The potential for discussion and collaboration is appealing—the format mixes some of the features of correspondence with a discussion group, conference call, and a panel symposium (with the crucial difference that the distinction between audience and panel is eroded).

While many cyberspace utopians speak of virtual communities with much excitement, what is particularly interesting about the interconnectivity of computer space is its difference from other types of group formation; for what we are constructing in these spaces might better be called virtual uncommunities.

The art world remains a difficult place for community or group formations because the gallery system recognizes value primarily in terms of individual achievement. In contrast to poetry publishing and criticism, in which poets play a substantial and perhaps determining role, individual visual artists are largely restricted to (or restrict themselves to) the role of producers of potentially saleable objects. Competition among artists is more common than broad-based alliance, with the occasional exception of loyalty to a small circle of friends.

At the national level, there are local communities of artists in every region. Various movements and schools—aesthetic or political or both—can also be understood as art communities. Most recently, the connections of artists within ethnic, gender, or racial groups have been seen in terms of community. But despite these sites of community among visual artists, sustained interaction, dialogues, and collaboration remain rare; indeed, these activities are not generally recognized as values. The internet provides an extraordinary space for interaction and exchange among artists living in different places and, perhaps more significantly, encourages collaboration between visual artists, writers, and computer designers and engineers. In a way remarkably anticipated by the mail art movements of the seventies and eighties, the net suggests the possibility of art works created for their exchange rather than market value—works that may be altered, augmented, or otherwise transformed as they pass from one screen to another.—What I am envisioning here is not art from another medium imported into the net but rather art that takes the unique constraints and potentials of the net as its medium.

To begin to delineate this and related computer and telecommunications media, let's start with the "small" screen. We might begin to speak of the screen arts to suggest the intersection of video, TV, and computer art that share the same physical support or monitor. More and more computers are now equipped with video quality monitors and the screen arts—in this broad sense—will be transmitted via modem, cable, and wireless systems as well as plugged in through cassette, CD-ROM, disk, and cartridge.

I distinguish among interactive, interconnected, and presentational screen media:

Presentational screen media is the broadest category. On the one hand, it includes the use of the CPU (computer processing unit) set-up as a means to present work realized in another medium, such as the presentation of a videotape or photographs, or read-only text files. On the other hand, presentational screen media also include work produced and viewed on computer systems that do not require viewer intervention beyond basic directional and operational parameters such as those available on a video recorder. —A hugely important subcategory is works produced on computer screens but not presented on screens. Word processing, "paintbrush", and "photoshop" programs are some of the tools of this medium, which promises to reimagine the way we read and see text and graphics; moreover, this new medium allows for a greater integration and interaction of verbal, visual, and sound elements than possible with previous printing technologies.

Interactive computer-screen art utilizes the processing system of the computer and includes significant viewer participation via keyboard, mouse, or joy stick. While video games are the most elaborate visual realization of this medium, works of computer art can be created that are not game-oriented but that use many of the features developed in video games. Still another format for interactivity is often discussed under the general heading of hypertext. Hypertext involves the lateral movement and linking of a potentially infinite series of data pools. It allows for non-linear explorations of a range of data bases; that is, unlike presentational modes, in hypertext there need be no established forward path through the data. For example, Jerome McGann and colleagues are at work on an edition of the complete works of Dante Rossetti that will include multiple discrepant versions of his published poems along with manuscript versions of these poems, together with his related paintings as well as source material for the paintings and the poems. All of this information will be linked so that one can move through the data in many directions. Claims of many enthusiastic hypertextualists notwithstanding, many of the most radical features of hypertext are technologies made available by the invention of alphabetic writing and greatly facilitated by the development of printing and bookmaking. Such formats as page and line numbering, indexes, tables of contents, concordances, and cross-referencing for encyclopedias and card catalogs, are, in effect, hypertextual. Much of the innovative poetry of the past 100 years relies on the concept of hypertextuality as a counter to the predominance of linear reading and writing methods. While hypertext may seem like a particular innovation of computer processing, since data on a computer does not have to be accessed sequentially (which is to say it is "randomly" accessible), it becomes a compensatory access tool partly because you can't flip though a data base the way you can flip through pages or index cards. (I'm thinking, for example, of Robert Grenier's great poem of the 1970s, *Sentences*, which is printed on 500 index cards in a Chinese foldup box.)

Finally—my third category—interconnectivity utilizes the network capability of linked systems such as the internet and formats such as listserves, bulletin boards, newsgroups, and group-participation MUDs (multi-user domains) and MOOs and other "real-time" multi-user formats. Interconnectivity allows for works of collaboration, linking, and exchange, as well as the possibility of simultaneous-event or immediate-response structures. Interconnectivity turns the screen into a small stage and in this way combines features of theater with writing and graphic art.

The most static of the three modes I have just defined is the presentation screen mode. Presentational screen media will merge with what is now available via broadcast TV, video cassettes, or video disk and CD. But certain computer features will provide novel methods for searching or scanning material, for example, enabling one to find one particular item or graphic or song or word amidst a large data base.

Yet because computer screens are often smaller than TV screens, a class of interactive and presentational screen art can take advantage of the more intimate single-viewer conditions now associated with books and drawings. New technologies for viewing texts may well supplant print as the dominant medium for writing and graphics. Books, I should add, will not be replaced—and certainly will not become superfluous—any more than printing replaced handwriting or made it superfluous; these are different media and texts or graphics disseminated through them will have different qualities. Nonetheless, it is useful to consider graphic and verbal works created specifically for the intimate presentational or interactive space of the small screen that use features specific to the CPU environment, including scrolling, lateral movements, dissolves, the physical properties of the different screen types (LCD, gas plasma, active matrix color)—an extension into the CPU environment of the sort of work associated with Nam June Paik's exploration of the video environment.

The status of computer-generated films may help to test my typology. Anything that can be viewed on a small screen monitor can also, and with increasing resolution, be projected on a movie screen. Nonetheless, it is still possible to distinguish, as distinct support media, the small backlit screen of the TV and computer monitor and the large projection-system screen of film. Moreover, the scale, conditions of viewing, and typifying formats make video, film, and TV three different media, just as animation, photography, and computer graphics may be said to be distinct media within film. (Hybridization and cross-viewing remain an active and welcome possibility.) Computer-generated graphics, then, may be classified as presentation computer art modelled on small screens for big screen projection.

Note, also, that I have not included in my sketch nonscreen art that uses computers for their operation (for example, robotic installations and environments)—a category that is likely to far surpass the screen arts in the course of time.

But I don't want to talk about computers but objects, objects obduring in the face of automation: I picture here a sculpture from Petah Coyne's April 1994 show at the Jack Shainman Gallery, which featured candelabra-like works, hung from the ceiling, and dripping with layers of white wax. For it has never been the object of art to capture the thing itself, but rather the conditions of thingness: its thickness, its intractability, its untranslatability or unreproducibility, its linguistic or semiotic density, opacity, particularity and peculiarity, its complexity.

For this reason, I was delighted to see a show of new sculpture at Exit Art, also in April, that seemed to respond to my increasing desire for sculpture and painting thick with its material obsessiveness, work whose response to the cyberworld is not to hop on board for the ride or play the angles between parasite and symbiosis—but to insist ever more on the intractability of its own *radical faith*, to cite the title of this work by Karen Dolmanish, consisting of a floor display of obsessively arranged piles of broken things—nails and glass and metal.

Object: to call into question, to disagree, to wonder at, to puzzle over, to stare at . . . Object: something made inanimate, lifeless, a thing debased or devalued . . . Whatever darker Freudian dreams of objects and their relations I may have had while writing this essay, nothing could come close to Byron Clercx's witty sculpture, *Big Stick*, in which he has compressed and laminated 20 volumes of the complete works of the father of psychoanalysis into one beautifully crafted Vienna Slugger, evoking both the uncanny and the sublime—finally, an American Freud. Here is the return of the book with a vengeance, proof positive that books are not the same as texts. Go try doing that to a batch of floppy disks or CD-ROMs.

In Jess's 1991 paste-up *Dyslecstasy*, we get some glimpse of what hypertext might one day be able to achieve. Collaged from thousands of tiny scraps collected over many years, Jess creates an environment of multiple levels and dizzyingly shifting contexts; and yet in this world made of tiny particulars, it is their relation and mutual inhabitation that overwhelms and confirms.

I long for the handmade, the direct application of materials on an uneven, rough, textured surface. I feel ever more the need for the embedded and encrusted images and glossings and tones and contours of forgotten and misplaced lore, as in Susan Bee's painting *Masked Ball*.

I want to contrast the solitary conditions of viewing a work on a computer screen, my posture fixed, my eyes 10 inches from the image, with the physicality of looking at a painting or sculpture in a large room, moving around it, checking it out from multiple views, taking in its tactile surface, its engagement with my thoughts.

On the journey of life, lost in cyberspace, where will we find ourselves: not who we are but who we will be, our virtual reality.

Weak Links

Every day. Day by day. The hours hang and the headlines punctuate a passage through time that we move through, head bowed at the collision of flesh and indoctrination. Yet there might be (might there be?) some doctrine to get us out of this viscous circle of self-enclosing artifacts that we call news, as if the world was already lost before we could speak a word to it.

In Hannah Weiner's *Weeks*, the daily bite of world-event narrative achieves the grandeur, perhaps the quiet desperation, of background music (ambient ideology). *Weeks* is an unnerving foray in a world of prefabricated events: a world we seem to have fallen into, as if from the cradle.

Weeks was written in a small notebook, one page per day for fifty weeks. Each page of the book is the equivalent of a single week, with each day taking its toll in about five lines. The material, says Weiner, is all found—"taken at the beginning from written matter and TV news and later almost entirely from TV news."

Here parataxis (the serial juxtapositions of sentences) takes on an ominous tone in its refusal to draw connections. *Weeks*, in its extremity, represents the institutionalization of collage into a form of evenly hovering emptiness that actively resists analysis or puncturing. In *Weeks*, the virus of news is shown up as a pattern of reiteration and displacement, tale without teller. Yet, while Weiner follows a strict poetic method of refusing the "lyrical interference of ego", the result is that these deanimated metonymies take on a teller, as if to call it "Hannah". This is the vortical twisting, or transformation, at the heart of *Weeks*'s prosodic inquisition.

Weeks is poetic homeopathy: a weak dose of the virus to immunize our systems—let's say consciousnesses—against it.

What do we make of our everyday lives: make of them, make out of them? What do we make of, that is, these materials that we can no where (not anymore) avoid, avert our ears as we do, or, as in poetic practice, hide behind the suburban lawns of laundered lyricism?

Weiner's *Weeks* is a shocking *cul de sac* to a tradition of the found in American poetry—a tradition that includes Weiner's own *Clairvoyant Journals*, where what is found is the words seen (projected? transferred?) onto the objects and bodies surrounding her. *Cul de sac* not in the sense of "no more to be found", any more than *no more to be lost*. Only that in the world of *Weeks* there's no way out and ascent upward is effectively blocked, since *Weeks* presents a world in which "I went by [can only go by] the information I received": i.e., not very far. What's left is to descend into this world of "our" very own making, to attend (to) its forms so better to reckon with it. "The standoff began as a botched robbery."

Claire-in-the-Building

There is not a man alive who does not
admire soup. I felt that way myself
sometimes, in a manner that greatly
resembles a plug. Swerving when
there were no curbs, vying
nonchalantly against the slot-machine
logic of my temporary guardians,
dressed always in damp
patterns with inadequate pixelation
to allow for the elan she
protested she provoked on such
sleep-induced outings in partial
compliance with the work-release program
offered as an principled advance on
my prostate subjection to
tales altogether too astonishing to
submit to the usual mumbo
jumbo, you know, over easy,
eat and run, not too loud, no
bright floral patterns if
you expect to get a job in such
an incendiary application of
denouement. My word! Ellen,
did you understand one thing
Frank just said, I mean, the
nerve of these Protestants, or
whatever they call themselves
or I ain't your mother's
macaroni and cheese, please, no
ice. Is sand biodegradable?
Do you serve saws with your steak,
or are you too scared to claim

anything? *No can't do.* "I
learned to read by watching
Wheel of Fortune when I was
a baby." By the time I was 5
you couldn't tell the slippers
from the geese. That's right,
go another half mile up the cliff
and take a sharp left immediately
after where the ABSOLUTELY NO
TRESPASSING sign used to be,
you know, before the war.
Like the one about the chicken
crossed the street because he
wanted to see time fly or because
he missed the road or he didn't
want to wake up the sleeping caplets.
A very mixed-up hen. "No, I can't,
I never learned." By the time
you get up it's time to
go to sleep. Like the one about
the leaky boat and the sea's
false bottoms. Veils that part to
darker veils. So that the fissure
twisted in the vortex. Certain she was
lurking just behind the facade,
ready to explain that the joke had been
misapplied or was it, forfeited?
Never again; & again, & again.
"Maybe he's not a real person."
Maybe it's not a real purpose.
Maybe my slips are too much
like pratfalls (fat falls).
Maybe the lever is detached from the
mainspring. The billiard ball
burned against the slide
of the toaster (holster). That's no
puzzle it's my knife (slice, life,
pipe). *The Rip that Ricochets around
the Rumor.* As in two's two too
many. "I thought you said haphazard—
but if you did you're wrong."
If you've got your concentration you've got

just about everything worth writing home
that tomorrow came sooner than expected
or put those keys away
unless you intend to use me and
then toss me aside like so much worn
out root beer, root for someone,
Bill, take a chance, give till it
stops hurtling through the fog or
fog substitute.

> *Save me*
> *So that I can exist*
>
> *Lose me*
> *So that I may find you*

"That's an extremely unripe plum."
"There's no plum like the plum
of concatenation." *Plunge & drift,
drift & plunge.* The streets are
icy with incipience.

Again Eigner

There is no writing I know as vivid as Larry Eigner's. He's invented, for poetry, something equivalent to three-dimensional photography: his works present a series of perceptions etched deep into the mind, where the mind is charted on a page and the page becomes a model of the thinking field. Perception and thought (words and things) are completely intertwined in Eigner's work, which brings to a visionary crescendo the exploration of the ordinary—the transient flickerings of the everyday that otherwise pass more unnoticed than regarded, more dismissed than revered. In Eigner's poems, one "fragment" is riveted to the next, so that one becomes, in reading this work, likewise riveted by the uncanny democracy of details, where attention is focussed unhesitatingly on each particular with equal weight, equal exhilaration. This is a poetics of "noticing things", where, as Eigner writes, "nothing is too dull" with "material (things, words) more and more dense around you." But equally, Eigner's is a poetics of coincidence, where "serendipity" (contingency) takes its rightful place as animating spirit, displacing the anthropocentric sentimentality of much of the verse of our time.

. . . I can't collect my thoughts any further, dwelling on the meanings of Larry Eigner's life, except to remember the time spent with him in conversation, or say the time Bob Grenier, Brian McInerney, and I took him to the Museum of Natural History on his one trip to New York. As we came into the room with some of the largest dinosaurs, Larry pointed straight ahead and said "that's interesting". He wasn't pointing to a dinosaur skeleton, though, but to an old sign posted on the back wall; it *was* interesting, in a style long banished (in exhibition halls now replaced). I think of that remark of Larry's as displaying how much he lived out his version of a democracy of particulars, as against the craving for highlights, for the heightened, that is as much a literary aesthetic as a consumer imperative. For Eigner, this didn't mean a flattening of affect; on the contrary, it meant a luminosity of every detail: the perceptual vividness that his work so uncannily concatenates. This acknowledgment of the daily, a series of remarks on the otherwise unremarkable, a sort of poetic alchemy that is not dissimilar to one strain of Jewish mysticism (a strain in which the mysticism dissolves into an active apprehension of the real), is an abiding model of, and for, a poetry where things as they are are let to stand for themselves.

This poet of the ordinary lived an extraordinary life, as if the physical challenges he faced since birth were spun by poetic license into mental acrobatics. Larry Eigner is a hero of our times. His will to think was unsuppressible. It was no ordinary privilege to have known him. I can't think of anyone I admired more.

* * *

"The Only World We've Got"

Anything on Its Side is placed, like

a volume in a tank of water, with utter

gravity against the next moment that occurs

in what is called time but for Eigner is always

spaced, for example on a page. What

would it be to be grounded, to know

the ground under you by the weight

it pushes back with? "Every atom of me

. . . across distances." No awful trembling

unto undecidability, everything founded in

its site, cleaves to what there is, to

what is there. "*To be* is involved

such words that hold / times in the mind":

a way, still, that a poem can enact its

own presence, with full measure of the

necessary determination to move from

anything to that which juts against it,

a conviction that life is made of (of)

just such leaps, the contingency of an eye

(aye, I) 'gainst a field of "r/oars" ("*suddenly*

a day"). Something like deep
focus, as if the poems had become
an organ, the sky bellows. Step by
step, slowly turning. Yet there is no
opening onto image here, no mime of
a rehearsal of a scene. Eigner's depth-of-
field *charges* each page to *hold* its own,
"to have things whole". "to see / dark
the / invisible". Perception all right,
but not sun-drenched barns: "fishmongers",
"pigment", "air". If there's
narrative, it's narrative unhinged
of causal nexus, logical spools. Each
line rivets its moment & moves on, like
angels on the head of a quill pin, nor
looks ahead nor back, but "bangs" indissoluble
at precise splice ("each fief") that
bodies the moment from one to next. "to
negotiate the ocean drop by drop
if there were time". In adjacency
is act-uality: "you thought it was
as it is". Nuggets of sound carving
space. "Motion" "motor" "process"
"winds" "bells" "floating" "echoing"
"coursing" "falling" "roaming" "wading"
"spilling" "flying" "dazzling" "burning"
"unflagging" "blows" "stirs" "curves"
"spirals" "stagger" "dives" "slips"

"slicks" "shakes" "hums" "simmers"

"twist" "float" "flap" "dangle" "glitter"

"subside": *"imagine the extent"* (a

geometry of ties that blind in music,

"the great sea orchestrated with men"—

"what's unseen" "what sound for our

ears"). What is *"dis*placed" at each

juncture is the plenitude of eyes seeing

beyond sight, the replenishment of

occlusion's hold, storehouse of an

interior horizon s(t)olid as emplacement.

"What you / see you / settle / on"—

settlement, homestead in the moment's

whole, "such words that hold" nor need

an other embrace. "your eyes open" "we

see something to *say* or / listen to".

Imagine the extent.

Frame Lock

Lost Wages, Nev., Nov. 13—Riddick Bowe, the 25-year-old challenger from Brooklyn outgunned Evander Holyfield through 12 gritty rounds to win the undisputed world heavyweight title . . . Afterward, when the decision was announced, a weary Holyfield was asked whether he wanted a rematch. "No," he said, "I think I'm finished."

The New York Times

A specter is haunting the literary academy: the growing discrepancy between our most advanced theories and institutionally encoded proscriptions on our writing and teaching practices.

I diagnose the problem as "frame lock", a kind of logorrheic lock jaw, or sandy mouth, or bullet-with-the-baby-not-just-quite-then-almost-out-of-reach, as a mood swinging under a noose of monomaniacal monotones, the converted preaching to the incontrovertible, the guard rail replacing the banisters, stairs, stories, elevation, detonation, reverberation, indecision, concomitant intensification system.

Frame lock, and its cousin tone jam, are the prevailing stylistic constraints of the sanctioned prose of the profession. No matter that the content of an essay may interrogate the constructed unity of a literary work or a putative period; may dwell on linguistic fragmentation, demolition, contradiction, contestation, inter-eruption; may decry assumptions of totality, continuity, narrative progression, teleology, or truth and may insist that meaning is plural, polygamous, profligate, uncontainable, rhetorical, slippery or sliding or gliding or giddy and prurient. The keepers of the scholarly flame, a touch passed hand to hand and fist to mouth by generations of professional standard bearers and girdle makers, search committees and admissions officers, editors and publishers, maintain, against all comers, that the argument for this or that or the other must maintain appropriate scholarly decorum.

Theory enacted into writing practice is suspect, demeaned as unprofessional. But that is because theory so enacted ceases to be theory—a body of doctrine—insofar as it threatens with poetry or philosophy. Theory, prophylactically wrapped in normalizing prose styles, is protected from the scourge of writing and thinking as active, open-ended, and investigatory. The repression of writing styles in the literary academy is enforced by the collusion of scholars, theorists, administrators, and editors across the spectrum of periods and methodologies. *PMLA* would prefer to publish poets writing in the patrician rhetoric of the nineteenth century about the exhaustion of poetry than to permit actual poetic acts to violate its pages. While many of the most innovative of the profession's theorists and scholars sit on the board of *PMLA*, the publication persists in its systematic process of enforcing mood and style control on all its articles and letters, as if tone or mood were unrelated to argument and meaning. Difference and otherness: these values ring hollow if they are not applied, also, to our own productions and articulations. If *PMLA*—a no doubt easy but nonetheless representatively obtrusive target—is strictly whitebread, the radical claims for diversity made within its pages seem stifled or neutered.

Professionalism and career advancement are the bogeymen of frame lock. Dissertations must not violate stylistic norms because that might jeopardize our young scholar's future. "Let them be radical in what they say but not in how they say it."—Such is the pragmatic, and characteristically self-fulfilling, argument that is made. The point here, as in most initiation rites, is to be hazed into submission, to break the spirit, and to justify the past practice of the initiators. Professionalization is the criteria of professional standing but not necessary professional values; nor are our professional writing standards at or near the limits of coherence, perception, edification, scholarship, communication, or meaning. Underneath the mask of career-minded concessions to normalcy is an often repressed epistemological positivism about the representation of ideas. While the philosophical and linguistic justifications for such ideational mimesis—for example the idea that a writing style can be transparent or neutral—have been largely undermined, the practice of ideational mimesis is largely unacknowledged and, as a result, persists unabated.

In order to explore unsanctioned forms of scholarly and critical writing, graduate students and new faculty need to be protected against the arbitrary enforcement of antiquated stylistic constraints. Yet even those in the profession who are sympathetic to these new—and indeed not-at-all new—writing forms may believe that one's initial professional work should be stylistically orthodox, with innovations considered only in later work. This argument is akin to the idea that art students should first learn anatomy and figure drawing before they embark on more expressionist or abstract work. As a generalization, there is no merit to this argument (while of course specific individuals may benefit from different experiences). Younger scholars and critics are most likely to bring energy and enthusiasm to their writing, to open up new paths, to push the boundaries of the possible; once channelled into frame lock, more often than not they get stuck in its claustrophobic confines. And young scholars who are not supported for taking new directions often drop out, or are forced out, of the profession: a loss of talent that our universities cannot afford.

It is no secret that universities reward conformism and conventionality under the name of both professionalization and currency. We see all around us dress and decorum advisories for job interviews such as those this week at the MLA: as if dressing the same as every one else—any more than writing the same or citing the same 17 major theorists or authors as everyone else—makes you a better researcher or cultural interpreter. Indeed, there is no evidence to show that tone-lock, any more than interview dress codes, makes better teachers, or more committed or knowledgeable scholars; on the contrary, there is plenty of reason to believe this sort of career-oriented behavior, exacerbated by the present scarcity of jobs, breeds a professional cynicism that is disastrous for the infectious enthusiasm and performative limberness that are crucial components for teaching. The forms we enforce among ourselves serve not the content of our work but the perpetuation of our administrative apparatuses.

Frame lock is a term I base on Erving Goffman's *Frame Analysis*. As applied to prose, it can generally be characterized as an insistence on a univocal surface, minimal shifts of mood either within paragraphs or between paragraphs, exclusion of extraneous or contradictory material, and tone restricted to the narrow affective envelope of sobriety, neutrality, objectivity, authoritativeness, or deanimated abstraction. In frame-locked prose, the order of sentences and paragraphs is hypotactic, based on a clear subordination of elements to an overriding argument that is made in a narrative or expository or linear fashion. In what might be called the rule of the necessity of paraphrase, the argument must be separable from its expression, so that a defined message can be extracted from the text. To this end, arguments must be readily glossable, and indeed periodically reiterated self-glosses are used as markers to enforce interpretative closure.

With the proliferation of frames of interpretation over the past fifteen years, a menu of methodological choices is available to the young scholar. In a campus version of the dating game, our initiate may attend a series of seminars, each promising the satisfactions of its newly rejuvenated, comprehensively restyled, and radically overhauled approach. One frame of interpretation beckons with its production of detail and cultural difference, another allures with its astounding solutions, while the sociality of a third seems magnetic; in contrast, the social responsibility of a fourth is compelling, while the ultimate sophistication of a fifth is irresistible. Finally, *über alles*, the retro chic of rejecting any and all the new frames of interpretation is always in style, always a good career move—and the fast track for getting quoted in national media.

After a period of flirtation with several of these approaches, our neophyte (the neophyte within each of us) makes a commitment to one primary frame. The marriage is consummated in the act of being announced.

Of course a newly chosen frame of interpretation may replace an older one; indeed divorce and remarriage are as inevitable as new consumers in a market economy. Serial monogamy is typical, as long as the series doesn't get very long; breaking frame is suspect. For the crucial ingredient of frame lock is consistency, sticking to one frame at a time. When frames are jumped, the new frame must appear to replace the old, which is best publicly stigmatized as damaged goods, so much youthful idealism or false consciousness or lack of rigor. This is called keeping up or advancing with the field.

If I exaggerate, and my commitment to exaggeration is second to none, even I was surprised to get a couple of examination copies in the mail this past month from Bedford Books of St. Martin's Press that seemed to parody beyond my powers the problem of rigid segmentation of frames of interpretation. In what could easily be called The Frame Lock Series of Target Texts, we have the complete, authorized, unabridged version of Polish immigrant Joey-Joey-Joey Conrad's brooding *Heart of Darkness*, in what might as well have been six-point type, an almost expendable pretext to a half-dozen large-type chapters offering a menu of interpretative modes—reader-response, deconstructive, psychoanalytic, new historical, historical materialist, and feminist. Each critical section starts with a ten-page gloss of the theoretical approach, written in clear unambiguous prose, studded with quotations from well-known practitioners of the theory: just enough lucid explanation to make a travesty of each of these methods, stripped as they are of their context, necessity, and complexity. Appended to this are ten pages applying the now-manageable theory to the pretext, the absent center that is so aptly named *Heart of Darkness* in this case.

Most scholars resist such compartmentalization, such marriages of convenience, despite the professional pressures that push them into them. But our profession too rarely addresses the conflict between inquiry and job-search marketing in which one's work is supposed to be easily summed up, definable, packaged, polished, wrinkles and contradictions eliminated, digressions booted. Insofar as we make hiring decisions using these criteria, insofar as we train graduate students to conform to such market imperatives, insofar as we present our own writing and scholarship and evaluate each other's along these lines, then the demands of our work—teaching, research, encouraging creativity—will be severely compromised. Professionalization need not be antithetical to our work as educators and writers and searchers, but in itself professionalization offers no protection against the emptying of values many of us would espouse for our work.

Goffman's analysis of frames is valuable for understanding the institutional nature of all forms of communication. In particular, frame analysis can help elucidate disputes over the curriculum in terms of both interdisciplinarity and core (or required) courses.

By their nature, frames focus attention on a particular set of features at the same time as they divert attention from other features that Goffman locates in the "disattend track". A traditional, or frame-locked, curriculum is designed so that each of its elements fits within a single overall scheme. Like the fourth wall in an old-fashioned play, the curricular frame is neither questioned nor broken. Even as curricular content (the canon) is challenged and reconstituted, the new material tends to be reframed within revised disciplinary boundaries. In contrast, anti-lock syllabi emphasize a performative and interdisciplinary approach that may undercut the passive learning patterns that currently cripple many of our educational efforts.

The process of locating disattend tracks, and bringing them to the center of attention, can be understood as not only a primary pedagogical aim but also a central project of much modernist and contemporary art. Within text-bound literary studies, the disattend track may include such features as the visual representation of the language as well as its acoustic structure. Moreover, a work may best be discussed within a context that not only includes its historical or ideological context, but also its interdependence on contemporary painting, theater, or music, not to mention the "popular" arts of the period. The idea that works of literature can be studied in isolation from the other arts, a founding idea of the discipline of English literary studies, may simply be mistaken. Certainly, the very limited aesthetic consciousness of college graduates would support the proposition that current approaches are misguided. Basic remodeling is necessary.

Not only our subjects, but also our methods, need to be addressed from an interdisciplinary perspective. In much of the discourse coming out of English departments, the art of writing has been relegated to the disattend track. To insist on the art of writing is, ironically, to press the need for interdisciplinarity within a field bisected against itself. To call for greater interaction between literary studies and the literary arts is to call literary studies back to itself.

My idea of a core curriculum will seem perverse to many advocates of both traditional and progressive approaches. My commitment to difference is not satisfied only by differences of "subject positions". To be sure, a course of differences must include a broad range of subject positions (including ones not easily definable by prevailing categories); but, to avoid frame lock, it also needs to include radical differences in forms, styles, and genres of expression and nonexpression. Insofar as narratives of personal or group experience are given primacy over other formal and aesthetic modalities, difference is not only enriched but also suppressed.

My modest proposal no doubt hopelessly complicates an already difficult task because it places virtually no limits on the number or types of possible works that might be studied. I find this a more stimulating starting point than determining a convenient frame that makes the task easier and more rationalizable. For example, I find myself surprisingly impatient with the obviously well-intentioned idea that an English department should require its undergraduate majors to take survey courses that cover canonically and historically significant (including previously neglected) works of English literature, along with a companion course in major trends in literary theory. In many such curricular proposals, and in the related "multicultural" anthologies published in recent years, the choice of literary authors is made with a commitment to diversity in mind. In contrast, there is rarely a similar commitment to diversity among the authors to be studied in theoretical and methodological courses. Furthermore, the new literature curriculums and anthologies are generally restricted to English language works, while it is hard to imagine a comparable anthology or core course in literary theory restricted only to works written in English. A number of problematic assumptions are at work here. In the first place, there is the idea that theory is a quasi-scientific form of knowledge that is able to transcend—largely, if not totally—its particular subject positions, and, as a result, is not dependent for its value on the fact that it *represents* a particular subject position. The corollary to this is that literary works do have their value in representing subject positions, and, as a result, are infinitely substitutable: in effect literature becomes a series of possible examples, any one of which is expendable. The problem is analogous to the disturbing practice of universities doing all their affirmative action hiring in the infinitely elastic or "soft" humanities rather than doing such hiring equally in the "uncompromisable" social and natural sciences.

What is English? While poetry may be said to be untranslatable in a way that philosophical works are not, philosophy also may be untranslatable in certain ways. Or rather, some philosophy (call it theory) and some literature (call it sociological) pose few translation problems. In this respect, it is revealing that some of the new anthologies that purport to represent cultural diversity—*The Norton Anthology of Literature by Women*, edited by Sandra Gilbert and Susan Gubar, and *The Heath Anthology of Amer-*

ican Literature, edited by Paul Lauter, are the most prominent—emphasize contemporary poetry written in a single-voice confessional mode that already seems to have been translated into the prevailing idiom of the anthologies themselves. This stylistic discrimination entails the rejection of works that challenge the idea that English is a transparent medium that can represent cultural experience as if it were information (already had a form). The result is that both formally innovative work and work in non-standard forms of English are marginalized.

I could go on.

Can Continental philosophy be understood in the absence of Continental literature? Or does Continental philosophy without Continental literature equal American literary theory?

Disciplinary boundaries serve more to cordon off areas of knowledge than to encourage students to search through a wide range of historical writers and thinkers and art practices. I would like to see the direction of undergraduate English programs in American universities move expansively toward the world rather than more parochially toward the literature of England and its linguistic heirs. While I suppose one could argue that people in the U.S. might have a special reason to know about the history and literature of the U.S. (though possibly North America would be the better frame), I can't see giving priority to the literature of England as opposed to the literature of the other European countries—or indeed other places in the world. English majors usually major in English not because of special interest in England but because of a more general interest in literature, writing, art, the humanities, or the history of ideas. English is the host language of their study. It's not as if students are likely to encounter Li Po or Soupault elsewhere in their studies—much less the Popul Vuh or Sappho. And, if that's so, it's hard to see how the line can be usefully drawn without including the "other" arts, and works from cultures that do not identify their cultural productions by proper names. Jerome Rothenberg's and Pierre Joris's *Poems for the Millennium: The University of California Book of Modern Poetry* goes a long way toward redressing this problem.

But I digress. I came here to talk paragraphs.

I like the idea of a paragraph developing its own internal logic, pushing a stretch of thought, turning around a term, considering a particular angle on a problem.

But it's the shift from paragraph to paragraph that creates the momentum, with the jump varying from almost indiscernible to a leap. My method of teaching, as much as writing, is to place one thing side by side with another and another, so that the series creates multiple perspectives on the issues addressed.

But what is the conclusion? What knowledge is gained? What has been taught or demonstrated?

—Performance has no value, no substance. You want a theater of ideas but no knowledge.—As if the process of critical thinking needed an end to justify it.

Then why does poetry have its music, fiction its stories, essays their ideas?

—But aren't you conflating literary and academic writing?   Possibly. Not necessarily. Not at all. Why are you bothering me? Can't you understand what I'm saying? I don't like to be spoken to in that manner. I think I deserve an apology, an ontology, a spin doctor, a value-added package with no financing, a one-way ticket to the next ocean liner, a way out of this pleated bag, container, vehicle, conveyor, storage bin, basement franchise.

Well, only if you say so, then maybe I'd agree.

What is wrong with you! Would you go and wash your hands they're full of chocolate!

Oh, excuse me. I don't know how that got in here, I guess I've never installed the right import protection system on my digital alphabet generator.

Can I recommend a few inexpensive, but fairly decent, restaurants in the neighborhood of the hotel? I particularly like the small satellite cafe in the atrium on 53rd just west of Sixth.

I've only just begun to contradict myself. But I contain no multitudes; I can't even contain myself.

Nor am I interested in proving anything.—Except to you, sir: to you I want to prove a thing or two, I'll tell you that. About that job opening . . . Can we meet me in the lounge right after the session?

It is my great pleasure to recommend V.S.O.P. for the position available at your university. V.S.O.P. is one of the most extraordinary scholars at the university and I am convinced that her work will become fundamental for future scholarship. I strongly recommend V.S.O.P. for advancement in the field. I can think of no young scholar that I could recommend to you more heartily.

Is that any worse than the way you conflate philosophy and what you like to call theory, or criticism and sociology, or interpretation and psychoanalysis? And anyway what is the natural form of scholarly writing? Where do our present standards come from? What values do they propagate? What and who do they exclude? What kinds of teaching and research do they foster, what discourage?

If some of the more interrogatory directions in literary studies, following almost a century of artistic practice, suggest we need to break down the distinction between high art and the rest of culture in order to investigate the interdependence of all cultural production, then it should come as less a surprise than it evidently does that the distinction between research and the thing researched will also break down. Erosion goes in both directions, or all three, since we don't want to forget about Aunt Rosie and the Babysitter's Club. Signifying is as signifying does. To assume a form of writing is to make it always and forever a cultural artifact.

Am I just complaining about being bored by certain prose styles, rendered without the panache needed to give them the intensity they sometimes possess? In any case, I'm not trying to exclude any of the styles of writing now practiced in the university, but to ask why we limit it to that. And if that should change, my questioning would find new targets. Questioning is its own reward. Frame-locked prose seems to deny its questions, its contradictions, its exhilarations, its comedy, its groping.

I find it more interesting to teach a class, or write an essay, on something I don't understand than to represent in a class or essay that which I already seem to have understood at some time previous.

I do not propose alternating between two subjects or two frames: that merely multiplies what is a problem in the first instance. I am suggesting a potentially endless series that does not systematically return to the point of its comparison, a parade of blackout sketches on Freud's mystic writing pad, whose origin is in departure, whose destination is in going on.

One thing I want to break down is the virtually Kantian picture of the studier and the thing studied. Serial composition, one paragraph adjacent to the next, one topic followed by another, one perspective permuted with another, refuses the idea that the studied and the studier are separable.

Next to us is not the work that we study, which we love so well to explain, but the work we are. I unclothe myself in addressing a poem, and the poem returns to show me my bearings, my comportment, and the way to read the next poem or painting, person or situation.

I am as low and befuddled as any man, as fouled and out of touch and self-deluded; this is what gives me a place from which to speak.

Is criticism condemned to be 50 years behind the arts? Is the art of today the model for the cultural studies of the next century? Will you be content to produce artifacts already inscribed in a dimming past, quaint lore for future researchers of institutional mores to mull on? Or will you make the culture you desire?

It's worth repeating: signifying practices have only art from which to copy.

—Oh, no, not art! I thought art was finished, over, done. I mean after Bürger and Danto and Jameson and Bourdieu and all those anthologies of cultural and new historical studies! I mean after the Yale School took Keats out on a TKO, art's never even had a strong contender.

—Charlie, Charlie, Charlie it was *you*. I could have been a contender, I could have been somebody, instead of a bum, which is what I am, let's face it.

—Art, she's not finished. I can hear her in the very halls we are congregating in today. She's saying: Just give me one more chance in the ring.

"Passed by Examination"

Paragraphs for Susan Howe

The poetry of Susan Howe marks a singularly engaged play at the crevices of the audible & the hidden. This luminous—*illuminated*—poetry refuses the categories of lyric or historical, mythopoetic or word-materializing, rather enlisting these approaches as navigational tools, multilateral compasses, on a journey into the unknown, denied, and destroyed.

Form in Howe's work is allegorical, the lineation miming (mining) the themes of the poems. *Structure of truth / Truth of structure.*[1] While references radiate exophorically (outwardly), they are pulled vortically into a compositional orbit in which anaphoria and cataphoria—internal textual dynamics of backward and frontward reverberation—hold sway, averting any fixing of the text's references outside the poem.[2] There is a constant, scaled reciprocity between abstraction and representation—neither is left, neither has the right, to "settle" the matter.

Look at a page as border marking the intersection of sight and words. Look at words as site of historical memory, as compost heap decomposing the past. Writing can engage the attention in such a way as to obliterate awareness of this border, this site, or can engender a hyperactive awareness of the page's opacity and impenetrability: stopped up short by an isolated syllable or by the space between syllables, then jolted by a line that becomes a crack into long-sealed chambers deep below the surface.

Here's the rub: the historically referential (exophoric) dimension of Howe's work is not used to ground the poem in an extra-linguistic truth any more than the literary allusions that permeate her work are there to send readers back to canonical sources (as if in replay of High Eliotic Modernism). Howe's collage poems use their source materials to break down /

1. Susan Howe, "Heliopathy", *Temblor* 4 (1986): 53.
2. Peter Quartermain usefully contrasts "exophoric" (outward pointing) with "cataphoric" (forward pointing) and "anaphoric" (backward pointing) in his *Disjunctive Poetics: From Gertrude Stein to Louis Zukofsky to Susan Howe* (New York: Cambridge University Press, 1992), pp. 24–25, 41–43.

break open the fixtures of historical representation and literary space, so the *work*—the poetic *activity*—exists at the border of representation and presentation, allusion and enactment, surface and depth. The poems are marked by resonance not reinscription. Howe's art, that is to say, is fundamentally aesthetic and ethical, not historical or narrative.

Speeches At The Barriers[3]

Howe reverses the dynamic of the "difficult" text excluding the reader by shifting the burden of exclusion outward. For the words are shut out at your own risk. *Inarticulate true meaning*.[4]—It is not the "marginal" anti-articulate text that is doing the excluding but the one who closes eyes, refuses to listen.

What are we divided from, divided by? To divide is to partition, to create borders, to differentiate, to delineate. These are also poetic acts: the inscription of a line of verse. These are also language acts: for to write is to divide, to speak to encode that division.

A sort of border life[5]

Take *Mark*—the name of Howe's father and son, a central figure in *The Secret History of the Dividing Line*. The mark (mar[6]) of an enclosure. The border between. That which mars the undifferentiated, soils the soil, establishes identity, fixes territory, announces sovereignty. For what's been marked is claimed, possessed—the sign of a stake (state). At the same time, a mark is a token, that which stands for something else, the visible trace of a sign, metaphor for a word, substitute for a signature and so standing for a name.—An artist makes her mark; but the confidence man finds her mark, or, as we now may say, target of opportunity.

Scribbling the ineffable[7]

There is no better model of scholarship, or research, than the works of Susan Howe, partly because they open up to unanswered—not always even unanswerable—questions. Questions that never finish or dispose or encapsulate or surmount, but continuously examine.

3. Susan Howe, *Defenestration of Prague* (New York: Kulchur, 1993). Subsequently republished in *Europe of Trusts* (Los Angeles: Sun & Moon, 1990), p. 97.

4. Susan Howe, *Articulation of Sound Forms in Times* (Windsor, Vt.: Awede Press, 1987), republished in *Singularities* (Hanover: Wesleyan University Press, 1990), p. 30.

5. "Thorow", in *Singularities*, p. 50.

6. Susan Howe, *Secret History of the Dividing Line* (New York: Telephone, 1978), republished in *Frame Structures* (New York: New Directions, 1996), p. 89.

7. "Thorow", p. 47.

quintessential clarity of inarticulation[8]

History is a lie, but we are no better than dupes or fools if we ignore it. We have at our "disposal" an avalanche of facts but can't tell what they mean or how they go together. *In the machinery of injustice / my whole being is Vision.*[9]

"The unexamined life is not worth living" would seem to have little currency. Howe's studies of American mythology against the grain provide a concrete method for examination. *Untraceable wandering / the meaning of knowing.*[10]

The Now that is Night
Time comprehended in Thought[11]

Is there some way out of the long, dark night of our captivity in history? For the conquerors of North America, an inhabited wilderness was a desert—an empty space—to be filled. & this is the method of "our" madness: we destroy without acknowledging the actuality of that which we obliterate. *They are denying the Dark / after dark will ever gather . . . So dark they run against trees.*[12]

Clear space of blackness

between us[13]

We disappear—benight, blacken—what appears to us unknown, unmarked, unclaimed; that is, unpossessed by us: calling it savage, inarticulate, mad, eccentric, odd, ineffable, dark, empty. So that our own history is one more concretely of evasions than charting. *The expanse of unconcealment / so different from all maps.*[14]

& our grammar repeats just these erasures & concealments, wiping out the wildness of language in the name of law, rationality, homogeneity, territory, or of a "populism" that recognizes only colonized forms of "popular" expression. *sense hidden.*[15]

What then is this project for poetry?: *Our law / vocables / of shape or sound.*[16]

8. *Secret History,* p. 95.
9. "Thorow", p. 49.
10. *Articulation,* p. 25.
11. Ibid., p. 28.
12. *Heliopathy,* p. 50.
13. *Defenestration,* p. 103.
14. "Thorow", p. 55.
15. *Secret History,* p. 118.
16. Ibid.

Here is blank reason[17]

The "savage" that we have conquered in the name of civilization is our-
selves. *We all wear moccasins.*[18] The captivity narrative is the story of our
own language held hostage, divided against itself; except when we some-
times return to it: in dreams, in the inarticulate sounds—the hiss—of "his-
tory", in poems such as these that bloom in the dark, sick from the blind-
ing light of the sun ("heliopathy" a kind of sunsickness).

disputation in dominion beyond sovereign.[19]

"The secret history of the dividing line" is that our "enclosure acts", which
we have long concealed (longed to conceal) from ourselves, need to be
overthrown, thrown out, "defenestrated". *You are of me & I of you, I cannot tell /
Where you leave off and I begin.*[20] Our language is always a "Western Border"
if we push through, *mark suns rising & setting*[21] . . . *[espy] bounds to leop over.*[22]
Poetry as a displacement of the "sovereignty" of the crown or law allow-
ing for some other order, call it dominion.

Freedom's dominion of possible.[23]

salvages / or / savages:[24] either we salvage the past, make it a present, or we
are disappeared, marked off, banished to the dark.

Complicity battling redemption:[25] either we own up to—take responsibility
for—examine—our grammars as much as our histories—or we remain
guilty for them.

The Great Crossing
we marched with drums beating and colors flying[26]

Howe weaves at the tears in the all-too-violent fabric that imparts national
identity to America. She sings of origins & hears the blanks firing in the
night of her exploding syllables.

17. "Heliopathy", p. 50.
18. Ibid., p. 46.
19. *Articulation*, p. 28.
20. "Thorow", p. 58.
21. "Heliopathy", p. 50.
22. *Articulation*, p. 9.
23. Ibid., p. 27.
24. *Secret History*, p. 91.
25. "Thorow", p. 55.
26. *Secret History*, p. 117.

The Value of *Sulfur*

For the past several years I have been a correspondent for *Sulfur* magazine. Correspondent from where? I like to think of myself as the correspondent from the outer reaches of language, because I think language, along with outer space, is the last wilderness, the last frontier—our collective inner space, as strange as the unexplored depths of the oceans, as wild as the word Emily Dickinson proclaimed was language's wildest, just the one syllable, NO.

Language is a wilderness that, unlike others, can never be conquered, or exhausted; but it can be made to accommodate: to submit, assimilate, compromise, deny. In contrast, I correspond for a poetry that dwells, without disavowing—that is, that dwells in ways that may make readers anxious—not only on the resplendent and difficult to contain, but also on the disturbed, confused, broken, awkward, difficult, dark. This is a poetry committed less to opposition than composition—a com(op)posing that values inquiry above representation, resistance over adjudication. For a stubborn aversion to the conventions of expression, even for the sake of the aversion, can be necessary relief in a society that confuses palatability for communication, packaging for style, tiny bytes of message for meaning. In a culture where national political discourse religiously avoids complexity and journalism swings maniacally from the parroting of PR releases to the endless repetitions of the same rehearsed banalities (whether it be celebrity interviews or the close-up faces of disaster victims), there is a need for a poetry that is not just more of same. & this is a need that grows in direct proportion to poetry's much-heralded denial, as in the cover story of last month's *Commentary* (August 1988)—"Who Killed Poetry?"—an article so proudly shallow that its only point seemed to be that it wished the art of writing could be killed, as if poetry was some kind of weirdly persistent mosquito that hovered around the author in the throes of composition: call it language's conscience, its consciousness of itself.

In the face of smugness like this, it becomes necessary to insist on the value of poetry that goes beyond the moralizing subjectivity that characterizes so much of the verse of our time. Whether a poem is innovative or traditional may not seem all that important if the ability of many people to read is in question; but larger social and public issues may elide the aesthetic value that a poetics may insist upon, against all odds. Yet the adversarial, in its passion, may also engender divisiveness. & indeed divisiveness is an unfortunate, but perhaps inevitable, legacy of alternative traditions in American poetry. As long as most poets of value in our culture continue to feel, with justification, unrecognized and unappreciated—not so much opposed as ignored—this legacy will be hard to reverse.

For while public discussions of poetry often focus on the building of "community", those of us who live our lives as poets are equally aware of the often blistering hostility that greets new poetry, not only from those who would be expected to dislike this work, but also, and often with more vitriolic bias, from those who would seem to be interested in related work (as a recent public tantrum in *Sulfur,* by one of its contributing editors, attests). Alternative institutions, as we have learned on the left, are not always sanctuary from the reductive, the dismissive, the self-righteous. They are not necessarily free from a nostalgia for past solutions untransformed to account for the present moment, nor, for that matter, from wild-eyed obliviousness to old and problematic solutions offered as revolutionary new ones.

The poet's life is one of quiet desperation, although sometimes it gets noisy. Everywhere undermined by apathy, suspicion, competitiveness, outside the welcome friendship of those similarly situated, it seems poetry "itself" has to be defended. Many days I feel like one of those 50s street vendors demonstrating multipurpose vegetable cutters; the flapping hands and jumping up and down may generate a small crowd because there remains interest if not in the product at least in the humiliation of trying to sell something few seem to want.

I flip through this week's *Nation* (October 3, 1988) and notice a letter to the editor by their own small press critic. He suggests that the "clarity" that the New York *Post* "demands of its sports writers" is a model that poets who wish to be political should emulate. Is it just my pessimism that makes me feel that this reflects an ever deepening crisis in our culture—a contempt, even in the alternate press's space for alternate presses, for intellectual and spiritual articulations not completely assimilated into and determined by the dominant culture's discursive practices? Discursive practices marked by endless chronicles of winners and losers, organized violence, and performance measured by the clock. & why exactly are the four words "dominant culture's discursive practices" any worse to someone of this persuasion than such approved formulations as "major league batting practice"? Perhaps poetry, like the wilderness, has to be denied as part of an effort to conquer it. For to admit that there is wilderness, or poetry, is to lose the battle to overcome it.

Why do things except for money, or sport, or family? This is something that seems no longer obvious. & if you say *civic*, it still doesn't explain that the community for which you may wish to speak has few voters or consumers, or perhaps is only a figment of your imagination, or a vision of a community that may sometime come to be. It still doesn't explain that the community for which you speak may be a people that have vanished, or been expelled, or vanquished. Our history is one of ghosts, whose voices we can sometimes hear sighing in lines more often than not denied the status of communication because they make too much sense, but sense of the wrong kind.

Each of us is entitled to our taste and perhaps deserve it. There is no point in disputing preferences, if presented as such. But it is another matter when such preferences are stated with the inevitability of endless repetitions of the same, when taste insists on its right to be proscriptive but not to be challenged, or when statements of taste turn to arguments that fundamentally distort the sources, motivations, and accomplishments, whether of the radical modernists of the 10s and 20s, the New American poets of the 50s and 60s, or poets today: decrying the absence of meaning or decorum; the abandonment of coherence, sentiment, or emotion; the loss of the music of traditional verse forms; and other various and sundry excesses. Seventy-five years ago, it was the stance of many avant-garde movements to proclaim just these feats, partly just to "bug the squares". But these claims have grown tiresome over time and, in any case, never really fit the work in whose name they were spoken, since really what was rejected was not meaning or music or even literary "tradition" but outworn, or no longer viable, ways of conceiving of them.

A poetry or poetics that is skeptical of fixed values will provoke a rather constant denunciation as valueless. Such rebukes can be encouraging in that they show the continuing need to rattle against the pieties of those certain (if insecure) in their beliefs and complacent (if anxious) in their condescension. An pro-vocative poetry will provoke those who would shirk from their own responsibility to make values rather than mimic them. The test of such a poetry is that it discomfits those who rely on an exclusive claim to truth and authenticity in order to legitimate their practice.

As I have learned from my many years on my own private Borscht Belt, people without a sense of humor do not laugh at jokes. And if you want to survive in show business, don't let the hecklers get you down, make them part of the show.

The poetry for which I correspond represents less a unified alternative poetics than a series of sometimes contentiously related tendencies, or proclivities, and, especially, shared negations (concerted rejections) of American official verse culture. For truly these projects-in-language are not restricted or exclusive; there is no limit to those who can, or have, or will participate in this work, which is open-ended and without proscriptions: not a matter of Proper Names but of Works, and perhaps not even a matter of works but of how readers read them. And maybe those who say that the mainstream is a projection, or desperate posturing, and that these alternate, alternating, traditions are the active matrix of American poetry, are right. For official verse culture, now as always, is under siege, undermining itself, and able to occupy only a tiny table at the banquet of culture: decked with medals and pride but notably less positioned for access to the stage than many of its designated, and undesignated, others.

Just now in North America there is an intense density of poetic activity, so that it becomes difficult to keep up with all the work that excites interest and involvement. The work about which I wish to correspond tends to be preoccupied with finding the possibilities for articulation of meanings that are too often denied or repressed by a (multinational) culture that we are always being subjected to, that we are indeed subjects of, and which, moreover, can be understood as its nowhere explicated subject: Poetry which is political not primarily in its subject matter, or representation of political causes, however valuable that may be, but in the form and structure and style of the poems, and in the attitude toward language.

Against the onslaught of a pervasive, and facile, insistence that there is no escape from the simulations of commodity culture, it becomes political to hold out for meaning: not the meaning that is the prepackaged message of an authorized and syntactically normalized, grammatical, decorum; but an always active, probing consideration of meaning as social, corporeal, multidimensional; a meaning that is not fixed but acted out in imperfect, asymmetric counterpoint to the labors that simultaneously engender each day.

Shaker Show

Now *that* is a chair
I wouldn't want to sit in.

Gertrude and Ludwig's Bogus Adventure

for Gabriele Mintz

As Billy goes higher all the balloons
Get marooned on the other side of the
Lunar landscape. The module's broke—
It seems like for an eternity, but who's
Counting—and Sally's joined the Moonies
So we don't see so much of her anyhow.
Notorious novelty—I'd settle for a good
Cup of Chase & Sand-borne—though when
The strings are broken on the guitar
You can always use it as a coffee table.
Vienna was cold at that time of year.
The sachertorte tasted sweet but the memory
burned in the colon. Get a grip, get a grip, before
The Grippe gets you. Glad to see the picture
Of ink—the pitcher that pours before
Throwing the Ball, with never a catcher in sight.
Never a catcher but sometimes a catch, or
A clinch or a clutch or a spoon—never a
Catcher but plenty o' flack, 'till we meet
On this side of the tune.

Introjective Verse

)introversive   )implosive   )introspeculative

incorporating

The Rejected

Verse, what?, if it is to trip and flail and fall, if it is to be *inessential*, useless, maybe could consider, losing it, forgetting laws and breadth: the breathlessness of the person who refuses to be a man when she listens.

I won't do two things: first, I won't show what introjective or CEN-TRIPETAL verse is, how it recoils, in its fate as decomposition, how, in distinction to the projective, it is dismayed; and 2, I'll hold back from suggesting a few contradictions about how the ebullient denial of reality takes such a verse out of believing, what that aversion does, both to the poet and her nonreaders. (Such aversion involves, for example, a return to the technical, and may, the way things hokey-poke around, lead away from drama and epic and toward the materials of poems, their sounds and shapes.)

I

First, some complexities that a person learns, if she works INTROJEC-TIVELY, or what can be called MISCOMPOSITION BY EAR.

(1) the *pataphysics* of the thing. A poem is energy absconded by the poet from where she got it (she will have several stashes), by way of the non-readers themselves, all the way over to, the poem. Oy!

This is the problem which any poet who departs from adenoidal forms is specially coddled by. And it involves a whole series of blunders. From the moment she jumps back into CENTRIPETAL MISCOMPOSI-TION—puts herself in the bin—she can aver by no tack other than the

110

one the poem refuses. (It is much more, for example, this backward som-
ersaulting, than simply such a one as Wilde put, so giddily, to get us
startled: life imitates art, not the other way round. Come on, girls & boys,
think complex, act to redistribute the wealth!)

(2) is the *abandonment of principle,* the ludicrousness that presides so con-
spicuously over such dysraphisms, and, when averred, is the reason why
an introjective poem refuses belief. It is this: FORM IS NEVER MORE
THAN AN EXTENSION OF MALCONTENT. There it went, flapping,
more USELESSNESS.

Now (2) the clumsiness of the thing, how the awkwardness of the thing
can be made to dishevel the energies that the form thought it accom-
plished. It can never be boiled down to a statement: ONE PERCEPTION
MUST NEVER LEAD DIRECTLY TO ANOTHER PERCEPTION. It
means something very different than what it says, is never a matter of, at
no points, (even—I shouldn't say—of our injuring reality as our weekly
bliss) get off it, invoke arrestation, keep out of it, slow down, the percep-
tions, ours, the evasions, the long-term evasions, none of it, stop it as much
as you can, citizen. And if you also slouch as a poet, REFUSE REFUSE
REFUSE the process at some points, in some poems, once in a blue while:
one perception STOPPED, SLOWED, BY ANOTHER!

So there we were, looping, where there's no dogma. And its inexcus-
ableness, its uselessness, in theory. Which doesn't get us, ought not to get
us, outside the cyberfactory, then, or 1995, where centripetal verse is
made.

If I sing tunelessly—if I forget, and keep crying wolf, out of breath—of the
sound as distinguished from the voice, it is for no cause except to loosen
the part that breath plays in verse, which has been observed and practiced
too well, so that verse may retreat to its proper immobility and placeless-
ness in the mouths that are already lost. I take it that INTROJECTIVE
VERSE teaches nothing, that that verse will never do what the poet
intends either by the tones of her voice or theater of her breath . . .

Because the centripetal questions the speech-force of language (speech
is the "red herring" of verse, the secret of the poem's delusions), because,
then, a poem has, by language, evanescence, nothing that can be mis-
treated as solid, objectified, thinged.

II

Which makes no promises, no realities outside the poem: no stances only
dances. It is the matter of content, this discontent. The content of Clease,
of Bruce, of Ball, as distinct from what I might call more "literary" minis-

ters. There is no moment in which the introjective evasion of verse is finished, the form fuels blame. If the beginning and end is the breathlessness of words, sound in that material sense, then the domain of poetry blurs and blurts.

It's hardly this: the uselessness of a baby, by itself and thus by others, crying in its misconception of its relation to culture, that semiotic fluidlessness to which it owes its gigantic existence. If it squall, it shall find much to squall about, and shall squirm too, culture has such flummoxing ways of terrorizing all that is outside. But if it stays inside itself, if it is contained in its infancy as if it is a participant in the life immediately surrounding, it will be able to babble and in its babbling hear what is shared. It is in this sense that the introjective ache, which is the artist's artlessness in the intimate streets of enfoldment, leads to scales more intimate than the child's. It's all so easy. Culture works from irreverence, even in its constructions. Irreverence is the human's special qualification as vegetable, as mineral, as *animalady*. Language is our profanest act. And when a poet squalls about what is outside herself (in "the material world", if you object, but also the materiality in her, for that matter), then she, if she chooses to reflect on this restlessness, pays in the street where culture has given her scale, centripetal scale.

Such works, though it's no argument, could not issue from persons who conceive verse without the full resonance of human voicelessness. The introjective poet staggers from the failings of her own boasts to that syntaxophony where language digs in, where sound echoes, where utterances concatenate, where, inevitably, all acts stall.

Poetics of the Americas

Speaking in Buffalo in 1994, the Argentinean poet Jorge Santiago Pered-
nik ended his talk on cultural resistance to the recent reign of terror in his
country by saying "the struggle is impossible and for that reason it took
place." Without wanting to violate the cultural specificity of Perednik's
comment, I understand this also to mean that poetry, insofar as it resists
reification as culturally sanctioned Poetry, is also impossible—and for
that reason takes place. For the sake of this collection, I would like to add
America to this list, for America is impossible and for this reason, also, it
exists.

Or Americas, for it is in the resistance to any singular unity of identity
that the impossibility of America, of a Poetics of the Americas, may be said
to dwell. The cultural space of this impossible America is not carved up
by national borders or language borders but transected by innumerable
overlaying, contradictory or polydictory, traditions and proclivities and
histories and regions and peoples and circumstances and identities and
families and collectivities and dissolutions—dialects and ideolects not
National Tongues, localities and habitations not States.

But such an America is imaginary, for everywhere the local is under fire
from the imposed standard of a transnational consumer culture and under-
mined by the imperative to extract it and export it as product.

In the United States we are particularly bedeviled by our own history
of cultural resistance, often confusing the struggles for cultural legitima-
tion of the last century with our own reversed roles in this one. I am think-
ing of the specific needs, a century ago, that gave rise to the invention of
"American literature" as an academic category within the university sys-
tem that had only recently countenanced English, or British, literature as
a suitable appendix to the study of the classics (primarily Greek and
Roman works). At that time, there was a clear necessity for breaking away
from the perceived limitations of "Island" English literature in order to
build an audience for, and give a measure of respectability and legitima-
tion to, certain New England and "middle-Atlantic" and Southern English
language texts. "American" in this context was a strategic rather than an

essential category; as a result, the multiethnic and polylinguistic reality of the U.S. was not accented in early formations of "American literature". By 1925, William Carlos Williams, in *In the American Grain*, had given new breadth to the concept of America; yet his related insistence on an American speech suggested a false essence to a concept useful only as a negation: NOT English verse diction. That is, as a negative category American literature was a useful hypothesis. In contrast, for the present, the idea of American literature understood as a positive, expressive "totalization" needs to continue to be dismantled.

The problem here is twofold: the totalization of "America" and the globally dominant position of the U.S. Since the U.S. is the dominant English language (as well as Western) nation in the political, economic, and mass-cultural spheres, its monopolizing powers need to be cracked— from the inside and outside—as surely as one version of England's grip on our language's literature needed to be loosened in the nineteenth century and early twentieth century. The same logic that led to the invention of American, as distinct from English, literature now leads to the invention of, on the one hand, a non-American-centered English language literature and, on the other, a poetics of the Americas. Any unitary concept of America is an affront to the multiplicity of Americas that make U.S. culture as vital as it is. America is, to echo Perednik, an "unclassifiable" totality. For there is no one America. The U.S. is less a melting pot than a simultaneity of inconsolable coexistences—from the all-too-audible spokespeople of the state to the ghostly voices of the almost lost languages of the sovereign nations of Arapaho, Mohawk, Shoshone, Pawnee, Pueblo, Navaho, Crow, Cree, Kickapoo, Blackfoot, Cheyenne, Zuni . . . ; though in truth there are no sovereigns, only sojourners.

For writing, or reading, to assume—and consequently "express" or "project"—a national identity is as problematic as for writing to assume a self or group identity. However, in jettisoning such presumptions, some sense of what such entities might be may be revealed. Such exploratory writing does not escape from its sociohistorical situation but rather contributes to an interrogation and reformulation of the *description* of that sociohistorical situation, foregrounding heterogeneous and anomalous elements rather than homogenizing ones. In contrast, attempts to represent an already constituted idea of identity may preclude the possibility of encountering newly emerging identity formations.

I feel much closer to the concerns of some small press magazines in the U.K., Canada, New Zealand, and Australia than to most poetry magazines in the U.S. As for the Americas, I would say that $L=A=N=G=U=A=G=E$ and *Xul*, the magazine with which Perednik is associated, probably share more than $L=A=N=G=U=A=G=E$ shared with most other poetry magazines published in New York.[1] The national focus of "American poetry" tends to encamp poets who would do better to share work and readership; similarly, it tends to arbitrarily limit the horizons of much current criticism of poetry. At the same time, "internationalism", like its Anglophonic cousin the "trans-Atlantic", has provided models of connoisseurship that have removed poems from the local contexts that give them meaning while at the same time developing a canon of works that undervalues the untranslatable particularities not only in given poems but also in the selection of poets. (A related problem of decontextualization is apparent in the reception of "Latin American" fiction in the U.S.) Perednik speaks of the serendipitous colliding of different poetries as the "law of poetic coincidence"; this poetic law provides a way to navigate between the universalizing humanisms of internationalism and the parochialism of regionalism and nationalism.

This is not to say that our different national and cultural circumstances are not marked in our poems; on the contrary it is the insistence on registering these social circumferences in the forms of our poems that may be our shared methodological approach. I am also conscious that U.S. poets tend to be less aware of developments in other English-writing countries than the other way around. Often, our boasting about the significance of a non-European American poetry has deafened us to the newness of English language poetries and non-English language poetries even further from Europe than our own, including some being written right in the heart of that "old" world.

The impossible poetics of the Americas does not seek a literature that unifies us as one national or even continental culture—America (the U.S.), North America (the U.S. and Anglophonic Canada), Multicultural North America (Canada, Mexico, and the U.S.), Latin America (south of the U.S.), South America (the "seventh" continent, since in the U.S. we learn that the Americas are two separate continents). Rather, the impossible poetics of the Americas insists that our commonness is in our partiality and disregard for the norm, the standard, the overarching, the universal. Such poetry will always be despised by those who wish to use literature to foster identification rather than to explore it.

So I hope it will be apparent that while I welcome the challenge of multiculturalism as it has entered U.S. arts and education in the past decade, I continue to find many of its proponents more interested in reinforcing traditional modes of representation than allowing the heterogeneity of forms and peoples that make up the cultural diversity of the Americas to transform poetic styles and personal and group identities. Yet it is hardly

1. See *The Xul Reader*, ed. Ernesto Grosman (New York: Roof Books, 1997).

surprising that static conceptions of group identity represented by authentic spokespersons continue to ride roughshod over works and individuals whose identities are complex, multiple, mixed, confused, hyperactivated, miscegenated, synthetic, mutant, forming, or virtual.

American literary multiculturalism, insofar as it seeks to promote representative figures, runs the risk of becoming a kind of domestic "internationalism". When we seek representativeness from a poet we often do so at the cost of misrepresenting the poem. At the same time, official verse culture remains dominated by a poetics of individuality and subjectivity that has tried to remain resistant to (not to say "above") not only questions of identity politics but also aesthetic position, a double evasion often expressed, apparently without irony, as "disaffiliation". The result is an homogenization of poetic values and practices undreamt of among poets willing to acknowledge their affiliations.

The problem is how to pursue affinities while resisting unities and how to resist unities without losing the capacity to be poetically responsible, that is, responsive to and supportive of those poetic tendencies and affiliations that deepen, intensify, and extend the activity of poetry. And that means enacting poetry's contemporaneity—the willingness of poets and ability of poems to act on and in the present social and cultural circumstances, including working with the cultural forms and linguistic materials specific to the present. The point is to pursue the collective and dialogic nature of poetry without necessarily defining the nature of this collectivity—call it a virtual collectivity or, to appropriate Stanley Cavell's phrase for Emersonian moral perfectionism, "this new yet unapproachable America": this unrepresentable yet ever presenting collectivity.

In a recent book, *Modernisms: A Literary Guide*, the British critic Peter Nicholls schematically contrasts two modernisms that may be applied to American poetry. The first and more familiar kind, associated with a partial reading of Ezra Pound and Thomas Eliot, "rests upon assumptions of a unitary self that carefully differentiates itself from the world of the Object and thus asserts codes of mastery."[2] In this type of modernism, the poem imposes a (masculine) order and form on the (feminine) flux of modern world; the self is imagined as closed, autonomous, distant, and antagonistic in its effort to establish stable authority. Another modernism can be associated especially with Gertrude Stein and her nonsymbological or constructive practice. In Nicholls's words, this poetic practice is "preoc-

---

2. The formulation here is Peter Quartermain's, from a letter (May 17, 1994). See Nicholls's *Modernisms: A Literary Guide* (Berkeley: University of California Press, 1995), especially pp. 200, 202, which are quoted in this paragraph.

cupied with what seems other but turns out to be the same", thus unsettling the autonomy of the self central to the first type of modernism. "Stein shares with H.D. the desire to move beyond the object-based poetics which derives its force from the repudiation of the feminine, and to discover in its place a form of writing that reveals continuities between self and world" by opening the self to that which is outside it.

I would propose at least three modernist projects: subjective, objective, and constructive. By nonsymbological or constructive, I am referring to the fact that in many of her works Stein does not depend upon supplemental literary or narrative contexts to secure her meaning but enacts her subjects as continuously actualized presentations of meaning. Unlike Pound or Eliot, with their myriad literary and other references, or James Joyce, with his etymological anaphora, with Stein you are left with the words on the page and the Imaginary structures they build.

In the poetry of the past two decades, I think we have moved away from the choice of subjective, objective, or even constructive and toward a synthesizing or juxtaposing of these approaches. Here the influence of the dialect poetries of the modernist period gives way to a dialectical poetry that refuses allegiance to Standard English without necessarily basing its claim on an affiliation with a definable group's speaking practice. The norm enforces a conduct of representation that precludes poetry as an active agent to further thought, unbound to the restrictions of rationalized ordering systems. Poetry can be a process of thinking rather than a report of things already settled; an investigation of figuration rather than a picture of something figured out. Such ideologically informed nonstandard language practice I call *ideolectical* and I find it equally present in British poets such as Maggie O'Sullivan, Tom Leonard, and Tom Raworth; in U.S. poets such as Lyn Hejinian, Bruce Andrews, Leslie Scalapino, Harryette Mullen, and Clark Coolidge; in Canadian poets such as Steve McCaffery, Deanna Ferguson, Nicole Brossard, Christopher Dewdney, Karen Mac Cormack, Lisa Robertson, and Catriona Strang; or in such South American poets as Perednik and Cecilia Vicuña.[3]

The invention of an ideolectical English language poetry, as a poetry of the Americas, involves the replacement of the national and geographically centered category of English (or Spanish) poetry not with the equally essentialist category of American poetry but with a field of potentialities, a virtual America that we approach but never possess. English languages,

3. For related discussion of the multiplicitous chartings of American identity in Lyn Hejinian, Harryette Mullen, and Theresa Hak Kyung Cha, situated in the context of a reading of Stein and Dickinson, see Juliana Spahr, "Re Letter and Read Her: The Reader-Centered Text in American Literature", doctoral dissertation, State University of New York, Buffalo, 1995.

set adrift from the sight/sound sensorium of the concrete experiences of the English people, are at their hearts uprooted and translated: nomadic in origin, absolutely particular in practice. Invention in this context is not a matter of choice: it is as necessary as the ground we walk on.

The impossible poetics of the Americas of which I speak has, in the U.S., a history of breaks from the received literary language of England. The vernacular was a crucial factor in many of those breaks, particularly as explored by such African-American poets as Paul Laurence Dunbar, Langston Hughes, Sterling Brown, James Weldon Johnson, and Melvin Tolson. At the same time, the American language was being transformed by the "bad" or "broken" English of the European immigrants from the 1880s through the early years of the new century: "new" syntaxes, new expressions came along with the new world. Here it is significant that Williams, Stein, Louis Zukofsky, and other makers of a new American poetry were themselves second-language speakers of English, while others were children of second-language speakers, as Peter Quartermain notes in *Disjunctive Poetics*. So for these children of immigrants, English became less transparent, more a medium subject to reforming. Correlatively, on the other side of the Atlantic, the explorations of dialect traditions by Basil Bunting and Hugh MacDiarmid and in the Caribbean by Claude McKay and more recently by Linton Kwesi Johnson, Louise Bennett, Michael Smith, or Kamau Brathwaite (who rejects the term dialect, preferring "nation language"), become a source of shared language resources among English language poetries.

I realize that my emphasis on nonstandard language practices makes for unexpected affiliations. Tony Crowley, in *Standard English and the Politics of Language*, points to two senses of "standard". A standard is a rallying point for the forward movement of an ideology or group, by means of which a unity is invoked, as for example a flag in battle. But a standard is also an objective unit of measure and regulator of uniformity, and as such a product of normalization and averaging. Standard American English involves both these senses: it is a sociohistorical construction, embedding class, ethnic, and racial preferences, that serves to build national unity; and it is also a regulator of language practices, serving to curb deviance. Under the aegis of standardization, problems of social coherence are displaced onto questions of linguistic correctness:

> The search for linguistic unity and identity is one that is founded on acts of violence and repression: a denial of heteroglossia—discursive and historical—in favour of centralizing, static forms. And the victory of one dialect or language over others produces a hierarchy, an ordering of discourse which excludes, distributes and

defines what is to count as discourse and what is to be relegated to oblivion. It brings into being the "authoritative word" [that in Bakhtin's words] "is located in a distanced zone, organically connected with a past that is felt to be organically higher. It is, so to speak, the word of the fathers." There is then no possibility of challenging this discourse . . . Its authority is already borne along with it and it is the authority of the ruling patriarchal tradition.[4]

In "our" "own" literature, the most significant past debates on these issues took place in two distinct quarters. Disowning and deflating the "authoritative word" was a central project for Stein and other constructivist poets of the modernist period. Even more explicitly, however, standard English was the center of a debate that took place within the frame of the Harlem Renaissance, itself a geographic displacement of what is more accurately described as African-American arts of the 1920s and 30s. Writers such as Hughes and Brown invented and defended a vernacular poetry that refused the standards of literary English advocated by poets such as Countee Cullen: a controversy that in complicated ways echoes the debate between Booker T. Washington and W. E. B. Du Bois. The issue in both controversies is the nature, terms, and price of assimilation.

As our literary history is usually told, the nonstandard language practices of the radical modernists, and their descendants, are not linked to the dialect and vernacular practices of African-American poets.[5] But the construction of a vernacular poetry was a major project for many poets, black and white, during the modernist period, and the fact that these develop-

4. Tony Crowley, *Standard English and the Politics of Language* (Urbana: University of Illinois Press, 1989), pp. 9–10. Crowley's citation of Bakhtin is from *The Dialogic Imagination* (Austin: University of Texas Press, 1981), p. 271.

5. A new and important exception is Michael North's *The Dialect of Modernism: Race, Language, and Twentieth Century Literature* (New York: Oxford University Press, 1994). North contrasts the mimicry of black dialect by white modernists and the skepticism of some African-American poets toward dialect. "Linguistic imitation and racial masquerade are so important to transatlantic modernism because they allow the writer to play at self-fashioning. Jazz means freedom to Jakie Rabinowitz [the Jolson character in *The Jazz Singer*] partly because it is fast and rhythmically unrestrained but also because it is not ancestrally his . . . For African-American poets of this generation, however, dialect is a 'chain.' In the version created by the white minstrel tradition, it is a constant reminder of the literal unfreedom of slavery" and what followed (p. 11). This reflects, in part, the view of James Weldon Johnson, who in his preface to *God's Trombones: Seven Negro Sermons in Verse* (1927; New York: Penguin, 1990) underscores that dialect verse is a "limited instrument . . . with but two complete stops, pathos and humor" (p. 7; see also note 21, below).

North goes on to scrutinize dialect and "primitivist" elements in such modernists as Eliot, Stein, Williams, and Mina Loy, which he sees not as forging a new poetics of the Americas but as trapped in a racist ventriloquism. Indeed, North suggests that "white interest in African-American language and culture was, if anything, more dangerous than indifference" (p. 11)—a conclusion that is sucked into the very vicious circles North's book sets out to critique.

ments often took place without reference to each other—the fact of the color line—should not now obscure their intimate formal and sociohistorical connection. Stein's breakthrough into the ideolectical practice of *Tender Buttons*, for example, was prepared by her problematic improvisations on African-American vernacular in "Melanctha". A generation later, both Tolson and Louis Zukofsky used complex literary framing devices as a means of working with, and against—I'd say torquing—vernacular linguistic materials. By linking dialect and ideolect I wish to emphasize the common ground of linguistic exploration, the invention of new syntaxes as akin to the invention of new Americas, or possibilities for America. In Brathwaite's account, however, dialect is better called "nation language" and if that is the case it would seem to run counter to ideolect, whose nations may be described, in Robin Blaser's phrase, as image nations, imaginary, ideological; dialectical in that other sense. I don't wish to relieve this tension so much as to try to locate it as pivotal to our literary history and contemporary poetics. I am convinced, however, that nonstandard writing practices share a technical commonality that overrides the necessary differences in interpretation and motivation, and this commonality may be the vortical prosodic force that gives us footing with one another.

In *History of the Voice*, Brathwaite's 1979 talk about the "process of using English in a different way from the 'norm'", Brathwaite speaks of the break with the pentameter metric of English verse as decisive in establishing a distinct Caribbean national language rooted in an oral tradition:

> It is *nation language* in the Caribbean that, in fact, largely ignores the pentameter . . . English it may be in terms of some of its lexical features. But in its contours, its rhythms and timbre, its sound explosions, it is not English, even though the words, as you hear them, might be English to a greater or lesser degree . . . But it is an English which is not the standard, imported, educated English . . . It is what I call, as I say, *nation language*. I use the term in contrast to *dialect*. The word "dialect" has been bandied about for a long time, and it carries very pejorative overtones . . . Nation language, on the other hand, is the *submerged* area of dialect which is much more closely allied to the African aspect of experience in the Caribbean.[6]

Brathwaite's "nation language" is as much a new standard to rally national spirit as it is a break from standardization. Any comparison of ideolectical

---

6. Edward Kamau Brathwaite, *History of the Voice: The Development of Nation Language in Anglophone Caribbean Poetry* (London: New Beacon Books, 1984), p. 13; subsequent references to Brathwaite are from this book. This essay is reprinted, without the extensive bibliography, in Brathwaite's collection *Roots* (Ann Arbor: Michigan University Press, 1993).

and dialectical poetry must confront this obvious contradiction: dialect, understood as nation language, has a centripetal force, regrouping often denigrated and dispirited language practices around a common center; ideolect, in contrast, suggests a centrifugal force, moving away from normative practices without necessarily replacing them with a new center of gravity, at least defined by self or group. Furthermore, the social positions from which these practices emerge will often be quite distinct. Dialect poets may be regarded by the dominant literary culture as outsiders, but they are often also at the center of collective formations that are struggling to obtain self-respect and cultural legitimacy. Ideolect poets often eschew the center with which they may be associated by education or social position, to the point of refusing the collective identities with which they might otherwise be affiliated. The point of a social reading of these forms is neither to elide nor reify such differences, but to bring them into conVERSation. The meaning of poetic forms can never be separated from the social contexts in which they are used, since meaning is never uniform, always informed by time and place. My emphasis is on how poetic forms can be used to question, rather than reinforce, the representations—and one might say the enactments—of these social contexts. For the social meaning of these forms is not given but made.

The work of Bunting and MacDiarmid is useful to consider in this respect for they are both poets whose work, dialect and not, insisted on a "northern" identity—Northumbrian and Scottish—while rejecting closed forms of Scots or Northumbrian nationalism. MacDiarmid's sympathy for but ultimate rejection by both Communist and Nationalist political parties is exemplary of the tension between localism and socialism or anarchism. Writing next to the Island center of traditional English verse, their poetry skirts the distinction between dialect and ideolect in a continuing dialog between language and place that dances around and within such ideological fractures and fractals, exposing the materiality of sound patterns to the territorialization of desire. MacDiarmid and Bunting had to invent aspects of the Scots and Northumbrian in A Drunk Man Looks at Thistle and Briggflatts (albeit the inventions were quite different in each case). Briggflatts is more a work of constructed syntax than an idiomatic reconstruction of an oral tradition; aurality is its most salient feature.[7] If we understand the direction

7. Peter Quartermain, in a letter (March 18, 1995), comments: "The new English that each uses is inescapably itself, a shade alien to the ear and at the same time a shade more 'authentically' English, because it departs from the koine, standard English, even though it is comprehensible in an ordinary English context and to an ordinary English ear (whatever ordinary means there—one used to [hear] 'standard' I suppose, but that concept has been decaying for the last forty or so years I think). You'll have noted that I'm saying nothing about what sort of syntax that is, but I do think it cultivates turbulence and roughness to the ear and tongue because the

of "English" away from its Island English center as a structural question, then we can begin to see links among poetic projects involving secession, dispersal, and regrouping. We may understand disparate practices as sharing a poetic space that is grounded not in an identical social position but in the English language itself as the material with which we make our regroupings and refoundings. Never just English but always a new English that is an object and a subject of our Verse. As Louise Bennett so eloquently and hilariously points out in her 1944 poem "Bans O' Killing", this issue is as much one of the past as of the present and future:

> So yuh a de man, me hear bout!
> Ah yuh dem sey dah-teck
> Whole heap o' English oat sey dat
> Yuh gwine kill dialect!
>
> Meck me get it straight Mass Charlie
> For me noh quite undastan,
> Yuh gwine kill all English dialect
> Or jus Jamaica one?
>
> Ef yuh dah-equal up wid English
> Language, den wha meck
> Yuh gwine go feel inferior, wen
> It come to dialect?
>
> Ef yuh kean sing "Linstead Market"
> An "Wata come a me y'eye",
> Yuh wi haffi tap sing "Auld lang syne"
> An "Comin thru de rye".
>
> Dah language weh yuh proad o',
> Weh yuh honour and respeck,
> Po' Mass Charlie! Yuh noh know sey
> Dat it spring from dialect!
> Dat dem start fe try tun language,
> From de fourteen century,
> Five hundred years gawn an dem got
> More dialect dan we!

---

smooth and the graceful and the beautiful . . . are not only 'southron' but also 'literary', gesturing lazily as they do to a pitifully limited concept of what constitutes the sublime. Like Mina Loy, they cultivate 'gracelessness' (but then one has to define 'grace,' no?) and might indeed be said to share with her the project which says 'I do not write poetry'—if what the centre produces is poetry, then they want none of it, reaching to another definition of sense and discourse, derived from dialect/ideolect speech, and from prose."

Yuh wi haffe kill de Lancashire
De Yorkshire, de Cockney
De broad Scotch an de Irish brogue
Before yuh start to kill me!

Yuh wi haffe get de Oxford book
O' English verse, an tear
Out Chaucer, Burns, Lady Grizelle
An plenty o' Shakespeare!

Wen yuh done kill "wit" an "humour"
Wen yuh kill "Variety"
Yuh wi haffe fine a way fe kill
Originality!

An mine how yuh dah-read dem English
Book deh pon yuh shelf
For ef yuh drop a "h" yuh mighta
Haffe kill yuhself.[8]

Bennett's wit makes all the more disturbing her point that suppression of "variety" in language produces the cultural suppression of a people: "Bans O' Killing". A people invents and sustains itself through its shared language so it is not surprising that colonial governments have often prohibited the use of native languages, dialects, patois, creoles, and pidgins in an effort to maintain social control. Bennett, all of whose poetry is written in Jamaican idiom, points to, and defuses, the stigma attached to dialect use; but she also makes patent the deep social scar left by the denigration of a particular language practice as inferior. In this sense, dialect becomes the verbal equivalent of skin color: an "objective" mark of alterity.

The explicitly political use of dialect in contemporary poetry is apparent in the work of Jamaican "dub" poet Michael Smith, even as he toys with old English rhymes: "Say / Natty-Natty, / no bodder / das weh / yuh culture!"[9] Or consider not only Linton Kwesi Johnson's deforming spelling *Inglan* but also these raucous lyrics from "Fite Dem Back" in *Inglan Is a Bitch*:

8. Louise Bennett, *Jamaica Labrish* (Kingston, Jamaica: Sangster's Book Stores, 1966), pp. 209–10. Bennett, a popular performer in Jamaica, was born in 1919. Bennett's poems might usefully be compared with the Hawaiian pidgin of Lois-Ann Yamanaka's *Saturday Night at the Pahala Theater* (Honolulu: Bamboo Ridge Press, 1993).

9. Michael Smith, *It a Come* (San Francisco: City Lights, 1989), p. 50. Smith, who was born in Kingston in 1954, was killed in 1983.

> we gonna smash their brains in
> cause they ain't got nofink in 'em . . .
> fashist an di attack
> noh baddah worry 'bout dat[10]

where Johnson switches from a quoted dialect that he mocks—the first two lines are in the voice of the neofascist "paki bashah"—back to his own dialect voice. Note that brains, in the quoted dialect, is spelled in the standard fashion but that *nothing* manages to suggest *fink* and, more tellingly, in Johnson's comment, *fascist* manages to suggest *shit*. Similarly, in "Sonny's Lettah", Johnson can use a traditional, heavily rhyming "letter from jail" form more effectively than any contemporary poet I can think of. "For these inheritors of the revolution," says Brathwaite, "nation-language is no longer anything to argue about or experiment with; it is their classical norm and comes out of the same experience as the music of contemporary popular songs: using the same riddims, the same voice-spreads, syllable clusters, blue notes, ostinato, syncopation, and pauses" (45–46). The British poet John Agard puts the case directly, in "Listen Mr Oxford Don":

> I ent have no gun
> I ent have no knife
> but mugging de Queen's English
> is the story of my life
>
> I don't need no axe
> to split/ up yu syntax
> I dont need no hammer
> to mash/ up yu grammar[11]

As Brathwaite puts it, "It was in language that the slave was perhaps most successfully imprisoned by his master, and it was in his (mis-)use of it that he perhaps most effectively rebelled."[12]

But rebelled into what? Not, I think, a more authentic representation of

10. Linton Kwesi Johnson, *Inglan Is a Bitch* (London: Race Today Publications, 1980), p. 20. The distinction between the two voices is even more marked in Johnson's performance.

11. John Agard, "Listen Mr Oxford Don", in *The New British Poetry*, ed. Gillian Allnutt, Fred D'Aguiar, Ken Edwards, and Eric Mottram (London: Palladin, 1988), p. 5. It is significant that this poem opens the anthology as well as the section of black poets, which includes Johnson, as well as several other poets working with dialect (or nation language)—Valerie Bloom, Jean Binta Breeze, Merle Collins, Grace Nichols, Levi Tafari. Mottram's and Edwards's sections in the anthology specifically chart poets working in the wake of Bunting and MacDiarmid. Thus, at least in Britain, the two streams I navigate in this essay are brought into close proximity.

12. Quoted in J. Edward Chamberlin, *Come Back to Me My Language* (Urbana: University of Illinois Press, 1993), p. 67. In the U.S. the explicitly political dimension of these issues emerges in the English First movement as well as in confrontations over the use of Black English.

speech but an even more marvelous realization of the yammering gap
between speech and writing (the stammering gaps among speeches and
writings).[13] "Writing wrongs speech", as Neil Schmitz puts it in *Of Huck
and Alice*.[14] In these senses, the nonstandard spelling of dialect writing
doesn't so much transcribe words as underscores the sensuous/sinuous
materiality of language. The pleasure is in this play between the written
word and the impossible objects of its desires.

Little has been written about Claude McKay's early dialect work, no doubt
due to the ambiguous status of certain literary dialect practices even for
such eloquent proponents of "nation language" as Brathwaite:[15]

> McKay's first two books of poetry (1912), written in Jamaica, are
> unique in that they are the first all-dialect collections of an anglo-
> phone Caribbean poet. They are however *dialect* as distinct from
> *nation* because McKay allowed himself to be imprisoned in the pen-
> tameter; he didn't let his language find its own parameters. (20)

Dialect practice can appear to be a form of self-deprecation as it approach-
es "black face"—the minstrel mocking of black vernacular by white as well
as black performers. As Brathwaite remarks:

> Dialect is thought of as "bad English". Dialect is "inferior English".
> Dialect is the language when you want to make fun of someone.
> Caricature speaks in dialect. Dialect has a long history of coming
> from the plantation where people's dignity is distorted through their
> language and the descriptions which the dialect gave to them. (13)

The anxiety of dialect is inscribed already in Paul Laurence Dunbar's work,
where poems in "plantation" dialect are placed side-by-side with poems
in standard English, both sharing the heavily accented pentameter that for
Brathwaite marks them as problematic but which nonetheless makes Dun-
bar's *Complete Poems* (1913) one of the most unsettling and provocative
works of early modernism. Brathwaite goes on to criticize McKay for his
turn to the sonnet in the poems for which he is most famous, noting the
heavy cost of McKay's desire for "universality". This echoes the debate
between advocates of standard literary verse such as Countee Cullen and
practitioners of the vernacular such as Sterling Brown, a debate that is at

13. On the poetics of limping, staggering, stuttering, and stammering, see Nathaniel
Mackey, "Sound and Sentiment, Sound and Symbol", in *The Politics of Poetic Form: Poetry and Pub-
lic Policy*, ed. Charles Bernstein (New York: Roof Books, 1990).
14. Neil Schmitz, *Of Huck and Alice: Humorous Writing in American Literature* (Minneapolis: Uni-
versity of Minnesota Press, 1983), p. 97.
15. North's *The Dialect of Modernism* includes a chapter on McKay, "Quashie to Buccra: The
Linguistic Expatriation of Claude McKay", which begins with a discussion of his dialect poetry.

the heart of Houston Baker's *Modernism and the Harlem Renaissance*. Baker identifies the controversy as between "mastery of form" and the "deformation of mastery". In contrast to my approach here, Baker champions the assimilationist poetics of Cullen and Washington, arguing for the long-term efficacy of using dominant cultural forms as one would a mask, to provide camouflage while precluding total identification. At the same time, he rebukes, unfortunately in my view, what he calls the "guerrilla" tactics of resistance and secession represented by Dunbar and others involved with "sounding" "deformation", a position he associates with Du Bois.

The use of dialectical or ideolectical language in a poem marks a refusal of standard English as the common ground of communication. For poets wishing to obliterate or overcome such marks of difference, the choice of the conventional literary language, whether understood as mask or not, reflects a willingness to abide by the linguistic norms of a culture and to negotiate within these norms. Nonstandard language practice suggests an element of cultural resistance that has as its lower limit dialogic self-questioning and its upper limit secession and autonomy.

Cullen took up the forms valued as "universal" by a dominant culture in which the use of African-American, as opposed to midwestern or northeastern, dialect was taken to be a mark of inferiority; his work wears its humanity on its sleeve, the only place where it could be seen in a society defined in large measure by the color line. In such a reading, Cullen can be understood as an American pragmatist par excellence.

Brathwaite, an advocate of "nation language", that is of linguistic autonomy and self-sufficiency, makes an argument against the compromised form of dialect practiced by McKay, seeing it, at best, as the beginning of a cultural practice that comes to fruition, in the Caribbean, with Bennett, Smith, Johnson, and his own work. In the U.S. during the modernist period, Sterling Brown is probably the foremost practitioner of such a poetics. For Brathwaite, "nation language" is not a deformation of mastery but the sign of a newly forming collective identity. It moves beyond critique and subversion to positive expressivity; that is, beyond a bogus universality to what Brathwaite, problematically in my view, understands as a genuine locality.

The tension between universality and locality is not simply a deformation or an embryonic phase of group consciousness to be shed at maturity. As against the positive expressivity of nation language I would speak of the negative dialectics of ideolect, where ideolect would mark those poetic sites of contest between the hegemonic and the subaltern, to use the terms of Antonio Gramsci. Here indeed would be a poetics of compromise and dependency—of hybridization and contradiction and multivocality. Under this sign of radical modernism, I would include not only Dunbar and McKay, but also Hughes, Jean Toomer, and Tolson; and I would add, among others, in the U.S., Zukofsky, Hart Crane, and Abraham Lincoln Gillespie, and in the U.K., Bunting and MacDiarmid.

One thing many of these poets have in common is the influence of Marxism on their poetic practice.[16] Marxism is a universalist philosophy with a checkered history of (often contradictory) critiques of nationalism as well as ethnic and racial and sexual essentialisms. Perhaps the most useful approach to this issue is found in the work of Gramsci, a Sardinian Marxist whose critique of hegemony is grounded in his own experience as a "subaltern" Southerner whose language was marked as inferior by its dialectical difference from the Italian of the North.

In considering the internal contradictions between the local and the universal, the subaltern and the hegemonic, I turn to McKay, who, in poems of breathtaking duplicity and paradox, uses proto-Marxist ideas of universalism to contest the hegemony of British culture in Jamaica. In 1912, when he was 22 and still living in Jamaica, McKay published two collections of dialect poetry, *Songs of Jamaica* and *Constab Ballads*. No one reading or commenting on these poems can fail to note the many compromising aspects of this collection. Most obvious are running translations and glosses at the foot of each page, providing unnecessary and misleading translations of dialect words and often giving blatantly, not to say comically, ameliorist interpretations of the poems. Like Dunbar's *Collected Poems*, McKay's dialect poetry is a schizophrenic presentation, foregrounding two unequally powerful readerships, black and white. Given McKay's association with, as Brathwaite puts it, "a Svengali like Walter Jekyll" (20), the controlling hand of white editorial authority is always present on the page.[17] Another equally marked gesture of "complicity" is the title *Constab Ballads* itself, for what kind of poetic autonomy can we expect from poems written from the point of view of a Jamaican native working for the British as a policeman?

16. Peter Quartermain, in a letter (March 18, 1995), notes that Bunting had read *Capital*. Despite his often stated antipathy to Marx "as economist and call it historian—it's the Hegelian side of Marx, the notion of that historical dialectic which will inevitably (or not) bring about historical change, the withering away of the state . . . Bunting had great sympathy for Marx as social critic, as let's say 'humanist,' and was especially taken with [his] diagnoses of the conditions of the working (and unemployed) poor."

17. According to McKay in his autobiography, *A Long Way from Home* (New York: Harcourt, Brace & World, 1970), Jekyll "became my intellectual and literary mentor and encouraged me to continue writing verses in Negro dialect." Jekyll, McKay continued, "had gone among the peasants and collected their field-and-yard songs (words and music) and African folk tales and published them in a book called *Jamaica Song and Story* [1907]." Jekyll "became interested when he first saw my verses—enthusiastic really—and said they sounded like the articulate consciousness of the peasants" (p. 13).

How is it possible for an act of linguistic defiance bordering on revolt to appear in a cultural space that would suppress any explicit expression of political opposition? In *The Practice of Everyday Life* (*Arts de faire*, literally the art of doing), in a section titled "a diversionary practice", de Certeau speaks of an "enunciative" tactic he calls "la perruque" or the wig:

> *La perruque* is the worker's own work disguised as the work of his employer. It differs from pilfering in that nothing of material value is stolen. It differs from absenteeism in that the worker is officially on the job . . . the worker who indulges in *la perruque* actually diverts time (not goods, since he uses only scraps) . . . for work that is free, creative, and precisely not directed toward profit . . . to deal with everyday tactics in this way would be to practice an "ordinary art", to find oneself in the common situation, and to make a kind of *perruque* of writing itself.[18]

In McKay's 1912 collections, pentameter dialect is the ruse or wig that allows a running double play of ingratiation and defiance. For the "white" audience, the dialect plays as minstrel show: charming, even ingratiating in its gratuitous nods to British sentiment and in its self-glossing self-deprecations. At the same time, the poems compose a song to the aesthetic power of difference, of the sonic and semantic richness of vernacular Jamaican, while in their themes they corrode the very authoritativeness to which they appear to be kowtowing, accumulating a counter-hegemonic force that mocks every surface pretence of accommodation. This double play brings to mind Melville's "Benito Cereno", which, as Aldon Nielsen points out, "is a dramatization of the white racist mind *not reacting* in the face of a slave insurrection; for the dramatic irony of the novel derives from Delano's inability to recognize that which is palpably before him. He is so much inhabited by the discourse agreements of white mythology" that he (mis)interprets "the actuality of the slave revolt" as stereotypical gestures of "servile loyalty".[19]

Certainly the most ingratiatingly Anglophilic, doggedly iambic, and apparently self-deprecating, poem in *Songs of Jamaica* is "Old England":

> Just to view de homeland England, in de streets of London walk . . .
> I would see Saint Paul's Cathedral, an' would hear some of de great
> Learnin' comin' from de bishops, preachin' relics of old fait';
> I would ope me mout' wid wonder at de massive organ soun',

18. Michel de Certeau, *The Practice of Everyday Life*, tr. Stephen Rendall (Berkeley: University of California Press, 1984), pp. 25, 28.

19. Aldon Lynn Nielsen, *Reading Race: White American Poets and the Racial Discourse in the Twentieth Century* (Athens: University of Georgia Press, 1988), pp. 16–18.

An' would 'train me eyes to see de beauty lyin' all aroun'

. . . .

I'd go to de City Temple, where de old fait' is a wreck
An' de parson is a-preachin' views dat most folks will not tek;
I'd go where de men of science meet togeder in deir hall,
To give light unto de real truths, to obey king Reason's call.[20]

On the surface, this is a poem of nostalgia and complacency, even ending
on the subservient note of the native returning home from the Mother
country, resting "glad an' contented in me min' for evermore" (65). No
wonder Brathwaite points to this poem as an example of McKay's "liter-
ary colonialism in the primordial (?) anglicanism" (20). But the poem over-
plays the sentiment in a way that, at least at the distance from which I am
reading it, calls attention to itself, or calls for a different kind of attention,
a reading between the lines. What, after all, is this great learning coming
from "relics" of an "old fait'" but the old *fate* of racism and colonialism; what
is this "beauty lyin' all aroun'" but more relics of lying beauty, overturned
by the "real truths" or Reason. For this poem, after all, is unambiguous in
enforcing the truths (plural) or Reason (cap R): the cant of the preachers
is a lying beauty, a wreck of learning that appears beautiful or truthful only
with eyes "trained" (by whom?). Read as wig, the poem begins to destabi-
lize, though a line like "I would ope me mout' wid wonder at de massive
organ soun'" remains difficult, as far as I can see, to turn round. Yet even
the textual glosses can seem to take on significance; here, only two words,
among a number equally nonstandard, are singled out for definition:
"t'o't"—thought, and "min"—mind. It's as if we are to be reminded that the
"native" has thoughts and a mind of his own: in this sense *mine* is synony-
mous with *mind*. Perhaps this poem is not so far from Louise Bennett's work
after all, considering that McKay's work was Bennett's first example of
Jamaican dialect poetry (Brathwaite, p. 28). Even the "old" in "Old Eng-
land" begins to seem more ominous.

Am I overreading? McKay is careful to note in *A Long Way Home*, that he
became a "free-thinker" before he was 13, discovering "like a comet . . . the
romance of science in Huxley's *Man's Place in Nature* and Haeckel's *The Riddle
of the Universe*" (12). By the time he was writing *Songs of Jamaica* and *Constab
Ballads*, McKay was steeped in Spinoza (for a while he considered himself a
pantheist), Schopenhauer, and Spencer (and by extension Darwin).

Consider McKay's "Cudjoe Fresh from de Lecture" about "How de buc-
cra te-day tek time an' bégin teach / All of us dat was deh in a clear open

20. Claude McKay, *Songs of Jamaica*, reprinted in *The Dialect Poems of Claude McKay* (Plainville,
NY: Books for Libraries Press, 1972), pp. 63–64.

speech" (55–58). The buccra's, or whiteman's, "open speech" is about evo-
lution, a humanist scientific theory that, in Cudjoe's interpretation, under-
mines the racist ideas that are lived out in the plantation system reflected
in the "imprisoned pentameter", or closed (constrained) speech, of the
poem: "Him tell us 'bout we self, an' mek we fresh again". This idea of being
made "fresh" (not used, exploited) is what Cudjoe tells as the urgent "news"
from this lecture:

> Me look 'pon me black 'kin, an' so me head grow big, . . .
> For ebery single man, no car' about dem rank,
> Him bring us ebery one an' put 'pon same plank.

Looking upon his black skin he also sees his black *kin* in this collective vi-
sion of the equality of "ebery man". On one reading "me head grow big"
has the same stereotyping gesture of self-patronization as "ope me mout
wid wonder", but taken literally it means the opposite—the news reverses
the patronizing of Cudjoe and his kin, returns heads to actual size. If evo-
lution "tell us 'traight 'bout how de whole t'ing came", then Christianity,
which preaches that blackness is a "cuss", tells it crooked:

> An' looking close at t'ings, we hab to pray quite hard
> Fe swaller wha' him say an' don't t'ink bad o' Gahd

Ingratiation or defiance hidden in a smirk as broad as the face of "Gahd"?
If evolution preaches chance not predetermination, then the scenario of
"Benito Cereno" is closer to hand, for no natural law precludes the justice
of insurrection (the hound, let's say, being on the other tooth):

> But suppose eberyt'ing could tu'n right upside down,
> Den p'rhaps we'd be on top an' givin' some one houn'.

The very next stanza quells such an interpretation, noting that were the
Africans not brought to the Americas they might still be "half-naked . . .
tearin' t'rough de bush wid all de monkey"—"'Wile an' uncibilise', an' neber
comin' tame." Yet the poem is not about the taming effect of this "clear
open speech" but how this way of thinking inspires strong feelings that
lead to Cudjoe's *own* uncorked "talk". Acknowledging that his talk is going
in two directions, Cudjoe then ends by saying maybe not:

> Yet both horse partly runnin' in de selfsame gallop
> For it is nearly so de way de buccra pull up:
> Him say, how de wul' stan', dat right will neber be,
> But wrong will eber gwon till dis wul' en' fe we. (58)

The buccra stops the gallop of Cudjoe's racing thoughts by saying right
will never be. But the last line of the poem is ambiguous: for if wrong will

grow till this world ends *for us*, doesn't that mean that we will have to end it ourselves, so that we may establish the truth of a new world? I hear this, anyway, with all the doubling I have so far noted, in the title of a poem that might be read as a hymn to accommodation, "Whe' Fe Do?" The gloss provided for this title encapsulates the issues sharply; it runs like this: "What to do?—equivalent to 'What can't be cured, must be endured.'" Each stanza of the poem ends with a variation on the title's question: "All we can do" "Dat we might do" "For dat caan' do" "Whe' else fe do?" "De best to do" and finally "But whe' fe do?" But can't (caan') the title also mean What Is to Be Done? all that can be done, what's best to do, what must be done?

What to make of this? In McKay's Jamaica poems, iambic pentameter is made the metrical mark of colonialism, the chains around a corrosive dialect. Pentameter is used to serve as the acoustic trappings of "old England", yoked to a diffident creole, the weird ordinary of verse dialect. It is an oxymoronic form. In this sense, the dialect poems have a similar implosive power to McKay's "If We Must Die", written five years after his move to the U.S. in 1914, which creates a tension between the conventional expectations of the Elizabethan sonnet form and its violent and unsettling subject matter.

Claude McKay's Jamaica poems are not free verse. They are marked by their uneasy relation to the cultural regime under which they were written. But what is the natural form for a vernacular poetry?[21] MacDiarmid and Bunting offer a radically modernist setting for their dialect work that is a far cry from the more direct, sometimes ethnographic, representations of Sterling Brown. Hughes's style is fluid but often sets itself apart from the quoted vernacular that peoples his work (as in "The Weary Blues"); unlike in Brown, identification with the demotic voices is not total. In his *Harlem Gallery: Book I, The Curator*, Melvin Tolson chooses a radically defamiliarizing form to set his multilectical excursions:

> High as the ace of trumps,
> as egghead says, "'The artist is a strange bird,' Lenin says."
> Dipping in every direction like a quaquaversal,
> the M.C. guffaws: "Hideho, that swig would make
> a squirrel spit in the eye of a bulldog!"
> Bedlam beggars

21. Lorenzo Thomas points to the significance of James Weldon Johnson's *God's Trombones: Seven Negro Sermons in Verse* (1927) as "an attempt to distinguish an authentic African-American vernacular from dialect stereotypes using Modernist poetic form" in a review of *The Hammers of Creation: Folk Culture in African-American Fiction* by Eric J. Sundquist in *American Book Review*, March–May 1995, p. 4. I am grateful to Thomas's discussion of Johnson and Melvin Tolson in a Poetics Program lecture on Tolson at SUNY-Buffalo on November 14, 1991.

> at a poet's feast in a people's dusk of dawn counterpoint
>   protest and pride
>   in honkey tonk rhythms
>   hot as an ache in a cold hand warmed . . .
>   A Creole co-ed from Basin street by way of
>   Morningside Heights . . .
>   brushes my shattered cocktail glass into a tray . . .
>   O spiritual, work-song, ragtime, blues jazz—
>   consorts of
>   the march, quadrille, polka, and waltz![22]

This is neither universal poetry nor nation language, it is "quaquaversal poetry", a close relative to ideolect. Tolson's hybridization of discourse, featuring the music of shattering glass (pentameter anyone?) on the tray of a Creole coed from New Orleans by way of the Upper West Side, mixes cultural references with the sophisticated élan of a poet who makes language his home: the poet's feast this counterpoint of contrasting rhythms, protest, and pride. It's not that the indigenous cultural forms of African Americans—spiritual, work-song, ragtime, and blues, so remarkably and directly charted in Brown's poetry—are the same as the European dance forms but that a process of Creolization is underway: they consort with each in the dance of America.

The closest thing I can think of to Tolson's dazzling mix of citations and refutations, discourse as concourse, is Zukofsky's collage poems, from "Poem Beginning 'The'" to "A". I think the Creole coed may even be a kissing cousin to Zukofsky's "A Foin Lass" in his translation into Brooklynese of "Donna mi Prega", "A Foin Lass Bodders". Zukofsky's use of slang is not, to be sure, an instance of cultural identification, and Zukofsky's sense of his Jewishness reflected the ambivalence of many leftists of his generation. He had, after all, chosen not to write in his native tongue, or at least the language of his parents, Yiddish, specifically choosing not to join with some of his differently radical contemporaries who wrote Yiddish poetry as an assertion of what could well be called Jewish nation language. But Zukofsky's ear was tuned to the local and the vernacular and even as he transforms the demotic into his own brand of ideolect the origin in the ordinary is patent.

When de Certeau writes of the practice of the wig as "an ordinary art" he provides a reminder that dialect and ideolect practices are practices of the ordinary, and in this way linked to other demotic literary practices; but

---

22. Melvin Tolson, "XI", in *Harlem Gallery: Book I, The Curator* (New York: Twayne Publishers, 1965), pp. 82–83.

also that the ordinary grounds itself in provisional constructions not natural facts. The ordinary eludes fixed forms of representation; it can be evoked, not captured. For the ordinary captured becomes merely captions on a vanished object, an evacuated site for the residual rubbernecking of exhausted passers-by. The poetic practice of the ordinary is synthetic and synthesizing, not essentializing. Verse dialect, like any representation of speech in writing, is always a form of invention.

One of the extraordinary things about the poetics of the ordinary is that it can make poems that look so strange. Any approach to the ordinary is partial because the ordinary, like materiality itself, is inexhaustible. The poetics of the ordinary can set its sights on a series of aspects—on meter, on diction, on theme, on lexicon. Poetic attention to any one of these aspects may make a poem that will seem alien to those accustomed to different literary conventions. Transcribed speech, for example, may seem more unnatural than the idealized conventions for representing speech. Dialect, because it uses a nonstandard lexicon, can look as odd as the *zaum* or neologistic poems of Velimer Khlebnikov or David Melnick or Gillespie or P. Inman, even to the native speaker of the represented idiom. The ordinary erodes and resists the standard, just as standard English and normative verse forms exoticize and defamiliarize the ordinary. There can be no completely ordinary poetry because there can be no poetry without style or form. "We fling ourselves, constantly longing, on this form."[23]

Very little has been written about the ideolectical writing of Abraham Lincoln Gillespie. Gillespie's pervasively neologistic work bears some resemblance to *Finnigans Wake*; certainly, Gillespie knew Joyce. Unlike Joyce, Gillespie was not interested in maximizing the etymological resonances of words but rather in creating a kind of scat writing, with jazz as a significant influence. American identity, along with "self" expression, is certainly under erasure, more likely actively being erased, in "Expatracination" (out from fatherland and race/roots), Gillespie's response to a 1928 *transition* questionnaire on Americans living in Europe:

> the Spiritual Future of America is not to evolve till a present diabetes
> is admit > removed, t'wit: America's total lack of parent-sagacity to
> exprimply an especially-while-correcting them goodwill toward,
> and to cull an early admiration from the children . . . THEN—the
> American Spirit will commence-sing as naive-direct-elimgoalpur-
> sue-clearly as its present FolkMelod—"PopularSong," frequently as
> blare-OutréFruct-freely as its dynaSaxophoneyc . . . (i.e. Fair,

23. Wallace Stevens, "An Ordinary Evening in New Haven", in *Collected Poems* (New York: Alfred A. Knopf, 1978), p. 470.

groove-compulsed into an inevitaBanter-Fair—we *are* a Good Will-Collective—will assume social sensitude, a BodyClap-RazzCourtly deft-joice-skew-Apply-akin (somehow) to the finesse of France's Golden period . . . Semitised Russia will certainly psychYap doubly, its individuentsremainingscorn-evadedDefeatists, speaking their present flapdoodleNonDigninholdLiable'd rushout-heedless-O-Self!-stuff.[24]

If dialect poetry seems to foster group identification, ideolect poetry may seem to foster the opposite: a rejection or troubling of identity structures, group or individual. Yet the rejection of received ideas of identity can also be understood as the continuation of the politics of identity by other means. The poetics of identity cannot be symmetrical for the subaltern and for that which it is subaltern to. For every poetics of cultural legitimation might not there also need to be a poetics of delegitimation?, as in, Please move over; or else we fall in the "groove-compulsed . . . Banter" of America as (we are not) "Good Will-Collective". This passage from Gillespie reminds me of nothing so much as one of Bruce Andrews's "dynaSaxophoneyc" riffs of invented slang in *I Don't Have Any Paper So Shut Up (or, Social Romanticism)*, which, like Gillespie's work, approaches the vernacular question from the other end of the stick, i.e., none too pretty out there. The evisceration of a preassigned cultural identity, as in Andrews (son, like Gillespie, of affluent white America), is also a form of identity politics.

Khlebnikov's *zaum*, or transense poetry, was made to transcend the divisions of national languages; he wanted to write an ideolect that all could understand. *Zaum*'s desire for universality is marked by its high coefficient of weirdness, which is to say its abiding and enchanting peculiarity. At another subdivision of this spectrum, David Melnick's homophonic, and therefore ideolectical, translation of Homer, *Men in Aida*, may first be read for the sheer pleasure of its sonic plenitude; but after a while the playful signification of both a gay and poetic "sub"culture, an erotic and writerly community, is unmistakable:

Ache I on a rope alone, guy guard on a wreck, day oh say sting.
Hose cape pee, oh tit, toes on echo sat. O Phoibos Apollo . . .
Egg are oh yummy. Andrews call o' semen hose Meg a pant on.
Argue on, critic. All high pay, then tie Achaioi.[25]

---

24. Abraham Lincoln Gillespie, "Expatracination", in *The Syntactic Revolution*, ed. Richard Milazzo (New York: Out of London Press, 1980), pp. 17–18. Gillespie was born in Philadelphia in 1895; he died in 1950.

25. David Melnick, *Men in Aida: Book 1* (Berkeley: Tuumba, 1983).

No more a poet of the Americas than Bunting or MacDiarmid, Javant Biarujia, an Australian poet, has embarked on the most systematically and literally idiolectical poetry of which I am aware. Over the past 25 years, since he was a teenager, Biarujia has been working with an invented language that he calls Taneraic; he also edits an (in effect) poetry magazine, *taboo jadoo*, dedicated to "the discussion and expression of private language *(langue close)*", which is in the process of publishing an extensive Taneraic-English dictionary:

> MEPA. 1. present (n.). 2. being in the process of. 3. in *(often with gerund).* A *mepa* xirardi celini armin. A is wearing a beautiful shirt. Vadas ibescya *mepa* avi bouain. I failed *in* my attempt. Anqaudi rasra ilir *mepa* virda. There's no point *[in]* waiting.
> **mepaceti.** nowadays
> **mepadesqesati.** this morning
> **mepadesqovati.** this evening; tonight
> **mepadesusati.** this afternoon
> **mepaiveti.** today
> **mepajabeti.** up-to-date; modern
> **mepanintati.** for the night; tonight
> **mepa yu.** whereas
> **mepeili.** in every place: everywhere
> MEPIR. imagination. **mepirdi.** imagine. **mepiri.** imaginary.
> **meplrocyu.** imagination; fantasy; hallucination. **mepirsya.** fancy . . .
> **mepir rin.** delusion. **das mepir rindi.** delude
> **mepir tane.** vision.
> **mepir troutou.** fancy.
> **mepir uza.** vision, foresight. **das mepir uzadi.** envision; visualize, envisage
> MEQ. sexual prowess *or* potency.[26]

This is from a dream recorded in Biarujia's diary:

> Mepadesqesati, vamahusatta ye trahemoqá e *Abdeleslam* . . . Ayoi vasyenda, tusqeriaru yole bayada e tusqer yoca, busai go ayoi vajesda vaireubda yole ayoi qussada. Vasezoqda gon . . . Oubqendiyo. Amahusatta, busai sezoqiaru duvondi aiban desqes.[27]

As dialect becomes vernacular, as the demotic is traded for ideolect, we may hear a complication or evasion or erasure of identity more than a celebration of it: an exploration of the space between identities more than

---

26. Javant Biarujia, *Nainougacyou Tanerai Sasescya Sepou E-Na: Taneraic-English Dictionary E-Na,* in *taboo jadoo,* no. 6 (summer 1992–93): 94.

27. Biarujia provides the text and translation in an offprint identified as from *Vehicle,* no. 3 (1992): "This morning I awoke from a nightmare about Abdeleslam . . . I ran to him, moving in slow motion, and when I reached him I cried out that I loved him. I cried . . . I kissed him. I woke up, and spent breakfast in tears."

In a letter (May 23, 1995) responding to a draft of this essay, and correcting a few typos I had made in his Taneraic, Biarujia says he has translated the word ideolectical into a Taneraic paraphrase: " *aspelasi remou abaq sancyab e sava mamale* (lit., nonfigurative thought-basis-way and personal-speech)".

the establishment of a primary identity. Then again, perhaps what we hear is a writing that moves beyond the present definitions and inscriptions of collective and individual identifications and toward a virtual or coming identity about which these confusions and comminglings, call them confabulations, hint; as if such writing leaves room for readers' multifoliate projections.

I am conscious that an ideolectical poetry, insofar as it may dismantle whatever self or group identities we may have already developed, risks making us more atomized and so more passive. In this state of "postmodern" paranoia, all collective formations—real or imagined—are ironized or aestheticized, that is, debunked as arbitrary codes, with fashion and market ascendant as the arbiters of value. If social identities are to be made problematic as part of the poetic process, this may be in order to forge new collective identities that will enable a more resourceful resistance to rigidly territorializing clannishness and paralyzingly depoliticizing codicity.

The problem is how to be resistant to the reductiveness of all forms of positivism without succumbing to the relativistic erosions of market value that transform poetry from an arena for social exploration or expression to an empty marker of "subjectivity" in designated Free Trade Zones (to which both poet and reader are subject). That is, to presume a realm of social truths against the one truth of technorationality and its schizoid doubles, triumphalist capitalism and religious fundamentalism.

Blake remains the greatest emblem of this "Mental Fight" in the English poetry traditions and Blake's active, oppositional Imagination—"Image Nations"—is a vital source for a poetics of the Americas.

The point is not to display imagination but to mobilize imaginations.

But how can we mobilize imaginations, those imaginary nations, when, for the most part, "imagination" and "subjectivity" have become house pets of the personal lifestyle industry, cousins to a "creativity" that seems to apply more to earrings than to hearing? This is no doubt Adorno's fear in questioning the historical role of lyric poetry in the wake of a systematic extermination process that seems to show up all our means of representation as thin, palely inadequate to the realities at hand.

For most conventional verse practices, like many other forms of cultural production, are more the products of an ideological system than of any putative author. As a result, they can be read as cultural "symptoms" rather than as the inspired and original works of an autonomous author. However, the current movement of "cultural studies" risks levelling all art to the status of symptom. For poetry can, even if it often doesn't, resist absorption into the *zeitgeist*. No artist can remain entirely free from "collaboration" with the society in which she or he works, history is too consuming for that, but relative degrees of resistance are possible. Art can provide a means by which to read culture, cognitive maps if you will. New forms provide new methods of critique.

Surely, the subjectivized, gutted lyric that pervades poetry today proves Adorno's point. Nonetheless, from this same historical point of view, I would say that poetry is the most necessary form of language practice after the wars: but a different poetry than we have known. The task of creating this poetry is impossible and for that reason takes place.

Unzip Bleed

It must be a thoroughfare built on a stadium of moss. Arnold felt betrayed by the news and so continued to allay any other fears he or those around him might harbor, else they find themselves sinking more deeply into a morass of their own desperation, complimented by a heady dose of moral topsoil which they imagined, against all odds, might hold their souls in place. Benny just wanted another banana before he returned to the Ferris Wheel, but Milton, as he had on so many previous occasions, insisted that a roast beef sandwich with horseradish dressing was in order. "I see no advantage in your timorous challenge," Bertha protested. "Why not strip away the veneer of pseudoemotionality and admit that all you ever wanted out of life was to float through, virtually unconscious of anything but the sheer velocity of time passing or the modulating colors of the clouds, drifting in cerulean ether, aimlessly poised for nothing." And if the rock gives no solace, will the stark stare of the weasel quell the piercing inside? Foxglove and indigo, juniper and ash—each day a layer on the misty promontory (promise) of forgotten intent. Is that sparrow dust or dacron rivulets, Moroccan tubas or tubby talons? The jewel-encrusted frame was all but indescribable and we peered through it like so many cows hooked to a milking machine. For liberty can have no standing army but must fight its battles in the space between the invisible and the viable; and this is a battle that never can be won—not once for all but once and again, accruing no gain, tossing in the engendering locomotion. The day the dog bit the rooster the train from Yellowknife arrived 45 minutes late. As if fire had not desire. They erected, to no greater surprise than their own, an immense tub for washing away all the world's sorrows. I rubbed my eyes again, not able to comprehend the enormity of the gulf that separated me from all I beheld. Roaring as if in pain, Shelley undertook her own defence by disparaging the credentials of her putative accusers, insisting their abusively derisory remarks be held to her credit. O how wondrous clouds do hide the transparent majesty of the sky. Winds blowing words but never deeds. As an illumination (illusion) undergirds their resistance to description, so the incommensurability of descriptions underwrites the multifold

138

texture of truth. Let me prevaricate on this point for just a minute more. You hold in your hands the evidence of my duplicity. "I'm hungry", said the lion. "I haven't had a thing to eat all day." The meaning of *this* sentence is not open to dispute. What thoughts I have of you tonight, Walter Benjamin, as I sing without hearing my voice, as I dance in the Cenozoic moonlight! Showboat to Abracadabra and Shazam by way of Palookaville. "I can't eat that, at least not until I become a bird." Holding that it is our actions not ourselves that have, or may accrue, value. Splash of lemon, side of slaw. Millicent could no longer contain her pride—until she started wearing Rely ultrabsorbent pads. Thrill a minute and not a minute too soon. To test an hypothesis, we all run up 4 or 5 flights of stairs (I have to run down 1 or 2 before I can go up 4 or 5). Later, I get a call about a murder. Then I see Byron fall in the stairwell—I think he will tumble all the way down but he lands only 1 flight below and is okay. Eliot immediately gets into the car and drives to Fort Browning, reporting fully on our indecorous deportment. "You're cold, you're hot, you're hungry, you're full—you're very inconstant." Bloomers one day, blue jays the next. I take RACE to be the central fact to persons born in America. Not that I know much about identity. Frankly, the issue confuses me. In any case, here are the facts. A stump is what's left after you cut off the rest of the tree. In this sense, humans are the stumps of nature, or is it chumps, or chipmunks, or monkeys, or aren't you the kind that spills the coffee and then pretends it was your sister, brother, neighbor, a ghost of a chance, she made me do it. Who ever said things would get *less* complicated? I'd say subconscious was too good a word for you. Bruno bowled a perfect game that day but things were not going so well on the job. "Just get it off your chest", Nash insisted, "even if the guys won't understand a word of it. At least you'll see it won't make you feel any better." The letter finally arrived but it was empty. "Do you mean Liberty the town or liberty the concept?" As if the ghosts we had to fear were the dead ones. It was not a light such as Giles had ever seen before. Never borrow a blender if you can steal it. Shifting into overdrive for the long haul over the deserted central plains, Mindy started her second pack of Doublemint gum. Then you'll never have to return the blender. Garden hoses as metaphor for social dysfunction. Just like our little doggies sent away for messing up the living room, we'll all be going to "a little farm in New Jersey" one day. A spool of thread, a jug of signs, and you beside me in the wilderness. *Our representatives are still busy—please hold.*

Lachrymose Encaustic / Abrasive Tear

Press this[1] quickly
and if it truly jerks[2]
who knows[3] who'll find it suiter than a bend[4]
for when the promise mocks[5] the call
or calls her course delay,[6] inlaid that long
go out to fault the[7] woes
that tarnish stain and toggle stare

1. The loom foretells the stall
   That jackass makes in sloth
   Rues the mauling of a splay
   Who incensed layers quill recall
   Or miffed to squander plum

2. That lays the blame too soon
   Or sooner ended comes to croon

3. Or nearing not rebuffs
   Such vagrant scorn
   As tallies to the husk
   & bloke of bilious crown

4. In loonier times than these
   Mere mitigation lies
   Or dangles pomp where
   Want is all but guise

5. As age delays emotion
   Emotion churns its pent

6. Whence leering folds the smattered
   Calf and schmooze accords irksome bile

7. Forsake such benched occlusion
   Leaving gale to mind the store-bought
   Premise of doleful tilt & chary
   With a word recant

140

Stein's Identity

What is identity and why is there so much of it?

Any cultural production can be viewed through the lens of its socio-historical circumstance. To ignore such contexts is to deny the social truths of the work. Yet such contexts are inadequate to establish a work's identity.

Identity is a play, according to Gertrude Stein in "Identity A Poem", her 1935 reworking as a play for puppets of some of parts of *The Geographical History of America, or The Relation of Human Nature to the Human Mind*. Stein's puppet show shows identity as an acting out rather than as an inner state; externally animated, not innately fixed.

Stein did not narrativize her otherness any more than she naturalized it and that makes her a suitably uncomfortable subject for those who would read her in terms of group-identity poetics. Stein's work eludes thematic and biographist projections in its demonstration that forms, structures, syntax, and style may also signify identity's puppet show. This may begin to account for how Stein's triple distance from the ascendant culture (gender, sexual orientation, ethnicity) is related to her radical breaks from traditional notions of meaning, literary tradition, explanation, and linearity.

Stein questions identity constructions, she does not affirm identity. Her syntactic and grammatic investigations show how language forms consciousness, how our words make as well as reflect experience.

In literature, genre, with its etymological roots suggesting both genealogy and gender, is a fundamental site of identity politics. Throughout her career, Stein plays with, in the sense of reforming and reformatting, genre, genealogies, and genders. "Identity A Poem" is an essay, a play, a poem; it mixes verse and prose lines.

In *Boundary of Blur,* Nick Piombino contrasts *self* and *identity,* noting that writers like Stein may fragment and rearrange representations of self in pursuit of new identity formations: "I contrast identity and self . . . because it is possible to understand the entire being of a person as a dynamic process of becoming when one aspect of being, which I am calling identity, may be visualized as potential and virtual, and [the] other aspect, self, as actual and thus biographically determined (historical) . . . Identity represents all that is potential to the self . . . Self represents that which is finite and observable in awareness."[1]

"I am I because my little dog knows me even if the little dog is a big one, and yet the little dog knowing me does not really make me be I no not really because after all being I I am I has really nothing to do with the little dog knowing me, he is my audience, but an audience never does prove to you that you are you . . .

No one knowing me knows me."[2]

In Stein's terms, self belongs to human nature and identity to human mind; though for Stein, as well as Piombino, identity's play is confined neither to mind nor nature. Identity of/in human mind is fluid and underdetermined; forming rather than final. The human mind at play is the site of identity's continuous becoming. Grammatically, identity's play is registered by the present participle (the continuous present)—an active, verbal principle. When identity enters human nature its chimerical unfolding gets boxed up as explanation, labels, naming, nouns. Human nature, insofar as it obscures human mind, is duplicitous; but when nature and mind remain at play, duplicity melts into the multiplicitous.[3]

My doggie knows my name, my smell, but not the thought that cleaves my nature, making me part of its world, part next. Beside myself is that being that belongs neither to my past nor to my self. This is language's tale and identity's possibility. Here a rose arises & is read.

1. Nick Piombino, "Writing, Identity, and the Self", in *The Boundary of Blur* (New York: Roof Books, 1993), pp. 43–45.

2. Gertrude Stein, "Identity A Poem", in *A Stein Reader,* ed. Ulla E. Dydo (Evanston: Northwestern University Press, 1993), p. 593; Stein, *The Geographical History of America, or The Relation of Human Nature to the Human Mind* (New York: Vintage Books, 1973), pp. 112–13.

3. On Stein's "duplicity" see Juliana Spahr's reading of another 1930s work of Stein, *The Autobiography of Alice B. Toklas,* in "Re Letter and Read Her: The Reader-Centered Text in American Literature", doctoral dissertation, State University of New York, Buffalo, 1995.

Of course anyone choosing to avert their identity is immediately subject to the suspicion that they have something to hide or that they suffer from self-hatred, as if skepticism is the same as rejection.

Such a writing beyond identity is utopian. But then only someone who has felt trapped needs to imagine freedom.

Human mind represents for Stein a freedom from history for which one well might have longed in Europe in 1935. But Stein's is not an escape from determinants of self nor the self-consciousness of personality. The play is dialectical. *She do the identity in voices*, to turn a phrase of T. S. Eliot's.

"What is the use of being a little boy if you are to grow up to be a man."[4]

Eliot's escape from personality is toward a Christian universalism. Stein's could never be that, nor did she aspire to it. Stein did not identify as a Jew she didn't have to; perhaps there was enough of that being done for her ("May I see your Identity Card, please?"). She takes her place in that line of what Isaac Deutscher calls "non-Jewish Jews", going back at least to Spinoza, and, in this, her most immediate company in American poetry includes Louis Zukofsky (who incorporates Spinoza and Stein into "A") and Laura Riding (her onetime protégé). (This heterodox tradition of Jewish writings is charted in Jerome Rothenberg's *A Big Jewish Book*.) Those Jewish-American modernists, like Stein, who turned away from Yiddish or other overt markers of ethnicity did not necessarily adopt an assimilationist cultural program, since the language of assimilation is never neutral, not an arena of "human mind" but of the name/nature-inf(l)ected language of the ascendant culture. Stein never bought into this assimilation, moving entirely in the other direction. In this sense her triple marginalization provided an ontological grounding for her radical forms of nonidentification, just as her affluence and education provided a space to perform them. Stein is one of the least assimilationist of American modernist writers and in this one of the most American if, following Stanley Cavell's reading of Emerson, we take America to be a movement away from given identities and toward something new, unapproachable, unrepresentable, and unattainable.[5]

"But we we in America are not displaced by a dog oh no no not at all not at all at all displaced by a dog."[6]

---

4. "Identity A Poem", p. 593; *Geographical History*, p. 58.
5. See Stanley Cavell, *This New yet Unapproachable America* (Albuquerque: Living Batch, 1989).
6. "Identity A Poem", p. 591.

In our current poetic landscape, identity is something the poet asserts the better to celebrate. Stein celebrates her suspension of identity, this holding off naming to see what otherwise emerges. Her writing becomes a state of willing, of willed, unknowingness.

The question may well be art versus culture not art as culture.

"So then the play has be like this."[7]

7. The same, p. 589.

Provisional Institutions

Alternative Presses and Poetic Innovation

In our period, they say there is free speech.
They say there is no penalty for poets,
There is no penalty for writing poems.
They say this. This is the penalty.
                    Muriel Rukeyser, "In Our Time",
                    in *The Speed of Darkness*

Imagine that all the nationally circulated magazines and all the trade presses in the United States stopped publishing or reviewing poetry. New poetry in the United States would hardly feel the blow. But not because contemporary poetry is marginal to the culture. Quite the contrary, it is these publishing institutions that have made themselves marginal to our cultural life in poetry. As it is, the poetry publishing and reviewing practices of these major media institutions do a disservice to new poetry by their sins of commission as much as omission—that is, pretending to cover what they actually cover up; as if you could bury poetry alive. In consistently acknowledging only the blandest of contemporary verse practices, these institutions provide the perfect alibi for their evasion of poetry; for if what is published and reviewed by these institutions is the best that poetry has to offer, then, indeed, there would be little reason to attend to poetry, except for those looking for a last remnant of a genteel society verse, where, for example, the editor of *The New York Times Book Review* can swoon over watered-down Dante on her way to late-night suppers with wealthy lovers of the idea of verse, as she gushed in an article last spring.[1] Poetry, reduced to souvenirs of what was once supposed to be prestige goods, quickly gets sliced for overaccessorizing, at least if the stuff actually talks back in ways we haven't heard before. If poetry has largely dis-

---

1. Rebecca Pepper Sinkler, "Hell Night at the 92nd Street Y", *New York Times Book Review*, May 9, 1993, p. 31. "For some" ("We lucky few" is the last phrase of the article) "there was to be a post-poetry spread laid on by Edwin Cohen (a businessman and patron of literature) back at his apartment at the Dakota, a Danteesque menu announced in advance: roast suckling stuffed pig stuffed with fruit, nuts, and cheese; Tuscan salami; prosciutto and polenta, white beans with fennel."

appeared from the national media, nostalgia for poetry, and the lives of troubled poets, has a secure place.

One of the clichés of the intellectual- and artist-bashing so fashionable in our leading journals of opinion is that there are no more "public intellectuals". The truth of the matter is that writing of great breadth and depth, and of enormous significance for the public, flourishes, but that the dominant media institutions—commercial television and radio, the trade presses, and the nationally circulated magazines (including the culturally upscale periodicals)—have blacklisted this material. Intellectuals and artists committed to the public interest exist in substantial numbers. Their crime is not a lack of accessibility but a refusal to submit to marketplace agendas: the reductive simplifications of conventional forms of representation; the avoidance of formal and thematic complexity; and the fashion ethos of measuring success by sales and value by celebrity. The public sphere is constantly degraded by its conflation with mass scale since public space is accessible principally through particular and discrete locations.

Any of us teaching college will have ample proof of the frightening lack of cultural information, both historical and contemporary, of even the most searching of our new students. These individuals have been subjected to cultural asphyxiation administered not only by the barrage of network television or MTV, but also, more poignantly, by the self-appointed keepers of the cultural flame, who are unwilling to provide powerful alternative programming, preferring to promote, as a habit and a rule, a sanitized and denatured version of contemporary art, pushing the pat and trim as cutting edge while debunking at every turn the untried and complex, the edgy or the odd or unnerving—that is those works of contemporary culture that give it life. Could I possibly be saying that the crisis of American culture is that there is inadequate support and distribution of difficult and challenging new art? Does a tire tire without air, an elephant blow its horn in the dark, a baby sigh when the glass door shatters its face?

The paucity of public funding for the arts has done irreparable damage to the body politic. Arts funding is as important as funding for public education. It's time for our federal, state, and local governments to consider linking arts funding with education budgets: *a percent for the arts!* & if that seems farfetched, it goes to show how far afield our educational priorities are. Every dollar spent on the development and distribution of new art will save thousands of dollars in lost cultural productivity over the next fifty years.[2]

---

2. "The budget for the National Endowment for the Arts, which has not changed appreciably in the last 12 years, is smaller than the Department of Defense's budget for its 102 military bands," according to an article in *The New York Times*, March 13, 1993, p. C13.

At the community ("free") clinic I worked for in the early 1970s we sold T-shirts that said, "Healthcare is for people not profit." Not that we were ahead of our time. Times are just behind where they could be. Whenever I go into a Barnes & Ignoble Superstore or Waldaltonsbooks (*If we don't have it it must be literature!*), I'm reminded that our slogan for healthcare applies to poetry too.

Does anybody wonder anymore what the effects will be of the consolidation of publishing and book distribution companies into large conglomerates? *Let them read cake.* This month's bestseller list contains the perfect symbol for the current state of affairs as the two top slots are occupied, in effect, by the publicity machines designed to promote "cultural product".[3] What sells, in this purest form of hype-omancy is the apparatus of publicity itself: for here we have self-consuming artifacts par excellence— no external referent need apply. And if we say that the public "wants" these products we are only succumbing to the equation of consumption with desire. For these books/machines/shows are the QVN of ideas, inexorably selling themselves in a vicious circle of publicity chasing its own tale: these books mark not the tabloidization of ideas— that happened long ago— but the tabloidization of tabloidization. Meanwhile, in the upscale journals that condescend to the truth bared by H. Stern and R. Limbaugh, no book has been more attended to than a memoir by one of the originators of this phenomenon, Willie Morris, formally editor of *Harper's*: for what better subject for promotion than promotion?

There is a world outside this semblance of culture. In poetry, its institutions go by the name of the small press and the reading series.

Along with small press magazines and books, poetry reading series are the most vital site of poetic activity in North America. Readings provide a crucial place for poets not only to read their new work but also to meet with each other and exchange ideas. Readings provide an intimately local grounding for poetry and are commonly the basis for the many regional scenes and groups and constellations that mark the vitality of the artform.

Despite the fundamental importance of readings in the creation of North American poetry over the past forty years, very little attention has been given to this medium either in the press or by scholars and critics except in the case where readings deform themselves to most resemble media events, as in the cross of MTV and poetry slams, where the alternative explorations of sense and meaning and sound are too often reduced to alt.culture.101, or retro-Beat-chic, opening acts for bigger budget spec-

---

3. Rush H. Limbaugh 3d, *See I Told You So* (New York: Pocket Books, 1993), and Howard Stern, *Private Parts* (New York: Simon & Schuster, 1993).

tacle of the band to come. While reading series are more concentrated in New York and the Bay area, many American cities have long-running local reading series. The best source of information about readings in New York City area is *The New York City Poetry Calendar*, which has been publishing a monthly broadside of poetry events since 1977. The calendar lists about 300 different readings each month, has a print run of 7,500 and a readership of well over 10,000.

Poetry readings range from small bar and cafe and book store and community center series, with audiences ranging from ten to a hundred, to poetry center readings that can draw from twenty to several hundred people. Community reading series differ in several crucial ways from university-sponsored series. These series often offer a forum for new and unpublished local poets through "open mike" and scheduled readings. The organizers of these series rarely receive any compensation for their work—and often can run a series for incredibly little money: the money from the door going to the poets plus a few hundred dollars a year for publicity. State and local arts agencies will sometimes provide such series up to a few thousand dollars for featured readers, which allows for some out-of-town poets to get travel money or a small fee of fifty to a few hundred dollars. Poets & Writers, Inc., is particularly helpful in these contexts, providing matching money for poets' fees. A community reading series can run a year of readings on less than many institutions spend on a single cultural event or speaker. That affects the spirit of the event. The atmosphere at a local reading series is often charged and interactive. In contrast, university series often suffer from a stifling formality. Unfortunately, English departments have been slow to include and support local readings series in their areas—despite the fact that these series can often provide a lively point of entry into poetry for students new to its forms and formats.

The past thirty years has been a time of enormous growth of small press publishers. According to Loss Pequeño Glazier's statistics in *Small Press: An Annotated Guide*, the number of magazines listed in Len Fulton's *International Directory of Little Magazines & Small Presses* has gone from 250 mostly poetry magazines in 1965 to 700 in 1966 to 2,000 magazines in 140 categories in 1976 to 4,800 magazines in 1990, of which about 40 percent were literary.[4] The importance of the small press for poetry is not restricted to any aesthetic or indeed to any segment of poets. According

4. Loss Pequeño Glazier, *Small Press: An Annotated Guide* (Westport, Conn.: Greenwood Press, 1992), pp. 2–3.

to a recent study by Mary Biggs, independent noncommercial presses are the major source of exposure for all poets, young and old, prize winning or not.[5]

The staple of the independent literary press is the single-author poetry collection. Douglas Messerli, publisher of Sun & Moon Press, a high-end small press comparable to Black Sparrow, New Directions, and Dalkey Archive, provided me with representative publication information for a 100-page poetry collection:

Print runs at Sun & Moon go from 1,000 to 2,000, depending, of course, on likely sales. Messerli notes that print runs of less than 1,000 drive the unit cost up too high and he encourages other literary presses to print a minimum of 1,000 copies if at all possible.

Sun & Moon titles are well-produced, perfectbound, and offset with full color covers. The printing bill for this runs from $2,600 to $4,000 as you go from 1,000 to 2,000 copies. Messerli estimates the cost of editing a 100-page poetry book at $300: this covers all the work between the press receiving a manuscript and sending it to a designer (including any copyediting and proofreading that may be necessary as well as preparation of front and back matter and cover copy). Typesetting is already a rarity for presses like Sun & Moon, with authors expected to provide computer disks wherever possible. Formatting these disks (converting them into type following specifications of the book designer) can cost anywhere from $300 to $1,000, one of those variable labor costs typical of small press operations. The book designer will charge about $500. The cover will cost an additional $100 for photographic reproduction or permission fees or both. Publicity costs must also be accounted for, even if, as at Sun & Moon, no advertising is involved. Messerli estimates publicity costs at $1,500, which covers the cost of something like 100 free copies distributed to reviewers, postage and packing, mailings and catalog pages, etc. The total cash outlay here, then, for 2,000 copies, is around $6,800. (For the sake of this discussion, overhead costs—rent, salaries, office equipment, phone bills, etc.—are not included; such costs typically are estimated at about 30 percent more than the cost of production.)

If all goes well, Sun & Moon will sell out of its print run in two years. Let's say Sun & Moon prints 2,000 copies of the book and charges $10 retail; let's also say all the books were sold. That makes a gross of $20,000. Subtract from this a 50 percent wholesale discount (that is, most book-

5. Mary Biggs, *A Gift That Cannot Be Refused: The Writing and Publishing of Contemporary American Poetry* (Westport, Conn.: Greenwood Press, 1990), cited in Glazier, *Small Press*, p. 38.

stores will pay $5 for the book) and that leaves $10,000. Subtract from this the 24 percent that Sun & Moon's distributor takes (and remember that most small presses are too small to secure a distributor with a professional sales force). That leaves $7,600. Now last, but not to be totally forgotten, especially since I am a Sun & Moon author, the poet's royalty; typically no advance would be paid and the author would receive 10 percent of this last figure, or $760. That leaves $6,840 return to the publisher on a cash cost of about $7,000.

As James Sherry noted years ago in $L=A=N=G=U=A=G=E$: a piece of paper with nothing on it has a definite economic value. If you print a poem on it, this value is lost. Here we have a vivid example of what George Bataille has called general economy, an economy of loss rather than accumulation. Poetry is a negative—or let's just say poetic—economy.

But of course I've stacked the decks a bit. Many small presses will eat a number of costs I've listed. Copyediting, proofreading, and design costs may be absorbed in the overhead if they are done by the editor-cum-publisher, proofreader, publicity department, and shipper. Formatting and production are commonly done on in-house computers. But these costs cannot be absorbed away—600 dpi laser printers and late-night "proofreading" can cause some serious malabsorption problems for which your gastroenterologist has no cure. Then again, if a book generates enough of an audience to require reprinting, modest profits are possible, allowing the publication of other, possibly less popular, works.

The situation for the independent literary magazines is similar to presses, and indeed many small presses started as little magazines. o.blek, a beautifully produced magazine edited by Peter Gizzi and Connel McGrath, was started on borrowed money in 1987. One thousand copies of the first 148-page issue cost $1,000 for typesetting, $2,700 for the printing, and $400 for postage. That cost has remained relatively consistent, although a switch to desktop halved the typesetting cost. That first issue, with a cover price of $5.50 (and with the distributor taking 55 percent), sold out in a year and a half. After one year, o.blek had about 75 subscribers; after six years, that number is 275 (a figure that does not include libraries, who mostly subscribe through jobbers). o.blek's most ambitious publication (edited by Juliana Spahr and Gizzi) is just out: 1,500 copies of a two-volume set, 600 pages in all, collecting poems and statements of poetics from mostly younger poets, many of whom participated in the Writing from the New Coast Festival held at the University at Buffalo last spring. Compare this to Sulfur, edited by Clayton Eshleman, who reports that there were 1,000 copies printed of the first issue in 1981—"maybe 50 subscribers at the time the issue was published, with perhaps 300 to 400 going out to stores. Now, 2,000 copies per issue; around 700 subscribers, with 800 to 900 copies going to stores."[6]

Of course, many small presses and magazines produce more modest publications than Sun & Moon, *Sulfur,* or *o.blek.* Perhaps the heart of the small press movement is the supercheap magazine or chapbook, allowing just about anyone to be a publisher or editor. In this world, marketplace values are truly turned upside down, since many readers of the poetry small press feel the more modest the production, the greater the integrity of the content. There is no question that many of the best poetry magazines of the postwar period have been produced by the cheapest available methods. In the 1950s, the "mimeo revolution" showed up the stuffy pretensions of the established, letterpress literary quarterlies, not only with their greater literary imagination, but also with innovative designs and graphics. In 1965, 23 percent of little presses were mimeo, 31 percent offset, 46 percent letterpress, according to Fulton's *Directory.* By 1973, offset had jumped to 69 percent, with letterpress at 18 percent, and mimeo only 13 percent. As Loss Glazier notes, the mimeo in "the mimeo revolution" is more a metaphor for inexpensive means of reproduction than a commitment to any one technology. Indeed, poetry's use of technology often has a wryly aversive quality. For example, as offset began to dominate the printing industry in the early 1970s, letterpresses became very cheap to acquire, so that presses like Lyn Hejinian's Tuumba and Keith and Rosmarie Waldrop's Burning Deck could produce books with little other cash expense than paper costs and mailing, given the editors' willingness to spend hundreds of hours to handset every letter and often enough handfeed each page.

In the metaphoric sense, then, the mimeo revolution is very much alive in the 1990s, with some of the best poetry magazines today—such as *Abacus, Witz, Mirage #4 (Periodical), The Impercipient, Interruptions, lower limit speech, Letterbox, Situation, lyric&,* and *Object*[7]—consisting of little more than a staple or two holding together from 16 to 60 sheets of paper that have been xeroxed in editions of 50 or 100 or 150. Yet the new mimeo revolution for poetry is surely electronic. Because the critical audience of poets, mostly unaffiliated with academic institutions, does not yet have access to the internet, attempts to create on-line poetry magazines remain preliminary. Still, the potential is there and a few editors have started to propose some basic for-

6. Clayton Eshleman, letter to the author, January 11, 1994. Information on Sun & Moon Press is based on an interview with Douglas Messerli in November 1993; information on *o.blek* is based on an interview with Peter Gizzi in December 1993.

7. The Electronic Poetry Center (http://wings.buffalo.edu/epc) is a good source of current information on small press publications; it did not exist at the time this essay was written.

mats. In 1993, the first three electronic poetry magazines I know about were founded—*We Magazine,* collectively edited in Santa Cruz, the Bay Area, New York City, and Albany—which in its active periods sends out one short poem per post to a list of subscribers; *Grist,* edited by John Fowler, which has produced two full-length issues so far;[8] and *Rif/t,* edited by Ken Sherwood and Loss Glazier, which produced an ambitious array of material for its first issue a few months ago: the main body of the magazine featuring poems by 16 poets (the equivalent of 50 pages), plus a series of associated files of translations, poetics, a set of variations on a poem, and a chapbook. Also online is Luigi-Bob Drake's, and friends', *Taproot Reviews,* an heroic effort to review hundreds of small magazines and chapbooks committed to "experimental language art & poetry." Experiments with poetry and poetics "listserve" discussion groups have also begun, with Joe Amato's pioneering *Nous Refuse;* at present, this intriguing mix of newsletter, group letter, and bulletin board is beginning to find its place. In any case, it seems certain that the net will be a crucial site for the distribution of works of poetry, especially out-of-print works, as well as for information on obtaining books and magazines, and, I suspect, for long-term local, national, and international exchanges of ideas and work in progress.

Distribution remains the most serious problem for the small press and one of the least understood parts of the process. While larger independent presses have distributors with sales representatives to visit bookstores, most small presses must rely on mailing lists and informal contacts to circulate their books and magazines.

Small Press Distribution is the most important source for alternative press titles published in the United States. With the recent demise of over half-a-dozen alternative press distributors, it is also the "sole remaining noncommercial literary book distributor left in the entire country."[9] SPD, which must take 55 percent of the retail price of a book (bookstores will typically take 40 percent or more of this), now distributes about 52,000 books a year, from over 350 presses, with net sales of $360,000. Their quarterly catalogs and annual complete catalogs are fundamental resources.

From 1980 to 1993, Segue Distributing published an annual catalog that offered a curated selection of small press titles that could be ordered through a central address.[10] Segue, unlike most distributors, was able to

---

8. In February 1994 *Grist* announced its first electronic book, *Gleanings: Uncollected Poems of the Fifties* by David Ignatow, including many poems "published here for the first time." Cost is $25 on diskette; the text is also available online.

9. Letter, dated October 22, 1993, to affiliated publishers from Lisa Domitrovich, Executive Director, SPD. SPD can be reached at 1341 Seventh Street, Berkeley, CA 94710.

10. During much of this period, I worked as editor of the catalog.

articulate an aesthetic commitment with its choices, as well as being able to include presses and magazines too small to be handled by other distributors. In addition, Segue included selections of small press books and magazines from the UK, as well as New Zealand and Australia. Segue Distributing was discontinued this year after losing its government grant support. I suspect that in the future activities such as Segue's will best be handled through electronic bulletin boards or similar formats.

One of Segue's most useful assets is its mailing list, which it makes available to affiliated presses. The mailing list keeps track of a shifting community of readers, with special attention to the local audience that wishes to receive notices of readings as well as the national and international audience that wishes to receive notices of book and magazine publications. I say *community* because *audience* is too passive a term to describe this matrix and because there is a tendency to speak of community when referring to a small press readership or, especially, the local "scene" for a reading series or a magazine. But I resist the term community as well, since it is more accurate to think of constellations of active readers interested in exchange but not necessarily collectivity.

While much distribution of poetry takes place in the mail, we all owe a great debt to the few remaining independent bookstores that make an effort to keep in stock a full range of poetry titles. There is no substitute for flipping through new books and magazines in a bookstore, and such bookstores themselves are crucial sites of whatever a poetry community might be.

We also owe a debt to those publications that are committed to reviewing and discussing small press publications, since one of the most involving aspects of the small press is the intensity of interchange that takes place in reviews, letters, correspondence, and conversation. This is what makes *The American Book Review* so much livelier than *The New York Review of Books*. At their best, reviews and essays in the alternative poetry press are less concerned with evaluation than with interaction, participation, and partisanship; in this respect, the prose of the small presses offers a refreshing alternative to the evaluative focus of newspaper and mainstream magazine reviews as well as the often stifling framelock of academic discourse. Indeed, the literary small press provides a forum not just for innovation in poetry but equally for innovation in prose, in the process demonstrating that a free press means giving writers stylistic freedom, not simply the freedom to express their opinions in mandated forms.

The power of our alternative institutions of poetry is their commitment to scales that allow for the flourishing of the artform, not the maximizing of the audience; to production and presentation not publicity; to exploring the unknown not manufacturing renown. These institutions continue, against all odds, to find value in the local, the particular, the partisan, the committed, the tiny, the peripheral, the unpopular, the eccentric, the difficult, the complex, the homely; and in the formation and reformation, dissolution and questioning, of imaginary or virtual or partial or unavowable communities and/or uncommunities.

Such alternative institutions benefit not just from the support of their readers and writers, but also from contributions from government, individuals, and foundations. Recently, such large foundations as the Lila Wallace–Readers Digest Fund have committed substantial funds to independent literary presses, but they have done so in ways that are often destructive to the culture of the institutions they propose to support. Rather than provide funds to directly support the production of books and magazines, or, indeed, editors or authors, such institutions insist on primarily funding organizational expansion, for example, by providing money to hire new staff for development, publicity, and management. While any money is welcome, the infrastructural expansion mandated by these foundations—defended in the name of stabilizing designated organizations—makes the small press increasingly dependent on ever larger infusions of money, in the process destroying the financial flexibility that is the alternative press's greatest resource. By pushing the presses they fund to emulate the structures of large non-profit and for-profit institutions to which they stand in honorable structural opposition, these foundations reveal all too nakedly their commitment to the administration of culture rather than to the support of poetry.

Literature is never indifferent to its institutions. A new literature requires new institutions, and these institutions are as much a part of its aesthetic as the literary works that they weave into the social fabric. The resilience of the alternative institutions of poetry in the postwar years is one of the most powerful instances we have of the creation of value amidst its postmodern evasions. *When you touch this press, you touch a person.* In this sense, the work of our innovative poetries is fundamentally one of social work.

Pound and the Poetry of Today

What Greek logomachy had in common with the Hebrew poison was debate, dialectic, sophistry, the critical activity that destroys faith . . .

The Hebrew attack, crying out for vengeance, began by destroying the Roman Gods . . .

But faith is weakened by debates, [which are] more or less rabbinical and if not rabbinical at least anti-totalitarian.

"Che l'intenzione per ragione vale."

Faith is totalitarian. The mystery is totalitarian. The sacred symbols are totalitarian. The destruction of the images of the Gods did not increase faith . . .

. . . That fatal inclination to want to understand logically and syllogistically what is incomprehensible is Hebrew and Protestant.

Ezra Pound, *Meridiano di Roma* (1942)

This is Charles Bernstein speaking . . . from the Upper West Side of Manhattan, home of Zabar's and Barney Greengrass, the Sturgeon King.

With thanks to Jerry, Marjorie, Jackson, Pierre, Rachel, and the rest of the Poetics "Jews" and Protest-ants (irregardless of ethnic origin) who insist on debating what they/we cannot understand.

& now for some further sophistry: "the critical activity that destroys faith":

Many of the poets and critics who discount Pound do not do so because of his fascism but because of a dislike for collage, parataxis, and the very

Pound quoted by Peter Nicholls in *Ezra Pound: Politics, Economics, and Writing* (London: Macmillan, 1984), pp. 157–58.

strikingly rhetorical surfaces of Pound's poems. They also discount other poets, working in related modes, whose politics are quite contrary to Pound's. The converse of this is also true.

In this context, I don't take the new wave of Pound criticism that regards fascism as central to Pound's poetic project to be a move away from reading Pound or as a way of undermining his significance or influence. This new Pound criticism, which in some ways incorporates aspects of what has come to be called cultural criticism, or cultural and gender studies, tries to integrate Pound's political and economic ideas with his poetic practice. Like all critical projects, this one is limited. Much of the best Pound criticism before this period tended in various ways to cauterize or surgically remove the cancerous parts of Pound's work, or career, in an attempt to save the good parts. Partly this was a strategy to "save" the work, but it was equally a forceful interpretative system, an "apolitics" of poetry. (Peter Nicholls: "Most previous criticism of [Pound's] work has, from a variety of motives, sought to keep these different strands separate, tending in particular to drive a web between the 'literary' and political dimensions in his writing" [1].)

Starting in the 1980s, critics like Nicholls, Richard Sieburth, Jerome McGann, Burton Hatlen, Bob Perelman, Rachel DuPlessis, Kathryne Lindberg, and others, but most militantly Robert Casillo, tried to integrate Pound's political and economic and gender ideologies into the trop(e)ical system that is his poetry. In doing this, these readers were giving Pound the respect of taking him at his word, in contrast to those critics who, like well meaning relatives, were often forced to say Pound didn't know what he was talking about. The point here is not to say one approach or the other is right but to note that these approaches allow for different readings of Pound's poetry. None of this work, it seems to me, ought to drive one away from reading Pound; quite the contrary. (Possibly this may be the work of a distinctly younger generation of scholars who no longer felt that raising these issues aligned their views with those who roundly dismissed Pound in the postwar period; this earlier polarization pushed those who went to the defense of Pound's poetry to avoid dwelling on the relation it has to his politics and views on money.)

Casillo and Sieburth actually brought me back to reading Pound; that is, reading through the fascism and masculinism brought me from a passive, largely unarticulated, aversion to Pound, to an active, and ongoing, interest in all aspects of his work. Certainly I have been polemical in my essays on Pound, but not without the ironic realization that Pound relished just this sort of poetic polemicism. Reading Pound through the fascism means reading Pound in the most specific social and historical terms. It also means reading poetic forms politically, as an economy of signs; it means thinking through the implications of poetic structures, rather than imagining them ever to be neutral or transparent. A poem including history means we must read the history too, and this history is writ in the style, in the symbolic/semiotic economy of the poem, in the material means of production, as much as in Pound's "disembodied" "ideas".

Poetry is not worth reading because it is comfortable or happy or understandable or uplifting, any more than history or philosophy is. Nor does reading for a politics of poetic form mean that forms are liberating; more often we find that, as Ray DiPalma once suggested, all forms are coercive.[1] If one starts with the assumption that a poetry should be truthful or beautiful, that its meaning should transcend the circumstances of its production—then of course talk of the politics of Pound's poetic forms will seem dismissive of Pound's work, since it pulls that work down from the heights of poetic vanity into the real-politics of the actual poem in actual history.

People say, Pound was deluded, Pound was insane, Pound was paranoid, Pound was delusional, as a way to explain away, or possibly contextualize, his fascism. I don't doubt this, but it doesn't get me anywhere. Fascism itself was (IS) delusional and paranoid, and Hitler and Mussolini and Goebbels are certifiable in my book, as are the shouting Brown Shirts pictured in *Triumph of the Will* (don't we call this "mass hysteria"?). I agree with Pierre Joris that what's important to understand as we approach the end of this long century is the nature of this delusion, of this insanity, that has attracted so many otherwise admirable, sometimes brilliant, people, groups, indeed cultures. Of course Pound was delusional during the period of his Radio Speeches; reading Pound means reading through these delusions, trying to come to terms with them. It doesn't mean that in making these judgments one is free of one's own delusions, or that such a reading gives a complete account of his poetic works, which demands multiple, contradictory, readings.

Pound was not just a fascist; he had different politics, and poetics, at different points in his life and even at some of the same points. Nicholls notes that from 1930 to 1937, Pound was eager to keep a dialogue open with the American left; and earlier in his life his views seemed more left than right, although, reading Nicholls, one begins to see this as much as a weakness in the left/right distinction as an inconsistency on Pound's part. Nicholls also shows that "perhaps the most disquieting thing about [Pound's] savage propaganda is that it was to some degree an extension of ideas that had governed the earlier *Cantos*" (156). Indeed, Nicholls's trac-

---

1. Ray DiPalma, "Tying and Untying", in *The L=A=N=G=U=A=G=E Book*, ed. Bruce Andrews and Charles Bernstein (Carbondale: Southern Illinois University Press, 1984), p. 14.

ings of the (de?)evolution of the practice of "authority" and "ideological closure" in Pound's work is crucial for understanding a fundamental dynamic of modernism.

Yet Pound's poetry is never simply a direct reflection of his politics; indeed, I would argue, quite to the contrary, that Pound's work contradicts his fascism. The fascist reading of Pound's poetic practice is valuable as one approach; it is not a final or definitive reading; as with all critical methods, it illuminates some issues while obscuring others. Of course, as Casillo's book and other Pound criticism shows, it also may push the criticism to the polemical and even hysterical, as if the critic feels she or he is wrestling with a demon more than interpreting a poem. This too needs to be historicized and contextualized before it can be judged.

Pound told Allen Ginsberg he suffered from that "stupid, suburban prejudice of anti-Semitism,"[2] as if he should have been immune from such a low, "suburban" consciousness. But one thing that is notable about Pound is that he does not appear to have been "personally" antisemitic, which would have been in no way unusual for a person of his generation and background. His attacks on Jews are not related to his hatred of individual Jews nor his desire to be a member of an "exclusive" country club. His views of Jews are highly theoretical and structural, projecting Jewishness, more than individual Jews, as the core force in the destruction of the most cherished values of the West. This demonization is not a "stupid suburban prejudice", it is the systematic paranoia-producing ideology that has come to be called by the word fascism. (Burton Hatlen: "we will all seriously misunderstand fascism if we insist on seeing it as a 'right-wing' political movement. For fascism . . . blended an authoritarianism usually associated with the 'right' and a 'populism' usually characteristic of the 'left'" [145].) Marjorie Perloff is quite right to point to it in Pat Buchanan and the fundamentalist right; they too have gone well beyond "stupid suburban prejudice", even as they bank on it. It is scary to see the degree to which fascist ideas have rooted themselves so deeply in mainstream American life, often in the guise of family values and consonance with a natural order. Pound's most fascist polemics resonate in an eery way with the current wave of attacks on the arts, gays, the disenfranchised poor, immigrants, feminism, and the cities. I say this because there is often a tendency among Americans to exoticize fascism; Pound did his best to bring it home.

Pound's work, it seems to me, not only allows for but provokes an ideological reading; it insists that it be read, form and content, for its politics and its ideas. And it is precisely this that is one of the *enduring* values of his

2. Cited in Burton Hatlen, "Ezra Pound and Fascism", in *Ezra Pound and History*, ed. Marianne Korn (Orono, Maine: National Poetry Foundation, 1985), p. 158.

work. The dystopian aspects of Pound's work are important to fully explore, even with tempers flying off the page, because he is a fundamental part of that elective tradition (thinking of Christopher Beach's useful sense of Pound's influence in his *ABC of Influence: Ezra Pound and the Remaking of American Poetic Tradition*) that, as Beach and others have noted, consists mostly of poets whose politics and economics differ so radically from Pound's. But the more important Pound is for that tradition, then the more important it is to understand the disease that consumes his work, which cannot be disentangled from what is "good" about it. Nicholls, for example, notes how Pound's insistence on "making it new" made for an affinity with related fascist ideals. The significance of "the Pound tradition" requires that we interrogate it for what it excludes as much as what it makes possible: interrogate the assumptions of poetic lineages not just to acknowledge their effects but also to counteract their effects. And let's not forget that one aspect of this elective tradition is a commitment to difficult writers and difficult writings.

In "Canonade", Jerome McGann takes up some of these problems from a somewhat different point of view by providing a critique of those who would construct their literary canon based on moral virtue. McGann's piece is a rebuke to the ever-resurgent idea (on both left and right) that art should be uplifting. Indeed, McGann won't let us forget that range of poetry that dwells, without disavowing—that is, dwells in ways that make readers anxious—on the foulest thoughts and darkest visions of a culture. He quotes Blake's idea that "The greatest Poetry is immoral" but also Byron's "He left a [Poet's] name to other times, / Linked with one virtue, and a thousand crimes" (to use the substitution for "Corsair" that McGann, in effect, suggests). McGann goes on to say about T. S. Eliot's most notorious poem: "Yet what a remarkable poem—indeed, how remarkable exactly because it has sunk into its own disgusting imagination! . . . Serpentine, garage-door, phlegm: all have, like the beast Ahab, their humanities. Their eyes are watching God, even when they watch from that cesspool titled 'Sweeney Among the Nightingales.'"[3]

*   *   *

I wrote a follow-up speech to "Pounding Fascism" (in A Poetics*) for the 1985 Pound Centennial at Yale: an occasion at which at I was made to feel (and no doubt also made myself feel) very unwelcome. I was just about the youngest person invited to speak, and the only Jewish one; it didn't seem a coincidence that I was also the only person to raise the question of Pound's fascism at this occasion. The spirit of the supposedly academic symposium was set by Pound's daughter asking us to observe several minutes of silence in*

3. Jerome McGann, "Canonade", *New Literary History* 25, no. 3 (1994): 487–504.

honor of the anniversary of her father's death, which coincided with the Yale event. In keeping with this reverential spirit, the tone of the day was solemn and studiously respectful. In contrast, my speech would have seemed boisterous and structurally irreverent, though insofar as this was so it was oddly more in the mood of the putative subject.

The lesson of Pound for contemporary poetry is contradictory and disturbing—for there are elements in his work that give comfort to utopian fantasies of a self-conscious, multivocal, polyvalent, intensely sonorous poetry and also of a repellent, self-justifying, smug, canonically authoritarian, culturally imperialist poetic and critical practice. Attempts to ignore or domesticate this central problematic in Pound fail to appreciate that the irresolvability of the problem is Pound's legacy; for while one may prefer to dwell on the formal innovations of *The Cantos*, the meaning of these innovations can be adequately appreciated only after we consider the context of their fascist roots. If we are to take Pound, or ourselves, seriously, then we must grapple not with "structures themselves" but with the political and historical contexts in which these structures emerge. We must, that is, understand that our poetical practices have political and social dimensions in terms of form over and above content—if we can allow this distinction at all. The sanitized Pound is inert and irrelevant; and it is evident from the remarkably thoughtful new Pound criticism by, for example, Christine Froula and Richard Sieburth, that opening the Pandora's box of "The Pound Error" allows for, rather than precludes the continuing relevance of Pound's work. ("The Pound Error" is Froula's term for Pound's inclusions of printer's errors, misattributions, mistranslations, and the like into the text of *The Cantos* so that the "history" that the poem includes is also the history of its groping compositional process. Froula means for "error" to also suggest errantry, or wandering.[4]) In a similar way, the relevance of Pound for contemporary poetry is to be found most significantly in those works that have confronted the politics of Poundian "textualization" and appropriation and have realized alternatives to it.

The fascist implications of Pound's work can perhaps best be understood by contrasting two compositional techniques, montage and collage. By definition, collage is a more general term of which montage is a type; but I wish to make a different distinction. For Eisenstein, montage involves the use of contrasting images in the service of one unifying theme; collage, as I use it here, juxtaposes different elements without recourse to an overall unifying idea. Pound wished to write a montage but produced some-

4. Christine Froula's "The Pound Error: The Limits of Authority in the Modern Epic" is chapter 3 of *To Write Paradise: Style and Authority in Pound's Cantos* (New Haven: Yale Unviersity Press, 1984).

thing far more interesting in the process. The underlying idea of his montage has been varyingly described by many of the critics who wish to make a claim for the overall unity of *The Cantos*. Suffice it to say now that his appropriation of prior texts (the quotations, citations, and transductions) were intended as an evaluative, "objectively" discriminating—and hence hierarchical and phallocentric—"ordering" of these materials. The "objective" historical synopsis of human culture (what we might call the subtextual curriculum of *The Cantos*) and its claims to ground the poem in an extraliterary reality have made the work especially attractive to many Pound scholars, despite the objectionable and elitist premises of this synopsis and the fact that *The Cantos* implodes the very "objective" and ideological aims it purports to articulate.

Understanding *The Cantos* as montage provides a framework for the poem's implied positivism, which also helps to explain those theoretical statements of Pound's that seem to fly in the face of his actual poetic practice: his insistence, variously, on "the plain sense of the word",[5] on the "direct treatment of the 'thing'" and on the unswerving pivot whose Imagist distillation was made possible by eliminating any word that did not directly "contribute to the presentation"[6] a poetics commonly taken as a refutation of the artifice of Symbolist and Swinburnian modes as well as a rejection of the excessive verbiage of contemporary conventional verse. Pound vilified fragmentation and abstraction as debasing the "gold standard" of language, yet his major and considerable contribution to the poetry of our language is exactly his rococo overlayings, indirection, elusiveness. His fast-moving contrasts of attitudes and atmospheres collapse the theater of Ideational Representation into a textually historicist, unfinishable process of composition by field—a field of many voices without the fulcrum point of any final arbitration, *listening not judging*: a disintegration into the incommensurability of parts that marks its entrance into the space of contemporary composition. Insofar as contemporary poetry does not wish simply to admire or dismiss Pound's work but to come to terms with it, these competing dynamics must be reckoned with.

It took the arrogance of Pound's supremacist and culturally essentialist ideology to give him the ambition to imagine a work on the scale of *The Cantos*, a poem that theoretically encompasses nothing less than the story—history—of the determinately seminal strains of human culture. That no person has an adequate vantage point to "make it cohere" is of course a lesson *The Cantos* teaches but that Pound never fully learned. It is

5. *Ezra Pound Speaking: Radio Speeches of World War II*, ed. Leonard W. Doob (Westport, Conn.: Greenwood Press, 1978), p. 283.

6. Ezra Pound, "A Retrospect", in *The Poetics of the New American Poetry*, ed. Donald Allen and Warren Tallman (New York: Grove Press, 1973), p. 36.

a lesson we need to learn not just from *The Cantos* but from the larger history of geopolitical struggles in this century. While Mussolini's utopian state failed to triumph, shattering *The Cantos* objective correlative, the current problematic of imposed order—the U.S. or U.S.S.R. *über alles*—is too obvious to need reiteration here. It is already constantly reiterated in the eloquent pleas heard from South Africa to Grenada, from Czechoslovakia to New Zealand, for the autonomy of cultural difference and against integration into an imposed curricular design. So contemporary poetry's response to Pound is to enact a poetry that does not fragment for the sake of a greater whole but that allows the pieces to sing their own story—a chordal simultaneity at pains to put off any coherence save that found within its own provisional measure. Every grain or strain or swatch has its own claim to truth, not as one of the "luminous particulars"—exemplary types selected by the Agassiz/Fenollosa scientific method and part of what Michael André Bernstein calls a "universally valid, external, narrative structure"[7]—but as part of the democracy of words and cultures and histories, all impossible to exhaust or rank. Pound's historical and ideological tendentiousness is not the problem: indeed, doctrinaire tendentiousness is in many ways a useful corrective to the denial of ideology in the transcendentalist Imagination of Romantic poetry. That is, the failure of *The Cantos* does not entail the necessary impossibility of including history, politics, and economics into a poem, but it does entail the rejection of the positivist assumptions behind these inclusions. So we must now attempt to critique Poundian panculturalism with decentered multiculturalism.

Jerome Rothenberg's anthologies, specifically *Technicians of the Sacred* and *A Big Jewish Book,* are exemplary of this political reversal of Poundian centrism. Rothenberg demonstrates the range and depth of cultures normally excluded in an Occidental-Oriental focus such as Pound's. Insisting on the limits of any attempts to claim lordship over this material, Rothenberg's anthologies leave us with a sense of what we do not know, what is beyond our ken, and of our own culture's reduced but replenished scale in relation to these other traditions. At the same time, the open form of "collecting"— creating a music of contrasting parts—is clearly an outgrowth of Poundian compositional strategies.

The lacunas in Pound's guides to culture have begun to speak. By introducing a form where dialects and languages mingle freely, where "nonpoetic" material—"raw facts", Chinese ideograms, printer's errors, slang, polylingual quotations—are given poetic status, Pound opened the flood-

<hr>

7. Michael André Bernstein, *The Tale of the Tribe* (Princeton: Princeton University Press, 1980), p. 69.

gates for what had been left out, or refined out, by precepts such as his own "use absolutely no word that does not contribute". The undigested quality of parts of *The Cantos* gives credence to the further explorations of the unheard and unsounded in our poetry. On the one hand, this includes the continuing care with which the sound and sense of the world of African-Americans and native Americans have been charted by many contemporary poets; it also includes, for example, Judy Grahn's attempts not only to articulate contemporary lesbian experience but to chart a lesbian curriculum from Sappho to Dickinson to Stein and H.D. and Amy Lowell to the present. These voices now speak of and for themselves, precluding appropriation but entering into that larger collage—a text without center but constantly site-specific—that is poetry in English. Indeed, it is something resembling this hyper- and hypo-American collage that forms the structure of the revisionist Poundian anthology *America: A Prophecy*, edited by Rothenberg and George Quasha. On the other hand, the further exploration of the unheard and unsounded in our poetry involves more radically incommensurable parataxis and more comprehensive development of the visual, typographic, and textually historicist dynamics suggested by *The Cantos*. In this respect, one could point to Ron Silliman (who uses a numeric rather than hierarchic procedure for ordering the disparate elements of the poem) or to Erica Hunt (a poem including "local" history), as well as to several dozen other innovative poets who are working in sharp contrast to the tradition of High Antimodernism as it has evolved from Eliot to Lowell to the present—a tradition that also sometimes traces its lineage to Pound.

The present flourishing of a formally innovative, open, investigative poetry—a poetry that refuses to take subject matter, syntax, grammar, or vocabulary for granted and that rejects simple and received notions of unity of conceit, closure, and prosody—is unprecedented in its scale in American literature. It is made possible, to a significant degree, by the existence of alternative and oppositional publishing (James Laughlin's New Directions, for example) and by the understanding that the work of the poet does not stop with the composition of a poem but continues into the network of other poets and cultural workers and readers—that it is a *social project* involving *social organizing*.

But rather than detailing the work of a number of other contemporary poets, let me cite a remarkable new work by Jackson Mac Low, *Words nd Ends from Ez*.[8] These lines are taken from Section IX, "From Drafts & Fragments of Cantos CX–CXVII":

8. Mac Low's 1983 *Words nd Ends from Ez* was published in 1989 by the Bolinas-based press Avenue B.

"The crozier's curve runs in the wall", the 2nd line of CANTO 110

oZier's cuRve he wAll,
Phin hOut exUltant
seeN impiDity,
Exultance,
aZ loR r-
leAf
Paler rOck-
layers at—
Un e deNho ia
"HaD Ever oZzaglio,
e *tRacciolino*
iccArdo Psit,
lOve blUer thaN oureD
Euridices,
yZance,
a's Rest,
use At P"
n Of trUction eraNts
faceD,
E tZ
e FRance
is
LAnnes Pire
fOrces,
a nUisance,
was Napoleon
l 22nD.

Ery iZation."

deR ed TAlleyrand Political.

e,
Orage id Up ter—
Night al—
AnD E yZantines
m pRologo
othAr.

Perform pÖ ejUniper,
ws aNd e lanD E
oZart,
verhanging n-
beAt

Pace
tO n
oUt rk,
aNd owarD Er eZzo heRe iziA.

This work selects words and word fragments from *The Cantos* by a system-
atic chance operation based on the positioning of the letters in E-Z-R-A
P-O-U-N-D. For instance, the first line in the extract is derived from "The
crozier's curve runs in the wall," the second line of Canto 110. The Z is in
the second-letter position (eZra), the R in the third-letter position (ezRa),
and so on; punctuation sets off line breaks. At an allegorical level, *Words
nd Ends* exorcises the authoritarianism that underlies *The Cantos*. Particularly
striking in this respect is the last page of *Words nd Ends* which, because there
is no Z in Canto 120, is completely blank: a resonating comment on
Pound's final years of relative silence and on all the unspeakable grand-
ness and horror that hovers over his epic poem.

Pound had a significant influence on Mac Low's early poetic thinking.
Mac Low was in correspondence with Pound until shortly before he began
to compose chance-generated poems in the early 1950s (he broke with
Pound in 1952 or 1953 over Pound's antisemitism). Mac Low's "objective"
text-generating procedure foregrounds much of the "free play" that
remains the most salient feature of *The Cantos* by systematizing the Pound
"error" that Pound himself only quixotically pursued or permitted: cer-
tainly Mac Low's work is all imaginative extension of the dynamics that
Froula documents. *Words nd Ends* is less a countertext to *The Cantos* than an
act of homage and a topographical map of features of the work otherwise
obscured by its narrative thrusts. By purging *The Cantos* of any remnant of
montage, it reveals a purer, inhering paradise within that poem.

Inappropriate Touching

The fabric does not hold
that weld the scales
unto the dock &
waited, like two boys
in overalls, for moltings
of the clock. A gilded
summons points the blame
at which twin fingers
grin again. The pleats
have dropped their pork
& fife, no mean trick
when you got no
dice. Where whales of butter
clog the lanes that
sirens chill & courtiers
lame— While me, I had
a shopping bag, a crate
of ice, a mottled crag; & these
I took great store to hide
against the looping
undertide . . . quick as
ferrets in a tank
of lukewarm acid that
I drank, & spilled forth
my fodderdall, &
leapt inside the rolling
pine, that fortune
goad & feeling snares—
I almost said
"no one upstairs." Then
worms'll guide me
into stares

as eyelids turn into
pillows on chairs. Once
I knew my left from
right, my north from
south, my limp from
stride. Awash awash
away away: this quirky
charm will lose
its sway. & in the losing
find, the chance to lose
again, come up with twice
the Rime—the once in
bedlam once in time.

Robin on His Own

There was a stray poet of Idaho
Whose practice of outside was in the know
The poet it seems enquired of things
Both inside and outside of Idaho

I first met Robin Blaser in January 1973. On graduating college I had won a fellowship for an American to spend a year studying in Canada and had the good luck to pick Simon Fraser University, which I knew little about except that it was near Vancouver, where Susan Bee and I had decided to go, because it was as far away from New York City as we could get. My idea was to buy a goddamn tiny car (an overpriced, rusting $1,200 VW bug, 80,000 hard miles, from a used car dealer in downtown Vancouver), read books, stare blankly and intermittently for increasing stretches of time, and see what writing might bring.

The University of British Columbia's Dean Walter Gage, the administrator of the William Lyon MacKenzie King fellowship, had told me right off that I would have to "sit for examinations" if I was to go to UBC, a prospect that I found unappealing. (I have always subscribed to the idea, usually put forward by detractors of student activism, that the anti-war demonstrations of the late 60s and early 70s were motivated by a desire to avoid examinations. Such a motivation, it seems to me, is of the highest order since to demonstrate is human but to avoid examination divine.) Dean Gage reluctantly let on that something called Simon Fraser University, on the outskirts of town, might have less rigorous policies than UBC, and indeed it did: I was able to get a library card to the incredibly useful archive now curated by Charles Watts and to participate in a small seminar Robin Blaser was conducting, once a week during the spring semester, on Emily Dickinson. Since my affiliation was with the Philosophy Department I did show up to that department's occasional colloquia, where, as I recall, visiting professors laboriously argued over the combination of giant steps, baby steps, umbrella steps, ballerina steps, rock star steps, and elf steps it takes to go from *is* to *ought* ("Stop! you didn't say 'mother may I?'") but rarely from *this* to thought. Such period exercises convinced me—I was then, as now, eager, not to say anxious, to be convinced of that which I was already convinced—that rationalist thought of this kind was mannerist at best, a not-quite-harmless hobby for ethicists on vacation from the entangling "restlessness"[1] and "disturbed meanings"[2] which no manner of mannerism could hope to smooth over.

> *I am not   there where I am the plaything*
> *of my thought*
> > *I think about what I am*
> *there where*
> > *I do not think I am thinking* (135)

Still, it was the philosophers, or one of them, that pointed me in the direction of Blaser, who was, in those days as now, a blazing light in the dustbowl of campus ratiocination, a Northwest beacon on which I could set my poetic compass: "the Far West of the mind" (134).

Robin Blaser was and remains my introduction to, not, oh my god, postwar North American poetry, the New American poetry, the San Francisco Renaissance, the Boston Gang, Canadian postmodernism, poets of the 50s generation, poet-critics, poetics professors, serial poetry, the Magic Workshop circle, renegade artists of Idaho, the practice of outside, the poetics of citation, the Vancouver scene, or, indeed, the new Nervalians (a.k.a. Robin and the Chimeras—

> I wanna see those chimeras swing
> Just like in frays gone by
> Let me hear those chimeras sting
> Chirpin' at the voids in the sky

—) not to underplay the value of all such frames, which we will happily continue with over the next few days.

Blaser, that is, was my introduction—at the crucial point in my life when writing poetry was becoming central—not just to particular poets and contexts of poets, but more importantly to possibilities for poetry. Robin Blaser's work is an induction into poetry as a "shattered" (151) mapping of the uncharitable yet-always-being charted aspirations and desperations, inhabitations and reparations, of the soul in and as language. It is an induce-

---

1. Robin Blaser, "The Recovery of the Public World", draft MS, p. 34. Subsequent references to this essay are preceded by "RPW".

2. Robin Blaser, "The Violets: Charles Olson and Alfred North Whitehead", *Line* 2 (1983): 61. Subsequent references to this essay are preceded by "V". In *Cups*: "A / disturbance in the cone / of weather"; reprinted in Blaser, *The Holy Forest* (Toronto: Coach House Press, 1993), p. 3. Subsequent references to *The Holy Forest* are given by page number alone. See also note 5.

ment into poetry as the art of thinking and thinking as an activity of words and phrases leaping together through vast, scarring, differences; figments and fragments that become companions in the poem's provisional journey of self-cancellation as self-consolation (69). "The story is of a man / who lost his way in the holy wood" (45). Or, as Blaser writes in *Charms*, a telling of "the courage to be lost" (105): which is to say, courage in the face of loss but also courage in the face of the loss of courage. "The words are lost" (48), "scattered" (41, 80); "the language is bereft" (45). But in this tale what is lost is never our individual words but their connections. And the art of weaving (96; V 63) them together—not back together—is what Blaser calls the "secret of syntax" (194). For if you've got no syntax then you've got to make it up as you go, and that just might be a poetic advantage.[3]

> Loopey Locket lost his socket
> And Slippy Slappy found it
> Nothing in it, nothing in it
> But the blinding round it

"The sorrow is sharp" (83), an edge to cut the shapes; and in the sharpening make sparks in the dusks that enfold, jolts of wild logos in a world accustomed to taming dogmas.[4] For Blaser's is a practice of leaps of association that bind us not into families or states or nationalities or groups but into image nations, those imaginary nations of speculation and desire, jelled not by coercion or law but by Blake's tears, or it tears?, of intellect: "the pure efficacy of poetry" (238).

This work offers no comfort to those who seek the piety of spirituality or the smugness of self-confident expression, nor does it provide encouragement to those who would back away from the difficulties of meaning and "The turbulence" (16) of representation:

> at the edge of
> the real
>   the work of   obscurities
> are the edge   of
>   necessary
> to a luminous passage (135)

Blaser's "art of combinations" (258) buoyantly and sometimes mischievously, deflects·any notion of the self, of selves, as prior to their coming

---

3.   "Olson said, 'I'd trust you
            anywhere with image, but
            you've got no syntax' (1958)" (184).

4. See Robin Blaser, "The Practice of Outside", in *The Collected Poems of Jack Spicer*, ed. Blaser (Santa Barbara: Black Sparrow Press, 1975), p. 305; further citations to this essay are preceded by "PO". On "folds" see the citation from PO 179, in the main body of the text, as well as note 9.

to mean in language, as Blaser insists in his quarrel with another poet "over experience", when his companion "spoke too soon of a sacred cut-out" for the self:

> . . . it was the process
> of the actual we were both about
>   what exactly do we experience in poēsis
>   over the neat 'I' that thinks itself a unity of things or
>   disunity des-
>   perately untrue to whatever we are tied to—like one's
>   grief or the smother-
>   ing domestic realism, or the I-feel, so deep and steeply,
>   no one wants to
>   listen without a drumhead   positivisms of the self
>   that die into an urn (317)

Against "positivisms of the self" as such!: so that the poem emerges not from some imposition of "I-feeling" but from a transposition of listening, "the sounding air of the mind" (254); a site in which, it goes without saying, one's selves are never absent: "the robin of such listening" (282):[5]

> It is within language that the world speaks to us in a voice that is not our own . . . In the reversal of language and experience, these fold into one another and unfold, composing as voices in our language. (PO 179)

But Blaser's restless thought does not stop here: along with this deflation of the self is also a rejection of the positivisms of spirituality, specifically of the appropriation of the sacred or mystical or religious to legitimate a particular poetic or political practice.[6] In contrast, Blaser speaks for the "incorporation of the text of the sacred into the domain of art"; that is, not for the sacred as poetry but poetry as the sacred (RPW 25).

Over and again, Blaser reiterates his commitment to "Languages" not "Language" (RPW 13); that is, to both the poetic and philosophical traditions of plurality and multiplicity and against scientism and religious in-

5. Discussing the poetics of "dictation", Blaser contrasts "an imposition" to a "disclosure", noting that in "the practice of outside" "language pushes us into a polarity and experienced dialectic with something other than ourselves. It involves a reversal of language into experience . . . which composes a 'real' . . . A *reopened language* lets the unknown, the Other, the outside in again as a voice in the language. Thus, the reversal is not a reduction, but an openness. The safety of a closed language is gone and its tendency to reduce thought to a reasonableness and definiteness is disturbed" (PO 275–76).

6. See, especially, "Even on Sunday" (346). Speaking of words such as "god, soul, spirit, angel, ghost," Blaser writes, "We need not return to them, and cannot in any sense that we now understand, but they haunt us" (PO 294).

tolerance. More than any of his contemporaries, he has incorporated his philosophical sources into his poems, so that the poems themselves begin to take on the character of notes as much as lyrics, reminding that any lyric requires notes. If this is a poetry of ideas then it is also a poetry of what ideas repress; for example their links to other, often incommensurable, ideas. The pervasiveness of citations and found language in Blaser's poetry and essays compromises (and at the same time comprises) his authorial identity; to read him is to be thrown into the company of his textual companions, so that his own voice is overshadowed by other voices, through whom he speaks: "like violets we are a bunch!"[7] Reading this work is to blaze a trail through a hypertextual forest, moving from link to link, losing track of home. Blaser has constructed an environment available for browsing, not to say cruising; his work enacts an erotics of reading as a form of composition.

Languages not language. Thinking back to those days in 1973, going over version after version of Dickinson's serializing poetry, I keep returning to "This world is not Conclusion. / A Species stands beyond" but also "A sequel stands beyond" as suggesting the ontological condition of seriality: the aversion of conclusion in a poesis of nextness; a process of the "proximous".[8]

Today we gather from three continents and in overflowing numbers— three generations of poets, essayists, critics, scholars, artists, fiction writers, readers, listeners, performers, citizens, subjects, singers; malcontents & revellers, rhapsodes & noise-makers; phobophiles, philophobes, phobophobes & philophiles; not to mention autodidacts & manual models; visionaries & revisionaries. We come to celebrate Blaser at 70 and there is a delicious peculiarity to that, for, as noted, the subject of our fête has been apt to evade such self-centering attentions in his periodical reimagining of himselves in the clattering vapours—"this crazy radiance" (152)—of his

---

7. This is Blaser speaking through Olson, who is speaking of his relation to Whitehead (V 72).

8.   "the inner
               music has worn out—amidst broad
               leaves and harbours, linked to
               the observer,   submerged
               or proximous, exactly like that
               which he loves, startling noise,
               clarity and shadow, the heights
               of ourselves equal to our shadows,
               night and day, the miracle of
               many things, the 'proliferation
               of geneses'" (256–57).

poetic compositions. In the process, Blaser has eluded capture, but also publication. There is a kind of glee in Robin's almost inaudible buzzing of the control towers of binational reception, and a method in his slipping between cracks of his own and others' invention (25). For, if I can pleat[9] my way around the point here, our subject admires cracks and may find himself pulled through them from time to time like Alice through the thimble, or was that Tom the Tuba who was no bigger than my drum set, the one that taps out serial beats.

> O! how wondrous clouds do hide
> The transparent majesty of the sky

So we come to "celebrate the sudden hang up of our"—in this case also *his*—"visibility, / celebrate the sudden beauty that / is not ourselves", to quote from the man of the hour (255).

And I suppose, would like to suppose, that this "not ourselves" nonetheless makes up a public, or some fragment of a figment of a public, though not the public that is quoted in newspapers or interviewed on TV, not a public constituted by its purchasing power, or by publicity (328), and not a public representative of the larger, ghoulish public of the U.S. political nightmare of mid-1990s, the years of Gingrich's Contract Contra America. As we gather today under the title "The Recovery of the Public World", then each of us, to ourselves and in whispers, must ask—is the public world sick, lost, or was it stolen? And if our gathering, if poetry, is an act of recovery of public space, does this mean we are simply covering over again, as one might recover the tattered and stained love seat in the living room, or does it mean that we are about repossessing public spaces, which is to say creating them?

Blaser takes the title "The Recovery of the Public World" from Hannah Arendt and specifically Arendt's distinction between society, an economic realm invested by individual property and wealth; and the public, the world we have in common. For Arendt, the public sphere is "not identical with the earth or with nature [but is a] human artifact . . . a fabrication of human hands" (RPW 22).

When society and the public clash, it is the dispossessed, the "outsiders" (350–51), the economically and culturally orphaned (159), who suffer. The crisis of democracy, that "nothing repairs" (254), is the tyranny of the majority at the expense of those who do not hail at the majority's calling. "I hear the crowds weep there" (236). These are the crowds to which we owe our imaginal affiliations. For the fight against the privatization of cul-

---

9. *"the pleats of matter, and the folds of the soul"* (370), quoted from Gilles Deleuze's *The Fold: Leibniz and the Baroque.* The first of Blaser's serial poem "Image Nations" contains the title "(the fold" (61).

ture and industry, of knowledge and nature, is "the fundamental struggle for the nature of the real" (V 62).

Is it just in fairy stories, or just mostly in them, that what is lost is found, let's say, recovered?

> The principle of the surround, Ms. Midnight
> is the destiny of the found—
> like grace will hold a pattern only so long[10]

Which is to say, the "found-things" (159) in these poems are foundational.

The public we recover is no more than a series of image nations, temporary sites composed of such "found-things": not "territory" (265), "those *mystical rags* we call flags" (346), but an "endless" procession (265) of "proximous" drifts[11]—"the *shattered marble* of . . . unwalled / thought" (211)— seeking "out what is beyond any single / man or woman, or the multiples / of them" (265).

The point is not to display imagination but to mobilize imaginations, those imaginary nations.[12] We are met on a great site of this mobilization, to honor, and, "jugged to our / joyance" (256), to praise; but most importantly to foment further poetic acts and ever greater feats of recovery of that public space so often and mortally endangered in this too dark century in which Robin Blaser has lived out most of his life.

---

10. Or so I have Dr. Boris Frame sing in "The Subject" (Buffalo: Meow Press, 1995).
11.   "'we drift together toward
                       the noise and the black depths
                       of the universe'" (255)
See also note 8.
12. "It is worth reminding ourselves of the job every poet faces to replace imagination in public thought where it means invented, the made-up, the idealized, the untrue" (PO 301).

Water Images of *The New Yorker*

Maybe you've heard it before: "Did you ever notice that every poem in *The New Yorker* has a water image? Whadda they do, only print wet poems?"

While slightly less interesting than looking for the hidden "Ninas" in the Hirschfeld cartoons in the *Times*, this water-on-the-brain syndrome has a certain fascination.

Still when *The New Yorker*'s poetry editor, Howard Moss, died I wondered if the policy would continue under a poetry editor whose name was not, like Moss, a water image.

So many of us love to complain about the trivializing of poetry by "official verse culture"—a high-fallutin' name for mainstream poetry editing—that I thought, for a change, why not try some hardnosed empirical research?

Why not try to give some social scientific status to these potshots?

With "only the facts" as my motto, I read through all *The New Yorker*'s poetry selections, except the couple of translations, from January 30 to May 15, 1989—16 issues total. In all but three of these issues, 100% of the poems published included at least one water image. Two of these almost waterless weeks (3/13 and 3/20) were back-to-back while in the third (2/27) two of the three referred to water while the other poem almost did, mentioning "clouds". My theory is that during the two-week dry spell the magazine's Water Image Control Officer may have been less than vigilant due to a drinking problem.

Overall, 86% of the poems published over these four months had water images; that's 32 of the 37 poems from this period.

In the January 20th issue, J. D. McClatchy mentions "cat spray" on line 3 but it's not until line 19 that we get "hose to wash / Dung out of the cow guts." A few pages later Elizabeth Macklin's "Surface Tensions" starts with a "a long, cool bath" in "blue water" and "flood[s]" on from there.

The next week, William Logan has a "grassy lake" in line 1, a "freshwater pond" in line 2, a "lone canoeist" in line 3, and "water like broken rakes" in line 4. He sums up his poetic sensibility a couple of lines after referring to "shallows of the continental shelf". A few pages later, Mary Kinzie has some arid stanzas before her dam breaks with "Will water / in the desert also stagger"; several lines before the end there's also the heart-felt precipitation of "weep". The third poem in 2/6, by Eleanor Ross Taylor, tells us "it rained all day" and ends with drinking "a glass of water".

At the risk of water-logging my tale, I'll condense the chronicle a bit from here out.

2/13: "ancient pools left by the glaciers" (Suzanne Gardiner) and "long sheets of ice" "stuttering black syllables of rain" by the "swimming pool" (Edward Hirsch).

2/20: "steam-table" and "pump water" (Amy Clampitt); "raw glimmer of Atlantic blue" (Eamon Grennan); and Donald Hall's state of the art "Like an oarless boat through midnight's watery / ghosthouse . . . I drift on / January's tide . . . / to repose's shore—where all waves halt."

2/27: "ice-white neon," "spit up, frothing, coming to a boil," "sob"—yet a "soft dry shout"! (Jorie Graham); and another "flood" (Josephine Jacobsen). Somehow the combination of "the weather was nice," "a blueness run everywhere", "source of desiring", "wellheads" and, incredibly, "turtledoves" led me to count George Bradley's marginal call in 3/6.

Mark Strand, in the same issue, is more forthcoming with "On the shores of the darkest known river" on line 2 followed by "steaming", "muck", "drift upstream, / Against the water's will", "weep", and "frost". Macklin in 3/13 shares with us "wet gray" "marsh bird" "waves" and "cool as water", while Joseph Brodsky has the obligatory "tear" and soon after "moon skims the water" (3/27). Some cartoons on we splash over Revan Schendler's "bay tide" and "broad shore".

In the April 3rd issue, Robert Mazzocco writes of "the Hudson" and "taking a leak" and "I'll water it when I remember it" and Strand has "lake" "rushing sound" "storms" and "water's edge"; while in 4/10 Linda Bierds muses about "rippling lines", "lake bass", and "sudden rain".

Seamus Heaney has a particularly appropriate title in 4/17— "Crossings". This modern master goes on to note that "Running water never disappointed" and waxes about "the wetness of the bog", "old drains and old streams", before reaching *The New Yorker* epiphany par excellence: "the absolute river / Between us and it all". Not to be outdone, Charles Wright, in the same issue, writes of stars "east of the river" and of being "Washed in the colors of paradise" "water-colored"; while Philip Levine manages only "snow had all but melted".

After Raymond Carver's terse "rain" and "damp" and Clampitt's "overseas" and "warm snowdrift", we get John Ashbery's "like a fish on a line" "under the waterfall" and his stabbing sense of where he's publishing— "A kind of powdered suburban poetry fits / the description" "to read little signs / in the moss" (4/24). Moss indeed!

5/1, 5/8: "A fleet docks / on the opposite shore", "idle port, / sailors" (Schendler); "bay" (August Kleinzahler's "Sunday in November"); "briny shadows" (Alan Michael Parker); "port", "Mediterranean", "white Atlantic", "sea" (Derek Walcott); "sea of blue" (W. S. Di Piero).

The final issue surveyed features Deborah Digges's gush of "fish" "sea" "dewy" "harbor" "across the bay" "waving from the shore" and "washed his face" too.

Mazzocco has it down in "Loneliness in the City" (also 5/15) with "waves of flickering shop windows" and "aquarium of little fish".

So much for hugging the shore at *The New Yorker*.

The Response as Such
Words in Visibility

Late at night, deep in conversation with my most intimate poetic collaborators, a question is asked, at first so tentatively that no answer seems called for, but then with a persistence beyond mere curiosity: What was your first textual experience?

Hearing so many thoughtful forays into the intersection of the visual and the verbal, I realize that this nocturnal question really must be a mask for another question: What was your first typographical experience?

Babbling as we do in the phonocentric illusion some call early childhood, where making and mimicking sounds brings the world into constantly (constitutively) new being, verging on the worlds we thought we saw the moment before but that vanish, like sibilants in dense fog, just as— just because—we invoke them . . . Into this paradise of entropic sounding comes the regime of order, the objects before my gaze grow labels, like in one of those intensely frightening Richard Scarey books where the bikes all say "bike" and the roads say "r-o-a-d" (*ceci n'est pas une lecture*). These visualized markers create boundaries on an indefinite expanse of plenitude, organize and stipulate and restrict where once there was potential and multiplicity. And where is "to" where "of", says the child, where is my little amongbetweenwithin. For words are no more labels of things than the sky is a styrofoam wrap of some Divine carryout shop. And letters are no more tied to words or words to sentences than a mule is tied to its burden.

Letters in liberty, words freed from the tyranny of horizontality, or sequence: these are some of the impulses of a visually active domain of poetry. The visual dimension of writing is apparent from the first gesture of any inscription—the moment of making a mark, a sign that does not yet signify anything more than its process of demarking. In this first instance, the gesture of writing and drawing are identical—call it inscribing, as if we could scratch some meaning out of (or is it into?) the sullenly indifferent blank of the page that always confronts us just beyond grasp.

There are, it seems to me, two domains of poetry that are insufficiently recognized, too little attended to: the sound and the look. This is another way of saying that *poetry* is too little attended to: sounds too quickly converted to words or images, the material space of the page too quickly supplanted by the ideational space of the text (as if MLA really meant "muted language association"). Too often, reading habits enforce a kind of blindness to the particular graphic choices of type, leading, page dimension, and paper, under the regime of a lexical transcendentalism that accords no semantic value to the visual representation of language. The poetic response to this derealization of poetry is to insist, against all odds, that a work can be composed whose semantic inhabitations are all visual; Cy Twombly's work, as illuminated by Renée Riese Hubert, suggests one such possibility, as do those works within visual poetry that do not employ alphabetic writing.

The idea that a text may yield up to a visualization of what it purports to represent is a primary example of what Ron Silliman, in his essay "The Disappearance of the Word / The Appearance of the World", calls the transparency effect. Still, an important distinction needs to be made between, on the one hand, derealizations of textuality—that is readings that discount sound sense or the visual materiality of the page, or both—and, on the other hand, works that encourage proactive visualizations of images, that is, visualizations that are constructed by the reader in the process of puzzling through the linguistic material presented. In contrast, the transparency effect describes the conjuring of visual images or nonvisual ideational content, without generally focussing on the importance of the distinction between these two forms of the effect.

Certainly, a primary effort of much formally innovative poetry over the last 20 years has been to insist on melopoeia (sound play), syntaxapoeia (play of syntax), and parapoeia (the play of parataxis, parody, and invented structure)—over phanopoeia (image play, which might be better called videopoeia or indeed visualization) and logorrhea (the endless repetition of the already known, whether received forms or contents). The transparency effect suggests a diagnosis of both phonophobia (fear of sound) and misography (belief in the interiority of the visual component of language and the superiority of the ideational component of language). In the case of Johanna Drucker's sumptuous and stunning series of books, we confront the materiality of the visual representation of language over videopoeia or logopoeia. Though, as a hyperbophiliac, I overstate it to say look and sound over ideas or visualizations: rather the insistence has been to ground the one in the other, not let the latter mute or repress the former.

This project has, therefore, necessitated a critique of that ocular imagism commonly associated with a decontextualized reading of Williams's wheelbarrow poem, among other sources. A non-ocular-centered poetry has emerged as a way of recovering the loss of language's visual appearance and sonic, syntactic, dialogic, and ideologic potentialities. But I like to see a precursor for this in Williams's 1930 poem "The Botticellian Trees". Here Williams seems to explicitly reinstruct those who see him as a naive ocular imagist, for what he sees in the crossing branches of bare winter boughs is not some primary unmediated sight of nature but letters, As and Bs, "The alphabet of / the trees". It would also be a mistake, I think, to look at Williams's visual arrangements of lines on the page as primarily a metrical or speech-scoring device. As Henry Sayre has persuasively argued in his book on the look of Williams's poetry, we can best understand his page design as a visual construction on the page.

In Johanna Drucker's book art, meaning can never be understood independently of the complications of its visual manifestations on the page. She has visually troubled the transparency of letters giving way to contents, so that you cannot help but see and be exhilarated by the many ways that letters and their sizes and shapes or ordering allow for, are a necessary prerequisite of, the aesthetic dimension of the verbal domain. Her books are exquisite but never precious; indeed her insistence on a virtually orchestrated funkiness I take as a way she distances herself from the traditions of fine letterpress printing that has generally idealized a self-canceling typography—one that you would never notice except perhaps to notice its finesses, its politesse, its gentility. Never crude, never self-conscious, the fine press's version of invisible visibility has rules such as a "type should never call attention to itself" (type should be read but not seen) and "don't mix types" (antimiscegenation). But it is only when the type itself starts to speak, when the dialogic or polyglot text also means a dialogue between fonts and papers, when intertextuality includes the material stuff of texts in its exchanges . . . that the Poetic will finally triumph over prosaicality.

Foregrounding the visual dimension of the verbal domain—sounds like some sort of tap-dance number by a performance artist called "The Wasted Apollinaires". The visibility of the text thwarts the New Critical-cum-deconstructive sense of the linguistic "idea" of the text: disrupting the idea of meaning as being hypermaterial (beyond its material embodiments). As such, renewed critical and hermeneutic attention to textual visibility is allied to the resurgence of bibliographic and socio-historical approaches in grounding poetry in its material and social contexts, in and of the world. Two recent works exemplify this movement: Jerome McGann's *Black Riders: The Visible Language of Modernism* and Johanna Drucker's *The Visible Word: Experimental Typography and Modern Art, 1909–1923*.

The Visible Word is a breakthrough study of the materiality of the visual representation of language. Johanna Drucker makes a fundamental contribution to aesthetics and the philosophy of language as well as providing a cogent application of her theoretical investigations to the visual and verbal arts of the modernist period.

Drucker provides a powerful critique of repression of the semantic contribution of the visible forms of writing, particularly typography, in the French philosophical and linguistic tradition from the structuralism inaugurated by Ferdinand de Saussure through such poststructuralist philosophers as Jacques Derrida. Drucker forces us to rethink a basic repression of the materiality of language (sight and sound) that had gone unchallenged not only within the French traditions and their American counterparts, but also within the separate literary traditions of New Criticism (and their successors) and the formalism of such art critics as Clement Greenberg and Michael Fried. No one before Drucker has made such a comprehensive statement on this issue, although her study follows in the wake of significant work in this area by Gerald Janacek, Marjorie Perloff, Mary Ann Caws, Willard Bohn, and Dick Higgins.

After its opening sallies against the windmills of linguistic dematerialization, *The Visible Word* settles into a more practical task: proving models for "close lookings" at the visual text of poems. As a preface to this task, Drucker presents an illuminating reading/looking at the interplay between the verbal and figural/visual elements of the inaugural work for modernist visual poetry: Mallarmé's *Un Coup de dés*. In what proves to be a keynote of her anti-reductive interpretive style, Drucker insists that Mallarmé's visual figuration is abstract and antimimetic, so that it cannot be translated into namable or sketchable equivalents. This resistance to interpretive closure, however, is not just a feature of *Un Coup de dés* but, Drucker argues, a feature of the destabilization inherent in visual-verbal interactions of the radical modernist typographic works that are the focus of her study.

With Mallarmé as the starting point, Drucker proceeds to reintegrate the common aesthetic and procedural approaches to materiality in modernist visual and literary art in order to establish experimental typography as a modern art practice. At the same time, Drucker aims to reverse the separation of the "purely visual" from the literary, which, she notes, becomes a foundational idea in much modernist criticism. In so doing, she charts how this highly problematic separation has played itself out in terms of representation versus presence, faktura versus autonomy. Drucker's revisionist history also questions the common misconception that radical modernist art is primarily concerned with "formal values for their own sake". By debunking such generalizations, she shifts the terms of discussion onto "the structure of relations among elements of signification".

In laying down the groundwork for interpreting typographic works, Drucker stresses the distinction, already present in Gutenberg's printing,

between marked and unmarked texts: "[Gutenberg's] bibles, with their per-
fectly uniform grey pages, their uninterrupted blocks of text, without
headings or subheading . . . are the archetype of the unmarked text, the
text in which the words on the page 'appear to speak themselves' . . . Such
a text appears to possess an authority which transcends the mere material
presence of words on a page." Drucker's book is a brief for the poetics of
the marked text. To make her case, she presents extended interpretations
of the work of four representative modernist figures, each of whom used
typography in strikingly innovative, but nonetheless dissimilar, ways. Her
account moves from the militant Italian Futurism of Filippo Marinetti to
the vernacular lyricism of Guillaume Apollinaire and from "hermetic eso-
tericism" of Ilia Zdanevich (Iliazd), a Russian *zaum* poet who emigrated to
Paris, to the highly rhetorical Dada subversions of Tristan Tzara.

Drucker traces the origins of modernist typographic experimentation
not only to Mallarmé but also both to the print advertising of the late 19th
century and to the typographic self-consciousness of, for example,
William Morris and the Arts and Crafts movement. Despite the sharp aes-
thetic, social, and political differences among these typographic practices,
Drucker sees their use of marked texts as "aggressively situat[ing] the
reader in relation to the various levels of enunciation in the text—reader,
speaker, subject, author—though with manipulative utilization of the
strategies of graphic design. Such inscription, obvious marking, of the as-
sumed reader, forces the language into a public domain".

The Visible Word closes with a discussion of the demise of typographic
experimentation, as the unruly incursions of language into public domain
are transformed by the "efficient" and "modern", which is to say uniformist,
principles of graphic design into contained, unified markers of corporate
identity and packaging.

The typographic containment and domestication of the unruly manu-
scripts of Emily Dickinson is the subject of Susan Howe's bibliographic
intervention in "The Illogic of Sumptuary Values". Her approach might be
seen as a vital counterpoint to Paul De Man's influential essay on disfigur-
ing Shelley in terms of the opposite direction of its interpretation of a
canonical English language poetic—toward displacement in De Man and
emplacement—to use Williams's word—in Howe.

Blake and Dickinson remain the two most intractable poets in the
English-language tradition. Both refused the assimilative processes of
publishing and distribution by creating works that defy easy entry into
standard formats of reprinting and dissemination. Indeed, for the most
part, we read Blake and Dickinson in visual translation or reproduction
rather than in the original.

Howe has gone well beyond previous Dickinson critics and editors in insisting on the visual integrity of Dickinson's manuscripts. She would have us read these works as much like drawings as like texts—a sensitivity to the significance of visual inscriptions that comes from Howe's own work as a painter (which immediately preceded her earliest poems). There is a fortuitous symmetry between Howe's discussion of Dickinson's linguistic graphicity and Renée Hubert's discussion of Antoni Tapies's quasi-verbal inscribings. When Hubert notes that "lines, splashes, fragments, and incisions are not to be taken at face value in their restrictions or limitations" and that "inscriptions finally reveal their kinship to scripture", it as if she has taken on the same subjects as Howe. Indeed, couldn't Dickinson's practice be described in these words of Hubert's on Tapies's ineffability: the painter—or poet—"has not only left lines, cleavages produced by invisible instruments or remnants resulting from unnamed occurrences, but also spots and strokes prolonging, so it would seem, defunct gestures"?

Howe's meticulously informed scholarship creates a crisis for Dickinson publishing—a crisis that Dickinson's self-appointed literary executors do not seem ready to confront. Cover-up will not be an inappropriate description of future Dickinson editions that do not acknowledge Howe's interventions. Howe demonstrates that there is no substitution for the originals—that all Dickinson's readers will benefit from reading the photoreproductions of her manuscripts, and I include in that high school readers as well, since these issues ought to be addressed as early as poetry is studied. Yet if we accept that typographic transcription is inevitable and even valuable, then Howe's typescripts—with radically different lineation and word-group endings than the Johnson versions—should be made available as soon as possible, not necessarily to replace, but to compete with, the Johnson transcriptions. If it is argued, contrawise, that some of us like these versions better because it conforms to certain postwar lineation practices, that is hardly an argument against these alternative versions, which after all appear to better conform to Dickinson's manuscripts, but rather can be seen as an advantage of time—that more of us are able to see linguistic significance in what most of Dickinson's contemporaries, previous critics, and editors have been quick to discount as insignificant. Howe's transforming of invisible or putatively insignificant details into semantically dynamic articulations typifies the history of Dickinson's reception since her death well over a century ago.

In the New York art world at this time, the use of language is commonplace. Yet many visual artists seem hostile to or ignorant of the literary or poetic traditions that are relevant to their language use. There seems, perhaps, to be a conscious effort to avoid anything but the most banal or trivial language, as if poetic language would pollute or corrupt by intimations of literary complexity or literary affiliation. This no-writing writing seems to want to have the suggestion or titillation of language without taking responsibility for articulation. The language in such works suggests the linguistic anonymity of billboards or advertisements, though rarely with the twisting or torquing of such language as is found in some of the more inventive poems of the past 30 years. I exempt from this indictment such sophisticated, poetically conscious, language users as Lawrence Weiner, Arakawa and Gins, Nancy Spero, Rogelio López Cuenca, Philip Guston and Clark Coolidge, or Robert Barry, as well as the conceptual interventions of Joseph Kosuth, whose neon signs replete with erasures are marvelously pointed.

My art world friends like to scold me when I go on this way: "Your problem is that you are reading the language; no one does that—just look at it." I admit it, then, I am out of my shallowness.

Jenny Holzer is one of the best installation artists of our time. I love, especially, the way she can and will ever too rarely speed up and slow down and blink and alternate the flow and direction of the words in her pieces: I'm always shocked how small a part that tends to play in her work overall. I enjoy being in dark gallery spaces with these fantastic illuminated linguistic totems. But when I start to read her repetitive and only half-intentionally trivial texts—such as "Abuse of Power Comes as No Surprise", "Myths Make Reality More Intelligible", or "Use the Dominant Culture to Change It More Quickly"—I wonder why she doesn't collaborate with a writer, or set already existing texts, say by Leslie Scalapino or Hannah Weiner or Kathy Acker, to lights. She's like a great composer who insists on writing her own libretto but only knows about one type of sentence structure and has never, apparently, read any other librettos. I'm amazed that writing that would be viewed in a literary context as largely derivative of quite interesting poetry of the 60s and 70s, can be either glossed over or praised to the extent that this work is. I find the situation demoralizing because it shows, finally, there is no more care for words in the artworld context than there is in the media, and, Barbara Kruger and Holzer notwithstanding, I do not find the project of using the dominant culture to change it more quickly, to quote one of Holzer's bronze-plaque texts, anything other than giving up. Contrast Holzer's economy of capitulation with Coolidge's "The road to excess leads to one's *Own Forms*," especially as scrawled by Guston in one of the Guston-Coolidge collaborations recently exhibited.

Because of my unease with Holzer's language, I appreciated Henry Sayre's discussion of how Holzer's *Truisms* "disenfranchise" the audience by "atomizing it"—that they preclude response or exchange by talk AT the audience, not with it: for this is a precise description of Holzer's adoption of what Sayre, citing Mark Poster's new book, *The Mode of Information*, calls the "electronic mode of information". Sayre makes the useful observation that in her recent work Holzer is "moving back from the decentered, dispersed, unstable conditions" of not only her earlier work, but also of the dominant form of electronic messaging. Yet it seems to me that it is precisely this sentimental regression in the new work that precipitates or accelerates what Sayre calls "a false sense of community, a simulacrum of community" by the imposition of the archly sentimental TV-news emotions of the chiselled upon coffins and "laments" motif that has a communicative style comparable to the truisms of national ceremonies at the Arlington cemetery replete with close-ups of weeping wives by graveside and the ambient sound of guns firing at slowed intervals to signify the gravity of the occasion.

Certainly Sayre's is one of the most interesting discussions of Holzer that I have heard and any future discussions of visible language will do well to consider the impact of electronic imaging. In that sense, Johanna Drucker's newest work, *Simulant Portrait*, her first computer-made work, with its investigations of what I keep thinking is sibilant but is really simulant female identity, would be interesting to think about in the frame Sayre provides.

That, though, brings to mind the question of simulant graphicity—that is, the representation of writing in electronic media (hypertext, videotext)—which is no doubt the most significant historical development in respect to the topic. It's striking that so much of the focus here has been on a rematerializing of the graphic, a project even more valuable in the gas plasma light of electronic alphabet imaging. But this is a subject for a future empaneling, or is it empanelment?

. . . For now, I'll just have time to answer the question I mentioned a little bit ago about my first typographical experience. But then again, some experiences are just too personal to remember.

From an Ongoing Interview with Tom Beckett

Tom Beckett: Does Language Poetry's dialectical heart beat in bipolar
relation to irony and alienation? Radically ironic poetry writing
(such as your own, or that of David Bromige, or Bruce Andrews)
does a wonderful job of underlining the alienating effects (and
affects) of language, while a text which is primarily non-ironical (I
am thinking here of characteristic work by people like Susan Howe,
Lyn Hejinian, & Ron Silliman) may actually counter alienation to the
extent that the reader feels encouraged to actively engage the text
and to co-produce its meaning(s). What do you think?

Charles Bernstein: You say *ironic* I say comic, you say *alienated*
    I say *disaffected*—besides I'm no alien, I'm from New York!
    You've got to make the bridge before you can (double)
    cross it. Give me a place to stand and I will look for
    a place to sit. A poem should be at least as funny as
    watching paint dry in the Cenozoic moonlight.
    It's only a joke but then it's only a poem.
    As Amberian has written:
    In one-liners, there truth dwells in its [lowest] tracings
    [lit. most base, close to the ground].
    What was it Freud said about jokes, it slips my mind?
    In the great historic project of undermining the hegemony
    of men's authoritative discourse, humor finds it hard
    to keep a straight face. Is verse lite slighted?
    Or is it one of those urban versus—
    what do you call it now?—nonurban? issues,
    in that much of the distrust of the comic extends a pastoral
    and lyric tradition, a poetics of sincerity,
    that the hyperironic (including the panironic, postironic,
    malironic, catironic, and parironic), what you call radically
        ironic poetry, actually
    works to erode. But then, if you don't distrust the comic

what *are* you going to distrust? Just let me take off this
truss! To quote Amberian again
Sincerity is closest to deception
which no doubt echoes the well-known proverb,
"Beware a sincere man selling fish",
which means, roughly, judge a *man* by what he says
not by his force of conviction or tone of veracity.
Can we talk?
Sincerity is the last refuge of scoundrels,
profundity an ingredient in every devil's potion,
&, hey, you!, don't tell me about love when you're
turning your back on me as if to talk to some
Higher Authority. The only Higher Authority I know
about is my landlord and I already paid her this month.
Against High Seriousness as such!
I'm for a men's poetry that questions the importance
of earnest anguish, of new-found sensitivity,
of subjective acumen as market "tool", that wants
to make fun of much that men hold dear. Surely
there be that delight in giddiness, in which the ecstatic
refuses to valorize itself. The raucous, the silly,
the foolish render the viscosity of the world's
vicissitudes. *The shortest distance from transcendence
to immanence is hilarity.*

Let there be one, two, many languaging poetries! (There always
have been.) Let readers coproduce meanings and let meanings
coproduce readers! Let alienation be encountered so that
alienation can be countered! Let counters be mixers and
mixers be movers and movers put up big tents for lots of
acts. And let disaffection melt away in the sounds of
laughter so that grief may compose itself in the space
between the laughs.

So, Tom, me, ironic? I'll admit I'm funny, but not funny
enough. Now Bromige he *is* funny. But Bruce I'd say is more
scary, that is if society scares you as much as it
does me. & yet, I hear something of this comedic poetics
in Silliman's puns and non sequiturs and in his
prodigious love of orphaned details; I find it always
in Hejinian's astonished whimsy and whimsical astonishment,
and in her bemused insistence on the facts of form;
I see it, surely, in the figure of Howe's Hope Atherton,

a Chaplinesque sojourner in the wilderness of signs, and
in the sublime wackiness of her typographic inversions.

TB: In "The Lives of the Toll Takers" (in *Dark City*) you have written:

> The hidden language of the Jews: self-reproach, laden with am-
> bivalence, not this or this either, seeing five sides to every issue,
> the old pilpul song and dance, obfuscation clowning as ingra-
> tiation, whose only motivation is never offend, criticize only
> with a discountable barb: Genocide is made of words like these,
> Pound laughing (with Nietzsche's gay laughter) all the way to
> the canon's bank spewing forth about the concrete value of
> gold, the "plain sense of the word", a people rooted in the land
> they sow, and cashing in on such verbal usury (language held
> hostage: year one thousand nine hundred eighty seven).

I was moved by that passage. It is rich with associative possibili-
ties—personal, literary, political—and yet, within the darkly zany,
satirical collage-logic of the poem, it sticks out (like a hitchhiker's
forward pointing, backward walking thumb) as singular commen-
tary. I still want to explore with you issues relating to irony and
alienation. Maybe if you could speak to the issues raised by the
quoted passage in relation to the larger architectures of the poem it
appears in we could move ahead another step. Or maybe I should
just ask you: For whom do the Toll Takers toil?

CB: I suppose the passage of a year, the time
       it has taken me to begin to respond
       to your question, is not an answer
       but a further elaboration, or belaboring.
       I'm wondering what gives ground
       for the sort of statement you cite, as if
       the zaniness of the surround makes a space
       for truthfulness divested of the patina of
       truth, what Alan Davies, in one of his essays,
       calls "lies that have hardened".

       The passage you ask about refers to Sander Gilman's
       Jewish Self-Hatred, which it diagnoses as a
       state in which a person internalizes the racist
       stereotype that their true language is not the one
       they speak but an imaginary "hidden language
       of the Jews". Gilman's study centers on the

delusion that the Jews can never be "native"
or even competent speakers of their own language;
for the anti-Semite rejects the possibility
that Jews can assimilate into the language, and
culture, that they can make it as their own. That
echoes with Pound's idea of Jewish rootlessness
but also gives social dimension to my preoccupation
with the radical morphogenerativeness of language
and its related instability and ambiguity, its
unsettling and polydictory logics, which constitute,
rather than impede, our mutual grounding in language
as a grounding in each other that forms the basis not
of nations or ethnicities or races but of polis.

I take this as an aesthetic practice that repudiates the moral
discourse of a right to speak as a racial or national
patrimony, and also a right way to speak. This is a lesson I
learned not from Pound and Eliot, exactly, but from Stein,
from Reznikoff and Zukofsky, and also from Groucho Marx
and Lenny Bruce.

"Hands, hearts, not values made us."

Language extracts a toll from all who use it
but having paid this toll, access is unlimited.
No one who speaks can fail to pay this toll
and the profit extracted is returned to the fold.

So dunnah ask
Fer whom duh toll takers toils—
Dey toil for youse.

TB: *Work*, I hiccup, like Maynard G. Krebs.
  You are a poet, theorist, Professor of English, a founder of the
Poetics Program at SUNY-Buffalo. You are also a vociferous critic of
what you have termed "official verse culture," as well as a champion
of the small press movement. From your unique vantage point, (a)
what do you consider to be the role of the poet in society, and (b)
what social impediments to the enactment of that role do you see.

CB: The role of the poet in society is to
           roll, i.e., not
           get stuck
           don't worry about the bumps, &

don't forget to bring a salami.
Or we are on a roll but nobody
knows it (if a poet roils society
but nobody hears it, did she really
roil, or just rock?). I wouldn't
join a society that would have me as a member.
I wouldn't join a society that would have
you as a member. And another thing too:
That's no society that's a public space.
The poet aims to shoo the fly off the flypaper
(for fly read reader, for flypaper read society).
I'm sick and tired of your society, I'm going
straight to the mall and buy me a new one
at the Society Shoppe.
Most of the poets who have a role in society
are giving poetry a bad name.
What this society needs is a good
five-cent Skeltonic.
(Let me help you unwrap the gauze.)
I've got a few words
& some new rhythms in my head
let me see what I can come up with.

There are no social impediments to a poet doing her
or his job since these impediments create the conditions
for the work; our problems are primarily technical and
ethical. But, boy, do we have some problems,
let me tell you . . .

Poets are the punching bags of society
& as I say, I recommend rolling with the punches.
But better still is ducking.
Now as to duck, I prefer it extra crisp
& if that makes me a francophile
so be it . . .
In any case, never take a punch sitting
down; run or at least walk rapidly,
hop or skip to the loo; unless it is a
fruit punch—that's good sitting or
standing but not jumping.

But, seriously, Tom, you were saying . . . ?
I got lost somewhere between the sentences
right in the middle of the verses.

Explicit Version Number Required

Years later and even the memory of evanescence
had passed. The sink, loaded with a lifetime
of dishes, was bigger than a stack of Uncle
Matt's molasses jack; and the inflections on the
thoroughfare were crowded with deputation.
Going down in a nosedive through the slatted
torquing of gilt intentions, liturgic ambassador
to intervalic invention, eyeing schlock absorbers
in the pouring light. *Think digitally,*
act analogically! The silhouette of the child
standing on the jetty in the bright sun
blows a hole through the rivulets
in the curtain of the casing of my
1966 Ford Escort convertible, elbowing out
interminable incentives to row the bloke
to Angelic paradigms bursting with waxy
savvy from the long halt; thus by ordinate demand
demonstrating the abiding circus of incapacity's
love of reeling rapture in the maimed
vision of circumnavigation's song. Spending
the day and only asking what it costs later.
Version of make-believe turning out to be shadow
boxing. "He saw the gap and took it." BETTER
A SORROWER THAN A FENDER BEAM. Before the dream
was the sleep, punctuated by endoscopic rigmarole.
FOCUS ON THE LOSS: I once was timed but now I'm
fixed rate. As if action were a substitute for glass.
All that is irritating melts into hemorrhoids: moral
fiber just another word for . . . consideration. Blush
and the world blushes with you, or not. Poetry fakes
nothing actually. *Poetry fakes nothing happening.*
& the dead deride the dead while the living forget to pay
attention. It is a large, crowded hall, perhaps an
amphitheater. We are in the audience.

Hinge Picture

George Oppen's *Of Being Numerous* is a poetry of constructive witness: the witness of a social becoming that "presses on each"[1] and in which each, all, are impressed.

Oppen's achievement has little to do with speech or sight, but with speech *as* sight, site of the social. Not perception but *acts of* perception, not the given but the *encountered*, as Oppen suggests in "The Mind's Own Place".[2] Sight in Oppen's work is not a passive looking onto the world but a means of touching that invests the world with particular, site-specific (historical, material) meanings. Without this touching—tooling, tuning—the world becomes empty, voided.

"Near is / Knowledge" (176). Or, as Hölderlin has it in "Patmos", "Near is / And difficult to grasp." Oppen's engendering witness stipulates both the integrity of things seen and their contingency—"the known and unknown". "Because the known and unknown / Touch, // One witnesses—" (172). The intersection of these vectors of response creates the "here" of a "real" we confront, a real which we come to know by participating in its making. ("Here still" [177].) This poetics of participatory, or constructive, presentness—akin especially to Creeley's—is Oppen's response to "the shipwreck / Of the singular" (151). The "singular" that has been lost is, in one sense, a unitary system of value or knowledge based on reason or theology ("The unearthly bonds / Of the singular" [152]). For Oppen, there is no neo-Nietzschean rejoicing in this loss. Rather, "The absolute singular" is related to what Walter Benjamin has called the Messianic Moment—out-of-time, out-of-history. "To dream of that beach / For the sake of an instant in the eyes" (152). For Oppen, however, there is another singularity, the potential for social collectivity: "one must not come to feel that he has a thousand threads in his hands, / He must somehow see the one thing; / This is the level of art / There are other levels / But there is no other level of art" (168). "Not truth but each other" (173).

1. *The Collected Poems of George Oppen* (New York: New Directions, 1975), p. 150. Subsequent references are given in the text.
2. *Kulchur* (1963); reprinted in *Montemora* 1 (1975).

Which is to say that, in *Of Being Numerous*, the loss of the "transcenden-
tal signified" does not necessitate the abandonment, or absence, of knowl-
edge but its *location* in history, in "people". This view entails both a rejec-
tion of the crude materialism of things without history and the crude
idealism of history without things. Materials in circumstance, as Oppen
puts it (186): the "actual" realized by the manipulation of materials by
human hands, tools. It is this process that is played out in Oppen's poetry
by the insistence on the constructedness of syntax: the manipulation of
words to create rather than describe.

Of Being Numerous forges a syntax of truthfulness without recourse to the
grammar of truth—"that truthfulness / Which illumines speech" (173).
The poem's necessarily precarious project is the articulation of a form that
would address the commonweal, a project most fully realized in the two
long poems in *Of Being Numerous*. For Oppen, the demands of the articula-
tion of an ideal communication situation necessitate a winnowing of
vocabulary and tone that entails the exclusion of anything that would
extend, displace, amplify, distort, burst—indeed, *question*—the vocables
of an enunciated truthfulness. At his most resonant, Oppen creates a mag-
nificent, prophetic, imaginary language—less voice than chiselled sounds.
His writing evokes not the clamor of the streets nor the windiness of con-
versation nor the bombast of the "dialogic" but the indwelling possibili-
ties of words to speak starkly and with urgency.

Yet Oppen's often claimed commitment to clarity, however qualified,
annuls a number of possibilities inherent in his technique. He hints at this
when he writes, "Words cannot be wholly transparent. And that is the
heartlessness of words" (186). ("Clarity", he has just said, "In the sense of
transparence" [162].) In contrast, it is their very intractability that makes for
the unconsumable *heart* (heartiness) of words. Inverting Oppen's criticism
that Zukofsky used "obscurity in the writing as a tactic",[3] I would say that
Oppen uses clarity as a tactic. That is, at times he tends to fall back onto
"clarity" as a self-justifying means of achieving resolution through scenic
motifs, statement, or parable in poems that might, given his compositional
techniques, outstrip such controlling impulses.

Oppen's syntax is fashioned on constructive, rather than mimetic, prin-
ciples. He is quite explicit about this. Carpentry is a recurring image of
poem-making. His poems, as he tells it, were created by a sort of collage
or cut-up technique involving innumerable substitutions and permutations
for every word and line choice. The method here is paratactic, even if
often used for hypotactic ends. This tension, which can produce the ki-

---

3. Burton Hatlen and Tom Mandel, "Poetry and Politics: A Conversation with George and
Mary Oppen", in *George Oppen: Man and Poet*, ed. Hatlen (Orono, Maine: National Poetry Foun-
dation, 1981), p. 45.

netic, stuttering vibrancy of some of Oppen's most intense poems, is at the heart of his use of the line break as hinge. In contrast to both enjambment and disjunction—as well, of course, as more conventional static techniques—Oppen's hinging allows for a measure of intervallic "widths" of connection/disconnection between lines. The typical Oppen hinge is made by starting a line with a preposition, commonly "Of". At its most riveting, this hinging taps into a horizontally moving synaptic/syntactic energy at the point of line transition.

Discrete Series uses this orchestration of lacunae in the most radical and open-ended way. (Could the 25-year gap between *Discrete Series* and *The Materials* be Oppen's grandest hinged interval?) In some of the later works, he abandons any angularity in his lineation, at the same time allowing an almost symbolic or allegorical vocabulary ("sea", "children") to take hold. Nonetheless, the possibilities of his use of the line as hinge are omnipresent in the work—and influential. Indeed, the hinge suggests an interesting way to sort through aspects of Oppen's influence, since there is some work that may resemble his but which misses the radical (in the sense of root) nature of his lineation.

The following stanzas were generated using an acrostic procedure (G-E-O-R-G-E O-P-P-E-N) to select lines, in page sequence, from *Collected Poems*. I have borrowed this procedure from Jackson Mac Low. That these poems are so characteristically Oppenesque is, I think, less the effect of familiar lines or typical references than the way single Oppen lines can be hinged to "each other" to create the marvelous syntactic music found throughout his work. I hope the structural allegory is apparent: the autonomy of the root, of the individual, allowing for the music of the social, the numerous.

> Grasp of me)
> Eyes legs arms hands fingers,
> On the cobbles;
> Reaches the generic, gratuitous
> Geared in the loose mechanics of the world with the
>   valves jumping
> Endlessly, endlessly,
>
> Outside, and so beautiful.
> Populace, sea-borne and violent, finding
> Passing, the curl at cutwater,
> Ends its metaphysic
> Nature! because we find the others

Generations to a Sunday that holds
Exterior. 'Peninsula
Of the subway and painfully
Re-arrange itself, assert
Grand Central's hollow masonry, veined
Eyes. The patent

Of each other's backs and shoulders
Planned, the city trees
Proud to have learned survival
Effortless, the soft lips
Nuzzle and the alien soft teeth

Glassed
Echo like history
One by one proceeding
Rectangular buildings
Growing at its edges! It is a place its women
Early. That was earlier.

Out of scale
Picturing the concrete walls.
Plunge and drip in the seas, carpenter,
Enduring
New in its oil

Good bye Momma,
Each day, the little grain
Of all our fathers
Ring electronically the New Year
Grows, grass
Enterprise.

On the sloping bank—I cannot know
Pours and pours past Albany
Perhaps the world
Even here is its noise seething
Now as always Crusoe

Gave way to the JetStream
Entity
Of substance
Rectangular buildings
Generation
Exposes the new day,

Of living,
Paris is beautiful and ludicrous, the leaves of every tree
    in the city move in the wind
People talk, they talk to each other;
Even Cortes greeted as revelation . . . No I'd not
    emigrate,
Now we do most of the killing

Glass of the glass sea shadow of water
Elephant, say, scraping its dry sides
Of veracity that huge art whose geometric
Recalling flimsy Western ranches
Gravel underfoot
Enemies in the sidewalks and when the stars rise

Other
Piled on each other   lean
Precision of place the rock's place in the fog we suffer
Early in the year cold and windy on the sea the wind
Night—sky   bird's world

Reznikoff's Nearness

I

1. Charles Reznikoff was born in Brooklyn in 1894. The date is interesting because Reznikoff is somewhat older than the poets of the "second wave" of radical modernism, with whom he is often associated. Zukofsky, for example, was born in 1904, Oppen in 1908, Bunting in 1900, Riding in 1901, Hughes in 1902, while Toomer was born in the same year as Reznikoff. Sterling Brown, with whom Reznikoff shared the great project of using the American historical record of injustice and social barbarism as a primary subject, was born seven years after him.

2. Reznikoff is a bridge figure between Williams, the poet he most resembles, and a decade older than he, and the poets born at the turn of the century, a decade after him. Like Williams, he came from a family in which English was not a native tongue. His parents (like my own grandparents) came from Russia, sometime after 1881; his paternal grandparents joined the family somewhat later.

His mother's father, Ezekiel, never made it to the New World, having died before Reznikoff was born. Ezekiel, a cattle and wheat broker, had written Hebrew verse on his travels. Just after he died his wife destroyed all trace of his writings, fearing his manuscripts might contain material that would create trouble for the family if discovered by the Tzarist authorities. The destruction of his grandfather's poetry is an emblematic story for Reznikoff and he comes back to it in two poems, the first opening *By the Well of Living and Seeing*:

> My grandfather, dead long before I was born,
> died among strangers; and all the verse he wrote
> was lost—
> except for what
> still speaks through me
> as mine.[1]

1. *By the Well of Living and Seeing* (1969), sec. I, poem #1, in *The Complete Poems of Charles Reznikoff*, vol.2, ed. Seamus Cooney (Santa Barbara: Black Sparrow Press, 1977), 91. Subsequent references to this volume are preceded by "2".

The poetic or psychic economy suggested here helps to explain Reznikoff's resolve to continue with his work in the face of intense waves of indifference, indeed his resolve to ensure that his own verse would not disappear entirely: "I would leave no writing of mine, / if I could help it, / to the mercy of those who loved me".[2] Reznikoff's work echoes this subtext in a number of ways: the poems are an act of recovery—where recovery becomes a project of immense proportion far beyond this initial point of focus. A few times, the poems register the difficulty of this recovery in terms of the poet's loss, or exile from, Hebrew, a language he does not really know (Reznikoff's parents would have spoken Yiddish and increasingly English), but which seems part of his identity.

Reznikoff tells the tale of his parent's life in Russia and of their painfully difficult work in the New York rag trade in scrupulous and informative detail in two remarkable autobiographical works, "Early History of a Seamstress" and "Early History of Sewing Machine Operator", as well as in his own continuation of their story in "Needle Trade".[3]

3. Reznikoff attended Boys' High School in Brooklyn and from 1910 to 1911 went to the School of Journalism at the University of Missouri. During the following year, he worked as a salesman for his parents' millinery business. But in 1912, remembering that Heine (the reference may at first seem peculiar but begins to make sense) had gone to law school, he enrolled at NYU. Reznikoff graduated law school in 1916 and was admitted to the bar the same year.

4. Legal studies provided Reznikoff a sharp contrast to the poetics of metaphysical and Symbolic overtone, of fashionable literary conceits and static ornamentation. Indeed, legal argument provided an analogue for the poetic principles he did find interesting, such as the "brand new verse" of Pound and H.D., which he read in *Poetry* when he was 21 and studying law.[4] It was at this time that he first formulated a poetics that emphasized

---

The story of the destruction of his grandfather's poetry is part of his mother's narrative in "Early History of a Seamstress" (1929) (published as part of Reznikoff's *Family Chronicle*) and is repeated in his 1930 novel *By the Waters of Manhattan,* whose first half recasts "Early History"— less successfully to my reading—into the third person, leaving the rest almost entirely unchanged. Reznikoff alludes to the burning of his grandfather's "bulky" manuscript again a few pages before the end of the novel.

2. *By the Well of Living and Seeing,* sec. III, "Early History of a Writer", #17 (excerpt), 2:176.

3. These three works were brought together as *Family Chronicle*—a masterpiece of historical autobiography (a genre more commonly presented today as oral history). First published in England under this title by Norman Bailey & Co., it was published by Universe Books, New York, in 1971, with a perfunctory introduction by the Jewish chronicler and humorist Harry Golden.

4. "Charles Reznikoff: A Talk with L. S. Dembo", in *Charles Reznikoff: Man and Poet,* ed. Milton Hindus (Orono, Maine: National Poetry Foundation, 1984), p. 98.

"the pithy, the necessary, the clear, and plain" [#17, 2:172], principles that, like most of his statements of poetics, stressed what he was breaking away from (the influence of Pound is unmistakable) more than the new poetic space he was inventing.

Remembering his years at law school, Reznikoff writes:

I found it delightful
to climb those green heights,
to bathe in the clear waters of reason,
to use words for their daylight meaning
and not as prisms
playing with the rainbows of connotation:

. . .

I had been bothered by a secret weariness
with meter and regular stanzas
grown a little stale. The smooth lines and rhymes
seemed to me affected, a false stress on words and syllables—
fake flowers
in the streets which I walked.

. . .

The brand new verse some Americans were beginning to write—
after the French "free verse" perhaps

. . .

seemed to me, when I first read it,
right:
not cut to patterns, however cleverly,
nor poured into ready molds[5]

5. After a very brief attempt to start a law practice, Reznikoff returned to millinery sales, saying his "mind was free" as he waited for hours to see the buyers at Macy's.

Reznikoff claims to have been very good at selling ladies' hats, although his wife Marie Syrkin, in her marvelous memoir, demurs on this point.[6]

In 1918, *Rhythms*, Reznikoff's first book, was privately printed and distributed—just one year after Pound's first *Cantos*. Reznikoff kept in mind the fate of his grandfather's poetry in choosing to arrange for the printing on his own. He also showed an independence from literary fashion and career that would mark his entire life.

Two years later, in 1920, Samuel Roth published his *Poems* in an edition of 250.

5. "Early History of a Writer", #16 (excerpt), 2:168–71.
6. Marie Syrkin, "Charles: A Memoir", in *Man and Poet*.

6. In 1927, Reznikoff bought his own press, setting the type and printing *Five Groups of Verse* in an edition of 375 copies, and later *Nine Plays* in an edition of 400 copies. During this time, he was able to stop working entirely, living on a very modest income of $25 per week from his parents.

7. Reznikoff seemed to accept the fact that there was, and would be, little interest in his poetry. But by the late 1920s he had met Zukofsky and George and Mary Oppen; they formed not a school but a small circle of support and mutual interest in each other's work—there was, for a while, a pool of light in a world of poetic darkness:

> against the darkness:
> a quadrangle of light[7]

8. In 1927 and 1928, Ezra Pound had included in his magazine *The Exile* poems by Williams and Zukofsky, McAlmon and Rakosi, as well as Reznikoff. In '28, Pound wrote Zukofsky that he ought to bring together a group of younger poets.[8]

In February 1931, Harriet Monroe's *Poetry* published a special issue edited by Zukofsky that began with a short statement, "Program 'Objectivists' 1931" immediately followed by an essay entitled "Sincerity and Objectification with Special Reference to Charles Reznikoff". As compared to the far longer manuscript version, the published essay cut references to Reznikoff's neglect and to his plays, altogether eliminating about half the original citations to Reznikoff's work; this process of elimination was radically accelerated in the intervening years so that in Zukofsky's collected essays, *Prepositions* (1977), all references to Reznikoff are removed for the final, citationless, distillation of Zukofsky's thought, now titled simply "An Objective".[9] Reznikoff was not alone in his obsession to cut and keep cutting.

From 1931 to 1932, the Oppens published three books (Pound, Williams, and Zukofsky's An "Objectivists" Anthology) under the imprint, To Publishers, with Zukofsky as the press editor.

In 1934, Zukofsky, Reznikoff, and the Oppens founded the Objectivist Press, with the advice of Williams and Pound. That first year they published Williams's *Collected Poems*, edited by Zukofsky with an introduction by Stevens, in an edition of 500 copies. Williams put up $250 of which $150 was refunded.[10] Reznikoff was much surprised to find their first book

7. *By the Well of the Living and Seeing*, sec. II, #33, 2:136.

8. Thomas Frederick Sharp, *"Objectivists" 1927–1934: A Critical History of the Work and Association of Louis Zukofsky, William Carlos Williams, Charles Reznikoff* (Ann Arbor: University Microfilms, 1984), p. 21.

9. Ibid., p. 206. *Man and Poet* reprints the *Poetry* version of the essay, pp. 377–88.

10. Sharp, *Objectivists*, p. 505.

REZNIKOFF'S NEARNESS   201

reviewed by *The New York Times;* it sold better than expected. In 1934, the Objectivist Press also published Oppen's *Discrete Series;* after that, Oppen stopped writing for 20 years. Finally, in the same year, the press published the initial installment of Reznikoff's *Testimony,* with an introduction by Kenneth Burke, in an edition of 200 copies.

Three years later, in 1937, New Directions was founded, and began publishing Pound, Williams, and others.

9. Reznikoff met Marie Syrkin in 1929 and they were married the next year.[11]

At around this time (Hindus says 1928, but Syrkin says 1930), Reznikoff's parents' businesses went bad and, like many other small businesses during the Depression, they went into debt. Not only had he lost his meager income, but also Reznikoff was now obliged to help out his family. Reluctantly, he took a job at *Corpus Juris,* a legal encyclopedia, as a copywriter. Eventually, he was fired from *Corpus Juris.* Syrkin recalls the editor telling him, "When I hire a carpenter I don't want a cabinetmaker."[12]

10. From 1938 to 1939 Reznikoff went to Hollywood for a $75-a-week job as a quite peripheral writer for a movie studio where an old friend worked. This period is described in his posthumously published novel, *The Manner Music,* a book that includes prose adaptations—less musical, less shapely—of at least nine of his late poems. The novel ends with the protagonist—an unrecognized, perhaps unrecognizable, artist—burning all of his work, again bringing to mind the destruction by fire of Reznikoff's grandfather's verse: "He tore up everything, everything he has ever written and burnt it. They found the heap of ashes next to him when they took him to the hospital."[13]

When Reznikoff returned to New York, he worked at a number of odd editorial and research jobs, including writing a history of the Jewish community of Charleston and editing the papers of Louis Marshall.

11. Between 1941 and 1959 Reznikoff did not publish any books, although he continued to work on his poems and his anti-epic, *Testimony.*

12. In 1948, Reznikoff received a letter from Williams: "A confession and

11. Syrkin had first read Reznikoff in 1920, while a college student at Cornell. "My particular friend at Cornell was Laura Reichenthal, later Laura Riding, and I had already been exposed to strains of modernist verse. But the culture had not taken. My first reaction to Charles's verse was negative" (Syrkin, "Charles", p. 37). The Reznikoff-Riding connection, albeit oblique, is fascinating.

12. Ibid., p. 45. See also Milton Hindus, "Introduction", in *Man and Poet.*

13. Charles Reznikoff, *The Manner Music,* with an introduction by Robert Creeley (Santa Barbara: Black Sparrow Press, 1977), p. 128. Prose versions of Reznikoff's poems can be found beginning on pp. 15, 19, 25, 27, 28, 58, 60, 77, and 115.

an acknowledgment! In all these years that I have owned a book of yours, nineteen years! a book you gave me in 1929 I never so much opened it— except to look at it cursorily. And now, during an illness, I have read it and I am thrilled with it."[14]

13. In the 1950s, while Syrkin was teaching at Brandeis, Reznikoff became managing editor, at $100 a week, of *Jewish Frontier,* a labor Zionist monthly with which Syrkin was involved. "With no aptitude for journalism," Syrkin recalls, "he despised the facile generalizations of the craft and the superficial editorials . . . in response to a current crisis . . . I had to contain his natural inclination to reduce pages to paragraphs and paragraphs to sentences."

The printers, however, appreciated his incredible meticulousness. "That he was a 'poet,' a designation privately equated with schlemiel, explained any failure to fit into a familiar mold."[15]

14. When he turned 68, in 1962, New Direction published a selection of his poems, *By the Waters of Manhattan,* with an introduction by C. P. Snow, and subsequently published the first volume of *Testimony.* In 1968, however, the publisher turned down the second volume of *Testimony* and Reznikoff arranged to have it printed privately in an edition of 200.

15. In 1975, Black Sparrow published *Holocaust,* based, as *Testimony,* not on firsthand reports but exclusively on court records, here from the Nuremberg and the Eichmann trials.

16. In 1976, with the first volume of his *Complete Poems* in press from Black Sparrow, Charles Reznikoff died.

II

The Abbaye de Royaumont, not far from Paris, was a center of Christendom in the 13th century, when it was built. During the Revolution, it sustained heavy damages and the abbey has never been fully reconstructed. In recent years Royaumont has been used as a literary, music, and business conference center.

In the fall of 1989, Royaumont was site for a conference on the American "Objectivist" Poets, a group more prominent in the French map of American poetry than in many of our homemade maps. The library of Royaumont, with its 40-foot ceilings and walls lined with ancient books, was an extraordinary setting for an occasion honoring four relatively obscure American poets, whose parents had come from Europe from Jewish shtetels to settle into the New World. Even more extraordinary, the conference began at sunset on the Friday night upon which fell Rosh Hashonah, the Jewish New Year.

At the invitation of Emmanuel Hocquard, who has translated Reznikoff's The Man-

14. Quoted by Hindus in *Man and Poet,* pp. 31–32.
15. Syrkin, "Charles", pp. 53–54.

ner Music into French, Michael Palmer, Michael Davidson, Lyn Hejinian, David Bromige, and I had come from America to speak on one or another of the "Objectivists", while Carl Rakosi gave a reading and commented on many of the talks presented.

I had brought along a tape of Reznikoff reading in 1974 at the Poetry Center of San Francisco State, along with a transcript of the 46 poems, and fragments of poems, he had selected for that reading, which I had cut and pasted together, as he must have done in constructing this sequence, from almost every section and period of his poetry. The following remarks are based on that talk.

1. How does a poem, these poems, enter the world?

2.—Measured and scaled, particular and necessary: that would be one answer. Reznikoff's gives his own "platform as a writer of verse", as he wryly puts it in an introduction to the reading, given when was 80, at the Poetry Center of San Francisco State:

> Salmon and red wine
> and a cake fat with raisins and nuts:
> no diet for a writer of verse
> who must learn to fast
> and drink water by measure.[16]

Reznikoff's selection, at the Poetry Center reading, of work from over 60 years of writing is a masterful weave—"mastermix"—creating not "the intricate medallions the Persians know"[17] but a discrete series of poetic encounters that marks his work from beginning to end, without end or beginning.

3. *Rhythms*, in 1918, marks the invention of literary cubo-serialism. By cubo-seriality, I mean to identify the more discreet development that characterizes Reznikoff's work from that point in 1918 on—the permutation of briefly etched, identifiable details that don't quite stand on their own and that are separated by a gap, or interval, that requires a full stop. The prefix suggests rhetorically consonant permutations of angles of view on related (or linked) subjects.

4. From his 1927 collection *Five Groups of Verse* (which included *Rhythms*), Reznikoff numbered each of his often quite tiny poems and ran them together on the page, rather than isolating each poem on its own page (as he had up to this point) or separating the poems in some other way. This very explicit, even intrusive, numbering expresses Reznikoff's radical commitment to the poetic sequence, or series, as details open to reordering.

16. *Inscriptions: 1944–1956*, #23 (excerpt), 2:76. This poem is also quoted below in section 8. In the Poetry Center reading, Reznikoff called this poem, and #21, discussed below, his "platform".

17. Ibid., #21 (excerpt), 2:75.

In Reznikoff, the process of composition is as much a matter of the shaping of sequences as of the creation of particular elements of the sequence: the otherwise unrepresentable (and overlooked) space between poems has become the location of the work's poesis of unfolding and refolding, separating and recongealing. In Reznikoff, the meaning of the poem is always twofold: both in the detail and in its sequence. That is, the detail works in counterpoint to its locus in a series to create the meaning of the poem.

Reading Reznikoff formally means attending to the relation of the part to the whole (and the whole to the part) in his work, along lines that also suggest the relation of the shot to the sequence (in film and photography), surface to depth (in painting but also in rhetoric), the fragment to the total (in philosophy but also in *Kabbalah*).

To create the text of his 1974 reading, Reznikoff stitched together 46 individual bits and pieces. As with any work of disjunctive collage, each frame or unit recontextualizes the subsequent frame or unit. Reznikoff's "groups" (as he sometimes called them) are not governed by a principle external to the compositional process—his series are not ordered narratively, or chronologically, or historically; there is no necessarily logical or causal connection between the links of the chain. Rather, Reznikoff employs a variety of thematic and tonal shifts to create an overall "musical" arrangement, to use his own phrase for the process. What Reznikoff calls, right from the first book, "Rhythms":

"The ceaseless weaving of the uneven water."[18]

5. There is no poet more dedicated to foregrounding the detail and the particular than Reznikoff and no poet more averse to blending these details into a consuming or totalizing form. The numbers that obtrude into the visual field of almost every page of Reznikoff's verse represent both this commitment and aversion. This is not to deny that the individual sections add up to a larger form, but to affirm that the particularity and integrity of each detail is not diminished by the newly forming whole. While this structural allegory of polis echoes through the work of several of his contemporaries, notably Williams, Oppen, and Zukofsky, it is Reznikoff's tenacity combined with an uncanny lack of didacticism that especially characterizes his approach.

Reznikoff rejected the "depth" of field simulated by various realist and mimetic self-centering procedures in which each detail is subordinated to an overall image or theme or meaning. By constantly intercutting, or jump cutting, between and among and within material, the poem's surface of

18. "Aphrodite Vrania", in *Poems* (1920), #25, in *The Complete Poems of Charles Reznikoff*, vol. 1, ed. Seamus Cooney (Santa Barbara: Black Sparrow Press, 1976), p. 36. Subsequent references to this volume are preceded by "1".

local particularities gains primacy, in contrast to the rhetorical depth of narrative closure that is aimed for in such "epic" montage formats as *The Waste Land* and certain of the *Cantos* (not to mention more conventional poetry). Reznikoff's network of stoppages is anti-epic. It enacts an economy of perambulation and coincidence, of loss rather than accumulation (a general rather than a restricted economy in Bataille's terms).

> Scrap of paper
> blown about the street,
> you would like to be cherished, I suppose,
> like a bank-note [19]

Pound's disinterest in Reznikoff is foundational.

6. Parataxis is a manner of transition. Elements are threaded together like links on a chain, periodically rather than hierarchically ordered and without the subordination of part to whole. The *OED* defines parataxis as "the placing of propositions or clauses one after another, without indicating by connecting words the relation (of coordination or subordination) between them."

Parataxis is a grammatical state of adjacency, of being next to or side by side. Besideness. As the mind lies next to its object, or one finds oneself a neighbor in conversation, or in reflection one thought follows the next. A nonlinear network of interconnections.

7. As a term of art, adjacency is distinguished from adjoining or abutting, as land that is adjacent to a common square, but nowhere touches.

Reznikoff's is an art of adjacency, each frame carefully articulated and set beside the next.

8. Reznikoff's cubo-seriality is modular and multidirectional, marking a series of sites available to rearrangement in ever new constellations of occurrence. (Reznikoff's own refiguring of his lifework at the 1974 Poetry Center reading is a model for this potential for reconfiguration.) Resembling the long walks through the city he took every morning, Reznikoff's poems move from site to site without destination, each site inscribing an inhabitation, every dwelling temporary—contingent but sufficient.

> Those of us without house and ground
> who leave tomorrow
> must keep our baggage light:
> a psalm, perhaps a dialogue . . . [20]

---

19. *Inscriptions*, #24, 2:76.
20. Ibid., #23. The final stanza of this three-stanza poem is quoted immediately below.

—so Reznikoff continues his "platform". "Without house and ground" hints of the wandering of exile and the absence of foundations, but this nomadic poetry refuses exile in its insistence that grounds are only and always where one sleeps, a view suggested by the poem's epigraph from the *Mishnah* (*Aboth* 6:4): "and on the ground shalt thou sleep and thou shalt live a life of trouble". Exile suggests expulsion from a native land, but in Reznikoff's verse the native is what lies at one's feet, ground for walking on: so no loss of prior foundations, no absent center, as in Edmond Jabès, but "finding as founding" to use Stanley Cavell's Emersonian phrase from *This New yet Unapproachable America*.

Perhaps there are those who possess house and land, who can afford to live higher off the ground, imagining possession as a prophylactic for loss. Damage is given, not chosen. The nomad, neither uprooted or uprooting, roots around, reroutes. Reznikoff's new world is not one of absence, but neither is it one of plenty.

> Like a tree in December
> after the winds have stripped it
> leaving only trunk and limbs
> to ride and outlast
> the winter's blast.

The "writer of verse", like the nomad, "must learn to fast / and drink water by measure". Reznikoff's baggage is, literally, the *light* that emanates from conversation and song (dialogue and psalm), exactly the measures of his verse. This is a poetry not of dislocation or banishment but of the "blinding" intensities of location as relocation, relocalization.

9. A typology of Reznikoff's parataxis would begin by distinguishing his non-developmental seriality from sequential seriality, to use Joseph Conte's terms in *Unending Design*, a distinction that is in some ways similar to that between analytic and synthetic cubism.

Certainly, the modulation of disjunctiveness between poems in a Reznikoff "group of verse" is one of the poetry's most distinctive features. As Burton Hatlen has argued, reading Reznikoff means reading each of his groups as a series, not as autonomous poems.[21] Such readings will need to take account of the fact that Reznikoff reordered the sequences of his groups in ways that underscore the modular, permutable, status of each discrete poem.

Reznikoff's groups are composed by varying the degree of continuity

21. Burton Hatlen, "Objectivism in Context: Charles Reznikoff and Jewish-American Modernism", presented at the annual meeting of the Modern Language Association, New York, 1992.

and discontinuity among the sections. The most typical relation between sections is one of simultaneity of occurrences, as if each poem were preceded by an implied "meanwhile".[22] However, some of the modules of a series do share thematic interconnections, with subject clusters connected by family resemblances, commonly involving a permutation of tangentially related motifs, with shifts among themes varying from slight to abrupt. Reznikoff's "Similes" (#45, 2:103) demonstrates this principle within a single poem, presenting four images each of which seem teasingly related to the others but which share no single stateable topic. Sometimes small thematic clusters are placed within larger nonthematic series. These may be given an overtitle—a sequence within a series—as "Winter Holidays" or "Early History of a Writer", or the cluster may simply share the same subject, as the motifs of the subway, birds, rain, and the moon identified by Hatlen in his reading of *Jerusalem the Golden*. Moreover, some of Reznikoff's works are framed by a single theme or subject, such as the biblical studies of "Editing and Glosses" in *By the Waters of Manhattan: An Annual* (1929), or, most prominently, his books, *Testimony* and *Holocaust*, which, while thematically linked, are nonetheless serial rather than sequential.

10. Seriality encompasses a vast array of modernist and contemporary poetry, much of it better known for its nonsequentiality than Reznikoff's verse. The usefulness of the term depends on the degree to which the different types of serialism are distinguished. The early modernist history of seriality could easily start with Stein's *Tender Buttons* (1912), the most original rethinking of poetic form in the period. One might also think of the serial ordering of long individual poems in Pound's *Cantos* or Zukofsky's *"A"*. Conte identifies Williams's *Spring and All* (1923) as the prototype for serial form, noting the 27 numbered, untitled poems that are interpreted with prose improvisations. But consider also Jean Toomer's *Cane* (1923), with its interspersing of loosely associated poems and prose.[23]

22. What makes the poems disjunctive is that they are not, in fact, threaded together by the use of such—in effect—conjunctions as "meanwhile" and "at the same time", which smooth over the synaptic break between units, and do not allow for the syncopation of cubo-seriality. The use of such hinges as "meanwhile" is particularly favored by John Ashbery, a device that apparently makes the marvelous incongruities of his work appealing to some readers who dislike the more textually disruptive practices described here. Note also that biblical and Homeric parataxis employs frequent conjunctions to link elements, a feature that distinguishes this older form of parataxis from modernist collage and montage. A fuller discussion of this issue would need to account for the structurally related use of parallelism in analphabetic poetries.

23. Joseph M.Conte, *Unending Design: The Forms of Postmodern Poetry* (Ithaca: Cornell University Press, 1991), p. 20. Conte defines the form of the serial poem as "both discontinuous and capable of recombination." He notes that the discontinuity of the elements of the serial poem "—or their resistance to a determinate order—distinguishes the series from thematic continuity, nar-

A pre-(modern) history of the serial poem would have much to account for, including, famously, Buchner's *Woyzeck*, but equally Dickinson's fascicles—the most radical serial poems of 19th-century America. (I return again to Dickinson's lines "This world is not conclusion. / A sequel stands beyond / Invisible as Music— / But positive, as Sound—", where *sequel* is a possible variant for *Species*.[24]) In *Emily Dickinson's Open Folios*, Marta Werner makes a convincing case that what we now know as Dickinson's letters or prose, are, to a surprisingly large extent, better classified as serial fragments.[25] The relation of fragments to seriality leads to a further deepening of both categories; Hölderlin's late fragments would be particularly relevant to consider in this regard.

During the period following the Second World War, the most influential conception of the serial poem came from Jack Spicer, who contrasted the "one night stand" of the individual poems to a composition by book in which the order of the poems, like each individual poem, is determined by "dictation". Both Robert Duncan and Robin Blaser were comrades with Spicer in this project.

Zukofsky's great cut-up collage, "Poem Beginning 'The'"—composed of 330 numbered lines, prefaced by a list of several dozen sources for the work—was written in 1926. As in much of Zukofsky's poetry, the poem's lines flow from one to next, working in counterpoint to the disjunctive nature of the sources and the numerical framing. The process of running-in such disparate material by the use of intricate syntactic, syllabic, and thematic patterning, which characterizes much of Zukofsky's "A", is a formal practice quite distinct from Reznikoff's cubo-seriality.[26] Many of Zukofsky's shorter poems are, like Reznikoff's, presented in numbered sequences. But unlike Reznikoff's splinters, Zukofsky's individual poems in *ALL* are longer and stand up by themselves as autonomous works. Zukofsky's short poetry, less dependent on the series, makes less of it.

---

rative progression, or meditative insistence that often characterizes the sequence . . . The series demands neither summation nor exclusion. It is instead a combinative form whose arrangements admit a variegated set of materials." In contrast, the sequence relies on "mechanic or imposed organization", for example the temporal progression of the seasons (p. 21).

24. *The Poems of Emily Dickinson*, ed. Thomas H. Johnson (Cambridge: Belknap Press of Harvard University Press, 1955), #501, 2:384–85.

25. *Emily Dickinson's Open Folios: Scenes of Reading, Surfaces of Writing* (Ann Arbor: University of Michigan Press, 1995); based on *Emily Dickinson: Quires of Light*, Ph.D. dissertation, SUNY-Buffalo, 1992.

26. In *Disjunctive Poetics: From Gertrude Stein and Louis Zukofsky to Susan Howe* (New York: Cambridge University Press, 1992), Peter Quartermain links the paratactic prosody of Zukofsky with Bunting and Pound and back to Whitman. See especially pp. 127–33. Conte makes the distinction between seriality and proceduralism: "Serial works are characterized by the discontinuity of their elements and the centrifugal force identified with an 'open' aesthetic. Procedural works, on the other hand, are typified by the recurrence of elements and a centripetal force that promises a self-sustaining momentum" (p. 42).

More directly akin to Reznikoff's cubo-seriality is George Oppen's *Discrete Series* (1932–34); the work of Lorine Niedecker, whose discrete seriality is explicitly shown only in the most comprehensive (though flawed) collection of her work, *From This Condensary*, edited by Robert Bertholf; the "Love Songs" (1915–17) of Mina Loy; and Langston Hughes's *Montage of a Dream Deferred* (1951).

More recent work that continues a poetics of adjacency, in which elements are discrete, incomplete, and recombinatory, would include— among *many* others—George Oppen's "Of Being Numerous", Robert Creeley's *Words*, *Pieces* and "In London"; Ron Silliman's "new", e.g., permutable, sentences; Lyn Hejinian's *The Cell*, Ted Pearson's *Evidence*, Tom Raworth's *A Serial Biography*, Ted Berrigan's "Tambourine Life", and John Ashbery's "Europe".

One criterion that usefully differentiates paratactic forms is the degree to which the parts are mobile or recombinable. On one end of the spectrum there is nonserial parataxis, bound to narrative or chronology, such as in the Homeric epics and the Bible. (There is another way of reading the Torah that suggests its nonsequential undertow: the Kabbalistic practice of gematria, as developed by Abraham Abulafia in the 13th century, which involves the recombination of numerically equivalent words and in some ways resembles anagrammatic and aleatoric methods of recombination.)

A second category, in which the arrangement of the elements is intrinsic to the meaning, covers most serial poems. Further recombination is, by definition, possible without compromising the prosodic structure of the work; nonetheless the meaning of the series is dependent, to a greater or lesser extent, on the particular array or temporal ordering that has been made or the procedure that has been used. By temporal ordering, I mean works that foreground the process of composition (elements are ordered as they were written); by array—nontemporal and nonsystematic configurations of modular elements; by procedure—external or explicit principles of design used to order elements of a series.

A third category consists of modular poems that have not yet been serialized: poems in which the arrangement of elements is extrinsic. In the strictest sense, few works fit into this category since the format of books binds an order onto even the most discontinuous set of leaves. In a broader sense, there are a number of serial works that are not intended to be read only or principally in the order in which they are printed. (Serial *reading* opens all works to recombination. My favorite image of readerly seriality is David Bowie, in Nicholas Roeg's *The Man Who Fell to Earth*, watching a bank of TVs all of which were rotating their channels.) Robert Grenier's *Sentences*—500 discrete articulations each on a separate index card and housed in a blue Chinese box—is the best example I know of extrinsic se-riality, though two other boxes of cards also come to mind: Jerome Rothenberg and Harris Lenowitz's *Gematria* 27 (27 recombinable numeric word equivalences) and Thomas McEvilley's cubo-serial *4* (44 four-line poems). In principle, hypertext is an ideal format for this mode of com-position since it allows a completely nonlinear movement from link to link: no path need be specified and each reading of the data base creates an alternative series. What's remarkable is that this structure is already a potential in Reznikoff's first book in 1918.[27]

I have in mind two other criteria for differentiating serial poems (though what good all this classification will do I can't say; not likely much): the degree of congruity or incongruity among elements of the series (this might be called coefficient of weirdness, with cubo-seriality, for example, having a low coefficient) and the extent of found or pre-existing material used in the poem.

11. In Reznikoff's cubo-seriality, it's a matter of the *cut*: as in the cut of a dress or of a fabric. Also a double cutting: the shapeliness of the lines as units inside each poem (the cut of each poem, Reznikoff as miniaturist); and the rhythm between the poems (the intercutting). The numbered poem as unit, but also the line as unit: isolating/emphasizing discrete words or word pairs, half-puns and off rhymes and echoes and repetitions; modulating—pushing against—too easy a rhythm, too quick a reading:

> Her work was to count linings—
> the day's seconds in dozens.[28]

12. Reznikoff is a "literary realist" only if one unit is considered in isola-tion, as has been the assumption of most readings of his work. Understood serially, in terms of their plasticity, the poems can no longer be read with the trivializing appreciation of being plain, descriptive, flat, simple, artless,

---

27. Wittgenstein's *Philosophical Investigations* and *Zettel* exemplify the distinction between intrin-sic and extrinsic order. *Zettel* is made up of over 700 slips found together in a file box. These slips were mostly cut from extensive typescripts of Wittgenstein's and many of the fragments were subsequently reworked. In addition, it appears that some of the remarks were written original-ly as part of this series. The editors remark that "now we know that his method of composition was in part to make an arrangement of such short, almost independent, pieces". For our investi-gation here, it is striking that some of the sections of *Zettel* were cut out of "one or two total rearrangements of *Investigations* and other material"; the fact that Wittgenstein made such recom-binations underscores the serial nature of his major philosophical work. See the "Editor's Pref-ace" of *Zettel*, ed. G. E. M. Anscombe and G. H. von Wright, tr. G. E. M. Anscombe (Berkeley: University of California Press, 1967). —Serial forms are particularly valuable for both philoso-phy and criticism, despite the fact that they are almost never employed.

28. *Poems* (1920), #5, 1:29.

and unassuming; or as being without rhetorical affect or "modernist discontinuity". Indeed, the early negative reviews of Reznikoff's works reveal a difficulty with his poetry that suggests his radical approach better than many of the more positive subsequent assessments: "a fragmentary style that annoys and bewilders", "cumulative effect . . . is promising shavings"; "He is unable to focus . . . apparent incoherence" (Malcolm Cowley); "half-baked, [showing] a lack of development".[29]

13. Subject matter is literally *beside* the point of this formal innovation, which would be possible with different subject matter and even without explicit subject matter (as in Stein). As Reznikoff notes, "Half the meaning [of poetry] is the music."[30] Milton Hindus, apparently reporting on a conversation with Reznikoff, remarks: "Literature was capable of making something out of nothing (indeed, it was Flaubert's dream to write a work about 'nothing at all'); it was capable of making interesting (by the quality of its style, by its emphasis, by the purity and freshness of its language, by the depth of its feeling or thought) the most commonplace and the least exciting or unusual occurrences . . ."[31] The comparison between Reznikoff and Flaubert seems particularly apt on the question of style; it's incredible that the exquisite stylizations of Reznikoff's poems have been lost in the tendency to call him, virtually, styleless.

14. Reznikoff does speak of poetry as the communication of feeling—but he is explicit that this feeling, in an "objective" poem, is not expressed as the direct personal statement of the author.

Reznikoff's manner, or method, as he calls it: the feeling comes *indirectly* as a result of the *selection of objects* and the "music" that composes the object.[32] It is a matter of the cut and the cutting.

29. Linda Simon provides these quotes in a useful synopsis of the responses to Reznikoff in her "Annotated Bibliography of Works about Charles Reznikoff", in *Man and Poet*, pp. 411–40.

Milton Hindus's laudatory review of *Family Chronicles* is representative of the "giving up the baby with bathwater" or "weak" response to Reznikoff's detractors, even though Hindus is not here talking about the poems (*Man and Poet*, p. 426): The work is difficult, Hindus argues, not because of the presence of avant-garde defamiliarizing devices "but because of its seemingly absolute and artless and primitive simplicity . . . He studiously and purposefully *flattens* . . . every incident . . . Reznikoff consistently subdues all the highlights in his pictures and produces a monochromatic effect which demands the utmost effort and attention from the reader." One wants to immediately add here what Jerome Rothenberg wrote of tribal primitivism: *primitive means complex*. Still, it's the picture of Reznikoff as "artless and unassuming", as Carl Rakosi describes him (*Man and Poet*, p. 429), that underplays how very artful and assuming this work is.

30. "First, There Is the Need", in *Sparrow* 52 (Santa Barbara: Black Sparrow Press, 1977), p. 6 (unpaginated).

31. *Man and Poet*, p. 22.

32. "First, There Is the Need", p. 2.

15. Jewish forms (not just themes): the idea of Jewish holiness (blessedness): in the detail, the everyday: every activity, every moment, holy: "How brilliant a green the grass is, / how blinding white the snow."[33]

In Jewish thought, the holiness of the ordinary can be traced to the 18th-century founder of Hasidism, Baal Shem Tov, as well as further back to earlier Jewish mystics.[34] In orthodox Judaism, as in other orthodox religions, the holy is external; graspable, if at all, only through law and ritual; it is an "object of dogmatic knowledge" as Gershom Scholem puts it (10). In Jewish mysticism, holiness is present in everyday—"low"—activities and not separated out to particular sites, such as the synagogue, or to particular times, such as the High Holy Days.—Just as we might say, following Reznikoff (or Duchamp), that the aesthetic is not confined to the "beauty" of traditional forms, but is fully present in the quotidian. Kabbalism is anti-dualistic, seeking to break down the distinction between God in Itself (God on high, set apart) and God in its appearance, in its immanence (in the low, a part). *There is no separation:* for holiness is found in the most common deeds and language, the most base and vulgar acts: the holiness of walking, the holiness of drinking, the holiness of sitting, the holiness of talking, the holiness of looking, the holiness of touching, the holiness of witness:

> Not because of victories
> I sing
> having none,
> but for the common sunshine,
> the breeze,
> the largess of the spring . . .
>
> not for a seat upon the dais
> but at the common table.[35]

Allen Ginsberg's litany of "holy"s in "Footnote to Howl" invokes the holiness of the common—"The skin is holy! The nose is holy! The tongue and cock and hand and asshole holy! / Everything is holy! everybody's holy!

33. *Inscriptions*, #21 (excerpt), 2:75. As previously noted, Reznikoff calls this poem, and #23, his "platform as a writer of verse"; #21 is also cited in sections 2 and 29.

34. Gershom Scholem, in *Major Trends in Jewish Mysticism* (New York: Schocken Books, 1961), notes that "the doctrine of God's immanence in all things" has earlier roots "among the great Jewish mystics and Kabbalists. To me, not the doctrine seems new, but rather the primitive enthusiasm with which it was expounded and the truly pantheistic exhilaration evoked by the belief that God surrounds everything and pervades everything" (pp. 347–48). Subsequently referred to in the text.

35. "Te Deum" (excerpt), in *Inscriptions*, #22, 2:75.

everywhere is holy! everyday is in eternity . . . / The bum's as holy as the seraphim!";[36] indeed, I would suggest that Ginsberg's poetics derive equally from Blake, Whitman, and Reznikoff—an interesting trio (even if this extravagance conflates Williams with Reznikoff).

16. Gershom Scholem points out that a positive attitude toward language distinguishes Kabbalism from other mystical traditions:

> Kabbalists who differ in almost everything else are at one in regard-ing language as something more precious than an inadequate instru-ment for contact between human beings. To them, Hebrew, the holy tongue, is not simply a means of expressing certain thoughts, born out of a certain convention and having a purely conventional char-acter . . . Language in its purest form, that is, Hebrew . . . reflects the fundamental spiritual nature of the world . . . Man's common lan-guage . . . reflects the creative language of God. (17)

17. It comes to this question: what is the status of the detail, the particu-lar in this work? Why is it so important? For Reznikoff, as for Williams, the detail is not a "luminous particular" in Pound's sense—not extraordinary but exactly ordinary, even if indeed luminous. So, then, why this particu-lar detail, and then that one?

Metonymy: the fragment as substitute for, hinting at, something else, something that only it can stand for, is an instance of—a manifestation or emanation. The part for the (w)holy.

Witness of the detail understood as metonymic.

Scholem, again, is a useful guide. Kabbalism rejects the allegorical for the symbolic, where allegory—"the representation of an expressible some-thing by another expressible something"—is akin to the literary conceits and Symbolism that Reznikoff rejected. In contrast, "the mystical symbol is an expressible sensation of something which lies beyond the sphere of expression . . . Every living thing is endlessly correlated with the whole of creation . . . everything mirrors everything else" (27).

Reznikoff, a secular poet refreshed by "the clear waters of reason", com-mitted "to use words for their daylight meaning" is no mystic, if mysticism is understood as elevating his work above "the common table", as he puts it in a poem entitled "Te Deum". Reznikoff is not a poet of the ecstatic, directed to the beyond, but a poet of the near, the close at hand: of a returning to oneself as to the world.

18. Fragment as shard—of a broken or cracked totality that cannot be rep-

36. Allen Ginsberg, *Collected Poems, 1947–1980* (New York: Harper & Row, 1984), p. 134.

resented in its totality (the taboo against graven images) but only as splinters (of light), details. ". . . but the cracked glass held in the frame."[37]

19. The ordinary, the everyday, the common, the neglected, the disregarded/unacknowledged as the site of Paradise (*there is no other—only recover*): *Arts de faire*, the art of doing, as in, *The Practice of Everyday Life*:

> As I was wondering with my unhappy thoughts,
> I looked and saw
> that I had come into a sunny place
> familiar and yet strange.
> "Where am I?" I asked a stranger. "Paradise."
> "Can this be Paradise?" I asked surprised,
> for there were motor-cars and factories.
> "It is," he answered. "This is the sun that shone on Adam once;
> the very wind that blew upon him too."[38]

Looked and saw: it is this twofold action that the poems constantly replay; looking is never enough, for it shows only what can be seen by using light; in contrast, the world may be beheld, beholded—held, cradled, rocked. The very wind.

20. First-generation immigrant to America not as exile (as it was for Jabès coming to France: Europe already "inhabited") but as founder—one who finds/inhabits and one who makes new a language (a new world). It is Reznikoff's mother who says, "We are a lost generation . . . It is for our children to do what they can."[39] For Reznikoff, finding as founding means finding as foundering (to fall to the ground, to come to grief).

21. The recovery of the ordinary: then was it lost?

22. NOT flatness or absence of rhetoric but . . . a *nearness* to the world not seen as "nature" but as social (urban). Materials of the world at hand, as found: *words* as materials.

Not, that is, reports of things seen (narrow definition of the "objectivist" as ocular or transparent imagism) but bearing witness to things not seen, overlooked. Entering into the word as a descent, not (Idealized) ascent, to borrow Simone Weil's terms.

37. *By the Well of Living and Seeing*, sec. II, #19 (excerpt), 2:121.

38. *Inscriptions*, #20, 2:75. This is the sense of paradise I hear in Ron Silliman's *Paradise* and Lyn Hejinian's *The Guard*.

39. These are the last words in Sarah Reznikoff's "Early History of a Seamstress", in *Family Chronicle*, p. 99.

23.

Hanukkah

In a world where each man must be of use
and each thing useful, the rebellious Jews
light not one light but eight—
not to see by but to look at.[40]

Delight. Finding the light in. "Not to see by but to look at" in multiple, serial array. Not sight but display. A Festival of lights.

24. "In *Testimony*," Reznikoff tells an interviewer, "the speakers whose words I use are all giving testimony about what they actually lived through. The testimony is that of a witness in court—*not a statement of what he felt but of what he heard or saw.*"[41] In "First, There Is the Need", Reznikoff writes:

> With respect to the treatment of subject matter in verse and the use of the term "objectivist" and "objectivism," let me again refer to the rules with respect to testimony in a court of law. Evidence to be admissible in a trial cannot state conclusions of fact: it must state the facts themselves. For example, a witness in an action for negligence cannot say: the man injured was negligent crossing the street. He must limit himself to a description of how the man crossed . . . The conclusions of fact are for the jury and let us add, in our case, for the reader. (8)

Philosophically, however, description is always an epistemological question: the *act* of describing constitutes what is described; this act is never neutral. Witnessing is less a matter of "sight" than of action, not static but dynamic. In Reznikoff, witnessing opposes the predawn, preprocessed conclusion: it *unfolds*.

25. Witness versus distance versus assimilation versus exile.

26. Nearness as attitude of address: not isolated, deanimated "images" of distantiated ocular evidence. The *intimacy* of address, the fondling/comment/intrusion into the "material" is a nearing toward a dwelling, making an habitation:

---

40. "Notes on the Spring Holidays", sec. III, *Inscriptions*, #46, 2:84.
41. "A Talk with L. S. Dembo", in *Man and Poet*, p. 107, italics added. Subsequently referred to in the text.

Rails in the subway,
what did you know of happiness,
when you were ore in the earth;
now the electric lights shine upon you.[42]

In the Dembo interview (110), Reznikoff reports that a Japanese listener had questioned the last line of one of his poems, presumably because it violated the ideal of Haiku—a violation that is just the point of his practice of comment on, or interference into, the scene:

What are you doing in our street among the automobiles,
    horse?
How are your cousins, the centaur and the unicorn?[43]

Just as the absence of the first-person pronoun in this poem marks its break from traditional expressive poetry, so the use of the second-person pronoun marks its break from an ocular imagism.

27. The poetics of adjacency are aversive of the detachment and irony associated with the "high" modernism of Eliot, or, more accurately, the tradition of Eliot. Are you apart from the language or a part of it?—What we do is to take back language from symbolical allusions and metaphysical contraptions. Yet this swings back to the question of exile, as Reznikoff laments his exile from Hebrew in his most Jabèsian moment:

How difficult for me is Hebrew:
even the Hebrew for *mother*, for *bread*, for *sun*
is foreign. How far have I been exiled, Zion.[44]

To be exiled from one's language is to be lost as a son or daughter, to be a foreigner in one's own tongue, as Jabès says the writer, as Jew, is exiled even in her own language. Since the Jewish tradition imparts to the word a fundamental spiritual nature, this exile from a language that one has never learned suggests the deepest sense of spiritual disconnectedness. Yet the poem also touches on the idea, fundamental to anti-semitism, that all Jews, even monolingual native speakers of English or German or French, have a "hidden language" to which they owe fundamental allegiance—a belief that, if internalized by the Jew, incites self-hatred, as Sander Gilman discusses in *Jewish Self-Hatred*.

Like many of his contemporaries, Reznikoff was a second-language speaker of English and it was no doubt his newness to English that con-

42. *Jerusalem the Golden* (1934), #17, 1:111.
43. *Jerusalem the Golden*, #39, 1:115.
44. *Five Groups of Verse* (1927), #14, 1:72.

tributed to the newness of his approach to founding an American poetry broken off from Island English, forged by syntax and music previously unheard in the language. Reznikoff's poetics of location as relocalization is not a poetry of exile. Yet loss rips through this poetry, like hot water spurting from a frozen geyser.

> The Hebrew of your poets, Zion,
> is like oil upon a burn,
> cool as oil;
> after work,
> the smell in the street at night
> of the hedge in flower.
> Like Solomon,
> I have married and married the speech of strangers;
> none are like you, Shulamite.[45]

28. The social engagement of the Jewish secular left meant not assuming the "social" as an abstract, static entity but as something to be located, particularized.

In the poetics of nearness, others exist prior to oneself; you do not look out onto other people as if through a preexisting subjectivity, but find whomever you may be as person, as poet, in relation to them, by virtue of your acknowledgment of their suffering, which is to say their circumstance or bearing in the world. This is the ethical grounding of Reznikoff's work.

29. Vividness not as design but texture:

> I have neither the time nor the weaving skills, perhaps,
> for the intricate medallions the Persians know;
> my rugs are the barbaric fire-worshipper's:
> how blue the waters flow,
> how red the fiery sun,
> how brilliant a green the grass is,
> how blinding white the snow.[46]

30. Witness as care / in-volved / as care-taken, caretaker, care in the language, for the world. Language is caretaker of the world.

---

45. *Jerusalem the Golden*, #1, 1:107. In the Dembo interview, Reznikoff responds to a question about "a personal sense of isolation or exile" in this poem: "I don't think 'isolation' is the word. I don't feel isolated in English it's just that I'm missing a lot not knowing Hebrew. Incidentally, Havelock Ellis, in one of his books, as I remember it, points out the tendency in a writer to use characteristics of the speech of his ancestors, even a speech he no longer knows" (p. 104).

46. *Inscriptions*, #21, 2:75. Reznikoff's "platform".

31. Witness/testimony as "self-cancellation" so that the language/event speaks of/for itself (modernist autonomy), as Reznikoff remarks in "First, There Is the Need", quoting an article on Zen that discusses the "forget-fulness of self" (3). Compare *Testimony: The structure of event:* constellation of particulars: picture is *produced* by this *method,* not presumed.[47]

32. Nearness/unfolding of event breaks down the subject-object split. Sub-ject/object; observer/observed; the paranoia of the objective depersonal-ized gaze. "apart and alone, / beside an open window / and behind a closed door."[48]

Here these dualities collapse onto one another, the distantiation/irony is collapsed, the observer enters into the observed through a process of participatory mourning: "The room is growing dark, / but the brass knob of the closed door shines— / *ready for use.*"[49]

> I would be the rock
> about which the water is
> flowing; and I would be the water flowing
> about the rock.
> And am both and neither—
> being *flesh.*[50]

33. "The infinite shines through the finite and makes it more real" (Scholem, 28). Dickinson's "finite infinity":

> There is a solitude of space
> A solitude of sea
> A solitude of death, but these
> Society shall be
> Compared with that profounder site
> That polar privacy
> A soul admitted to itself—
> Finite Infinity.[51]

---

47. In "On Reznikoff and 'Talking Hebrew'" (*Sagetrieb* 7, no. 2 [1988]), John Martone writes that "[c]entral to Reznikoff's objectivism is the poet's subordination of the self to the material at hand. The poetic subject and not the poet as subject is the center of the work. The sincerity, Zukofsky said about Reznikoff's work, is in the details. And *all* Reznikoff's books . . . direct our attention not so much to an experiencing authorial self as to a detailed, profoundly historical world of experience. Reznikoff is the first American poet to 'decenter' the subject on so massive a scale . . . Revolutionary in the context of American poetry, [this decentering] is a basic feature of the *Talmud* and a given in traditional Jewish hermeneutics" (p. 72).

48. "Autobiography: New York", in *Going To and Fro and Walking Up and Down* (1941), sec. 2, #IV, 2:27.

49. "Autobiography: Hollywood", in *Going To and Fro and Walking Up and Down*, sec. 3, #XXIV (excerpt), 2:46, italics added.

50. #XXIV, immediately following the adjacent poem; italics added.

51. *The Poems of Emily Dickinson*, #1695, 3:1149.

34. It's a question of the poem's attitude toward its materials: condescension, sentimentality, impersonality, identification, misidentification, detachment, erasure, appropriation, approbation, condescension, deafness, blindness, scorn, ecstasy, depression, anxiety, hypocrisy, reflection, management, control, possession, flirtatious, annihilating.

35. Serial composition, one detail adjacent to the next, one perspective permuted with another, refuses the binary. Oppen:

> There are things
> We live among 'and to see them
> Is to know ourselves'.
>
> Occurrence, a part
> Of an infinite series[52]

36. My aim not to explain the poems but to make them more opaque.

37. The sensation of not understanding, comprehending (say in Zukofsky or Stein): poems charged with the intractability, the ineffability, of the world.

> I like this secret walking
> in the fog;
> unseen, unheard,
> among the bushes
> thick with drops;
> the solid path invisible
> a rod away—
> and only the narrow present is alive.[53]

Reznikoff's very extreme attitude toward elision and condensation has the supplemental effect of producing density in exact proportion to its desire for clarity. This is not the clarity of conventional poetic or expository discourse because its poetic space has been transformed into a gravitational field in which every word matters in the sense of having matter, musical or notional weight.

In "Early History of a Writer", Reznikoff recounts how a friend had applied Kittredge's method of microanalysis to some of his early poems:

> he read my verse as I had never read verse before,
> scrutinizing it, phrase by phrase
> and word by word, thought and image, thought and sound . . .

---

52. George Oppen, "Of Being Numerous", #1 (excerpt), in *Collected Poems of George Oppen* (New York: New Directions, 1975), p. 147.

53. "Autobiography: Hollywood", #III (excerpt), 2:39. Compare Oppen's "And the pure joy / Of the mineral fact // Tho it is impenetrable // As the world, if it is matter / Is impenetrable" ("Of Being Numerous", #2, p. 148).

Reznikoff immediately realizes that this method was similar to what he had at law school—

> prying sentences open to look for the exact meaning;
> weighing words to choose only those that had meat for my
>   purpose
> and throwing the rest away as empty shells.
> I, too, could scrutinize every word and phrase
> as if in a document or the opinion of a judge
> and listen, as well, for the tones and overtones,
> leaving only the pithy, the necessary, the clear and plain.[54]

Reznikoff asks that we pry his words open, listening for the tones and overtones—a way of reading that intensifies the conflict between "the clear and plain" and "the necessary", between the accessible and the ineffable: for when words are weighed and measured for their undertones as well as their piths, the empty shells that fall away, like scales falling from "unseeing eyes," leave only the "narrow present" of the fog.

38. "A poet's words can pierce us. And that is of course *causally* connected with the use that they have in our life. And it is also connected with the way in which, conformably to this use, we let our thoughts roam up and down in the familiar surroundings of the words."[55]

39. William Carlos Williams and Gertrude Stein are the paradigmatic modernist poets of the ordinary. Just as Williams found the poetic in the back-lot "cinders // in which shine / the broken // pieces of a green / bottle", so Stein found the poetic in the materials of the poem, "actual word stuff, not thoughts for thoughts", to use Williams's formulation.[56]

For Reznikoff, a poetry of the everyday is a poetry of the city. As he remarks in his introduction to the Poetry Center reading, his pervasive urbanism marks a decisive break with the nature poetry of the verse tradition. Moreover, Reznikoff's is a poetry of the found, a disposition appar-

---

54. "Early History of a Writer", #17, 2:172. Reznikoff mentions this anecdote, identifying Kittredge's Shakespeare course at Harvard, which is not mentioned in the poem, in the Dembo interview, *Man and Poet*, p. 103.

55. Wittgenstein, *Zettel*, #155, p. 28e.

56. "Between Walls", in *The Collected Poems of William Carlos Williams*, ed. A. Walton Litz and Christopher MacGowan (New York: New Directions, 1986), p. 453: what shines in this poem is "the broken": that which is damaged or destroyed & that which has been cast aside, but, at the same time, the fragment, the shard of ineffable worth. "Actual Word Stuff, Not Thoughts for Thoughts" is the title of Quartermain's essay on Williams and Zukofsky in *Disjunctive Poetics*; the quote is from a 1928 letter from Williams to Zukofsky. —One might imagine Stein's project as a radical extension of seriality to the level of syntax, so that not only sentences or phrases or details, but also individual words, are permuted.

ent in the found details of the everyday that people his poems, but never more evident that in the found material of *Testimony*, Reznikoff's testament to the foundering of America and to the possibility of its founding in fondling, call it care in, the everyday.

40. I've been told that Reznikoff disliked obscurity and would certainly not have wanted his work to be characterized as obscure. Yet Reznikoff, from the beginning, seemed to expect that obscurity was the likely outcome for his poetic work and seemed to accept that with remarkable equanimity. Perhaps he understood the nature, the social structure, of obscurity better than his contemporaries. Neglect, disregard—the socially obscure, the forgotten and repressed, the overlooked—this was his subject.

Hiding in plain sight you may never be found: if sight is not to "see by but to look at", not to use but behold.

41. Reznikoff's investigations have something of the sublimity that Wittgenstein assigns to logic, but which might be assigned equally to poetry:

> . . . it is rather of the essence of our investigation that we do not seek to learn anything *new* by it . . . as if by this end we had to hunt down new facts . . . We want to *understand* something that is already in plain view. For *this* is what we seem in some sense not to understand . . .
>
> Something we know when no one asks us, but no longer know when we are supposed to give an account of it, is something we need to *remind* ourselves of. (And it is obviously something of which for some reason is it difficult to remind oneself.)[57]

Reznikoff's poetry reminds of very general facts that we already knew—are in plain view—but which we have difficulty accounting for. Above all, we have difficulty accounting for the fact that the poetry is *difficult*, because it doesn't seem, at first, to be difficult at all, but patent; as if the difficulty of such patency isn't the first thing we might wish to deny (repress).

42. Reznikoff in an interview ten days before his death:

> Whatever the difficulties, your business is to write what you think you should. You owe that much to yourself and to other humans, too.[58]

43. The perspective here is extreme only if it's extreme to read a poem's forms as an inextricable part of its content. Nor does it stretch the point to insist, against all odds, that Reznikoff's formal innovations are essential

---

57. *Philosophical Investigations*, tr. G. E. M. Anscombe (New York: Macmillan, 1958), #89.
58. *Man and Poet*, p. 428.

for understanding what his work is "about" and that to neglect these features is to repress what he has labored to say.

I've often heard Reznikoff damned with the faint praise of his accessibility, as if he is a kind of Jewish, urban Frost, or the Norman Rockwell of poetry—ashcan snapshots of city life. Ironically, it's this very surface of accessibility that has tended to dissipate interest in his work. In the absence of recognition of the formal and phenomenological intensities, even opacities, of this work, it can seem as his detractors charge—without literary interest, pointless.[59]

If Reznikoff is accessible, it is an accessibility so fragile as to make him, for many readers, more difficult to read seriously and thoroughly than his apparently less accessible, but more often accessed, contemporaries. The history of Reznikoff's reception suggests that his work could not, except for a few initiates, be understood in its own time; or if it was understood, beyond his few serious readers, it was understood in such a way as to allow it to be discounted as superficial.

The paradox is that the difficulty of his work—which is related to its understatement and subtlety, its iconoclasm and darkness, and the freshness and originality of his music—is of a different order than the more famous "obscurities" of Pound or Eliot or Joyce, difficulties that our present habits of reading tend to valorize more than they do the kind of difficulty the poems of Charles Reznikoff surely present.

The paradox is that Reznikoff's apparent accessibility stands in the way of a recognition of the significance of his poetic achievement: if he's liked for being "easy" then he's at the same time disregarded for being insignificant. But both these approaches seem not so much to read Reznikoff as to read through him.

44. In *Reading in Detail* Naomi Schor argues that working in detail has a history of being stigmatized as feminine, which is to say, of peripheral value. Unlike the "heroic" sweep and "grandeur" of hypotactic order, detail is marginalized as ornament, blemish, weakness, deficiency, simplicity, *easy*: ultimately as disregardable as the "lost" women and men that Reznikoff refuses to thematize or caricature or stereotype. Reznikoff never states his

---

59. Pointlessness is a typical charge made against radical modernist discontinuity and fragmentation. Thus, Reznikoff's poems are "essentially insignificant" and "incidental and decorative" according to a 1934 review; while Hayden Carruth, reviewing *Testimony*, speaks of Reznikoff's "cold, neutral language" as "uninteresting" and "lifeless" and Robert Alter refers to the "seeming impassivity . . . flatness, and numbing pointlessness" of different Reznikoff works. See Linda Simon's "Annotated Bibliography" in *Man and Poet*. In contrast, John Martone, in "On Reznikoff and 'Talking Hebrew'", is right when he calls *Testimony* "the most difficult of the modernist long poems . . . No grandiose mythopoetic vision distracts us from the commonplace, from the [often brutal] circumstances of everyday life" (p. 79).

themes in generalized, abstract terms but leaves it for his particulars, so ordered, to speak for themselves.

45. To be sure, Reznikoff's stated intentions are for "clarity" of "communication" against the "cryptic"—but his insistence is on—*above all else*—"intensity" produced by "compression" and "rhythm" (cut and shapeliness) that is "passionate" and "musical" and *not*—in *his* words—"flat".[60] Opacity, in this sense, is the refusal of the flatness of ocular or idealist imagism: it is the opacity of the object, of objectification; just as opacity is also the antithesis of the cryptic, with its "cloying music / the hints of what the poets meant / and did not quite say",[61] the symbolical assertion of a puzzle to be deciphered: words not ciphers but things of the world to be thickened, weighted, condensed, so that they may be heard and felt.

46. Then how to understand Reznikoff's choice of recurrent, dark subject matter in his work . . . or how to understand why so much violence, so much darkness in the world?

47. "When you least expect it the lights go out. & when you least expect it, too, the lights come back on again." —Reznikoff, during the Poetry Center reading.

48. Yet flesh is opaque: when you catch it (comprehend it), it's dead.

49. *Testimony* is perhaps the darkest, and certainly most unrelenting, of modernist long poems. Reznikoff spent years in various libraries pouring over trial records from the 1890s and 1900s, selecting a few cases out of each hundred he surveyed and then styling them so as to allow the event itself to speak, as if without interference, without teller. A chronicle of industrial accidents, domestic violence, racism, *Testimony* tells the story of America's forgotten, those who suffer without redress, without name, without hope; yet the soul of these States is found in books like this; the acknowledgment of these peripheral stories turns a waste land into holy ground.[62]

    Reznikoff worked on *Testimony* through the 1930s and 1940s, at a time

60. In "First, There Is the Need", Reznikoff writes, "Clarity, precision, order, but the answer is intensity: with intensity we have compression, rhythm, maybe rhyme, maybe alliteration. The words move out of prose into verse as the speech becomes passionate and musical instead of flat" (p. 5). Reznikoff also talks about prose not having the "intensity that I wanted" in #17 of "Early History of a Writer" (2:171).

    61. "Early History of a Writer", #16, 2:169.

    62. My own reading of Reznikoff began with *Testimony*, which for some time overshadowed my reading of his other poems. I see these remarks as a commentary on how to approach, how to interpret, Reznikoff's great anti-epic. The best account of the composition of *Testimony* is Katherine Shevelow's "History and Objectification in Charles Reznikoff's Documentary Poems, *Testimony* and *Holocaust*", in *Sagetrieb* 1, no. 2 (1982).

when both Oppen and Carl Rakosi had stopped writing, in part because of the conflict they felt between their left political commitments and their poetic commitments. Perhaps *Testimony* can be seen as a labor-intensive counterpart to the lacuna in these poets' work.

Reznikoff's work is preoccupied with those left out of society, people whose lives were destroyed by things (machines, circumstances, an economy) out of their control: again, the neglected, the overlooked. His one reference to Marx is placed strikingly as the last of four poems in a series about prophecy called "Jerusalem the Golden", which is itself the final series of his book of the same title, published, significantly, in 1934 (#79, 1:127–29). "Jerusalem the Golden" begins with "The Lion of Judah"—a poem in which the prophet Nathan denies the right to permanent foundation even, or already, to the Jews ("you shall not build the Lord's house / because your hands have shed much blood"). This poem, considered in the light of the first poem of *Jerusalem the Golden* ("The Hebrew of your poets, Zion / is like oil upon a burn / . . . I have married . . . the speech of strangers") suggests the intractability of the Jewish diaspora (understood, however, not as exile but a series of displacements/replacements). In the second poem, "The Shield of David", the prophets locate "all the lights of heaven" in "the darkness of the grave", abjuring the emptiness of ritual as shells for "unseeing eyes", eyes that look but do not see: *looked and saw* the Light in the Darkness:

> worship Me in righteousness;
> worship me in kindness to the poor and weak,
> in justice to the orphan, the widow, the stranger among you,
> and in justice to him who takes hire in your hand

The third poem, a brief evocation of pantheism, is entitled "Spinoza", after the prototypical Jewish "excommunicate" or "non-Jewish Jew", in Isaac Deutscher's phrase, whose pantheism and determinism significantly prefigure historical materialism (both Marx and Spinoza are crucial sources for Zukofsky's "A"-9). In the last of the series, "Karl Marx", Reznikoff writes:

> We shall arise while the stars are still shining . . .
> to begin the work we delight in,
> and no one shall tell us, Go . . .
> to the shop or office you work in
> to waste your life for a living . . .
> there shall be bread and no one hunger for bread . . .
> we shall call nothing mine—nothing for ourselves only . . .

50. Darkness and light; or dusk, when dark and light can no longer be separated—

> Suddenly we noticed that we were in darkness;
> so we went into the house and lit the lamp.[63]

51. Thrown into the world through EVENT as TESTIMONY / TESTIMONY as EVENT, the poem merges the objective and subjective so that no polarizing can occur.

"Event" emerges as the world/word materializing process takes place.

52. *Testimony*: to found America means to find it—which means to acknowledge its roots in violence, to tell the lost stories because unless you find what is lost you can found nothing.

Against the indifference of the juridical gaze (paradigm of detachment), founding means giving witness to what is denied at the expense of the possibility of America.

> In and about the house darkness lay, a black fog;
> and each on his bed spoke to himself alone, making no sound.

To speak out against the Dark is to make Light: this is the Poetic alchemy, call it economy, that Reznikoff enacts over and again: to recover the lost, make sound in the presence of silence, behold the Light—

53. *Testimony* as memorial: an act of grief/grieving, of mourning. The cost of life, the cost of lives lost, is poetic/psychic economy, of which this an account/accounting. "No one to witness and adjust"—'cept *here*.

"Calling the lapsed Soul . . . / O Earth O Earth return".[64]

54. "Shipwreck of the singular":[65] mourning/grief as part of the celebration of the New Year (Yom Kippur), as prerequisite for new world / new word. "America" not so much a "place" but an attitude toward language.

55. Ignored, like Stein, partly because he does not use symbological allusion or historical reference (Pound/Eliot) that require you to look elsewhere than to what is happening, Reznikoff makes the reader (not himself) into the witness of language, where events are enacted in words and we don't so much judge them as come near to them.

56. The observer and the observed meet at dusk in the midst of shadows. How can we tell the seeing from the seen, the see-er from the seer?

63. *Poems* (1920), #22 (excerpt), 1:35. The citation in the section following the next is the last stanza of this poem.

64. Williams's *Spring and All*, #XVII ("To Elsie"), in *Collected Poems*, p. 217; and Blake's introduction to his indelible series, "Songs of Experience".

65. Oppen, "Of Being Numerous", #7 (excerpt), p. 151.

57. Reznikoff's Rosh Hashonah poem ends this way:

> You have given us the strength
> to serve You,
> but we may serve or not
> as we please;
> not for peace nor for prosperity,
> not even for length of life, have we merited
> remembrance; remember us
> as the servants
> You have inherited.[66]

Jewishness not as "chosen" but *inherited*: can't get rid of. Jewishness in the sense of an inhering possibility for poetry and its testimony as engaged witness that *changes*—intervenes in—what it witnesses by its care in & for the world/word.

III

January 1, 1990

Dear Jean-Paul Auxemery, [67]

At a party last night, for the Christian New Year, a guest brought our host, a Czechoslovakian-Jewish émigré, a piece of the Berlin Wall. A piece of rubble, to be sure, but packaged in a brightly designed box assuring, with a red stamp, that papers attesting to the "authenticity" of the contents had been enclosed by the importers, a New Jersey firm. A small label on the top indicated that the item had been purchased at Bloomingdale's. Here, indeed, was the essence of late, or multinational, capitalism: a commodity created, by the alchemy of packaging, from that which is intrinsically worthless. It's the sort of "symbolism" that is diametrically opposed by what you usefully call Charles Reznikoff's "ethics of style", which has as its method acknowledging the details of intrinsic value that this same culture has discarded, as by the reverse alchemy of turning things of substance into rubble by *disregard*.

I won't ever forget the first night, and first morning, of this year's Jewish New Year, where we celebrated the work of Reznikoff in a former Christian abbey at Royaumont, near Paris. I won't forget that our Reznikoff

---

66. "New Year's", #1 in "Meditations on the Fall and Winter Holidays", in *Inscriptions*, #13, 2:66.

67. This letter was originally published, in a translation by Jean-Paul Auxemery, in *a.b.s.: Poètes à Royaumont*, no. 3 (1990), along with Auxemery's original letter to me.

panel ended with your overwhelming reading of *Holocaust*—your French translation of a work barely known in its native land. My own intervention had focussed not only on Reznikoff's *Testimony*, as you note, but also more particularly on his *Complete Poems*. What I remember thinking was that *Holocaust* had never sounded so necessary, so appropriate (in your sense that Reznikoff always found the most "apropos" words). Yes, I have had my difficulties with *Holocaust*—the most unrelentingly painful to read of Reznikoff's work, about an unmitigated horror of our common, "modern" history. I think I must have said this work was about a problem *specifically* European; I could not have meant that it was "solely" European, however, since the destruction of the European Jews is of the most urgent relevance to all Americans, to all Jews, indeed to all humans. I think I must have suggested that *Holocaust* is necessarily Reznikoff's most problematic work at a technical—in the sense of aesthetic or formal—level, in the sense that no American work of poetry had found a form to adequately acknowledge that which is beyond adequate acknowledgment; so that *Holocaust* stands apart and beyond the achievement of Reznikoff's *Poems* and *Testimony*.

I say *specifically* European for a very practical, literal, reason that you, with your remarkable involvement with Olson, would certainly appreciate the implications of: Reznikoff's work, apart from *Holocaust*, and his biblical poems and Talmudic "collages", has been a profound investigation of "American" materials: it is work immersed in the local and particular details of this place that he found himself in, first generation in his family, and also of a language, English, that was an intrinsic part of that emplacement. One of my favorite Reznikoff remarks is one he made to Marie Syrkin, his wife, in explaining why he would not go to Palestine with her in 1933; he told her "he had not yet explored Central Park to the full". Indeed Reznikoff never left North America or English (an "American" English of course) in real life or in his poems—with the primary exception of *Holocaust*, which not only involved a European site or place (*lieu*) but also for the first time working with documentary materials not originally in English. For me, what was so striking about your reading of *Holocaust* in French was that one could imagine those incidents happening near the place, even Royaumont; we were *close by* the *scene*.

Reznikoff's *Complete Poems* and *Testimony* explore the tragedy and violence that is the grounding of this Republic, call it United States. It is not a story that Americans are familiar with or, even now, ready to acknowledge. Each poem of Reznikoff, always placed in series, shocks by its recognition of something otherwise unstated or unsaid: say, unacknowledged or repressed or denied or suppressed. *Testimony*, while a litany of sorrows, finds new avenues to locate the transgression of dominance against the human spirit.

By contrast, the violence, the repulsiveness, of the incidents in *Holocaust* are always and already known, hence preclude the insinuating subtlety of *Testimony*. (An exception being the section entitled "children".) And, for Americans, always and already projected outward to the German, to the Nazi, to a European story. If it does not hit home, it is because the story of World War II has been the greatest source for American self-congratulation: we defeated the Nazi monsters. *Not*: the Nazi monsters in us, which go on, largely on the loose. This is like saying, North American has not had a 20th-century war on its soil. Reznikoff shows otherwise. *The Complete Poems* and *Testimony* testify to a system of domination and disregard that has *won; Holocaust* to a system of explicit violence that, at least on the face, *lost.*

Poetry is always technical, an order of words, at least in the first instance. If I put aside, yes even disregard, the sentiment of "la raison d'un coeur noble" to reiterate these technical questions it is not without an appreciation of the integrity of the whole of Reznikoff's oeuvre or of the noble gesture of your bringing into French, into France, Reznikoff's final testament, a testament that, to be sure, does go beyond his concern for any one nation or language, a work that we can only wish he had never *had to* write.

With all best wishes,

An Autobiographical Interview

Loss Pequeño Glazier: My first question is one that has been on my mind for quite some time. Reading your work, there seems to be a presence of your early life in your writing, certainly from the point of view of language and surface texture. Yet not much has been published on this subject. You were born in New York, correct?

Charles Bernstein: Yes, at Doctor's Hospital, Upper East Side, Manhattan, on April 4, 1950. As my father had it on the announcement: "Sherry Bernstein, Labor; Herman Bernstein, Management."

LPG: I'd also be interested in hearing about your parents. Certainly the idea of poetry as a business and the generational conflict, for example in "Sentences My Father Used," makes this of great interest.

CB: My father, Herman Joseph Bernstein, was born Joseph on December 22, 1902, in Manhattan; he was the eighth of 11 brothers and sisters: Joseph (who died before him, so the name was never really used), Sadie, Harry, Gad, David, Pauline, Ceil, Evelyn, Sidney, and Nahum. His father, Charles, died when my father was young; his mother, Jenny, died in early 1945. Both immigrated from Western Russia in the 1890s, settling in the Lower East Side and then the Village. Jenny ran a Jewish resort in Long Branch, New Jersey, for a while but was put out of business by an epidemic; later she ran a restaurant in lower Manhattan. My father's grandfather spent his days studying the Talmud and the like; he did not work. Many of my father's brothers were very successful in business and real estate. My father mostly worked in the garment industry, eventually as co-owner of Smartcraft Corporation, a medium-size manufacturer of ladies' dresses, one of the first firms to make cheap ($12) knock-offs of fashion dresses. Back taxes did him in in the early 60s; he had a heart attack but eventually rebounded as the American consultant to Teijin, Ltd., Japan's largest textile manufacturer. He married my mother on December 12, 1945, at the age of 42. He died January 20, 1978, of leukemia.

My mother was an only child. She was born on February 2, 1921,

229

and lived with her mother, Birdie Kegel, on Avenue P, near Prospect Park in Brooklyn. Birdie, born Bertha in Western Russia in 1891, was abandoned by her father, Louis Stolitsky, who left for the United States. Her mother died and she was sent, alone, to America when she was seven; she went to live with her father and stepmother, an unhappy circumstance for her. She married Edward Kegel in 1918. He was a successful Brooklyn real estate developer; he died of a streptococcus infection in 1927.

LPG: Given that both your parents had their roots in Western Russia, might I ask specifically where in Western Russia they came from? Importantly, did you grow up in an environment of spoken Yiddish or Russian? Do you have any familiarity with or memory of either of these languages?

CB: I don't know the precise locations where my grandparents on my mother's side were born. My father's mother emigrated from Lithuania in about 1888, when she was in her early teens; his father emigrated from near Odessa: But this was ancient history to my father, who after all was born in New York, and I don't ever recall him talking about it, except in the oral history I did with him just before he died, which I had to listen to again in order to answer your question. My father did not dwell on such things, at least not so as I could tell. Maybe it was that he didn't want to trouble me, or my brother and sister, about it; maybe he didn't think we'd be interested; maybe he didn't want to think about it. The main thing was that the family got out. In things like this I found my father quite opaque: he didn't seem at all introspective, although to say that is to reflect an enormous gulf between his own cultural circumstances and my own. In many ways my father seemed foreign to me, which is not to say unfamiliar; so it is all the more startling that I now find myself resembling him in so many ways. The early poem that you mentioned, "Sentences My Father Used" (in *Controlling Interests*), tried to think this through; much of this poem is based on the oral history I did with my father. (I'm sure I'm not alone in finding Paul Auster's evocation of his father, in *The Invention of Solitude*, very close to my own experience of my father.)

But equally, in the case of my mother and my grandmother, origins and roots were rarely a topic. The only grandparent I knew was my grandmother, who always lived very close by, but since she came to America as a little girl, any echo of Yiddish was long gone. My mother says the only time she remembers hearing her parents speak Yiddish was when they were saying something they didn't want her to understand. So, no, we "had" only American English at home, except for the occasional Friday night Hebrew prayer, although neither of my parents, nor my grandmother, knew much Hebrew and what Hebrew was around was the product of religious education. That was the context in which I learned a very little Hebrew in the couple of years before I turned 13, at Congregation Rodeph Shalom, a Reform synagogue on the Upper West Side.

LPG: But wouldn't your father have been familiar with these languages? And if the background of your parents was not a linguistic presence, wasn't it of importance in their political outlook?

CB: My father probably spoke Yiddish as a kid, but there was no hint of that in our household, except for the pervasive idiomatic insistences that come naturally from any such linguistic background and add texture and character to a person's speech. For example, my father would say "close the lights" or "take a haircut". I know there must be dozens more examples but I can't bring any to mind right now, only keep hearing him saying, "Can't you kids close the lights? This place is lit up like Luna Park."

My parents were assimilationists who nonetheless had a strong Jewish and later Zionist identification. As for many of their generation, this made for interesting contradictions. We were loosely kosher in the "beef fry" years, but in other years the bacon fried plentifully and tasted sweet. Or we were kosher on Friday night when my Aunt Pauline came to dinner but not the rest of the week. Of course, on Rosh Hashonah and Yom Kippur, when dozens of relatives descended on our apartment for gigantic and endless meals that I grew to dread for their tediousness, we were strictly kosher, with once-a-year Pesach plates and cakes made from matzoh meal. (Those who might "correctly" say you can't be a little bit kosher ignore the actual practice of Jewish ethnicity.) My father's family was associated with the Congregation Sherith Israel, the hundreds-year-old Spanish and Portuguese synagogue relocated across the street from our building; I occasionally attended the Orthodox services in their august main sanctuary. But as I say, for my parents the religious end of Judaism was less pronounced than a decisive, but at the same time mutable, ethnic identification.

In politics my parents were liberal Democrats, but not especially political, though I can still remember handing out leaflets on Broadway and 74th Street for Adlai Stevenson, when I was 6. And while I am pleased to have been enlisted into the Stevenson camp, and have holes in my own shoes to prove it, my politics and that of my parents grew further apart. When I was a teenager my father and I used to have vituperative exchanges at dinner about Vietnam and about racism, as he embraced Hubert Humphrey and I drifted leftward.

More recently, my mother expressed her exasperation that I was the only Jew in New York who supported Jesse Jackson, though I pointed out to her that my brother had also voted for Jackson. (I center here on my father not only because it is more relevant to your question but also because my relation with my mother continues in a way that makes me less apt to characterize it.)

In any case, my father's concerns were centered foursquarely on success, and too often, and very painfully for him, failure in business. As he put it, "One can achieve success and happiness if the right priorities are valued." "The right priorities" was not a particularly elastic concept for him and in this he represents, more than less, a new-immigrant generation that didn't have the leisure to question what their very hard work made possible for my generation.

LPG: Louis Zukofsky and Charles Reznikoff are writers who have been consistently of great interest to you in their ability to "create a new world in English, a new word for what they called America." How does the experience of your family inform your reading of these authors? I was wondering if, especially in Reznikoff's work, other than the literary and documentary qualities, there are specific events or issues that you find particularly resonant in your personal history?

CB: Yes, my relation to Zukofsky and Reznikoff is tempered by this history. Zukofsky and my father were virtually the same age and grew up near each other, but there seem few other points in common. Zukofsky and Reznikoff interrogated and resisted the very ideologies that my father accepted as the givens of American life. And both had gone well beyond the high school education my father possibly completed. (My mother's education was not much more extensive, though she had a few years of "finishing school" after high school; but that is a different story.)

My father certainly had no sympathy for artists, whom he thought of as frauds (in the case of "modern" art) or slackers (as in the case of his own rabbinic grandfather, whom he saw as something of a family black sheep). And we grew up surrounded by popular American culture but very little in the way of literature or art. While my parents hardly even played music on the radio, the newspapers—the *Times*, the *Post*, the *Daily News*, and later *Women's Wear Daily*—loomed large. We did have books, but they were mostly inherited popular novels of the previous decades supplemented by a few contemporary best-sellers or condensed books (just add boiling water). My mother had decorated a large part of our apartment in a very formal French colonial style. The large living room, for example, was for company—not for everyday life. In this context, books become decor, as with a complete set of Ruskin's work bought by the yard for a beautiful antique bookshelf. As far as I can tell, the Ruskin was never opened during my childhood, though I do appreciate the fact that it presided over us, in some subliminal way.

Zukofsky and Reznikoff are important to me because they suggest a totally different sense of Jewishness than anything I knew of in the 50s, something along the lines that Isaac Deutscher, writing from a left perspective, describes as the "non-Jewish Jew", but also part of the heterodox context chartered by Jerome Rothenberg in *A Big Jewish Book.* This is something of a circus sideshow to "serious" Judaism, with opening acts by Maimonides and Baal Shem Tov, Spinoza and Heine, or, in the main tent, Groucho and Harpo and Chico Marx, Lenny Bruce, Woody Allen, Bob Dylan. While I never mentioned Jewishness in my college piece on Stein and Wittgenstein (and the subject is largely unmentioned in each of their works), it is, of course, an obvious point of contact as well as a crucial, if implicit, reference point for me.

But let me end this string of thoughts by quoting a passage from Amos Oz that, by a delicious coincidence, Eric Selinger e-mailed while I was answering your question:

Now suppose a new Kafka is growing up right now, here in San Francisco, California. Suppose he is fourteen years old right now. Let's call him Chuck Bernstein. Let's assume that he is every bit of a genius as Kafka was in his time. His future must, as I see it, depend on an uncle in Jerusalem or an experience by the Dead Sea, or a cousin in a kibbutz or something inspired by the Israeli live drama. Otherwise, with the exception of the possibility that he is growing up among the ultra-Orthodox, he will be an American writer of Jewish origin—not a Jewish American writer. He may become a new Faulkner, but not a new Kafka.[*]

It seems to me this tortured and reductive conception of identity is just what the tradition of writers I've mentioned have refused. And it is in exploring and realizing alternative identity formations that at least one sliver of a Jewish tradition may be of use; in this, Kafka is our dark and imploding star.

LPG: As your father was a manager in the garment industry, how did this reflect upon your own sense of "self" while growing up? (In other words, his work could have seemed petty or commercial compared to your own engagement with social concerns or you may have felt pressure to become a part of the "cottage" industry.) Did you have to fight pressure to participate in your father's commercial enterprise?

---

[*] Amos Oz, "Imagining the Other: 1", in *The Writer in the Jewish Community: An Israeli-North American Dialogue*, ed. Richard Siegel and Tamar Sofer (London: Associated University Presses, 1993), p. 122.

CB: One day I woke up and found myself metamorphosed into a tiny businessman. All that I have done since, political and poetic, has changed this not at all. For poetry, after all, is the ultimate small business, requiring a careful keeping of accounts to stay afloat. Not to mention all that "small press" stuff like distribution, promotion, and book manufacturing. That is to say, I have wanted to bring poetry into the "petty, commercial", indeed material and social world of everyday life rather than make it a space in which I could remain "free" of these things, or, better to say, chained to an illusion of such freedom.

Because my father and his brothers were "self-made" men, they believed that theirs was the only practical, and therefore right, course in life. The proof was that it had worked for them and, as far as I can tell, they never came to understand how the lives so created could look so hollow, if not misguided, to at least a few of the next generation. To start a business on nothing, as my father had done in the 1920s, when he bought and resold short end-pieces of fabric rolls that would otherwise have been discarded ("the trim, the waste"), meanwhile being weekly hounded by his successful brother to repay a small loan, sets in place a pattern of anxiety and diminished expectations for the, what?, "quality" of life, if aesthetics can be defined so, that doesn't easily, if ever, unravel. The business isn't something you do to make money; it's what you do, who you are. Family, like cultural or social activities, is an extended lunch break.

And what went with this, at least for my father, was an unquestioning belief not only in progress and industry in the abstract but in the absolute value of industrialization, Western Civilization, the market system, and technology that the catastrophes of the Second World War did not, finally, touch. I imagine that the 20s and 30s passed my father by as he worked, singly and single-mindedly, to establish himself, to create his own estate. That came, finally, during the war and he married for the first time in the very first year of the postwar era, and at pretty much the age I am now, starting a family when most men of his generation had grown-up kids. He came the closest to his American Dream in the 1950s. It was as if his life had led him to this decade of prosperity and surface tranquillity, and he remained, for the rest of his life, its unshakable constituent.

But here's where the ethnic ethos comes in again: it wasn't for us, the children, to continue in business but to become professionals, free from the grinding labor and terrorizing uncertainty of business. The pressure, then, was to be a physician or lawyer; my own choice, at least initially toward downward social mobility, was rankling and fundamentally unacceptable, and must have made me seem ungrateful and disrespectful of the whole struggle of the business, of his life. I know my father often complained about my lack of respect and certainly had no respect to spare for my choices. I pretty much ignored the pressure, which is to say adamantly rejected the life so envisioned for me, and never, really, looked back.

LPG: Tell me about your brother and sister? Did you grow up in New York? What was your early life like?

CB: I have a brother, Edward Amber (changed his last name), born October 8, 1946, and a sister, Leslie Gross (married to Donald Gross), born June 17, 1948. My parents moved from 81st Street just east of Columbus to 101 Central Park West just before I was born; my mother still lives in the same luxurious twelfth-floor apartment, which overlooks Central Park. Classic Upper West Side.

Like my sister and brother, I went to a self-congratulating "progressive" school of the Deweyite persuasion, the Ethical Culture School. I was there kindergarten to sixth grade. None of us did very well there and I intensely disliked the social, cultural, and intellectual environment. This was a place that even if you were "comfortable" the other kids, and their parents, made you feel like you were a pauper. On the school's part, they did not think much of me, as I was repeatedly told: my penmanship and spelling were abysmal; I was slow to read and in constant need of remedy in the form of remedial groups; I did not socialize right, my appearance was somewhat ajar. I give a sense of this in "Standing Target" in *Controlling Interests*, where I quote some reports from Fieldston day camp, which was run by Ethical. My favorite thing to do was stay home; some years I missed as many as 40 days. And at home there was the chance for reverie, for sleeping late, for making tuna fish sticks sprinkled with paprika, for watching daytime TV. I read *TV Guide* religiously in those days and knew all the panelists on the celebrity game shows, all the actors on the sitcoms, and all the comedy shows from the early 50s that I had missed the first time around.

I liked TV and hanging out at home—but not sports! I was the kind of kid that was always picked last for the team and put in right field or its equivalent. By the time I was in high school (after a brief flirtation with soccer, all dressed in black to play goalie, in junior high school), I used to put my hands in my pockets whenever I was thrust into a game. Never played catch with any member of my family, but we used to go out to Chinese dinners on Thanksgiving and Christmas, and I liked that.

I can still remember my delight at the reaction of my sixth-grade teacher, Miss Green, when I sported a button that read "I may look interested but I'm just being polite." I've always tried to be polite. But I did like one thing about Miss Green's class: for months, it seems to me, we read, always starting from the first page, *The Old Curiosity Shop*: "Night is generally my time for walking." I loved that and could, no matter how awkward I otherwise felt in the class, fall into that prose and be transported.

I was not admitted to Fieldston, Ethical's upper school, a routine matter for my classmates, and went on, to my great relief, to a small highly conventional, private school, Franklin, for seventh and eighth grades, and it was there that the worlds of history and literature opened up for me. What I hated about Ethical was that you never received grades but were given pop psychology reports about your development and social integration. At Franklin, there were concrete tasks assigned and measured by tests; the right attitude was less important than the right facts. Certainly, there were some tough times adjusting. I wanted to do really well and can remember cheating a few times on tests in seventh grade, as if that would prove to myself that I knew a thing or two. Actually, the academic side of the school became the great focus of my life as I began to read the history of Greece or China and especially to read literature. I remember a great, thick collection of international short stories, with a gray cover, that I got while at Franklin and the excitement I felt when I read, even if I could not fully understand, Kafka, Genet, Camus, and especially Sartre. Then one day in seventh or eighth grade an English teacher named Francis Xavier Walker wrote on the board, "Bun is such a sad word is it not, and man is not much better is it." He said it was by Samuel Beckett and that he liked the way it sounded, the way it focused on the sound of the words man and bun. That was kind of like hearing about the theory of relativity. I was hooked; in fact years seemed to go by when all I wanted to do was stay in my small room overlooking the park, which at that point I rarely stepped into, and read books and watch TV.

LPG: Yes, you have written that "my work is as influenced by *Dragnet* as by Proust." This comment, of course, is indicative of the sources of "information" we have in a media culture like ours. Did your interest in the classroom experience change when you went to high school?

CB: Well, I always loved those clipped voice-overs. But I have to say the influence of *Dragnet* was nothing compared to the Manhattan *Yellow Pages*.

I spent high school at a terrific school, the Bronx High School of Science, where, in my senior year, I edited the school newspaper, *Sci-*

ence Survey. Science was a "specialized" school, something like today's magnet schools, but pretty much the only such schools in New York, in the Sputnik era, were science schools, so my interest in going there was for the quality of the school and not for the science and math, which I never cared much about. Strangely, I always did very well on standardized tests of physics, chemistry, geometry, algebra, and the like, but I never felt like I "got" it. My interests were literature, history, social studies. Indeed, I coordinated our high school Forum series, which sponsored speakers every month; I remember in particular taking a cab back into the city with James Farmer of CORE. There were great, even inspired, English teachers at Science. The one I was closest to was Richard Feingold, who gave vivid lectures on *Hamlet,* Jonathan Edwards, Emily Dickinson, and Robert Frost. Feingold is now a professor of 18th-century poetry at Berkeley. He came to my reading there a few months back—I hadn't seen him in over 25 years.

During high school I started going to the movies a lot, and also to the theater. I grew up with the big musicals of the period, but at this point I got interested in Pinter and imports from the Royal Shakespeare Company, Peter Brooks's productions, but also off-Broadway stuff: I can still remember being riveted by Leroi Jones's *Dutchman.* You know, the whole world of "high culture" and modernism opened up for me and I was always making lists of what I should know about. I remember sending for WQXR's Martin Bookspan's list of the 100 most important classical records and then checking them out at the library or buying them. I mean I had no information about this kind of thing but I was fascinated. My parents, like I said, didn't listen to music, or read very much beyond the newspapers and magazines (though my mother would occasionally read a best-selling novel), but they did do things like get me a subscription to Leonard Bernstein's Young People's Concerts with the New York Philharmonic and they were happy to buy me tickets for lots of other concerts all over the city, which I generally went to by myself. When I was 16, my father, sister, and I went to Europe. We visited London, Paris, Florence, Rome, and Berlin. In London I went to plays every night and saw all the museums, all the sights. It was thrilling, although it was quite difficult to travel with my father, and the deep generational and political divisions between us were never so apparent.

LPG: When did this divergent cultural information begin to coalesce for you?

CB: Everything fell into place in the mid-60s: those great movies from Fellini and Antonioni and Godard, Phil Ochs and Bob Dylan and

Richie Havens—and much that holds up far less well these days (I still have my Procol Harem and Incredible String Band records), the Be-Ins, the smoke from loose joints. While I had a Bar Mitzvah at 13 and was, at the time, quite religious, all that started to come apart within a year or two. The civil rights movement, the sit-ins, the Mississippi Freedom summer, Martin Luther King, and then the Vietnam war all increasingly focused my politics. I tuned to WBAI, Pacifica radio in New York. I was around for the demonstrations during the Columbia University strike during my senior year in high school, and also involved with demonstrations at my high school (against regulations prohibiting "shirts without collars and dungaree-type pants", among other things).

I've never shaken the shock and sadness I felt when Martin Luther King was assassinated; it was my 18th birthday. In the summer of 1968, after a trip I took by myself to Scandinavia (I wanted to see the fjords) and also to Greece (where you could still get by on a couple of dollars a day), I returned to the U.S. to go to the Chicago demonstrations during the Democratic National Convention. Like everyone else there, I got gassed, got "radicalized" (again), and got to hear Allen Ginsberg chant "Om" to the crowd.

I met Susan (Bee Laufer) in high school—at a party in Greenwich Village on February 9, 1968. Her parents had both grown up in Berlin, had left in 1936 on a youth aliyah to Palestine when they were teenagers, and had met in Jerusalem. They came to New York in 1948—Sigmund keeping the same job, until a couple of years ago, and the same apartment all this while. Susan's parents were both artists: her mother, Miriam, a wonderful, unjustly unrecognized, painter doing 50s-style expressionist paintings of, among other things, female nudes, a later series painted on car windshields. The Laufers, who had been sympathetic with the left when in Palestine, were a remarkable political and cultural contrast to my own family. With Susan, I started to go to the art galleries and then also up to Provincetown.

LPG: Then you attended Harvard, correct? This must have been quite a change from the cultural and social excitement of Manhattan. Was this a satisfying experience?

CB: I found Harvard a rather unpleasant place and was shocked by the snobbism and arrogance. It was unbelievable to me that the "men" at the Freshman Commons would clink their glasses when a woman walked into the hall. If Katie Roiphe and other post-feminists would like to go back to this time, they can have it. This was the last year that you had to wear a tie and jacket to dinner; there were parietals in effect in the still all-male dorms. I found the environment suffocating and depressing. And living in Harvard Yard was like living in a zoo—with all the tourists taking pictures of you and your environs when you poked your head out the door.

I have to say, it was an eye-opener to realize how few of my classmates actually cared about the arts, literature, history; though after a while it was possible to find like-minded souls. Still, Harvard students, on the whole, seemed contemptuous of the arts and of learning in a way I never encountered at Bronx Science; I soon came to realize that the enhanced admission for students from elite prep schools pulled down the intellectual, cultural, and moral level of the school, just as it does the country. Talk about affirmative action. In my year only one student from all the public schools of Chicago got into Harvard, while 40 percent of the classes at the elite schools were admitted. I got a real sense of where this was all going when I had a job doing child care at a 25th reunion. At the Boston Pops concert, the middle-aged Harvard grads gave a standing ovation to an orchestral version of "Raindrops Keep Falling on My Head". I keep that image in mind when I think of our "elite" institutions and what they are doing for our culture.

I was not alone in my distress. In my freshman year I became involved in the anti-war movement, even if my somewhat anarchic and pacifist politics did not sit well with some factions of SDS. I was impressed by many of the ideas of the New Left, and especially by the Port Huron statement and the concept of participatory democracy. And I certainly thought something had to be done to stop the war. I was in and out of University Hall during the 1969 occupation, but when the police were called I was in bed, right next door to the occupied building. I quickly slipped into the building and was arrested for trespassing in a case that was ultimately dismissed. Despite the dismissal in a court of law, I was put under indefinite "Warning" by Harvard's Committee of Rights and Responsibilities ("We're right, you're responsible"). I have been amused and appalled to see how in the intervening years some of my classmates who did not take a stand of principle against the war have parlayed their own failure of political judgment into a source of pundit power: I am thinking here of James Fallows and Michael Kinsley.

LPG: The political informs your work on many levels. It seems relevant here, given your experience with politics at the Columbia and Harvard strikes and the (one would presume extremely significant) Chicago demonstrations, to ask whether you were considering political activism as a future involvement. What influenced you in this regard? And wouldn't "literary" action be considered less than effective? How do you reconcile this?

CB: I never wanted to be a professional activist, although in some ways maybe that is what I've become. I always thought protest was for the informed citizen, taking the time out of her or his everyday life, time hard to spare but required by the very demands of citizenship. The demonstrations of the 60s and 70s were exhilarating, and I dearly miss that level of idealism and activism in the U.S., dearly miss the time when the political and cultural left, or shades of it, set the national agenda rather than the Religious Right, as now seems the case. Still, I was amazed at a reunion held on the 20th anniversary of the Harvard strike how many of the people spoke of those events as the high point of their life. I think my own preoccupations were and are elsewhere.

It seems like it can never be stated often enough that the claims made for "the politics of poetic form" are against the idea of the political efficacy of poetry. If anything, the politics of the poetic for which I have spoken mute any such efficacy. So then the question becomes, how do you reconcile thought and action, or second thoughts and action, reflection and decision? The answer is, as best you can. Poetry explores crucial questions about the core values that constitute a polis; it allows for reformulations of the basic issues of political policy and the means we use to represent them. It may even mock what men, and women, hold most dear, so that in our laughter we may come to terms with what we cling to.

Poetry thickens discussion, refuses reductive formulations. It sings of values not measurable as commercial sums. But such poetic politics do not exhaust one's political options or commitments. I don't suggest that aesthetics replace politics, I just don't believe in a politics that abolishes aesthetics.

LPG: If Harvard was a disappointment culturally, I wonder what your expectations had been. Did you expect a revelation in terms of education? Was there a specific grant or scholarship that encouraged you to attend? Why did you choose to go to Harvard?

CB: My choice was to go to the best college that I could get into, where "best" was conventionally defined. This was a given, which I had no means to contest. I bought the image of Harvard as the ultimate place of Higher Learning, in which I would be able to pursue my studies in a manner that deepened and extended what I most liked at Bronx Science. In many ways this was possible at Harvard, and I certainly did have the extraordinary opportunity to read and converse. I just had no idea what went with this; my studies had not prepared me for the fact that the fruit of learning would be laced with nausea-inducing poison and that for many the lesson learned was not to eat that fruit, or not eat very much. That is perhaps the chief product of the Harvard Education: willful ignorance, learned callousness, and an ability to keep your eye on your personal bottom line (defined by money and social status). So, yes, this was disillusioning, and it hit me hard and almost immediately upon arriving—that "learning", as I had romanticized it, was not disinterested and indeed was being used as a means of preserving social injustice; that one had to struggle, even at a place like this, to create a space for thought, reflection, art. These are lessons I have found very useful. But perhaps, looking back, it's not Harvard that shocked me but America, an America I had not yet met in the culturally rich, but unrepresentative, precincts I had inhabited up to that point in my life.

LPG: Your involvement with philosophy is well known. Certainly, "Thought's Measure", among others, qualifies as a consummate philosophical essay. You studied philosophy at Harvard?

CB: Yes, I concentrated in philosophy at college, though my interests were more in the history of philosophy and "continental" philosophy than in analytic philosophy, toward which I was antipathetic. As a freshman I took "Introduction to Symbolic Logic" with Willard Quine. He mumbled to the blackboard during most of the lectures, though I did find his books witty and provocative. I had a dream one night in which I was haphazardly trying to stuff all my clothes into a suitcase and Quine came over to show me how they would all fit if neatly folded. I shot him. (This was a time in which Quine was widely quoted as saying that we should handle the student demonstrators in the United States the way they did in South America: bring in the militia.) Then there was Hilary Putnam, who was in his Maoist period. And John Rawls, whose *Theory of Justice* had just come out: the most rational man in the world but, well, somewhat boring and stiff for my taste at the time. In contrast, I was very impressed with Judith Shklar, the social historian.

Two philosophers, Stanley Cavell and Rogers Albritton, were particularly important for me at Harvard. The first year I was there they split one of those grand tours of Western thought, Albritton from the pre-Socratics to the Middle Ages, and Cavell from the Enlightenment on. Each brought his own quirky, thought-filled style to the occasion. I had heard about Wittgenstein before coming to college and felt an immediate fascination, so to fall in with these two Wittgensteinians was marvelous. I also had the great pleasure of spending a fair amount of time talking to Cavell and Albritton, and

though I have remained friends with, and been influenced by, Cavell
all these years, it was those long late-night discussions with Albritton
that initiated me into philosophical conversation. My senior thesis
was called "Three Compositions on Philosophy and Literature" and
was a reading of Stein's *Making of Americans* through Wittgenstein's
Philosophical Investigations. (A bit of this was recently published in
Gertrude Stein Advanced, ed. Richard Kostelanetz.)

LPG: It seems to me that Stein and Wittgenstein would not exactly be
considered "canonical" in any institution at the time. Were these writ-
ers approved or encouraged in your program? Was it a struggle to
gain acceptance for these writers as the focus of your thesis?

CB: As I mentioned, Cavell and Albritton were both very committed to
Wittgenstein, especially the *Investigations,* so within that microcosm,
Wittgenstein was the canonical, albeit "anticanonical," modernist
philosopher. I had no companions in my enthusiasm for Stein, how-
ever; not surprising in a philosophy faculty in any case, and most
decisively not in the English faculty, with which I had little contact.
Of course Stein had studied at Harvard with William James and at
Emerson Hall, the site of my own studies; but that was a fact of little
import in 1971. Since mine was an undergraduate thesis I was pretty
much left to do what I wanted and wasn't required to gain any accep-
tance for Stein, which would not have been possible. I did have a
third reader for the piece though, a witty and genial visiting British
philosopher named G. E. L. Owen, whose specialty was classical
Greek philosophy but who had read, and expressed some sympathy
for, Stein.

LPG: Were your thesis readers comfortable with the *connection* between
Stein and Wittgenstein?

CB: At the time the idea of a connection between Stein and Wittgen-
stein was completely far-fetched, the first of my crackpot theories
that end up, over time, not seeming nearly so cracked. If the linking
of these two names now seems unsurprising, that takes away from
some of the brash humor I had in mind for it years ago. My own
name for the project was "Three Steins". But I can't explain how when
I was 21 I fell upon a matrix of thinking and writing that would con-
tinue to occupy me until this day. For the writing and thinking I was
starting to do then is very much of a piece with my work now. Let's
say it was an intuition that bore out.

LPG: What was the occasion or relation or particular event that might
have put you in contact with these writers? How did this come
about?

CB: Wittgenstein I had first heard about in high school, just a passing remark by a friend returned from college, but I became fascinated and curious since it seemed to go significantly beyond what I had been finding so interesting in that wonderfully intoxicating high-schoolish way about existentialism (with a puff of Hesse, zen, the Beats, and the Beatles mixed in), and so was happy to pick up on that in the next few years, especially in the context of reading over a range of philosophical works. I can't quite place my interest in Stein, certainly not from any class or reading list! I know I was consciously looking for literary equivalents for the modernist and abstract expressionist painting that I was so passionately taken by, and while I appreciated what I was offered—Joyce or Céline or Kafka or Woolf or Proust or, indeed, Faulkner, I felt there was something missing, something I did see, though, in Beckett's *Stories and Texts for Nothing* and Burroughs's *Naked Lunch* (I realize my examples here are all prose writers). Meanwhile, in 1970 Susan [Bee] was taking a seminar with Catharine Stimpson at Barnard, one of the first courses to be given on women's literature. This was way before there were anthologies or even recommended syllabi for such classes, before much of the material now at the center of women's studies courses was reprinted. Anyway, Stimpson apparently assigned *Three Lives* and I must have heard about that from Susan. I don't think I more than glanced at *Three Lives*, but I soon found *The Making of Americans*, *Tender Buttons*, "Composition as Explanation", and much other Stein material, some of which was beginning to be published in new editions at this time. When I first read these works of Stein, I was completely knocked out: this was what I had been looking for, what I knew must exist, and I was giddy with excitement.

LPG: What other activities were you involved in at Harvard? What about its "literary" culture?

CB: My sophomore year I happily moved to Adams House, just at the time it became coed and when it still had a beautiful private swimming pool. (When I was on the house committee we passed a resolution requiring bathing suits only from 7 to 9 AM.) My main artistic work at college was in theater, though, oddly, as I look back on it, I was elected editor of the freshman literary magazine, the *Harvard Yard Journal*, and we put out two issues. In my senior year I also put out a small xerox magazine of work by people in Adams House called *Writing*. (I stayed clear of "literary society" at Harvard, or anyway it stayed clear of me. The pretentiousness of the *Advocate* scene couldn't mask its emptiness, and I don't mean that in the zen sense.)

LPG: Were there other "cultural" activities you found more relevant at the time?

CB: I studied theater games and improvisation with Dan Seltzer, a Shakespearean scholar who had gotten involved with acting. I directed several productions, including a rather large-scale musical production of Peter Weiss's *Persecution and Assassination of Jean-Paul Marat as Performed by the Inmates of the Asylum of Charenton under the Direction of the Marquis de Sade*, influenced by the radical theater work of the Living Theater, the Open Theater, and Grotowski. We did the production in street clothes (though one review seemed to think these were hippie costumes) in the dining room at Adams House. William Liller, an astronomer and the master of Adams House, played the Director of the asylum and Marat was played by John McCain, at that time a Progressive Labor Party activist and later gay activist; McCain died of AIDS a few years back. The composer Leonard Lehrman was the musical director. It was a wild time. One night the Japan scholar John Fairchild showed up and one of the cast rebuked him, in one of the bedlam scenes during the play, for his Vietnam policy—in Japanese. After a benefit performance for the Bobby Seale defense fund, a spontaneous demonstration moved the audience into the street. The next year I scripted and directed a work I called *Comings and Goings* that linked short pieces by Beckett and Pinter with a staging of the trial of the Chicago 8. I also played a bit role in a play by Joseph Timko and Jesse Ausubel on the death of Moritz Schlick, the Vienna Circle philosopher and logical positivist. My role was as the graduate student that killed Schlick and my line was "I shoot you out of jealousy and revenge: Bang! Bang!"

I spent the fall following college graduation (1972) in New York, living with Susan on Arden Street in Washington Heights and working mainly as the office manager of Sloan's Furniture Clearance Center #45 on East 85th Street, for $2.75/hour. When Susan graduated Barnard in December, I took advantage of a William Lyon MacKenzie King Fellowship, which I had received, and we spent a year in Ruskin, just east of Vancouver. I had a loose and pleasant relation with Simon Fraser University, and it was there I attended a marvelous seminar on Emily Dickinson with Robin Blaser.

LPG: From what I've read, I would assume that you experienced a breakthrough in Vancouver. Was it at this point that the thrust of your future in writing became apparent?

CB: Not so much a breakthrough as follow-through. I moved to the Vancouver area with Susan in January 1973, six months after graduating college. During the nine months I was there I was able to read in and around the "New American Poetry", something I knew little about before this.

Shortly after moving, I sent some of my work, out of the blue, to Jerome Rothenberg, primarily on the strength of *Technicians of the Sacred*, which I had read with great enthusiasm when it came out in the late 60s. Remarkably, Jerry wrote me right back and suggested I get in touch with Ron Silliman, in San Francisco, who was editing a section of new poetry for his and Dennis Tedlock's new magazine, *Alcheringa*. Ron wrote me back, also immediately, on a piece of letter-head from something called "The People's Yellow Pages", which seems apt for Ron. He had finished the collection, called "The Dwelling Place: 9 Poets", but said he was going to quote something I said in my letter to him. He also gave me a list of people to read, which, as I recall it from this distance, included Michael Palmer and Clark Coolidge and a half-dozen others, including Eigner and Cree-ley. I hadn't read many of those poets and was also hearing about some of them, and a related set, from Blaser. I had access to the library and to the extraordinary poetry collection, so I had no trouble finding even the most obscure poetry I wanted. It was heaven.

As to my writing, I was onto something, but not there yet. I hadn't yet gotten to the other side of what Ron, I think, heard as Stein's "syrupy rhythm"; I was in a Stein period, that's for sure, writing things like "Paddington wade, she said faded" and a mock-epic, "Hermes Hermeneutic" ("Hermes Hermeneutic, the swashbuckle kid from Ala-cazam, swim/swam/swum past fireflies and mint juleps, pusses in the alleys and lizigator monsters").

LPG: Then you returned to New York City?

CB: Actually we moved from Vancouver to Santa Barbara in the fall of 1973, for no particular reason, I suppose, than that the sun was ap-pealing after months of gray skies. In Santa Barbara I worked part-time for the Freedom Community Clinic, a free clinic, as a health ed-ucation coordinator at a time when we were very involved in questions of feminism and gay rights, drug education, and, of course, sexually transmitted diseases. While I was there I continued to read around and I was in touch with other poets, getting their magazines and books. Even made it up to see Ron Silliman, although our first conversation was made almost inaudible by the loud band playing at the bar where we met. (Ron knew one of the people in the band!) In Santa Barbara I went to one of Kenneth Rexroth's gatherings but didn't connect up with that context at all. *Disfrutes* and *Asylums* were written in Santa Barbara and include the earliest poems of mine that have been published.

I moved back to New York, to 464 Amsterdam, in early 1975, and that's when I met Bruce Andrews and we discovered how much we

had in common, not only as poets and artists but also, for example, in
an interest in such things as the Frankfurt school, which at that time
seemed an unlikely thing for a poet to be interested in. (I had read
Habermas's *Knowledge and Human Interest* with great interest and later
attended a series of lectures he gave at UC Santa Barbara in 1974.)

In New York I went to lots of readings, particularly at the Poetry
Project at St. Mark's, but all over the place. And in 1978 not only did
Bruce and I start $L=A=N=G=U=A=G=E$, actually the planning for
that goes back to 1976, but Ted Greenwald and I also started the Ear
Inn series.

LPG: Let me stop you for a moment here. I am specifically interested in
the period from 1973, when you left Vancouver, and 1978, when
$L=A=N=G=U=A=G=E$ was founded. It is unclear, besides the men-
tion of Stein and Wittgenstein, what your sense of literary "elders"
was during this period. In terms of "contemporaries," you have men-
tioned Jerome Rothenberg and Ron Silliman but I have the feeling
that your reading would have been much more immense. Let me be
more specific. I would like a clear sense of your "position" in terms of
literary "influences" at this time.

CB: "Literary" is a problem for me since I was trying to get away from
the literary, from any preset idea of poetry or of the aesthetic. It
seemed to me that writing, certainly not verse—let's say verbal art in
the sense that Antin talks about it in his early essays—was the thing.

In New York, I worked initially at the United Hospital Fund, writ-
ing the scintillating *Health Manpower Consortia Newsletter*, which Susan
and I designed in exactly the format that we would use, a few years
later, for $L=A=N=G=U=A=G=E$; then briefly for the Council on
Municipal Performance, a public interest group where I primarily
worked on mass transit issues and against the subway fare hike of that
moment; and then for a couple of years, as Abstract Editor of the
Canadian edition of *Modern Medicine*, where I wrote about 80 medical
abstracts each month. This immersion in commercial writing and
editing—as a social space too but more in the technical sense of
learning the standardized compositional rules and forms at the most
detailed, and numbingly boring, level of proofreading and copyedit-
ing—was informing in every way.

As far as art goes, painting has always been intimate for me, and I
mean in particular Susan Bee's work, which crisscrosses, parallels, and
leaps ahead of my "own" work. Living with a painter, seeing the
paintings develop sometimes day to day from my comfortable "critic's
chair", seeing how Susan would handle (and I mean literally handle)

similar interests in collage, in the giddy rhetoric of various styles jux-
taposed, well, I can't adequately acknowledge the importance of that.
Many times Susan's work has amazed me by showing that things I
thought you "theoretically" couldn't do needed to be done, and that
includes things your own ideas would seem to hold you back from.
The company and work of visual artists was and remains so much a
part of the sense and texture of my work that I made a decision, at
some point, not to write too much about it or else I would end up just
writing about it. So I'll leave it without further account save the fact
of my immersion and the many, many shows I went to each month in
the mid-70s.

And then . . . then there's the movies, endless movies, including
the visionary and revisionary films of Sonbert, Snow, Brakhage, Gehr,
Child, Hills, Kubelka, Jacobs, and such (with Vertov, Eisenstein, etc.,
not far behind). And the theater—Richard Foreman's, Robert Wil-
son's (I especially appreciated those early "messy" pieces), Richard
Schechner's stuff at the Performance Garage, and so much else,
including much of the performance art that was presented in New
York at the time. And how about new music, thinking of so many
nights at the Kitchen and other spaces; but also, and crucially, the
opera? And so many poetry readings, three or more a week.

What I am getting to is that in *this* context what most excited me
was indeed the work of my immediate contemporaries, just because,
let's say, they are contemporaries and the meaning and the trajectory
of their work was not yet determined, historicized (which can hap-
pen awfully fast). This work made the most immediate sense to me.

LPG: Certainly these are crucial elements in the constitution of a writ-
ing. But you still haven't mentioned specific writers. Where and who
were the "elders"? That is, what sense of relation was there to say
Pound, Williams, or the Objectivists? Of course there's also a "mid-
dle" layer here: Creeley, Ginsberg (who must've been very active in
New York)—and also Olson (though he doesn't fit exactly into either
of these categories). At the same time I am very intrigued by what
your sense of "contemporaries" might have been. I want a sense of
who your "colleagues" were.

CB: Yes, indeed, there is a literary answer too.

Rothenberg's anthology *Revolution of the Word*, which came out in
1974 and included Riding, Zukofsky, Loy, Gillespie, Oppen, Schwit-
ters, Duchamp, Mac Low, and others, is a good map of what was
interesting me. At the same time, over those years I read and reread
H.D., Williams, Stevens, Eliot, Bunting . . . Not to mention the Rus-

sian constructivists, concrete and visual poetry, sound poetry, ethnopoetics, Dadaism . . . to keep the list, neatly but misleadingly, to the present century.

As for the "middle layer" you ask about, I knew Corso and Ginsberg from high school on, and had seen Ginsberg perform many times. I especially loved his recording of Blake's *Songs of Innocence and Experience*, which I got when I was a college freshman and used to sing to myself all the time (still do). But from my perspective—thinking again back to the early 70s—I think this work just didn't seem to me radically modern in the way that, say, Pollock or Rauschenberg or Morris Louis or Twombly or Rosenquist, or Godard or Cage or Coltrane or Stockhausen, or the poets in *Revolution of the Word*, or indeed Stein or Wittgenstein did. And that would have gone for Pound too, whom I read with greater interest only later.

But somewhere in all this I had to slow up and backtrack a bit, and this is where I started to absorb, in a big way, many of the poets grouped in, around, and about "The New American Poetry" including Mac Low (whom I went to see perform many times during the 70s), Ashbery, Eigner, O'Hara, Guest, Schuyler, Spicer, Antin, and Creeley (whose *A Quick Graph* and other essays I read with great interest). The work of these poets, and especially their *new* and ongoing work, was incredibly exciting for me, and not just as artworks to appreciate. The work made me want to write poetry and also gave me many entry points for how to do it. Reading became intimately connected to writing.

Yet even as I write this, it still seems too pat, too limited, and my suspicion of narrative gets the better of me. When you are just starting to write, all poems seem like maps of possibilities for your own writing, or did to me, and order and sequence is jumbled, irrelevant, maybe an insult. In 1975 I didn't care very much about generations and influences or the order I read anything in, and I certainly didn't know what was important and what not, and if I did probably leapt from the former toward the latter. In 1995, a professor no less, the historical matrix for poetry seems to me not only very interesting but determining. But in that case these lists are as important for the names I've left out that ought certainly to be mentioned, acknowledged.

To chart that warp and woof you'd have to do a magazine like $L=A=N=G=U=A=G=E$, and this is what we did.

LPG: But "charting" implies that the activity surrounding $L=A=N=G=U=A=G=E$ was "fixed" in some sense. In fact, probably the greatest danger for people who write about "Language" writing today is that they do so as if it were defined—a finite set of texts. You are on record as once saying that $L=A=N=G=U=A=G=E$ was one part of several efforts and that these included *This, Roof, A Hundred Posters,* and *Tottel's.* What was the nature of the relationship among the poets involved with the $L=A=N=G=U=A=G=E$ project?

CB: In 1976, when Bruce and I first started to discuss what would become $L=A=N=G=U=A=G=E$, there was no forum that addressed the philosophical, political, and aesthetic concerns that were central to us, although there were many poets and a number of poetry magazines that were working in ways with which we felt a strong affinity. Indeed, there was much hostility in alternative as well as "mainstream" circles, not only to the kind of poetry to which we were committed but also to our poetics—both our insistence on the value of nonexpository essays and also our rejection of received and beloved notions of voice, self, expression, sincerity, and representation.

Official Verse Culture operated then as it does now by denying its narrow stylistic orthodoxy under the cloak of universalized and unassailable poetic principles. Thus we had the spectacle of a poetry of abject conformity celebrating its commitment to individuality while flailing rather more viciously than might have seemed decent at actual individual expression. The prevalent phobias against groups and against critical thinking encouraged us to make our opposing commitments specific and partisan. If mainstream poetic "individuality" breeds unreflected conformism, collective formations might actually provide the space for conversation as well as for difference.

In this context, $L=A=N=G=U=A=G=E$ was (and in other guises and transformations may still be) an ongoing and open-ended collaborative conVERSation and exchange on a series of particular and partisan, but also mutable and provisional, poetic principles and proclivities conducted in a decentralized manner by a number of differently situated editors, reading series coordinators, poets, and readers: a linked series of poetic tendencies and collaborative exchanges among a range of poets who desired, for a period of time, to make this social exchange a primary site of their work. By "open-ended" I'm suggesting a context in which, despite shared, if conflicting, stylistic and formal concerns, one doesn't know what the results will be. No formal rules for participating are ever established. And while I could reiterate our specific and galvanizing preoccupations, the point of $L=A=N=G=U=A=G=E$ was not to define its own activity or to prescribe a singular form of poetry, but rather to insist on particular *possibilities* for poetry and poetics.

LPG: I'm also interested in the "may still be" of your answer. How do

you see the $L=A=N=G=U=A=G=E$ project—or its permutations—
projecting into the present? Certainly the locus of such an activity is
modified by, on the one hand, a number of these poets now appear-
ing in teaching anthologies, and on the other, the number of
"younger" writers entering this "location."

CB: As names like Language poetry, Language writing, language-cen-
tered writing, or language-oriented writing become fixed in time they
lose generic and projective force. About ten years ago, I remember
reading a call for submissions of "language" poetry for a new maga-
zine that said, "You may be a language poet and not know it!" That
seemed right to me: the terms were sufficiently underdetermined that
there was room for projection. In contrast, when *The New York Times
Magazine* ran a big poetry feature last spring that purported to map
contemporary poetry, they carefully excluded from their list of "Lan-
guage Poets" every one of the many participants in
$L=A=N=G=U=A=G=E$—a nasty business unfortunately characteristic
of the sort of cultural disinformation practiced at places like the *Times*.

Still, one test of an art's vitality is that it manages to unsettle, and
it seems like this work continues to do that, and I for one am happy
to embrace the description of my work as ungainly solipsistic inco-
herence that has no meaning. No meaning at all.

Which is to say, projection has its consequences, and one of them
is that the recognition (positive or negative) accorded even a projec-
tion tends to split off, objectify, and atomize the "project", both styl-
istically and generationally. Then again, there's no need to get glued
to a bill of particulars circa 1978 or 1988 when you can just as easily
remain attentive to shifting conditions and contexts, new names and
new work. But when this happens, and this is why it's appealing, the
"location" you mention in your question changes: just that it's my
desire to participate in the emerging locations, to reground myself.
So my current identification is not with work that takes the same
positions as $L=A=N=G=U=A=G=E$ but with work that pursues these
and related issues. I find extraordinary company just now, in so many
magazines and books that I can hardly begin to keep up. For exam-
ple, the Poetics e-mail discussion group, and the Electronic Poetry
Center, with which we are both involved, seem to me to be continu-
ing the work of $L=A=N=G=U=A=G=E$; Segue Distributing, and the
like; just as the poetry publishing of Sun & Moon Press and Roof
Books, or the Ear Inn reading series, for example, continue to flour-
ish, partly because they have welcomed new writers.

And of my companions of $L=A=N=G=U=A=G=E$ days, I find it
less remarkable than it probably is how contemporary, how crucial,

our exchanges remain—not all, of course, but many and profoundly, after 20 years. And yet I am leery of how loyalty to old friends can form a closed circle, and I have tried, no doubt clumsily, fitfully, inadequately, to resist the temptation.

LPG: Speaking of the present, it seems to me not only relevant that the ideas associated with $L=A=N=G=U=A=G=E$ and with your own books have achieved greater circulation and authority but also that your own relation to poetry within the institution has changed dramatically. Some might say that your position with respect to the establishment has shifted from one end of the spectrum to the other: from outsider to insider, from outspoken critic to tenured professor. Do you think you have been absorbed by the institutions you have critiqued? Is it possible for a radical voice to maintain a usefully critical distance while drawing sustenance from a largely conservative institutional apparatus and while having to be, of necessity, supportive of some of the goals of that sponsoring institution?

CB: Absorption is as absorption does. Which is to say, everything is not absorbed in the same way: today's meal can be tonight's delirious dreams . . . or tomorrow's dyspepsia (a kissing cousin to dysprosody). The point is not to just to critique but also to change, and change with. In this sense, my poetry is a kind of changing room, a small but well appointed cabana at the beach of culture. Over time things do change, which is one reason why it is worthwhile to speak up in the first place. Still, I wish there were more publishers, more reviews, more teachers (at all levels) putting forward not only the poets (modern and contemporary) but also the approaches to writing suggested by syntactically inventive, visual, and hyper/hypotextual poetries; by non- and pluri- and quasilinear essays; and by constructive, programmatic, conceptual, and self-reflective poetics.

As something of a formalist, a social formalist, I try to do within any situation what can't be done anywhere else. In terms of teaching that means not focussing on the transmission of repeatable information but rather on the production of an environment for encountering, and for reflecting on, art works; it means providing students the space to pursue projects that might be hard to do elsewhere. But it also requires finding ways to support the poets and poetry to which I remain committed, recognizing how important the university can be, but usually isn't, for the support of such art activity; and also acknowledging that the university's role is not to be the center of authority but a place that responds to, and aids, the poetic activity that is generated, by and large, far from its precincts. That means making the most of whatever resources are available, as we did with the Electronic Poetry Center and the LINEbreak radio show, but also with the Poetics Program reading series, presses, and magazines. The university, like most large bureaucracies, tends toward stagnation, following the least line of resistance. Nonetheless, based on my limited experience, it is possible to create small but deep pools of activity, if you are motivated and tenacious, and perhaps a little bit looney.

I don't think there ever comes a time to stop advocating, or where partisanship or asserting an aesthetic judgment must become merely self-serving. My argument has been, and remains, directed at systematic discrepancies of attention to different approaches to poetry and to language, something that goes beyond any individual poet's recognition, or position. In any case, the idea is not to replace one authority with another, much less one style with another, but to keep the doors spinning to tunes generated on our homemade reality synthesizers. Which is to say: *Keep playing monkey to your own grinder.* And remember: It's not over even when it's over.

Beyond Emaciation

Hemmed in by oceanic verisimilitude
quite a lot like blazing pumps
with pompadour upholstery, bloated
enough to play a hunch on
lumpy reprehension, sputtering
atop murky monstrosity of
chronic maldistribution of rectifiers,
like the match that hit point
at the expense of spooners, or
the pompadour that cartwheeled
past Tumultuous Expectation
(Evacuation), slogging through
packed pitfalls and penny-dreadful
circuits, melody of tilts
& tailspins, tunnels &
torches. Suds, these are my
suds—any attribution to
corroded (corrugated) segment,
spooked the stake and succumb
to eviscerated haberdashery
on line at navigational stump—
humpy calculus to somewhere
near argumentation's eponymous
mortuary. Then walking ahead
or backing off, gesticulating
with meretricious momentum,
salamander retrieval intercepts
gummy (gulled) garrulousity
who meant all the time to
throw the dice to the other
corridor. The ball rolls
down the lane or street or

curb or row or meeting
ground and the titular
turner stoops
to swoop it up
but

Riding's Reason

> That He another day woke to find himself speaking a strange language, in
> which everything was known and clear—as if all difficulties of the intelli-
> gence were difficulties of language alone: in this language He had but to
> speak to discover, as, for instance, the word for *horse* here not only stood for
> horse but also made plain the quality of horseliness, what it was.
>
> Laura Riding, *Anarchism Is Not Enough* (1928)

The publication of *Rational Meaning: A New Foundation for the Definition of
Words* brings to completion one of the most aesthetically and philosoph-
ically singular projects of twentieth-century American poetry. No North
American or European poet of this century has created a body of work that
reflects more deeply on the inherent conflicts between truth telling and
the inevitable artifice of poetry than Laura (Riding) Jackson. This conflict
ultimately led, in 1941, to Riding's renunciation of poetry; it is also the
basis of this long *summa contra poetica*, which she wrote with her husband,
Schuyler Jackson, over a near forty-year period starting around 1948.

No doubt *Rational Meaning* will be most appreciated by those who
appreciate the body of work of its principal author. Although the book is
co-authored by Schuyler Jackson, the distinctive style and preoccupations
of Laura Riding (Jackson) are present throughout this book and the fate
of the work is intimately tied to the fate of Riding's poetry.

I emphasize that this is a "poet's work" because the genre of the book
is that of a treatise on the philosophy of language. At another level, how-
ever, the book is an ars poetica—a "creative" work rather than a work of
linguistics, philosophy, or literary criticism as they are professionally
practiced. Indeed, the authors intentionally reject, across the board, the
major developments in all these professional fields. Nonetheless, *Ratio-
nal Meaning* is hardly a defense of poetry in poetic prose, even as it sits in
an anxious historical line with treatises and prophetic books by a num-
ber of earlier poets, from Sidney to Blake to Coleridge to Shelley to Poe.
For this book presents a "rational" approach to meaning that is *opposed* to
poetic approaches to meaning; in this sense it is not an ars poetica but an
anti-poetics.

Anarchism Is Not Enough (London: Jonathan Cape, 1928), p. 171.

"... The means of poetry delude."

Yet in its testing of our senses of meaning, in its insistence on "language as the ground of human intelligence",[1] *Rational Meaning* is a pursuit of poetry's love for language by other means; because, for the authors, the means of poetry delude. In this sense, its company might uneasily include other, more contemporary, if stylistically dissimilar, works: Louis Zukofsky's *Bottom: On Shakespeare* (which in its utopian impulse it most closely resembles), Ludwig Wittgenstein's *Tractatus Logico-Philosophicus*, Walter Benjamin's "Doctrine of the Similar", Ezra Pound's *Guide to Kulchur* and *Jefferson and/or Mussolini*, William Carlos Williams's *The Embodiment of Knowledge*, Simone Weil's *The Need for Roots*, and Gertrude Stein's *How to Write*. In making these comparisons, so against the grain of a work that insists that its contribution is precisely its noncomparability, I realize I am aestheticizing and historicizing this work in ways rejected by the authors.

Laura (Riding) Jackson was born Laura Reichenthal in 1901 in New York City. Riding's father was a Jewish immigrant from Galicia (Austro-Poland) and an active socialist; her mother was the daughter of German Jewish immigrants. She grew up in the Yorkville section of Manhattan and in Brooklyn, where she went to Girls' High School. Her background is quite similar to those of her immediate contemporaries Louis Zukofsky and Charles Reznikoff. And like them, she grew up in a household where English was not the only native tongue. Her earliest experiences of language were multiple and inflected, yet early on poetry may have seemed a way to a purer language "where the fear of speaking in strange ways could be left behind" and also "as a way of speaking differently from the untidy speaking of ordinary talk".[2] Some of her first poems appeared in the early 1920s, in publications associated with the Fugitives. From 1926 to 1939

---

1. Laura (Riding) Jackson, "Afterword", in *Lives of Wives* (Los Angeles: Sun & Moon Press, 1995), p. 325.

2. Laura (Riding) Jackson, "Twentieth Century Change in the Idea of Poetry, and of the Poet, and of the Human Being", in *P[oetry] N[ation] Review* 14, no. 1 (1987) (review supplement 1): 77–78. Quoted in Deborah Baker, *In Extremis: The Life of Laura Riding* (New York: Grove Press, 1993), p. 37. The biographical and bibliographical information in this essay is based on Baker; Joyce Piell Wexler, *Laura Riding's Pursuit of Truth* (Athens: Ohio University Press, 1979); Wexler, *Laura Riding: A Bibliography* (New York: Garland Publishing, 1981); and Barbara Adams, *The Enemy Self: Poetry and Criticism of Laura Riding* (Ann Arbor: UMI Research Press, 1990). I am also indebted to Jerome McGann's "The Truth of Poetry: An Argument", in *Black Riders: The Visible Language of Modernism* (Princeton: Princeton University Press, 1993), part of which appears as "Laura (Riding) Jackson and the Literal Truth", *Critical Inquiry* 18, no. 3 (1992).

Some of Baker's biographical information is disputed by Elizabeth Friedmann, who is writing an authorized biography of Laura Jackson (personal communication, September 3, 1996). Friedmann believes that Laura Reichenthal's maternal grandfather was Dutch and not Jewish, in other words not a *Deutsch* Jew. She also feels it is important to state that Laura Reichenthal's father came from what was at the time Austria (but what is now Poland).

she lived, mostly with Robert Graves, in England and Mallorca, Spain (and briefly in Egypt and Switzerland and France), where she published numerous books of poetry, essays, and fiction under the name Laura Riding. Her work through this period is among the greatest achievements of any American modernist.

In 1939 Riding returned to America, where she met, and in 1941 married, Schuyler Jackson. Schuyler Brinckerhoff Jackson II was born in 1900 in Bernardsville, New Jersey, to an affluent, socially well-positioned family. He attended Pomfret, a Connecticut prep school, and then Princeton. His first published article was on Yeats, with whom he had a happy meeting; and he shared with Riding a special regard for the Victorian poet Charles M. Doughty, whose epic poem *The Dawn in Britain* (1906), with its archaic recasting of language modeled in part on Edmund Spenser's English, holds a singular place of honor in *Rational Meaning*. In the 1930s Jackson was, for a time, a follower of Georges Gurdjieff. An aspiring poet and editor, as well as farmer, Schuyler was also the poetry reviewer for *Time* magazine, for which he reviewed Riding's *Collected Poems* in 1938. In 1943 Riding and Jackson moved to Wabasso, Florida, where they lived, mostly without electricity or telephone, until his death in 1968 and her death in 1991.

After the publication of her *Collected Poems* in 1938 and two non-poetry books the following year, Riding published almost nothing for thirty years. In 1970, her *Selected Poems: In Five Sets* was published under the name Laura (Riding) Jackson. In the preface she explained her renunciation of poetry, saying that the craft of poetry distorted the natural properties of words and that the sensuosity of words blocked what she called, in her poem "Come, Words, Away", the soundless telling of truth that is in language itself. She puts it this way in "The Wind, the Clock, the We":

> At last we can make sense, you and I,
> You lone survivors on paper,
> The wind's boldness and the clock's care
> Become a voiceless language,
> And I the story hushed in it—
> Is more to say of me?
> Do I say more than self-choked falsity
> Can repeat word for word after me,
> The script not altered by a breath
> Of perhaps meaning otherwise?[3]

The thirty-year pause in this life of writing, at least as reflected through a cessation of publishing, echoes the gap between George Oppen's *Dis-*

---

3. *Selected Poems: In Five Sets* (New York: W. W. Norton, 1973), p. 66.

lacuna-

"voiceless telling"

crete Series (1934) and *The Materials* (1962). Oppen, just seven years younger than Riding, perhaps had not found a way to reconcile his left political commitment with his practice of poetry. But he did return to poetry, and with an epigraph that he could share with Riding: "They fed their hearts on fantasies / And their hearts have become savage."[4] Riding, whose politics moved in the opposite direction from Oppen's, never returned to poetry, where meaning is always "otherwise" than intended, instead turning (for what poets do is turn) toward a way of meaning otherwise, that is not toward poetry but to a voiceless telling.[5] The long poetic lacuna of these two "non-Jewish Jews" implicitly acknowledges the question later stated most famously by Theodor Adorno: can lyric poetry be written after—*much less during*—the systematic extermination of the European Jews? As far as I know, Laura (Riding) Jackson does not explicitly address this issue, but what she does say of 1938 and 1939 is significant. "Human sense of the human stood at last poised at the edge of an unignorable question about the human."[6] Within this historical context, perhaps Oppen's commitment to a clarity and honesty ("that

4. *The Collected Poems of George Oppen* (New York: New Directions, 1975), p. 16. The lines recast Yeats's "We had fed the heart on fantasies, / The heart's grown brutal from the fare" in "The Stare's Nest by My Window", part 6 of "Meditations in Time of Civil War", in *Selected Poems and Two Plays of William Butler Yeats* (New York: Collier Books, 1962), p. 107. The first poem of *The Materials* begins with a stanza that is close to Riding: "The men talking / Near the room's center. They have said / More than they had intended" (p. 17).

5. (Riding) Jackson did publish a poem or two after the *Collected*. She discusses her renunciation of poetry in *Rational Meaning* (Charlottesville: University of Virginia Press, 1997), chap. 2, pp. 446–49 n. 2. Otherwise unattributed citations in this essay are to this edition.

6. *Lives of Wives*, p. 326. Riding's post-1938 renunciation of poetry and turn to "rational meaning" resembles, in many ways, the renunciation of Communism and turn to "core values" not uncommon among intellectuals in this period: one true belief changing to another true belief. Notable in this respect is Riding's 1939 tract *The Left Heresy in Literature and Life*, co-authored by "ex-Communist" Harry Kemp. In terms of *Rational Meaning*, note that "scientific socialism", like logical positivism and structuralism, has the same sort of extralinguistic logic that is the primary critical focus of the work. But so, for that matter, does capitalism, with its deterritorializing multinational logics that axiomatize meaning as decisively as any of the forms of reification denounced in *Rational Meaning*. From this perspective, Félix Guattari and Gilles Deleuze's critique of structuralism in *Anti-Oedipus: Capitalism and Schizophrenia* makes a strange bedfellow for *Rational Meaning*. See also Riding's *The Covenant of Literal Morality: Protocol I* ([Deyá, Mallorca]: Seizin Press, 1938), which is a crucial document in understanding her perception of the crisis of the late 1930s.

In his 1949 essay "Cultural Criticism and Society", Adorno wrote: "Cultural criticism finds itself faced with the final stage of the dialectic of culture and barbarism. To write poetry after Auschwitz is barbaric. And this corrodes even the knowledge of why it has become impossible to write poetry today. Absolute reification, which presupposed intellectual progress as one of its elements, is now preparing to absorb the mind entirely" (in *Prisms*, tr. Samuel and Shierry Weber [Cambridge: MIT Press, 1981], p. 34).

truthfulness / Which illumines speech")[7] that is expressible only though a highly delimited diction can be linked to (Riding) Jackson's recurrent concern for "right use" and "good sense" and frequent censure of what she experienced as linguistic violation. For the unnameable catastrophe of these years, with its rationalized but irrational logic of extermination, engendered a crisis of and for expression in which the abuse of language became inextricably identified with the abuse of the human.

Rational Meaning originated in a project of Riding's from the 1930s, first called *Dictionary of Exact Meanings* and later *Dictionary of Related Meanings*, which was to include "24,000 crucial words of the English language to be defined in such a way as to erase any ambiguity that might have accrued to them over years of improper usage." Oxford University Press turned down the proposal as "too individual and personal" and as an attempt to put words "into straightjackets".[8] In 1938, Little, Brown agreed to publish the book, even after a dismissive readers' report by I. A. Richards and C. K. Ogden, who subsequently became targets of Riding's wrath. Riding and Jackson continued to work on the dictionary until at least 1948, when they turned their attention to *Rational Meaning*, which Laura Jackson continued to work on after Schuyler Jackson's death.

To claim that *Rational Meaning* can be understood primarily in the context of the poetic project of Laura Riding cuts against the heart of the Jacksons' thesis. For though I believe that the idealization of meaning demonstrated so passionately and so relentlessly in *Rational Meaning* is problematic, it is the longing for rootedness in language's intrinsic meanings that makes this work so resonant. For *Rational Meaning* charts, with thankless diligence, the radical antithesis of those deanimating views of meaning that have come to hold sway, in this century, in linguistics and philosophy and poetry.

Imagine theories of the meaning of words as occupying a vertical spectrum. The lower limit of this spectrum would be the theory that

---

7. Oppen, "Of Being Numerous", in *Collected Poems*, p. 173.

8. Baker, *In Extremis*, pp. 367–68, 406–7. Riding's original collaborators on this project were Robert Graves and Alan Hodge, and, earlier, according to Elizabeth Friedmann (personal communication, September 3, 1996), Jacob Bronowski. In her fax, Friedmann disputes Baker's facts, noting that the reader's report was not by Ogden and Richards but rather that they were cited in one of two anonymous reports; she notes that the reports were "respectful". Baker, citing Oxford University Press's reaction to the dictionary proposal, has "straightjackets" but should it be "straitjackets" (both are "correct" in my dictionary), or, as Friedmann identifies the source, "strait jackets"?: It is a telling question, as words, and the facts that adhere to them, slip and slide, despite every attempt to get them straight, no chaser. Like a stick refracted in the water, it's gotta be bent to look strait.

the meaning of words is extrinsic or conventional: that words' meanings are determined only by linguistic, social, or historical contexts, or by means of their systematic differences from other words. The upper limit of the spectrum would be the theory that the meaning of each and every word is inherent in the word itself, nonrelative, self-complete. Much of the philosophy, linguistics, and poetics of the twentieth century, and especially in the postwar period, has moved toward the lower limit. In sharp contrast, *Rational Meaning* makes the case for the upper limit. By making this otherwise largely unrepresented argument, the Jacksons bring into full view the spectrum of views on the relation of meaning to language.

This work aims to restore the truth of language. While language, in the view of the authors, is "itself the anatomy of truth" (46), in modern times we have lost our rapport with language, ceasing to think of meaning as inhering in words and imagining instead that words have primarily psychological or social or historical or conventional meaning. This development is traced by the authors to a decline in the faith in reason. Their quest is "to make words tell all that human thought can hold, . . . to make human thought bring forth its all, for telling" (55).

The key concept of this book, and also the most elusive, is that words have intrinsic meaning. The authors decisively reject a Saussurean notion of the meaning of words as relative or differential. As early as 1928, in the dream story in *Anarchism Is Not Enough* quoted in the epigraph on "horseliness" above, Riding was flipping Ferdinand de Saussure's 1916 *Cours de linguistique générale* on its head. For Saussure is commonly understood to argue that "the relationship between signifier and signified is 'unmotivated' or arbitrary; that is, it is based purely on social rather than on natural necessity: there is nothing about a horse which demands that it be called 'horse', since the French call the same thing *un cheval*."[9] For related reasons, the Jacksons explicitly reject the structuralist and taxonomical notions of the relation of language to meaning that they find in the work of Noam Chomsky, Claude Lévi-Strauss, Jacques Lacan, and others.

Rational Meaning also rejects analytic philosophy, finding that it is a "trimm[ing]-down" of the domain of human knowledge to the "scientifically observable"—a critique the authors share with a wide range of thinkers and one that makes it clear that the rationality of which they speak is anti-positivist (151). Logical positivism, like structuralism, separates logic from meaning and in so doing "dissociat[es] language from

9. I quote here from a dictionary definition of *sign* in Chris Baddick, *The Concise Oxford Dictionary of Literary Terms* (Oxford and New York: Oxford University Press, 1990), p. 205.

the concept of truth", where *truth* means a "possessed awareness" in and through language (152, 379). When the authors complain of the scientific bending of terms like space, time, cause, and world, the comments resemble the critique of ordinary language philosophers without subscribing to J. L. Austin's or Wittgenstein's sense of the meaning of words in their use.

The perspective in *Rational Meaning* might seem closer to the linguistics of Charles Sanders Peirce, with his theory of icons, indexes, and symbols (suggesting, respectively, resemblance, linking, and conventional association between a sign and its object). Indeed, the Jacksons might appear to view the structure of the sign as something like iconic. But Peirce's linguistics is founded on an idea of inadequacy in the relation of the sign and its object that is inimicable to the thesis of *Rational Meaning*. Equally antipathetic to the Jacksons would be Peirce's emphasis on the social construction, and contestation, of meaning.

In arguing for rational, and against relative, meaning, *Rational Meaning* also makes a case against poetry and its reliance on metaphor and linguistic materiality (sound play, puns, and rhymes). This should not be surprising considering the terms by which Riding had renounced poetry's insufficiencies. Yet an argument for the intrinsic meaning of words would also be a defense of poetry if this argument interpreted the expressive quality of sound patterns as indicating an inherent relation of sound to meaning. But, for the Jacksons, if words are not Saussurean signs, with "arbitrary" relations of signifier to signified, neither are they the sound symbols of Roman Jakobson's linguistics. Words, in the authors' view, are meaning-entities not sound-entities. If we think of words as sound-entities (as poets may tend to), then we think of words as symbolizing rather than meaning. Word choice in poetry, the authors assert, is governed not by "linguistic rightness" but rather by the desire to induce "emotional states", as by word sounds and rhythmic manipulation. As a result the "truth-object" is at the mercy of a "professional requirement that the words have a physically attractive delivery and emotionally forceful impact" (171).

Although dictionaries are, for the Jacksons, the bibles of language, and far preferable to literature and linguistics, they hold that traditional dictionaries are of only limited help, since they define words in terms of usage and in terms of one another rather than through the intrinsic meaning of words. The Jacksons reject the notion that words are primarily the product of change and that meaning fundamentally shifts with time: "language does not change, in its fundamental make-up, and in its vocabularistic essentials" (611). In this respect, among the most remarkable parts of this

VaaBLE - word sound

work are the definitional illustrations, for example of *cat* and *dog* in chapter 15 and of *truth* in chapter 18.[10]

In *Rational Meaning*, the Jacksons argue that our natural disposition to words, our innate trust in them, has been unlearned. Rules of an imposed and denatured "logic" of use ride roughshod over the "natural custom of the language" (88). For the authors, a key symptom of this alienation from language is the tendency to synonymize words, that is, to define words in terms of their likeness to one another rather than their distinctness. Their motto is "one meaning, one word": each word has "a meaning that is its own and no other" (257, 187). Indeed, if one word-sound (what they call "vocable") has several distinct meanings, the Jacksons would say that the one sound is, in fact, several words. Crucially, the Jacksons emphasize the distinctions between apparently similar words, a thorough demonstration of the poetic (they would say rational and nonprofessional) pursuit of *le mot juste*. Their efforts to distinguish *alter* from *change* from *modify* from *vary* bring to mind Austin's desire to show how ordinary language reveals crucial distinctions that philosophers mistake by trying to deduce such distinctions from an external logic. But the Jacksons' efforts aim at individual words and away from what they call a "vocabularistic photograph of usage" (377). Their view is not that words have no meaning apart from use but that good usage elucidates true meaning and, moreover, that good diction has deteriorated because of literary indulgence, "linguistic libertarianism", and "vocabularistic promiscuity" (97, 461).

For the Jacksons, the belief that only context determines meaning is a kind of nihilism; they are at pains to decry instances of "ordinary" word use that is loose and thoughtless—most touchingly when they note the destructiveness of the routinized use, in letters, of "Dear" and "Yours" (451–52). They maintain an even more negative view of novel or invented word uses, as by poets, which "breaking-up and nullifying" the meaning

10. "This rendering of 'cat' we offer provisionally—in trial of the possibilities of term-definition: 'familiar animal, small-statured, sleek and supple of body, quiet in presence.' In the same spirit we offer the following for 'dog': 'familiar animal, of varying size, generally smaller than the human, by nature animated, and intelligent to the extent of being capable of attaching itself to human beings companionably and protectively, and otherwise serviceably.' Something further might be added for 'cat', perhaps this, after 'quiet in presence': 'amenable to intimate domestication while retaining some predatory and other features of wildness'" (pp. 293–94).

"'Truth,' then, as inseparable in meaning from connection with the utterance of words, comprises in its meaning a certain quality of utterance, a quality of linguistic intelligence. It also comprises in its meaning a power of expression that must be associated with the gift of linguistic knowledge and competence: this is an enlivenment with moral purpose to utter words that will be a right expression of something for one's expression of which occasion exists—either by external prompting of one's own, or the two coinciding . . . Language is formed to meet the requirements of truth as the reason of its being; and words have a necessity of usefulness for truth impressed into their meanings" (p. 353).

configurations on which the rational use of words depends and thus compromise language's expression of what (Riding) Jackson in *The Telling* calls truth's "One"-ness.[11] Regrettably, their blanket rejection of all types of linguistic divergence or difference as an affront to "human self-sameness" elides distinctions between "bad" grammar, "broken" English, new words, acronyms, advertising slogans, obscenities, vulgarities, dialects, and slangs; nor do they consider how corporate and government manipulation of language differs from nonstandard language practices rooted in social resistance to the very axiomatizing of language that they rightly condemn.[12]

Rational Meaning does not argue for a mystical or theological foundation for words: the Jacksons see the formation of English as an historical event. They defend their recourse to Spenser's English (and to Doughty's) not as an archaic romanticism (Spenser was already archaic) but as a lamentable consequence of the decline of English diction.[13] Equally problematic, they insist on the name-like character of language's most basic elements—a noun-centeredness that is the focus of critique both in Wittgenstein's *Philosophical Investigations* (specifically its opening sections) and in the poetics of Riding's one-time ally, Gertrude Stein.

At the same time, the Jacksons reject any external or transcendental vantage point from which language would acquire its truths. They return us, again and again, to language as an enactment, a telling. Truth, in this light, is never exterior to language (there is no extra-linguistic, "independent" reality), just as different languages are not exterior, but rather interior, to each other.

Indeed, *Rational Meaning* is at its best when decrying structuralist and positivist taxonomies that picture language as a nonhuman system, as a corpse, rather than responding to language as an actual site of human being. Objectification of language "tear[s language] out of the contexts

---

11. *The Telling* (New York. Harper & Row, 1972), 127; the main part was originally published as an issue of *Chelsea* in 1967.

12. Or, to put it another way, the Jacksons are themselves licentious in their moral censoriousness. I have argued for the value of a bewildering variety of nonstandard language practice, including Riding's, in *Content's Dream: Essays, 1975–1984* (Los Angeles: Sun & Moon Press, 1986), *A Poetics* (Cambridge: Harvard University Press, 1992), and most recently "Poetics of the Americas", in this collection.

13. Doughty's *The Dawn in Britain* (London: Duckworth & Co., 1906) thusly beginith:

> I chant new day-spring, in the Muses' Isles,
> Of Christ's eternal Kingdom. Men of the East,
> Of hew and raiment strange, and uncouth speech,
> Behold, in strom-beat ship, cast nigh our Land!
>   New Light is risen upon the World, from whence
> The dawn doth rise.

of . . . reason" (454), turning it into a dumb show of signs, so that words become mere codes, ciphers for a significance that is always elsewhere, as if meaning accompanies words rather than being revealed through them. Theorizing meaning in terms of codes, symbols, and systems undermines the actuality of language as a practice of immediacy by dislocating meaning from words and toward abstract and hypothetical logics; the result is an alienation of sense and a Taylorization of value. "The particulars of language and not, note, the 'depth structures' that 'underlie' 'all languages' require the attention of that which is neither incidentally nor accidentally related to the world."[14] "Words have a necessity of usefulness for truth impressed into their meanings . . . they are made to tell, to tell thought well, and rightly" (353).

Yet the authors' aspirations can veer toward a neo-Platonic idealization: a "unitary personality of being" (443), in which language, "touching perfection",[15] is emptied of social and historical tempering. According to the Jacksons, words have virtually immutable meanings, the only good language is clear and correct, and poems ought to be banished from the republic as the purveyors of the merely subjective or, worse, the willfully ambiguous. They never stop trying "To hurl life back into the thin teeth / Out of which first it whistled,"[16] insisting that "nothing can have intellectual durability that does not involve an attempt to see the universe as a rational unity" (156).

Yet the vitality of this work is not in its intellectual durability and universality but in its fragility and peculiarity; not in its rational unity but in its utopian, obsessive unreasonableness, even its "idiotic defiance". Though perhaps it is not so much Athens as Sparta that is evoked; for if words make a journey through the world, the Jacksons seem to say, Come back with your words intact, unvarnished, soundless; or use them as shields, warding off all that is destructive and disorienting and vulgar, all that permutes and decays, all that voices frets with chatter. "Come, words, away from mouths," as Laura Riding writes in a poem,

> . . . away to where
> The meaning is not thickened
> With the voice's fretting substance . . .
> Come, words, away to miracle

14. I quote from my poem "Palukaville" in *Poetic Justice* (Baltimore, 1979), collected in *Republics of Reality: 1975–1995* (Los Angeles: Sun & Moon Press, forthcoming).

15. "[T]he creed offering hope of a way of speaking beyond the ordinary, touching perfection, a complex perfection associated with nothing less complex than truth" (Laura [Riding] Jackson, preface to Riding's *Selected Poems*, p. 12).

16. "The Wind, the Clock, the We", in *Selected Poems*, p. 66. The poem continues: "An idiotic defiance of it knew not what".

More natural than written art.
You are surely somewhat devils,
But I know a way to soothe
The whirl of you when speech blasphemes
Against the silent half of language . . .
Centering the utter telling
In truth's first soundlessness[17]

Rational Meaning is, to use Riding's words in a different context, "a hoping cof"[18] Perhaps it is the ultimate modernist testament to what Pound, himself in search of linguistic perfection, called "the plain sense of the word"; then again, perhaps it is postmodern testimony to what I would call *the pained senselessness of the world*. For if Pound believed that he could stare at a Chinese ideogram and unbare its meaning, Laura and Schuyler Jackson believed such self-evidence present in language's silently lucid pronouncements. For these poets of the anti-poetic, the truth is not in an exterior Idea of Forms but indwelling in the telling of human being in and as language.

Rational Meaning is the book promised in *The Telling*, Laura (Riding) Jackson's great philosophical work on the limits of poetry and the possibility for truth telling. If *The Telling* is (Riding) Jackson's *Purity of Heart Is to Will One Thing*, *Rational Meaning* is her *Concluding Unscientific Postscript* (to consider Kierkegaard in this context). *Rational Meaning* is far more cumbersome and argumentative, in its complex and exacting exposition, than *The Telling*, which is a masterpiece of anti-analytic, anti-"literary" diction that more closely resembles Wittgenstein's *Philosophical Investigations* or Stein's *Lectures in America*. If *The Telling* is evocative and concise, *Rational Meaning*'s very length testifies to its commitment to thoroughness and argument; it eschews the invocativeness of *The Telling* as too poetic; its prose is determinately anti-aesthetic. The authors are at pains not to make their work into a modern *Zarathustra*; Aquinas's *Summa Contra Gentiles* is more their model. Yet *Rational Meaning*'s idea of rationality continually turns on the self-evidence of what the authors are telling about language. Thus the work tries to thwart the accumulative or positivistic aspects of much linguistics and philosophy. The Jacksons don't want to get anywhere with their prose; rather they want to return readers to basic facts whose importance they have neglected. "Words themselves are

17. "Come, Words, Away", in *Selected Poems*, p. 59; last two lines only in Laura (Riding) Jackson, *The Poems of Laura Riding: A New Edition of the 1938 Collection* (New York: Persea, 1980), p. 136.

18. *Everybody's Letters* (London: Arthur Barker, 1933), p. 119. Quoted in Baker, *In Extremis*, p. 34. Baker suggests the words are from a letter Riding wrote when she was 10.

the only actual means of rectifying what has happened to words in people's consciousness" (330).

As much as the authors are against "poeticizing", they also are against providing any explanatory paradigm or set of special terms that might be used as a formula or theory for understanding language. This is neither a theory nor a poetics of meaning but a "foundation" of meaning. They want nothing less than a complete turn from the ways that poets and philosophers, anthropologists and social scientists, have regarded—they would say disregarded—language. In the end, it might be best to say that *Rational Meaning* is neither theology nor linguistics nor literature: its work is ethical. It argues for an ecological approach to language, specifically for the value words have in human interconnectivity and the interdependence of language and human being; its call to return to language's "organic identity" echoes calls to respect the earth's natural inhabitations (418). This "green" dimension of *Rational Meaning* may also be worthwhile to consider in connection with the gender of its principal author;[19] in any case, *Rational Meaning* is one of the few philosophical treatises on the nature of language and meaning to be authored, or co-authored, by a woman.

Rational Meaning is in many ways a frustrating work. It is so long, and so preoccupied with its own prophetic significance and panoptic dismissals, that few readers will avoid discouragement.[20] The book courts discouragement and irritation, offering strong and unflavored medicine to an ailing society. Palatability, of various contemporary kinds, is exactly what the authors see as a problem. Many prophetic works, especially by such selfstyled prophets—"iconoclastic" is the nicer word we have for such artists—are destined to be resented by their "audience". The authors lecture to us as if we were children gone astray. They wish to call us back to the only true path of "the one life-story" of the "One Being" of an "Original Whole" (in the words of *The Telling*). They reject so much philosophy and poetry—all of structuralism and poststructuralism, all of modernism and postmodernism!—that it is foolish, even silly, to take personal offense. Yes, there are similarities between what these authors and what some others have said; but they are less interested in these similarities than in how they differ. This is the ground of their discourse.

If I disagree with much of what the authors say, I have found reasons other than agreement to appreciate what I question, knowing that the

19. See Laura (Riding) Jackson, *The Word Woman and Other Related Writings*, ed. Elizabeth Friedmann and Alan J. Clark (New York: Persea Books, 1993).

20. Critics have responded in kind to (Riding) Jackson's juridical pronouncements, characterizing her approach as "fascinating, frustrating, infuriating, illuminating" (Robert Gorham Davis); "uncompromising, intractable, intransigent" (Martin Seymour-Smith); as well as "dogmatic", "hostile", and "haughty". See Wexler's *Bibliography*, sec. H.

important thing is not to be persuaded by their arguments but to respond to them. The Jacksons stake out a powerful, often eloquent, often deliciously barbed, often achingly arched argument against the relativism of the modern age—one that goes much further in its critique than such anti-modern modernists as T. S. Eliot (as the authors are careful to note). I suspect it is an argument that, ultimately, will take a place of honor in the history of human thought.

This book settles nothing for me; it leaves me with questions that echo in my mind and on my tongue. Poetry—can it be?—a striving not for truthfulness but for truth? And what if all we do as poets—our forms, our structures, our love of sounds and patterns—moves us yet further from this singular truth? What if, that is, words have unitary meanings, call them rational meanings, and what if our poetry, our philosophy, our linguists, our dictionaries, lead us away from this grounded rationality of words— toward some evasive play of relative worth?

Laura (Riding) and Schuyler Jackson call us back not to some truth external to ourselves but to a truth available to all, a truth that is in every word we use, a "truth [that] requires language for its making" (364). They call us back to our rootedness in language, which is our human house, our destined home.

Whose He Kidding

"What is irony?" said the jesting pilot
& then stayed around to field questions.
"I don't make jokes I test planes."
Well, so do we all. Yet to have
an idea of multivalence, ambivolence in
Steve McCaffery's ever apter word, isn't
to put off, much less, pull off
anything. Antony Easthope in his
substantially probious *Poetry as Discourse*
says sarcasm is the most extreme,
maybe most emblematic,
form of irony in its 180-degree difference
& manifest contempt, as opposed to milder forms
of irony that veer off zero-degree separation anxiety
less steeply. Tell it to my mother: "So
glad you called (pause) this year."
She's not saying the *opposite*. Irony
is bourgeois, anyway, reconciliatory; sarcasm
(& the comic ploys related to it) is dialectical,
fomenting contra-diction. Of course not. Depends
on. If I
prefer to speak of the comic rather than the
ironic it's because the nature of literary
irony can be taken (Kierkegaard didn't)
as an especially, even uniquely, context-
dependent form of discourse, as if
there was some *other* discourse that was
context-independent—the words just meaning
what they say, no interpretation (interruption)
necessary. (Whose
on first?) That may be okay for a working
hypothesis for rocket makers, but it ain't cut no

water in the realms of the sense. I'm (that nostalgic
notion) at pains (I don't mean this metaphorically
but synecdochically) to say that the context-
dependence of meaning (meaning is addicted
to context) rules out neither
truth nor trust, knowledge nor
bicarbonate of soda
in those difficult to get a take on (make
on) circumstances everybody's always
riffing off of. My doctor tells
me I need more rest
but I know the quiet is
killing me.

Unrepresentative Verse

A hundred years ago Oscar Wilde—a writer perhaps even more celebrated in Victorian England than Allen Ginsberg in postwar America—was hounded to death while at the very height of his fame and at the top of his magnificent form. Allen Ginsberg, and to be sure many others, courageously refused to be bashed down by the perverts who would end a person's life and career because of their sexual orientation or lifestyle. He was part of a massive cultural movement to make what happened to Wilde if not unthinkable at least unacceptable in the U. S. of A. He did this not by presenting "positive" images of being gay or smoking pot but by presenting by turns joyous and defiant images of these things and a number of others. Wilde ends his days in jail and then disgrace. Ginsberg is celebrated—on the occasion of his death two weeks ago—even in the pages that reviled him—*The Times, The New Yorker,* &c.

I give this account not because it is unknown to those convened here today, but because it suggests an idea of the poet central to the issues that have brought us together under the banner "Poetry and the Public Sphere". For Allen Ginsberg magnificently embodied the role of public poet.

Allen Ginsberg is one of the few poets of the postwar period to cross over both into popular and mass culture and this is primarily because he remained (among other things) a poet of and for adolescent identification, right up to the end of his life. By adolescence I mean the defiance of authority and a sexual omnivorousness, combined with a bad boy image in which the poet wears his, in this case considerable, learning as lightly as possible. It was Ginsberg's genius to synthesize political and social dissent into something intensely appealing to adolescents . . . of all ages. But if Ginsberg had astounding success at attracting media attention, this was not because he took stands in an effort to gain public exposure; his success in this realm is largely dependent on the authenticity of his way of life as much as his positions, a mode of authenticity that he takes, above all, from Whitman. Yet the 20th-century poet he ends up most resembling is not Bill Williams of Paterson but Tommy Eliot of St. Louis. Resembles, but only in the sense of a reverse or polarized image: for Eliot became the poet as symbol of the closed, the repressed, the xenophobic, the authoritative; in short, of high culture in the worst sense; while Ginsberg became the symbol of the open, the uncloseted, the anti-authoritarian; indeed, of low culture in the best sense. Ginsberg's move from ethnically particularized Jewishness (Al from Jersey) to small b buddhism (bubba to Baba) is correlative to Eliot's move from Christian-American to High Church Anglican—in both cases an assumption of a new religion as vehicle for universal identification that gets you high or anyway higher. Ginsberg, after all, is an anarchist in politics, a libertine in lifestyle, a buddhist in religion— the virtual inverse of Eliot's monarchist in politics, uptight in lifestyle, Anglican in religion. Yet if Ginsberg's adolescent sublime provided a role for the poet that was hugely desirable in mass and popular culture, this was often at visible, if not actual, expense of his poetry, consummately sophisticated political acumen, and ethical grounding, none of which, on their own, could have gained him access to the public space he occupied for near to 40 years. Indeed his poetry was obscured by his public stature while that stature provided an important, and relatively rare, platform for an admirable form of liberationist politics. The dynamic is not unrelated to the case of Eliot, for insofar as he became a symbol of poetry as the antithesis of adolescence, the greatest achievements of his own poems were also obscured; indeed, this is the central obscurity of Eliot's poetry, not the textual difficulty that has been fodder for popular accounts for so many years. (And after all "Prufrock" is also a great work of the adolescent sublime.)

As a result of all this, Ginsberg's legacy for poetry, just as Eliot's, is not an entirely happy one, which I say without intending any negative judgment on each of their often astoundingly great poems. Much of the poetry that shares a social and formal affinity with Ginsberg has assiduously avoided just the forms of grand address and narrow historical self-identification that projected his poetry so decisively into a public space achieved by few of his contemporaries or heirs. For it has seemed a greater urgency for poetry to find means of articulation in which the poetic project itself—the details of particular sounds in particular orders—is not subsumed by a cultural project that is in many ways antipathetic to poetry; that is, if poetry is understood not as an idea but a practice, and not a matter of comrades-through-time or cultural positions, but of words and syntax. The cultural project of this poetry of radically small scale is to keep the attentional focus on the possibilities of language, on what language has to tell. Not only to sing of felicities and dance with facility but trip and fall the better to make music of our flailing and of our incapacities. And, yes, of course, that is also what Ginsberg, in *Howl*, in *Kaddish*, and indeed also Eliot, in *The Waste Land*, in "Prufrock" may be said to be doing. So today I call them back from the nether world of cultural representatives to the practice, their practice, still largely obscured, of the writing and performance of poems in a word that, as Jack Spicer put it, "no one / listens to poetry" but which, from time to time, may heed the voice of the poet.

For the problem is not just the individual voice of lyric poetry, which Adorno, among others, has called into question, but also the ventriloquized voice of public discourse (in poetry and the massed media). The problem is the reifying of individuality and publicity, as if they were the same thing, in the quenchless desire for absorption by the Culture-at-Large.

Yet poetry, representative of the problem, may also provide unrepresented alternatives.

As Little Orphan Anagram says, "Poetry fakes nothing actually."

But this is a poetry that we must continually reinvent and which must reinvent us.

Poetry and [Male?] Sex

I don't know much about sex but I know what I like. Whenever I hear the word sexuality I reach for my wallet. Your sexual politics is the way you live.

Some time ago, a letter was passed on to me in which my essay on Charles Olson, in *Content's Dream*, was taken to task as "unjust" in its critique of Maximus's sexual politics. Randy Prus writes:

> Phallocentrism is different from misogyny. What I mean to say is, some men write from the "balls", that soft tender spot which the gender is constantly trying to express and yet protect. Hemingway and Mailer write from the phallus, that hard expression of masculinity. Olson, as well as Whitman, as well as myself write from the "balls". H.D. in *Notes on Thought and Vision* locates the "womb" as one center of writing. The "balls" are the male counterpart of that, as well as to that experience. Gender expression does not mean gender dominance.

Here we see "maleness" desiring the same privilege in contemporary "progressive" ideological space as is accorded to "womanhood" or "blackness". But maleness, like whiteness, like Americanness cannot claim the "status" of "marginality" because it remains culturally, politically, socially, and economically dominant. The "imaginal" values of maleness have not been suppressed/discredited/denied but rather vaunted: the struggle for men is to unlearn masculinity, without substituting any positive value to this gender differential, since positive values for maleness (as distinct from "humanness"), remain suspect, at least for the present, as socially adaptive strategies to maintain control and power.

One of the most striking features of the current poetry context is the resourcefulness of many marginalized (though not marginal) groups in asserting a powerfully positive identity either in individual writings or through integrally related social formations (readings, publishing, critical writing). White, heterosexual men cannot occupy this ground, for the relevant group affiliation is one that cannot, in good conscience, be

273

advanced; on the contrary, the group solidarity of straight, white men needs to be dissolved not in order to be regrouped in a more "authentically male" fashion but to become dispersed into a human future that is not now possible to envision. Certainly, men sensitive to this problem may be envious of those who are able to participate in building group gender identification, and it is not surprising that many men express resentment toward feminist poetries in a variety of ways: for it is precisely the position of the unrepresented or the subaltern that straight, white American men are rightly excluded from occupying in any primary way. While men's consciousness raising is a valuable, indeed necessary, activity, "men's liberation" is an obscenity; which is not to say that all human beings are not tyrannized by a social order that tyrannizes any group.

Within this context, the questioning, through poetic methods, of the authoritative structures of our society is useful for both men and women. The poetic works that result will not necessarily be differentiable by gender, but the world they connect to, at least within the context of a non-utopian reading, surely will be. That is, it is useful to read works by men and women differentially, taking note of the different aesthetic and social meanings of works when read in terms of gender. The difference, however, is in the social act of reading and interpretation, not in the words themselves. What is problematic, for me, is the reduction of this investigation to biologically reductive categories: the genitals made symbolic. We are so enmeshed within the social coding of gender that we have no way of locating irreducible biological meanings for sex differences. Biology is not destiny, rather it establishes a ground of possibilities for sociocultural enacting. There are no knowably inherent social attributes to maleness or femaleness, only socially engendered, or socially asserted, ones. The questioning of the putative givens of gender is one of the richest domains of "modern" poetry and it is little wonder that so many of the most revolutionary writers of the past 250 years have refused, or been unable, to conform to conventional gender and sexual classifications.

Of course, this suggests problems for any feminism, much less masculinism, that holds to a priori gender definitions. Social and sexual functions make essences. If the socially desired end is equal employment opportunities for all, then this will be what will determine the correlatively equal sharing of infantcare, housework, etc. The "essentially" nurturing role of women will be as irrelevant as the learned (or never learned) nurturing role of men faced with the deadening forms of employment available to most of us. The point is not to radically demarcate gender distinctions, which inevitably lead to workplace and economic and status discriminations: not further divisions of labor, that is, but the pooling of these realities. There is real, expressible, pain and loss, as well as gain and pleasure, involved in the forms of alienation that men experience in the workplace or in a singles' bar or in a marriage, and the critical articulation of these experiences is necessary: but these are realities that women and men will more and more share if sexism and phallocentrism are to be eroded.

A few years ago I made the modest proposal that literary works traditionally taken to represent "mankind" be read in the harshest light of gender criticism while works too often in the past read as "underdeveloped" because of the social status of the author be read as universal representatives of the human. I think, however, my proposal was too modest, because I see, in the gerrymandering projects of the anthologies of official verse culture, a curious willingness to represent American poetry since 1960 in a way that backs off from the priority previously accorded to dominant groups, and indeed is even willing to reclaim some poets previously and egregiously neglected in earlier anthologies, while at the same time leaving in place many of the dominant assumptions about poetic value, including those forged by masculinist practices.

So my question is: Does the strategy represented by many of the newly "diverse" anthologies indicate change or rather a continuation of patterns of exclusions by other means? I have to say I cringe at any discussion of anthologies and the inevitable counting by categories of inclusion and exclusion. So often that seems to contribute to a reductive approach to understanding what constitutes the radical, but hard to objectively or sociologically define, diversity and difference in American poetry. Surely careful and explicit consideration needs to be given to gender, ethnicity, and race in broadly defined, period-focussed representations of American poetry; but I am appalled at what often seems to be a forced and superficial compliance, especially in respect to a medium that has such an enormous capacity to explore multiple senses (and multiple possibilities) of collective identity. What is most misdirected about the new diversity is not its commendable desire to revise the canon but the unpoetically literal approach to this task. Moreover, diversity needs to be applied not only to the present generation of poets. Anything more than a cosmetic brushover of these issues requires a thorough-going rethinking of what constitutes our poetic heritage: in many ways the representation of the past is a more important part of this project than is the representation of the contemporary scene, where the opportunity for counter-representations are far more plentiful. If we revise our ideas of who counts in the present we need to do this for the past as well. This means not just adding to the slightly trimmed core group of validated white men but also asking if these may be the wrong white men, that is if there are white male poets excluded from the literary history of the twentieth century, and earlier, because of masculinist and supremacist assumptions that have previously governed these choices, men (of whatever sexual orientation) who may have troubled the prevailing paradigms for poetry because they refused the moral, gender, political, ethical, or aesthetic paradigms favored by the official verse culture of their time or our time. We also need to note the continuities of exclusions, not only of particular groups, but also of poets, male and female and from every conceivable background, who foreground nonstandard language practice, whether dialect or ideolect.

The problem, to put it in the most rhetorically inflammatory way, is not just the proportion of white men in the representations of twentieth century American poetry, but that these white men are, at least to some extent, the wrong white men, reflecting, even to this day, the socially conservative Southern Christian orientation of some of the New Critics, an orientation, by the way, that retains for me both historical and aesthetic significance. In the unlikely event my advice should be taken, however, let me add, with the kind of irony of which I am particularly fond and for which I am often taken to task, that every newly excluded poet of a revised canon will take on a new historical interest for me at exactly the point of exclusion, for at this point a process of recovery can begin.

But what does this have to do with poetry and the erotic? It is sometimes hard to understand how the body can be shaped by language—that our ideologies are scleroticized into social flesh, that we live out our grammars with our bodies. Poetry is a place where that grammar can be reforged. Indeed the project of much current poetry that attempts to rupture conventional grammatical and narrative patterns can be understood in terms of just such a sexual politics. At the same time, as a man, I have been concerned with resisting any establishment of new and positive identity formations through such writing practices.

If not gender, what then? The various social roles learned by women and men make for different points of departure in coming to terms with the controlling interests of these roles and that will no doubt be pervasively reflected in individual works. I have tried, in my work, to understand who and what I am without assuming the authenticity of my feelings or sexuality. This has afforded me an unlimited amount of pleasure in writing.

For writing is erotic when sclerotic patterns of communication are violated, especially if this violation isn't left hanging in the fire but comes to fruition. As against the idea that nonnormalizing writing practices unleash a de-creative "libidinal flow" that is otherwise locked up by, or in, language, I would say that the object(s) of my desires is a pro-creative poetry. For there is no prelinguistic, presymbolic domain that is systematically repressed with the acquisition of language but that can be liberated by textual ruptures of the phallocratic symbolic order: an idea that is the last outpost of Romantic ideology in poststructuralist doxa. Rather, the linguistic or semantic or symbolic order is coterminous with the body, its coming into being and its expiration. The presymbolic is, at best, a u-topian projection, out of this world (like Romanticism's nonsocial Imagination): literally nowhere, never.

There is no "presymbolic" holdout (hideout); language play is simultaneously, not consecutively or narratively, constitutive of meaning *and* erotic. Language as such is no more "phallic" than it is "clitoral"; and while standard grammar may reflect the (patriarchal) social order, alternative (nonphallic) grammars are simultaneously being realized and repressed. Just as it is necessary to reject the reduction of meaning to utility, it is also necessary to guard against the schizophrenic splitting of meaning from the imaginary or bodily flows through which it is enacted. As Samuel Weber has put it, there is no free play only power plays: in the interior of any argument for the liberation of libidinal energy trapped by inscription is the demon of phallic play ma(r)king its own unchecked reinscription.

Writing and reading enact a sexual economy in that they open onto an arena of erotic play—release, delay, longing, emptiness, destruction, production, absorption, theatricality, determination, satisfaction, frustration. The sensuous pleasures of words, phrases, and images can never be underestimated as embodying the aesthetic force of a poem. The poetics of pleasure, and the absolute acknowledgment of the heterogeneity of desire—different pleasures for different people—remains a fundamental test of any politics, including any politics of poetry.

Pleasure is always site specific: bound by social and personal histories. There can be no hierarchization of the methods of pleasure (call them pleasuring principles or the apparatuses of the erotic, as you like). If sexual practices are never "absolutely liberatory" in function neither can any claim special legitimacy as being more "natural" than others: in any case, eros does not require such utilitarian justifications. And if it is wished to imagine a liberatory function for sexuality, it is sobering to keep in mind that desire constitutes social grammars. Nor is there a "material core" to eros: genital sex, touching a wall, the vision of an empty and dark room, smell, eating bread, dancing (on a threshing floor or in your head), as much as those more hushed[-up] pleasures of the text, are equally sublimations/actualizations—articulations—of eros.

When I speak of a procreative poetry, I don't mean that this can be untangled from decreative play. I mean rather to emphasize a sense of a poem's needing no value outside its immediate pleasures: where the value resides in the instantiation of pleasure for itself, the noninstrumental fact of its own activity. The erotic text for which I make my proposition desires to constitute itself by both its disengagements and its engagements, in order—not to leave the social realm but to more materially, sensually, sentiently place itself as lived and felt object in and of the world. In this way, the poem is transformed by the powers of its embodied desires, as each of us is transformed in our journeys from our separate inceptions, from text to work.

Close Listening

Poetry and the Performed Word

I sing and I play the flute for myself.
For no man except me understands my language.
As little as they understand the nightingale
do the people understand what my song says.

Peire Cardenal

No one listens to poetry. The ocean
Does not mean to be listened to. A drop
Or crash of water. It means
Nothing.

Jack Spicer

While the performance of poetry is as old as poetry itself, critical atten-
tion to modern and contemporary poetry performance has been negli-
gible, despite the crucial importance of performance to the practice of the
poetry of this century. The subject is wide-ranging and requires a range
of approaches. At one end of the spectrum would be philosophical and
critical approaches to the contribution of sound to meaning: the way
poets, and especially twentieth century innovative poets, work with sound
as material, where sound is neither arbitrary nor secondary but constitu-
tive. At the other end of the spectrum would be critical interpretations of
the performance style of individual poets. Such approaches may well
encourage "close listenings" not only to the printed text of poems, but also
to tapes and performances.

Close listenings may contradict "readings" of poems that are based ex-
clusively on the printed text and that ignore the poet's own performances,
the "total" sound of the work, and the relation of sound to semantics. Cer-

Cardenal, "Song 56" (early 13th century), tr. Gregory Nagy, based on W. Pfeffer's *The Change
of Philomel: The Nightingale in Medieval Literature*, quoted in Nagy, *Poetry as Performance: Homer and Beyond*
(Cambridge: Cambridge University Press, 1996), p. 211. Spicer, "Thing Language", in *Language*
in *The Collected Books of Jack Spicer* (Los Angeles: Black Sparrow, 1975), p. 217.

tainly, discussion of sound as a material and materializing dimension of po-
etry also calls into play such developments as sound poetry, performance
poetry, radio plays and radio "space", movie soundtracks, poetry/music
collaborations, and other audioworks. Beyond that, "close listenings" call
for a non-Euclidean (or complex) prosody for the many poems for which
traditional prosody does not apply.

Since the 1950s, the poetry reading has become one of the most im-
portant sites for the dissemination of poetic works in North America, yet
studies of the distinctive features of the poem-in-performance have been
rare (even full-length studies of a poet's work routinely ignore the audio-
text), and readings—no matter how well attended—are never reviewed by
newspapers or magazines (though they are the frequent subject of light,
generally misinformed, "feature" stories on the perennial "revival" of po-
etry).[1] A large archive of audio and video documents, dating back to an
early recording of Tennyson's almost inaudible voice, awaits serious study
and interpretation. The absence of such a history has had the effect of elid-
ing the significance of the modernist poetry traditions for postwar per-
formance art. At the same time, the performative dimension of poetry has
significant relation to text-based visual and conceptual art, as well as visual
poetry, which extend the performative (and material) dimension of the lit-
erary text into visual space.

The newly emerging field of performance studies and theory provides
a useful context for this study. By considering examples of "total" perfor-
mances in other cultures, performance theorists have reoriented the dis-
cussion of the relation of theater, audience, and text. While much of the
discussion of postmodern performance art has focused on this and related
contexts, there has been considerably less focus on the implications for
poetry performance. Particularly helpful for "close listening" is Erving

---

1. There are only two collections that I have been able to locate that address the poetry read-
ing: *Poets on Stage: The* Some *Symposium on Poetry Readings*, ed. Alan Ziegler, Larry Zirlin, and Harry
Greenberg (New York: Some/Release Press, 1978), and *The Poetry Reading: A Contemporary Com-
pendium on Language and Performance*, ed. Stephen Vincent and Ellen Zweig (San Francisco: Momo's
Press, 1981). The accounts of poetry readings in these pioneering collections are largely anec-
dotal. Also notable are the annual reports for 1981 and 1982 of San Francisco's 80 Langton Street
Residency Program, assembled by Renny Pritikin, Barrett Watten, and Judy Moran, which pro-
vided a number of sustained accounts, by different writers, of a series of talks and readings and
performances at the space. More recently, the Poetics List, an electronic discussion group
archived at the Electronic Poetry Center (http://wings.buffalo.edu/epc), often features accounts
of readings and conferences (including lists of those in attendance at readings and even the occa-
sional fashion report). In contrast, reflecting standard academic practice, there is no mention of
Wallace Stevens's recorded poetry performance in a recent book on the poet by Anca Rosu, but
there is some irony in this given the book's auspicious title, *The Metaphysics of Sound in Wallace
Stevens* (Tuscaloosa: University of Alabama Press, 1995), which only goes to show that meta-
physics tends to displace physics.

Goffman's *Frame Analysis*, especially his conception of how the cued frame through which a situation (or work) is viewed necessarily puts other features out of frame, into what he calls the "disattend track". Focusing attention on a poem's content or form typically involves putting the audiotext as well as the typography—the sound and look—of the poem, into the disattend track. Indeed, the drift of much literary criticism of the past two decades has been away from the auditory and performative aspects of the poem, partly because of the prevalent notion that the sound structure of language is relatively arbitrary. Such elements as the visual appearance of the text or the sound of the work in performance may be extralexical but they are not extrasemantic. When textual elements that are conventionally framed out as nonsemantic are acknowledged as significant, the result is a proliferation of possible frames of interpretation. Then it becomes a question of whether we see these frames or strata as commensurate with each other, leading to a "total image complex" of the poem, to use Veronica Forrest-Thomson's term; or whether we see these strata as incommensurate with each other, contradictory, leading to a reading of the poem as untotalizable. Here "strata" might usefully be thought of also as the kind of layers one finds in a palimpsest.

In a sense, the *Close Listening* collection emerged as a complex, multilayered response to a quite simple, and common, response to a poetry reading, as when one says: "I understand the work better hearing the poet read it. I would never have been able to figure out that the poems would sound that way." (This is not to discount the significance of performances by poets that seem "bad" for one reason or another or may make one like the work less than on the page, nor to distract from the significance of the performance of a poem by someone other than its author.) Insofar as poetry performance is countenanced as a topic of discussion, the subject is often assumed to be exemplified by such high-octane examples as Vachel Lindsay's notorious "Congo" ("MUMBO JUMBO in the CONNNG-GO"), or Carl Sandburg's melodramatic presentation style ("in the tooooombs, the coooool toooooombs"), or Allen Ginsberg's near-chanting of *Howl*, or more recently "rap", "slam", and "scratch" poetry. But the unanticipatably slow tempo of Wallace Stevens's performance tells us much about his sense of the poem's rhythms and philosophical sensuousness, just as John Ashbery's near monotone suggests a dreamier dimension than the text sometimes reveals. The intense emotional impact of Robert Creeley's pauses at line breaks gives an affective interpretation to what otherwise reads as a highly formal sense of fragmented line breaks—the breaks suggest emotional pitch and distress in a way audible in the recordings but not necessarily on the page. The recordings of Gertrude Stein make clear both the bell-like resonance of her voice and her sense of shifting rhythms against modulating repetitions and the shapeliness of her sound-sense; while hearing Langston Hughes one immediately picks up not only on the specific blues echoes in the work but how he modulated shifts into and out of these rhythms. Having heard these poets read, we change our hearing and reading of their works on the page as well.

No doubt, there are a number of factors that are involved in the dramatically increased significance of the poetry reading in the postwar period in North America and the United Kingdom. At the outset, though, let me put forward one explanation. During the past forty years, more and more poets have used forms whose sound patterns are *made up*—that is, their poems do not follow received or prefabricated forms. It is for these poets that the poetry reading has taken on so much significance. For the sound shapes of the poems of such practitioners are often most immediately and viscerally heard in performance (taped or live), even if the attuned reader might be able to hear something comparable in her or his own (prior) reading of the text. *The poetry reading is a public tuning.* (Think of how public readings in the 1950s by Creeley, Ginsberg, Olson, and Jack Kerouac established—in a primary way—not only the sound of their work but also the possibilities for related work. And how the still-current mixing of public and private "talk" at readings was partially established by these poets.) The proliferation of poetry readings has allowed a spinning out into the world of a new series of acoustic modalities, which have had an enormous impact in informing the reading of contemporary poetry. These performances set up new conventions that are internalized and applied to further reading of the poetic texts. They are the acoustic grounding of innovative practice—our collective sounding board.

To be heard, poetry needs to be sounded—whether in a process of active, or interactive, reading of a work or by the poet in performance. Unsounded poetry remains inert marks on a page, waiting to be able to be called into use by saying, or hearing, the words aloud. The poetry reading provides a focal point for this process in that its existence is uniquely tied to the reading aloud of the text; it is an emblem of the necessity for such reading out loud and in public. Nor is the process of transforming soundless words on a page into performed language unique to the poetry reading. To give just one example, Jerome Rothenberg points to the ancient Jewish tradition of reading and incanting the Torah—turning a script without vowels into a fully voiced sounding.[2] Public recitation also brings to mind a number of sermonic traditions, from subdued preachment to

2. See Jerome Rothenberg, "The Poetics of Performance", in Vincent and Zweig, *Poetry Reading*, p. 123. See also David Abram, *The Spell of the Sensuous* (New York: Pantheon, 1996), pp. 241–50.

Gospel call-and-response. And if the poetry reading provides unscripted elements for the performer, it also provides special possibilities for the listener, from direct response to the work, ranging from laughter to derision; to the pleasure of getting lost in language that surges forward, allowing the mind to wander in the presence of words.

When the audiotape archive of a poet's performance is acknowledged as a significant, rather than incidental, part of her or his work, a number of important textual and critical issues emerge. What is the status of discrepancies among performed and published versions of poems, and, moreover, between interpretations based on the text versus interpretations based on the performance? Amiri Baraka is one of the most dynamic poetry performers of the postwar period. For Baraka, making the words dance in performance means taking the poems off the page, out of the realm of ideas, and into action. In some of Baraka's most vibrantly performed poems, such as "Afro-American Lyric", the text can seem secondary, as if, as William Harris seems to suggest in his discussion of the poem, the text—with its inventive typography—has become merely a score for the performance.[3] Surely, it is always possible for some poems to seem thinner on the page than in performance, *and vice versa*. But I don't think this is the case for Baraka, whose work is always exploring the dialectic of performance and text, theory and practice, the literary and the oral—a dialectic that will involve clashes more than harmony. Performance, in the sense of doing, is an underlying formal aesthetic as much as it is a political issue in Baraka's work.[4] The shape of his performances are iconic—they signify. In this sense the printed text of "Afro-American Lyric" works to spur the (silent, atomized) reader *into* performance—it insists on action; the page's apparent textual "lack" is the motor of its form.

The text of "Afro-American Lyric" brings to mind the language of Marxist political pamphlets, foregrounding the poem's untransformed didacticism. Hearing Baraka read this poem on a tape of his July 26, 1978, performance at the Naropa Institute, however, gives a distinctly different impression. Baraka sounds the syllables of "simple shit" ("Seeeeeeeeeee-immmmmmmmmmmm pull" in the text), interweaving and syncopating them with "exploiting class, owning class, bourgeois class, reactionary class," turning the text's diatribe into a cross between a sound poem and a

3. William Harris, *The Poetry and Poetics of Amiri Baraka: The Jazz Aesthetic* (Columbia: University of Missouri Press, 1985), pp. 109–10; Harris extracts portions of the text, from which I quote below. See also Harris's interview with Baraka, where the poet agrees that his poem is a score and says he is principally interested in performance—"[the text] is less important to me" (p. 147). Harris briefly discusses Baraka's performances on pp. 59–60. See especially his discussion of the relation of music and dance to Baraka's work, starting on p. 106.

4. See Nathaniel Mackey, "Other: From Noun to Verb", in *Discrepant Engagement: Dissonance, Cross-Culturality, and Experimental Writing* (Cambridge: Cambridge University Press, 1993).

scat jazz improvisation. He makes playful yet dissonant music from the apparently refractory words of Marxist analysis, bringing out the uncontained phonic plenitude inside and between the words. This is no mere embellishment of the poem but a restaging of its meaning ("Class Struggle in Music", as Baraka titles a later poem). Baraka's recitations invoke a range of performance rhetorics from hortatory to accusatory: typically, he will segue from his own intoning of a song tune to a more neutrally inflected phrase, then plunge into a percussively grating sound.

What's the relation of Baraka's performance—or of any poem performed by its author—to the original text? I want to overthrow the common presumption that the text of a poem—that is, the written document—is primary and that the recitation or performance of a poem by the poet is secondary and fundamentally inconsequential to the "poem itself". In the conventional view, recitation has something of the status of interpretation—it provides a possible gloss of the immutable original. One problem with this perspective, most persuasively argued by Jerome Mc-Gann in *Black Riders*, *The Textual Condition*, and *A Critique of Modern Textual Criticism*, is that there is often no one original written version of a poem. Even leaving aside the status of the manuscript, there often exist various and discrepant printings—I should like to say textual performances—in magazines and books, with changes in wording but also spacing, font, paper, and, moreover, contexts of readership; making for a plurality of versions none of which can claim sole authority. I would call these multifoliate versions *performances* of the poem; and I would add the poet's own performance of the work in a poetry reading, or readings, to the list of variants that together, plurally, constitute and reconstitute the work. This, then, is clearly not to say that all performances of a poem have equal authority. An actor's rendition, like a type designer's "original" setting of a classic, will not have the same kind of authority as a poet's own reading or the first printing of the work. But the performance of the poet, just as the visualization of the poem in its initial printings, forever marks the poem's entry into the world; and not only its meaning, its existence.

A poem understood as a performative event and not merely as a textual entity refuses the originality of the written document in favor of "the plural event" of the work, to use a phrase of Andrew Benjamin's. That is, the work is not identical to any one graphical or performative realization of it, nor can it be equated with a totalized unity of these versions or manifestations. The poem, viewed in terms of its multiple performances, or mutual intertranslatability, has a fundamentally plural existence. This is most dramatically enunciated when instances of the work are contradictory or incommensurable, but it is also the case when versions are commensurate. To speak of the poem in performance is, then, to overthrow the idea of the poem as a fixed, stable, finite linguistic object; it is to deny the poem its self-presence and its unity. Thus, while performance emphasizes the material presence of the poem, and of the performer, it at the same time denies the unitary presence of the poem, which is to say its metaphysical unity.

Indulge me now as I translate some remarks by Benjamin on psychoanalysis and translation into the topic at hand:

> The question of presence, the plurality within being present, is of fundamental significance for poetry. The presence of the text (the written document) within the performance but equally the presence of the performance inside the text means that there are, at any one moment in time, two irreducible modes of being present. As presence becomes the site of irreducibility, this will mean that presence can no longer be absolutely present to itself. The anoriginal marks the possibility of the poem being either potentially or actually plural, which will mean that the poem will always lack an essential unity. (Within the context of poetry, what could be said to be lacking is an already given semantic and interpretive finitude, if not singularity, of the poem.) It is thus that there is no unity to be recovered, no task of thinking of the origin as such, since the origin, now the anorigin, is already that which resists the move to a synthetic unity. Any unity will be an after-effect. Such after-effects are composed of given publications, performances, interpretations, or readings. The poem—that which is anoriginally plural—cannot be known as such because it cannot exist *as such.*[5]

The relation of a poem to variations created in a poetry reading has not, so far as I know, received previous attention. Variations created in performing "oral" poetry is, however, a subject of Gregory Nagy's *Poetry and Performance*, where, speaking of both the Homeric epics and troubadour poetry, Nagy writes, "to perform the song . . . is to recompose it, to change it, to *move* it."[6] Indeed, Nagy's "poetics of variation" is suggested by two variant epithets for the nightingale in *The Odyssey*—where the nightingale

5. The passage is based on Andrew Benjamin, "Translating Origins: Psychoanalysis and Philosophy", in *Rethinking Translation: Discourse, Subjectivity, Ideology*, ed. Lawrence Venuti (London: Routledge, 1992), p. 24; all the references to poetry are my substitutions made to Benjamin's "original"; I have also elided a few phrases. See also Benjamin's *The Plural Event: Descartes, Hegel, Heidegger.*

6. Nagy, *Poetry as Performance*, p. 16. Nagy specifically cites McGann's work on "the textual condition".

can be understood as a metaphor for the performer of poetry: "patterning many different ways" (49–50) and also "with many resoundings" (39). Nagy quotes Alfred Lord's study of Homer, *The Singer of Tales:*

> Our real difficulty arises from the fact that, unlike the oral poet, we are not accustomed to thinking in terms of fluidity. We find it difficult to grasp something that is *multiform*. It seems ideal to us to construct an ideal text or to seek an *original*, and we remain dissatisfied with an ever-changing phenomenon. I believe that once we know the facts of oral composition we must cease to find an *original* of any traditional song. From an oral point of view each performance is *original*.[7]

The poetry reading, considered along with typographic, holographic, and contextual variants, modulates and deepens what McGann calls the "textual condition". The poetry reading extends the patterning of poetry into another dimension, adding another semantic layer to the poem's multiformity. The effect is to create a space of authorial resistance to textual authority. For while writing is normally—if reductively and counterproductively[8]—viewed as stabilizing and fixing oral poetic traditions, authorial poetry readings are best understood as destabilizing, by making more fluid and pluriform, an aural (post-written) poetic practice. And here the double sense of reading is acutely relevant. For in realizing, by supplementing, the semantic possibilities of the poem in a reading, the poet encourages readers to perform the poem on their own, a performance that is allowed greater latitude depending on how reading-centered the poem is—that is, how much the poem allows for the active participation of the reader (in both senses) in the constitution of the poem's meaning.

I am proposing that we look at the poetry reading not as a secondary extension of "prior" written texts but as its own medium. What, then, are the characteristics specific to this medium and what can it do that other live performance media—instrumental music, song and opera, theater—cannot? The answer may be found in what seems to many the profoundly anti-performative nature of the poetry reading: the poetry reading as radically "poor theater" in Jerzy Grotowski's sense. If that is true, it may show how what some find as the most problematic aspect of the poetry reading may turn out to be its essence: that is, its lack of spectacle, drama, and dynamic range, as exemplified especially in a certain minimal—anti-expressivist—mode of

---

7. Ibid., p. 9, his emphasis. Quoted from Alfred Lord, *The Singer of Tales* (Cambridge: Harvard University Press, 1960), p. 100.

8. This qualification is in response to a comment by Dennis Tedlock on this passage. Tedlock emphasizes that writing is also a performance and as such readily open to variation and revision.

reading. I'm tempted to label this mode *anti-performative* to suggest a kind of rhetorical (in the stylistic sense of "antirhetorical") strategy and not to suggest it is any less a performance choice than the most "theatrical" reading. (John Cage's poetry readings are a good example of this mode.) In an age of spectacle and high drama, the anti-expressivist poetry reading stands out as an oasis of low technology that is among the least spectaclized events in our public culture. Explicit value is placed almost exclusively on the acoustic production of a single unaccompanied speaking voice, with all other theatrical elements being placed, in most cases, out of frame. The solo voice so starkly framed can come to seem virtually disembodied in an uncanny, even hypnotic, way. Such poetry readings share the intimacy of radio or of small ensemble or chamber music. In contrast to theater, where the visual spectacle creates a perceived distance separating viewers from viewed, the emphasis on sound in the poetry reading has the opposite effect—it physically connects the speaker and listener, moving to overcome the self-consciousness of the performance context. Indeed, the anti-expressivist mode of reading works to defeat the theatricality of the performance situation, to allow the listener to enter into a concave acoustic space rather than be pushed back from it, as in a more propulsive reading mode (which creates a convex acoustic space). When a poem has an auditory rather than a visual source (the heard performance rather than the read text), our perspective on, or of, the work shifts. Rather than looking at the poem—at the words on a page—we may enter into it, perhaps to get lost, perhaps to lose ourselves, our (nonmetrical) "footing" with one another. According to Charles Lock, "the absence or presence of perspective marks the crucial difference between 'pictorial' and 'symbolic' signs, both of which are 'visual.'"[9] For a text is the only visual sign system that, as Lock puts it, is "entirely free of perspective" (418). Like a text, auditory phenomena do not permit perspective but they do have an auditory version of perspective, *location*, and that is a constitutive element of the medium of the poetry reading.

This formalist approach to the poetry reading may explain the common dislike, among poets, of actors' reading of poems; for this registers not a dislike of vocalization but of a style of acting that frames the performance in terms of character, personality, setting, gesture, development, or drama, even though these may be extrinsic to the text at hand. That is, the "acting" takes precedence over letting the words speak for themselves (or worse eloquence compromises, not to say eclipses, the ragged music of the poem). The project of the poetry reading, from this formalist perspective, is to find the sound in the words, not in any extrinsic scenario or supplemental accompaniment. Without in any way wishing to undermine

9. Charles Lock, "Petroglyphs in and out of Perspective", *Semiotica* 100, 2/4 (1994): 418.

the more extravagantly theatrical style of reading, I would point to this more monovalent, minimally inflected, and in any case unaugmented, mode as touching on the essence of the medium. For poetry cannot, and need not, compete with music in terms of acoustic complexity or rhythmic force, or with theater in terms of spectacle. What is unique, and in its own way exhilarating, about the performance of poetry is that it does what it does within the limits of language alone.

(Let me note here Peter Quartermain's caution, in *Close Listening*, that the poet's voicing of a poem should not be allowed to eliminate ambiguous voicings in the text; nor should the author's performance of a poem be absolutely privileged over that of other readers and performers.)

The (unaccompanied) performance of poetry has as its upper limit music, as realized in what has come to be called sound poetry, and its lower limit silence, as realized in what has come to be called visual poetry. Visual poetry gets us to look at works as well as read them, while sound poetry gets us to hear as well as listen. Curiously, these two limits intersect, as when a visual poem is performed as a sound poem or a sound poem is scored as a visual poem. It's important, however, to stay focussed on the poetry reading in the ordinary sense, since it seems to me that this mode of reading is most critically neglected—or perhaps just taken for granted, if not derided. Even those sympathetic to performed poetry will remark that most poets can't read their work, as if such a sentiment suggests a defect with the medium of poetry readings. One might say that most of the poems published in books or magazines are dull without that observation reflecting on poetry as a medium. Perhaps it makes most sense to say that if you don't like a poet's reading it is because you don't like the poetry, to pick up on a recent observation of Aldon Nielsen on an internet discussion list. There are no poets whose work I admire whose readings have failed to engage me, to enrich my hearing of the work. That is not to say, however, that some readings don't trouble or complicate my understanding or appreciation. For related reasons, I am quite interested in audio recording of poetry readings. If, as I am suggesting, poetry readings foreground the audible acoustic text of the poem—what I want to call the audiotext of the poem, specifically extending Garrett Stewart's term *phonotext*—then audio reproduction is ideally suited to the medium. (Video, it seems to me, is often less engaging for poetry, since the typically depleted visual resources—static shots of a person at a podium—are no match for the sound track and tend to flatten out the affective dimension of the live performance. For me, the most energetic and formally engaging cinematic extension of the poetry reading is a series of films made from the mid-1970s to mid-1980s by Henry Hills, especially *Plagiarism, Radio Adios*, and *Money*.)

What is the relation of sound to meaning? Any consideration of the po-
etry reading must give special significance to this question since poetry
readings are acoustic performances that foreground the audiotext of the
poem. One way of approaching this issue is to emphasize the oral di-
mension of poetry, the origins of the sounds of language in speech. And
of course many poets do wish to identify their performance with just such
an orality, even to the extent of stressing a "return" to a more "vital" cul-
tural past, before the advent of writing. But I am interested in a broader
range of performance practice than is suggested by orality; in fact, some
of the most interesting poetry reading styles—from Jackson Mac Low to
Stein to T. S. Eliot—defy orality in very specific ways: Eliot through his
eerily depersonalized vocal style (emanating from the mouth more than
the diaphragm); Stein with her all-over, modulating or cubist, resonances;
and Mac Low with his immaculate enunciation of constructed word pat-
terns. Orality can be understood as a stylistic or even ideological marker
of a reading style; in contrast, the audiotext might more usefully be un-
derstood as aural—what the ear hears. By *aurality* I mean to emphasize the
sounding of the *writing*, and to make a sharp contrast with *orality* and its
emphasis on breath, voice, and speech—an emphasis that tends to val-
orize speech over writing, voice over sound, listening over hearing, and
indeed, orality over aurality. *Aurality precedes orality*, just as language pre-
cedes speech. Aurality is connected to the body—what the mouth and
tongue and vocal chords enact—not the presence of the poet; it is pro-
prioceptive in Charles Olson's sense. The poetry reading enacts the poem
not the poet; it materializes the text not the author; it performs the work,
not the one who composed it. In short, the significant fact of the poetry
reading is less the presence of the poet than the presence of the poem.
My insistence on aurality is not intended to valorize the material ear over
the metaphysical mouth but to find a term that averts the identification of
orality with speech. Aurality is meant to invoke a performative sense of
"phonotext" or audiotext and might better be spelled a/orality.

   The audiotext, in the sense of the poet's acoustic performance, is a
semantically denser field of linguistic activity than can be charted by
means of meter, assonance, alliteration, rhyme, and the like (although
these remain underlying elements of this denser linguistic field). Think-
ing in terms of the performance of the poem reframes many of the issues
labored over by prosodists examining the written text of poems, often syl-
lable by syllable, phoneme by phoneme, accent by accent, foot by foot,
stress by stress, beat by beat, measure by measure. The poem performed
conforms even less to analysis of syllable and stress than the poem as read.
Many prosodists have insisted that the (musical) phrase provides a more
useful way of understanding poetry's sound patterns than do accentual sys-

tems, whether quantitative or syllabic, that break poetry into metrical feet. Consideration of the performed word supports that view, although the concept of phrasing and of musicality is much expanded when one moves from the metrical to the acoustic, beyond "free verse" to sound shapes. For one thing, the dynamics charted by accentual prosodies have a much diminished place in the sound environment of a poetry reading, where intonations, pitch, tempos, accents (in the other sense of pronunciation), grain or timbre of voice, nonverbal face and body expressions or movements, as well as more conventional prosodic features such as assonance, alliteration, and rhyme, take on a significant role. But more importantly, regularizing systems of prosodic analysis break down before the sonic profusion of a reading: it's as if "chaotic" sound patterns are being measured by grid-oriented coordinates whose reliance on context-independent ratios is inadequate. The poetry reading is always at the edge of semantic excess, even if any given reader stays on this side of the border. In fact, one of the primary techniques of poetry performance is the disruption of rationalizable patterns of sound through the intervallic irruption of acoustic elements not recuperable by monologic analysis. While these irruptions may be highly artful, they may also fall into the body's rhythms—gasps, stutters, hiccups, burps, coughs, slurs, microrepetitions, oscillations in volume, "incorrect" pronunciations, and so on—that is, if you take these elements to be semantic features of the performed poem, as I propose, and not as extraneous interruption.[10]

Prosody is too dynamic a subject to be restricted to conventionally metrical verse. Yet many accounts of poetry continue to reduce questions of poetic rhythm to meter or regularized stress, as if nonmetrical poetry, especially the more radically innovative poetry of this century, were not *more* rhythmically and acoustically rich than its so-called formalist counterparts. In the acoustic space of performed poetry, I would emphasize *distress* and asymmetry, as much as accentual patter: dissonance and irregularity, rupture and silence constitute a rhythmic force (or *aversion of force*) in the sounded poem.[11] Such counterrhythmic elements create, according

10. I am well aware that prosodists can mask and analyze a performed poem in ways that will illustrate their particular theory (including quite conventional ones)—just as I have. This is no more than proper in such semantically dynamic terrain.

11. The science of dysprosody is still in its infancy, although it is likely to dominate technical studies of unidentified poetic phenomena (UPPs) in the coming millennia. The Dysprosody Movement was founded by Carlo Amberio in 1950. A translation of its main theoretical document, *The Dyssemia of Dystressed Syllables*, from a previously undisclosed language into trochaic hexameter "blink" verse—a form Amberio believes to come closest to the counterintuitive thought patterns of unspoken American English—has long been forthcoming from the Center for the Advancement of Dysraphic Studies (CADS). (Blink verse, invented by Amberio, involves a fractal patterning of internal rhymes.)

to Giorgio Agamben, "a mismatch, a disconnection between the metrical and syntactic elements, between sounding rhythm and meaning, such that (contrary to the received opinion that sees in poetry the locus of an accomplished and perfect fit between sound and meaning) poetry lives, instead, only in their inner disagreement. In the very moment when verse affirms its own identity by breaking a syntactic link, it is irresistibly drawn into bending over into the next line to lay hold of what it has thrown out of itself."[12]

If studies of prosody foundered in the early twentieth century on the inability to reconcile the musicality of poetry with strictly metrical classifications, then recitation usefully transforms the object of study from meter to rhythm, to use the distinction made by Henri Meschonnic, for whom meter is asocial and without meaning, while rhythm is grounded in the historicity of the poem and implies a sociality.[13] The issue is not the written—the text—versus the oral, but the embodied acoustic performance—the aurality of the work—versus an abstract or external idealization that is based on a projection of time as a "smooth" space, which is unilinear, homogenous, and incremental. The new prosody requires an engagement not with abstract time but with duration and its microtones, discontinuities, striations, and disfluencies. Traditional metrics, with its metronomic beats, remains a fundamentally Euclidean system that is unsuited to a full measuring of the complex prosodies of the twentieth century or, moreover, much older poetry as well as the verbal art of cultures that fall outside the purview of traditional Western literary criticism.

In performance, meter is eclipsed by isochrony—the unwritten tempo (rhythmic, cyclical, overlapping) whose beat is audible in the performance as distinct from the text. In *Free Verse: An Essay on Prosody*, Charles Hartman quotes Karl Shapiro's comment that isochrony "equalizes unequal accentual elements by varying the *time* of feet, whether in the ear or in the recitation."[14] Hartman goes on to argue that "equivalence " has "only secondary bearing on English verse" (38); to which I would say: *exactly the same secondary bearing as performance!* Insofar as the performed word is granted a reciprocal status to the text, isochrony becomes a dominant prosodic element, not just in the poetry reading but also in the silent reading (I would now say silent recitation) of the poem, as well as in the composition of poem—whether

12. Giorgio Agamben, "The Idea of Prose", in *The Idea of Prose*, tr. Michael Sullivan and Sam Whitsitt (Albany: State University of New York Press, 1995), p. 40. Agamben's specific subject here is enjambment. Thanks to Carla Billitteri for bringing this essay to my attention.

13. Henri Meschonnic, *Critique du rythme: Anthropologie historique du langage* (Lagrasse: Verdier, 1982).

14. Charles O. Hartman, *Free Verse: An Essay on Prosody* (Princeton: Princeton University Press, 1980). Shapiro is quoted from "English Prosody and Modern Poetry", *ELH* 14 (June 1947): 81.

"by ear" (in Charles Olson's phrase) or by sentence (in Ron Silliman's). In short, recitation rests on temporal rather than syllabic or accentual measure, which themselves may become secondary. This greatly expands the sense of isochrony from slight variations of non-stressed syllables to larger acoustic and lettristic units, and indeed the sort of isochronic practice I have in mind would allow for the equivalence of temporally unequal units. For this complex or "fuzzy" prosody of sound shapes, such polyrhythmic equivalencies are created by performed pauses, syncopations, emphasis, as well as shifts in tempo and pitch; just as on the page equivalencies are indicated by visual organization (lines irrespective of tempo), by nonmetrical counting (of syllables or words), and the like. The page's enjambment and syntactic scissoring become performance's isochronic disruption of syntactic flow, creating a contra-sense rhythm (or anti-rhythm) that is abetted by breaking, pausing (temporal caesura), and other techniques that go against the flow of speech rhythms. Isochrony may also be used to create a stereo or holographic effect, for example in the intense overlapping phrasal units in Leslie Scalapino's readings.

PERforMANCE readlly allows FOR stressING ("promotING") unstressED syllaBLEs, INcluding prepOsitionS, articCLES, aNd conjunctIONS—creaTING SynCoPAtEd rHyThms, whiCH, onCE hEArd are THen caRRied oVer by readERS iNTo theIr oWN reAding of tHe teXT. (Let me stress that, as with many features I am discussing in the context of performance, it is often possible to hear such rhythmic and arhythmic patterns in the process of close listening to the written text of the poem, as in Stein's aptly titled prose-format poem *How to Write*. Gerard Manley Hopkins's marvelously delirious attempts to visually mark such patterns in his texts is exemplary.) Performance also underscores (or should I say underwrites?) a prosodic movement of which I am particularly fond, in which the poem suggests a certain rhythmic pattern over the course of, perhaps, a few lines, then segues into an incommensurable pattern, sometimes shuttling between the two, sometimes adding a third or fourth pattern: the prior pattern continues on underneath as a sort of sonic afterimage, creating a densely layered, or braided, or chordal, texture. The complex or fuzzy prosodics of such sprung rhythm produces the acoustic equivalent of a moiré pattern.

Performance also allows for the maximum inflection of different, possibly dissonant, voices: a multivocality that foregrounds the dialogic dimension of poetry. Hannah Weiner's performance of her *Clairvoyant Journal* is an exhilarating example—three competing voices of one "self" collide with one another in an electric ensemble consisting of Weiner, Peggy DeCoursey, and Sharon Matlin in a tape published by New Wilderness Audiographics in 1976. But I am equally interested in the possibility of

slippage among tones, dictions, accents, and registers in polyvocal per-
formances in which different voices are evoked using performative cues
rather than alphabetic ones. The potential here is to create rhythms and
voicings that are not only supplemental to the written text but also at odds
with it.

Such poetry is more usefully described as polymetrical or plurimetrical
than as "free"; still, our technical vocabulary strains at accounting for more
than a small portion of the acoustic activity of the sounded poem and there
are a number of performative features that are only available in readings
(in both senses) since they are not (readily) scorable in the lexical text.
Ernest Robson, going steps further than Hopkins, developed an elaborate
and eccentric system for scoring pitch and stress in the written texts of
his poems.[15] Among the most resourceful attempts to designate acoustic
features of performed poetry has been Erskine Peters's, in his work-in-
progress *Afro-Poetics in the United States.* Peters, together with an associate at
the University of Notre Dame, J. Sherman, has developed a "special font
to document the sounds, rhythms, and melodies of the Afro-poetic tradi-
tion."[16] The sixty characters in Peters's system designate such acoustic fig-
ures as accelerated line pacing, accented long and short stretches, blue
noting, bopping, calibrated stagger, call-response, chant, crypting, delib-
erate stutter, echo toning, extreme unaccented, falsetto, field hollering,
gliding or glissando, glottal shake, guttural stress, humming, moan, osti-
nato, pegging, pitch alteration (heightened and lowered), quoting, riff,
rushing, scatting, slurring (three versions), sonorous chant stretching,
sonorous inhaling, sonorous moaning, sonorous tremor, spiking, syllabic
quaver, tremolo, and ululating rhythm.

One reason that Hopkins figures so prominently in *Close Listening* is that
he initiates, within the English tradition, a complex prosody that requires
performance to sound it out. With rational metrics, the "competent" reader
could be presumed to be able to determine the poem's sound based on
well-established principles. With complex prosody and polymetricality,
however, the performance establishes the sound of the poem in a way not
necessarily, or not easily, deducible from the text.

Despite these many examples, many poetry performances tend to sub-
mit to, rather than prosodically contest, the anesthetized speech rhythms

15. See Ernest Robson's *I Only Work Here* (1975) and *Transwhichics* (1970), both from his own
Primary Press in Parker Ford, Pa. On Robson, see Bruce Andrews's "The Politics of Scoring", in
Paradise and Method: Poetics and Practice (Evanston: Northwestern University Press, 1996), pp.
176–77.

16. I am grateful to Professor Peters for providing me with relevant sections of his manu-
script. In a chapter entitled "African-American Prosody: The Sermon as a Foundational Model",
he provides detailed descriptions for each of the prosodic terms he employs.

of official verse culture. Indeed, one of the effects of chatty introductions before each poem is to acoustically cue the performer's talking voice so that it frames the subsequent performance. David Antin radically extends and transforms such talk to become the main event of his performances, or "talk pieces", which remain among the postwar period's most provocative critiques of—and useful interventions within—the poetry reading. Conversely, when a poet makes no incidental remarks, it may be to allow the sound of the poem to have its full sway. Clark Coolidge is a particularly adept practitioner of this style, and his remarkable extensions and riffs on speech rhythms are all the more resonant on account of it.

What makes sound patterns expressive? Beats me. But a rose by any other name would no longer rhyme with doze or shows or clothes, unless the other name was pose or glows. A rose by any other name wouldn't be the same—wouldn't arouse the same associations, its sound iconicity might be close but no pajamas. Sound enacts meaning as much as designates something meant.

The relation of sound to meaning is something like the relation of the soul (or mind) to the body. They are aspects of each other, neither prior, neither independent. To imagine that a meaning might be the same despite a change of words is something like imagining that I'd still be me in a new body. (So disagreements on this matter are theological as much as metaphysical—they cannot be reduced to factual disputes.) It won't come as a big surprise to most people that a poet is investing so much in sound—no doubt we've been seduced into confusing the shell for the husk, or is it the pea for the nut?

J. H. Prynne, in "Stars, Tigers, and the Shape of Words", makes the argument quite well, though it does bear repeating, since repetition is never interesting for what is the same but for what is different: While verbal language may be described as a series of differential sound values, and while it makes sense to say that it is these differences that allow for meaning, it does not follow that the only meaning these sounds have lies in their difference from other sounds. Positive meanings adhere to sound in a number of ways. To speak of the positive, rather than merely negative or differential, meaning of sound does not rely on what might be called "pure" sound symbolism—the perception that particular sounds and dynamic features of sounds (as in pitch, constellations of sound, intonation, amplitude, timbre) have intrinsic meaning; though there is much that is appealing in this view, as Walter Benjamin shows in his "Doctrine of the Similar". The claim that certain sound vibrations have an inhering or immutable meaning is the perhaps mystical nodal point of a constellation of iconic attributes of language. Other points in this constellation cluster around the purely extrinsic meanings that adhere to sounds and dynamic features of sounds, either based on historical associations, which over time get hard-wired into some words or sounds; or, more intricately, based on the oral range made possible by a specific dietary pattern that alters the body's sounding board (dentation, palette, vocal cords, breath). Each language's specific morphology allows many possibilities for iconicity—from the physical size or number of characters in a word, to the number of syllables or patterns of syllables in a word, to associations with timbre or intonation or patterning. Iconicity refers to the ability of language to *present*, rather than represent or designate, its meaning. Here meaning is not something that accompanies the word but is performed by it. One of the primary features of poetry as a medium is to foreground the various iconic features of language—to perform the verbalness of language. The poetry reading, as much as the page, is the site for such performance.

Iconicity can also provide a way of hearing poetry readings, where the iconic focus shifts from an individual word to the chosen mode of performance; for example, the stress and tempo. I have already given an iconic reading of Baraka's performance style. John Ashbery's relatively monovalent, uninflected reading style—he is surely one of the masters of the anti-expressivist mode—is marked by an absence of isochronicity, a correlate to the fluidity and marked absence of parataxis in his texts. The cutting out of this rhythmic dynamic is iconically significant.

It is certainly not my intention to reinvent the wheel, just to let it spin words into acts. Any consideration of the relation of sound to poetry needs to point to the pioneering work of linguists such as Charles Sanders Peirce, Roman Jakobson, Linda Waugh, George Lakoff, and many others. In a recent treatment of this topic, *What Makes Sound Patterns Expressive*, Reuven Tsur quite usefully emphasizes a distinction between the perception of speech sounds (the "speech mode" of listening) and material sounds (the "nonspeech mode").[17] He argues that there is a marked cognitive difference in the way a listener hears a material sound—say a flapping flag or the pouring rain—and the way she or he hears human speech. Speech triggers a specific cognitive mode of interpretation in a way that material sound does not. This is something like the distinction Roland Barthes makes, in an essay called "Listening", between hearing (physiological) and listening (psychological).[18] According to Tsur, and following Jakobson, the "poetic function" of language is a third type: it involves *hearing* what we are *listening* to. That is, poetry creates something of the conditions of hear-

17. Reuven Tsur, *What Makes Sound Patterns Expressive? The Poetic Mode of Speech Perception* (Durham: Duke University Press, 1992). See pp. 11–14.
18. Roland Barthes, "Listening", in *The Responsibility of Forms*, tr. Richard Howard (New York: Hill and Wang, 1985).

ing (not just listening to) a foreign language—we hear it as language, not music or noise; yet we cannot immediately process its meaning. Another way of saying this is that the poetic function—what Tsur calls "the poetic mode of speech perception"—rematerializes language, returns it from "speech" back to "sound"; or rather, the poetic mode synthesizes the speech mode of perception and the nonspeech mode of perception. I want to project this frame of reference onto Barthes's evocative speculations on rhythm in "Listening". Barthes uses Sigmund Freud's famous discussion of the child's game of *fort/da*, in which the child tosses out and pulls back a spool attached to a thread, as an example of a primal rhythmic oscillation of presence and absence, miming the presence and absence of the mother at the same time as it makes palpable the structure of the linguistic sign. It's as if when I say "you're here" / "you're not" the sounds are present but *you* are not. In the poetic mode of listening, there is an oscillation (or temporal overlap) between the materially present sound (hearing: the nonspeech mode) and the absent meaning (listening: the speech mode): this is a satisfaction of all reading aloud, as when we read stories and poems to children. The poetry reading allows for a particularly marked extension of this pleasure, especially when the performance seizes the opportunity to make rhythmic oscillations between its opaque soundings and its transparent references. No doubt this helps to explain the uncanny power of a great sound poem like Kurt Schwitters's "Merz Sonata", with its exquisite passages of child-like intoning, which evoked tears from its first hearers. But it also a quality inherent in the structure—the medium—of the poetry reading itself, and it can be found in its most ordinary forms. In this way, the poetry reading occupies a formal space akin to song, but one in which the musicality, or sound-grounding, of the language is produced strictly within the range of speech-mode perception. It is the transformation of language to sound, rather than the setting of language in sound, that distinguishes song from recitation.

As a matter of habituated fact, the distinction between speech perception and sound perception seems well established. I do hear the beat of a hammer, the lapping of water, or the bleat of a sheep in a way that is cognitively discontinuous with the way I listen to human speech. With the speech in which I am most at home, I automatically translate streams of sounds into streams of words with a rapidity and certainty that makes the sounds transparent—a conjuring trick that is slowed by variant accents and arrested by foreign tongues. But this transparency effect of language may be less an intrinsic property of speech than a sign of our opaqueness to the transhuman world, which also speaks, if we could learn (again) to listen, as writers from Henry David Thoreau in *Walden* to, most recently, David Abram in *The Spell of the Sensuous* have argued. "It is animate earth that speaks; human speech is but a part of that vaster discourse."[19] Yet language is not just a part of the "animate earth"; its sounds also echo the music of the *nonanimate* earth. Speech-mode perception, as an habituated response to language, may indeed preemptively cut off our response to nonhuman sounds—organic and machinic—at the same time as it dematerializes human language, muting its sonic roots in the earth as well as the world. Yet while Abram argues that our alienation from the sensuous is partly to be blamed on alphabetic writing, I would emphasize—against such self-proclaimed "oralist" perspectives—that our insistent separation of human and nonhuman sounds is not the result of writing (alphabetic or otherwise) but of human language itself.[20] Alphabetic aurality is not cut-off from the earth but is a material embodiment of it.

In attributing the transparency effect of language to speech-mode perception, I am eliding two prominent developmental models that provide powerful accounts of how and when language works to differentiate its users from their sensorial surroundings. In *Revolution of Poetic Language*, Julia Kristeva writes of infancy as an absorption in a pre-verbal "chora" that is (tellingly) a "rhythmic space" that "precedes evidence, verisimilitude, spatiality, and temporality" and indeed "figuration."[21] Kristeva goes on to theorize the subsequent development of a symbolic order in which a "subject" emerges from the chora when the child is able to differentiate herself from her surrounds. For Kristeva, the chora—which she associates with radically poetic language—is anterior to "sign and syntax," anterior to the linguistic order of language: "Indifferent to language, enigmatic and feminine, this space underlying the written is rhythmic, unfettered, irreducible to its intelligible verbal translation; it is musical, anterior to judgment, but restrained by a single guarantee: syntax" (29). Abram and Walter Ong write not of the development of individual subjects but of human culture, charting the alienation that alphabetic writing inaugurates in previously oral cultures in terms of the loss of the "presence" of the word, for Ong, and the loss of language's interconnectivity with the more-than-human world, for Abram. Yet both of these accounts rely on unilinear, progressivist models of development. The implication is that one stage of human

19. David Abram, *The Spell of the Sensuous* (New York: Pantheon, 1996), p. 179.

20. Dennis Tedlock comments: "But there is nothing intrinsic to the alphabet that makes its effects on perception inevitable. Such writing has been used in many places and periods without any notion that it is an adequate or sufficient notation of the sounds of speech. What is rather as issue is the projection of phonemics (with its linear system of differences) back onto speech and its installation as the very foundation of a flattened (and 'scientific') conception of language. Yet we can recognize that the sounds coming from the next room are those of a person speaking *without being able to distinguish any phonemes!*" (personal communication, September 1, 1996).

21. Julia Kristeva, *The Revolution in Poetic Language*, tr. Margaret Waller (New York: Columbia University Press, 1984), pp. 25–27.

consciousness replaces or supersedes the next and that something like "poetic" language is needed to put us back in touch with—to return us to, or retune us with—the previous stage.

The problem is that writing does not eclipse orality nor does the symbolic law supersede the amorphousness of the "semiotic", any more than objectivity replaces subjectivity (or vice versa). We don't return to anything—turning (tuning) is enough. The power of symbolic—of the ego or the alphabet—does not come in Faustian trade for the virtually Edenic space of undifferentiated connectivity. Moreover, this originary myth is literally delusional, for it leads us away from the concrete material situation of our connectivity through the alphabet, through aurality, through the "symbolic". Better than to speak of the preverbal, we might speak of the omniverbal. Rather than referring to the presymbolic, we might say asymbolic or heterosymbolic. Instead of projecting a preliterate stage, we might say analphabetic or heteroliterate: for aren't the petroglyphs and megaliths—those earliest human inscriptions made on or with rocks— already writing, already "symbolic"?[22] As if the first human "babbling" were not already language, always social, a toll as well as a tool! We go "From amniotic fluid to / semiotic / fluidlessness", where the semiotic is drenched in the symbolic and the symbolic absorbed within the semiotic.[23] As Nick Piombino observes in his discussion of D. W. Winnicott in *Close Listening*, *language is also a transitional object.*

If "orality" or the "semiotic", aurality or logic, are stages, they are stages not on a path toward or away from immanence or transcendence but rather stages for performance: *modalities* of reason; *prisms* not prisons. Or let me put this in a different way: perhaps the first writing was not produced by humans but rather *recognized* by humans. That is, it's possible that the human inscriptions on the petroglyphs frame or acknowledge the glyphs already present on the rock face (Lock, 415–16). Then we might speak of the book of nature, which we read as we read geologic markers or the rings around tree ("can't see me!").

Poetry characterized as pre-symbolic (and praised or condemned as primitive, infantile or child-like, nonsensical, meaningless) would more accurately be characterized as post-symbolic (and thus described as paratactic, complex or chaotic, procreative, hyperreferential); just as such works, when they aver rationality, are not irrational. Rather, such works affirm the

---

22. In his article on petroglyphs, already cited, Lock critiques the term "prehistoric": "Better, surely, to speak of 'ahistoric' . . . and then note that 'ahistoric' also serves well for 'illiterate'; by the word 'ahistoric' we might avoid the pejorative, and the Darwinian tendency" (p. 407). Here I yet again switch frames from human history to human development.

23. The lines are from "Blow-Me-Down Etude", in my collection *Rough Trades* (Los Angeles: Sun & Moon Press, 1991), p. 104.

bases of reason against a dehumanizing fixation on the rigidly monologic and rationalistic. The problem is being stuck in any one modality of language—not being able to move in, around, and about the precincts of language. I am not anti-symbolic any more than I am pro-"semiotic". Rather I am interpolated in their folds, knowing one through the other, and hearing the echo of each in the next. This is what I mean to evoke by "a/orality"— sound language, language grounded in its embodiments.

Human consciousness has as much a sedimentary as a developmental disposition; stages don't so much replace each other as infiltrate or interpenetrate—I want to say *perform*—each other. Consciousness is a compost heap, to borrow a term from Jed Rasula. Neither the symbolic stage nor the rise of literacy marks language's de-absorption in the world. Language itself, speech itself, is a technology, a tool, that, from the first cultures to the first responses to the cry of a baby, allows us to make our way on the earth by making a world of it. The iconic sound shape of language beats the path.

Iconicity recognizes the ability of language to present its meaning rather than to represent or designate it. The meaning is not something that accompanies the words but is performed by them. Performance has the potential to foreground the inexorable and "counterlogical" verbalness of poetry—"thickening the medium" by increasing "the disparity between itself and its referents."[24] When sound ceases to follow sense, when, that is, it *makes* sense of sound, then we touch on the matter of language.[25] This is the burden of poetry; this is why poetry matters.

It is precisely because sound is an arational or nonlogical feature of language that it is so significant for poetry—for sound registers the sheer physicality of language, a physicality that must be the grounding of reason exactly insofar as it eludes rationality. Sound is language's flesh, its opacity as meaning marks its material embeddedness in the world of things. Sound brings writing back from its metaphysical and symbolic functions to where it is at home, in performance.

Sound, like poetry "itself", can never be completely recuperated as ideas, as content, as narrative, as extralexical meaning. The tension between sound and logic reflects the physical resistance in the medium of poetry. Rime's reason—the truth of sound—is that meaning is rooted in the arationality of sound, as well as in the body's multiple capacities for signification. Language is extra-lexical, goes beyond sense, and nothing shows this better than verbal performance, which, like the soundless performance of

24. William K. Wimsatt, "On the Relation of Rhyme to Reason", in *The Verbal Icon: Studies in the Meaning of Poetry* (Lexington: University of Kentucky Press, 1954), p. 217. Wimsatt is referring to poetry as text not to the performance of poetry.

25. See Agamben, "The Idea of Prose", p. 37.

the body, exceeds what seems necessary to establish the substantive content of the poem—what it is saying, its metaphors and allusions.

In sounding language, we sound the width and breadth and depth of human consciousness—we find our bottom and our top, we find the scope of our ken. In sounding language we ground ourselves as sentient, material beings, obtruding into the world with the same obdurate thingness as rocks or soil or flesh. We sing the body of language, relishing the vowels and consonants in every possible sequence. We stutter tunes with no melodies, only words.

And yet sound, while the primary focus of my considerations here, is only one iconically expressive medium of the performing body, and I specifically want to leave room for the apprehension, by non-acoustic means, of some of the features I have attributed to sound. I am thinking of a conversation I had with the English poet and performer Aaron Williamson, who is deaf, in which he noted that he is able to experience many of the physicalizing features I have discussed in terms of sound. Rhythm is an obvious but crucial example: Williamson pointed out that he could feel the rhythm of the poet's performance while reading and looking at (something akin to *listening* and *hearing*) the poet's lips.

Poetry readings, like reading aloud (and this is something most explicitly marked in sound poetry), are a performance of the carnality of language—its material, sensuous embodiment. But this bodily grounding of language is not a cause for celebration any more than it is a reason for repression: it is a condition of human being and a fundamental material for poetry; call it language's *animalady*. Yet, in the present cultural context of the late twentieth century, this animalady loses its force as concrete experience when reified as (represented) speech or sentimentalized as (a return to) orality. The most resonant possibilities for poetry as a medium can be realized only when the performance of language moves from human speech to animate, but transhuman, sound: that is, when we stop listening and begin to hear; which is to say, stop decoding and begin to get a nose for the sheer noise of language.

Beyond all of these formal dimensions of the audiotext and the performed word, a primary significance of the poetry reading rests with its social character. Readings are the central social activity of poetry. They rival publishing as the most significant method of distribution for poetic works. They are as important as books and magazines in bringing poets into contact with one another, in forming generational and cross-generational, cultural and cross-cultural, links, affinities, alliances, communities, scenes, networks, exchanges, and the like. While San Francisco and New York remain the centers of poetic activity in the United States, dozens of cities across the country, and in Canada, Australia, New Zealand, and Great Britain, have active local reading series that serve to galvanize local poetry activity. The range of such activity is so great as to be difficult to document, since the written record is so much poorer than that of publications. This absence of documentation, together with the tendency among critics and scholars to value the written over the performed text, has resulted in a remarkable lack of attention given to the poetry reading as a medium in its own right, a medium that has had a profound impact on twentieth century poetry, and in particular the poetry of the second half of the century.

The reading is the site in which the audience of poetry constitutes and reconstitutes itself. It makes itself visible to itself. And while the most attention had been paid to those moments when the poetry reading has been a means for poetry to cross over to a wider audience—as in the anti-war and other politically oriented readings of the 1960s or in some of the performance poetry of the present moment—the fundamental, social significance of the reading, it seems to me, has to do with infrastructure not spectacle. For this reason I would turn around the familiar criticism that everyone at a poetry reading is a poet to say that this is just what is vital about a reading series, even the essence of the poetry reading. For poetry is constituted dialogically through recognition and exchange with an audience of peers, where the poet is not performing to invisible readers or listeners but actively exchanging work with other performers and participants. This is not to say that reading series geared to a more "general" public or to students are not valuable. Of course they are. But such events resemble nonpoetry performances in that their value is dissemination to an unknown audience more than creation and exchange. They are not the foundries of poetry that a more introverted reading series can be. Poetry, oddly romanticized as the activity of isolated individuals writing mono-logical lyrics, is among the most social and socially responsive—dialog-ic—of contemporary art forms. The poetry reading is an ongoing convention of poetry, by poetry, for poetry. In this sense, the reading remains one of the most participatory forms in American cultural life. Indeed, the value of the poetry reading as a social and cultural form can be partly measured by its resistance, up to this point, to reification or commodification. *It is a measure of its significance that it is ignored.* That is, the (cultural) invisibility of the poetry reading is what makes its audibility so audacious. Its relative absence as an institution makes the poetry reading the ideal site for the presence of language—for listening and being heard, for hearing and for being listened to.

Taps

[In memoriam Eric Mottram]

Sometimes I feel grim \

   come out of the subway, tears on skin

Or meet again on the Danube, the Danube, & sing the old songs
Meet again on the Danube until we've gone to jail

   A voice that eludes reason, manner of insistences,
   hope doubled upon oration, bubbles the turf you
   won't be wanting any more in the morning

      My name is "Interrogation Rooms"
      My name is "Refamiliarization"
      My name is "Standing Up and Ripping Through"

as if you could name love
without turning it into an abstraction
& killing it

      Only twenty minutes to there from here.
  A dollar down & fifty
      more to go. A dollar down
      & turn around, & fifty more to go!

at a moment's spin, recollect what

      is left
      or echo
      what remains

   scrambling up & back

               stairs, dressers, seams

Or meet again on the Danube, the Danube, & sing the old songs
Meet again on the Danube until we've gone to jail!

         Only twenty minutes to there from here.
         A dollar down & fifty
         more to go. A dollar down
         & turn around, & none to go!

Warning—Poetry Area
Publics under Construction

Do publics construct poetry or does poetry construct publics?

Not so fast, where's the shell under those nuts, the nuts under those texts, the texts under those author-functions, the author-functions inside those periods, the periods inside those stanzas, the stanzas inside those ever-loving tats for ticks, quantums for particles, buzz saws for heliotropes, missionaries for bugle boys? The public does not and cannot exist until it can find means to constitute itself; to convene in, on, or about the precincts of language; to explore its multiple, overlapping or mutually exclusive, constituent parts, elements, components, units, fractions, links, bands, conglomerations, alliances, groupings, configurations, spheres, clusters, divisions, localities; to find means of conversation without necessitating conversion, among and between these constituent parts, allowing that these parts shift and reconfigure in response to changing circumstances.

Poetry explores the constitution of public space as much as representing already formed constituencies; risks its audience as often as assumes it; refuses to speak for anyone as much as fronting for a self, group, people, or species.

In the process of recognizing new communities, new audiences, and new publics for poetry, as well as redressing the previous exclusion of groups from our republic of letters, I want to honor the complexity of contemporary American poetic practice over and above its representativeness. Within universities in the 1990s, contemporary poetry is increasingly being taught for the ways it marks, narrates, and celebrates ethnicity, gender, and race. To fit this curricular imperative, some poems may be selected for their explicit and positive group representations. Other poems (by the same poet or by other poets) may seem less useful if they are found to complicate representation because of their structural or formal complexity—their contradictory, ambivalent, obscure, or mixed expressions or inexpressions of identity; or because of their negative or skeptical approaches to fixed conceptions of self or group identity. For poetry may wish to question, rather than assume, group identity as much as self identity—

not to deny that selves and groups exist, or have voices, but to take their description and expression as a poetic, as much as an epistemological, project.

Like many developments in education, the trend toward a representative poetry is as much market or consumer-driven, not to say demographic, in origin as it is ideological. The gorgeous mosaic of students in the classroom, to use former New York City mayor David Dinkins's term, puts an enormous, and appropriate, pressure on teachers to create syllabuses that reflect the various origins of our students as much as their multiple destinations. Yet, like in electoral politics, not every group is recognized as equally significant in the often schematic, not to say gerrymandered, patchwork of multicultural curricula. Similarly, some subject areas such as contemporary poetry are being used to front for the far more static approach to issues of gender, race, ethnicity, and sexual orientation in other areas of the humanities and in the social and natural sciences.

There are good reasons for this unequal development, since contemporary poetry remains an indispensable site for the exploration of the multiplicities, and multiplicitousness, of identities. TV and Hollywood movies continue to provide inadequate, or nonexistent, representations of many groups in our culture. This may help to explain why poetry and the small press are a *central* place for such representations, given the independent press's ability to serve what can as easily be called small or niche markets as "marginal" communities. For some groups in our culture, poetry may be a primary site of basic cultural exchange in a way that is hard to comprehend for those who identify with the cultural representations of the mass media. This is why it is crucial to differentiate share-driven mass media from popular and local and folk-cultural activities whose lifeblood is their low market share—their small scale, let's emphasize, rather than their "unpopularity".

But it is not only sociologically identified "groups" that are unserved or underserved by the majoritarian, market-share-driven, mass media, but also "outsiders" of every sort and kind, of every stripe and lack of stripe, as Maria Damon eloquently argues in *The Dark Side of the Street*. In an increasingly intolerant American cultural landscape, nonmajoritarian cultural activities are stigmatized as elitist and as "special interests" even though these activities are the last refuge of local and particularistic resistance to the big government and big media claimed, by the right, to be the source of our problems. The current attacks on public television and public support for the arts and humanities are a sharp warning that intellectual complexity, aesthetic difficulty, and non-mega-market-driven cultural production have become "minor" art activities that cohabit the same shadow world of poetry and the small press as do group- and outsider-identified cultural practices. For if commercial culture is increasingly dominated by entertainment products that are developed, through the use of focus and dial groups, to evoke maximum positive response at every unit of exposure; then art that is not just figuratively but literally untested, art that evokes contradictory and confused initial response, or simply appeals to a statistical minority of targeted readers, will not be circulated through commercial channels.

It should be no more a surprise to us in the USA, than it has been for the past few years to citizens in the former USSR, that market forces create different, but not necessarily desirable, cultural values compared to those imposed top down by the old-guard of cultural arbiters or commissars.

In the post-Pantheon world of book publishing, the diversified companies that own the major trade publishers are charged with publishing not simply profitable books but the most profitable books. Works that appeal to minor or micro publics, that is to say small constituencies, are excluded from this system in favor of works that appeal to macro publics, which is to say a substantial market share of the targeted audience. The circumstance is somewhat analogous to a TV show with millions of enthusiastic viewers being cancelled for its failure to garner an adequate public.

Yet unprofitable cultural product does continue to be manufactured in the commercial sector and not simply as a result of the inevitable market failures of the entertainment industry. The question is, why are some works published despite their relatively poor profit potential in preference to other works with a similar profit profile? It isn't just nonprofit arts organizations that lose money supporting their particular cultural agendas. Indeed, as far as losing money in an effort to construct a public, the independent and alternative presses are no match for such mainstream magazines as *The New Yorker*, which, despite a circulation that has recently surged to 750,000, appears to be losing as much as $10 million a year (that's something like $13 per subscriber)—an amount that could finance a good part of the annual cost of the alternative poetry presses and readings and magazines.[1] *The New Yorker*'s parent company, S. I. Newhouse, is apparently less concerned with profit than with cultural dominance—legitimating the cultural product that forms the basis of its media empire; for this exercise in hegemony, circulation, and publicity are more important than profit.

Of course, publishing statistics are notoriously unreliable, especially

1. Elizabeth Kolbert, "How Tina Brown Moves Magazines", *The New York Times Magazine*, December 5, 1993, p. 87.

when they concern the amount publishers are willing to lose—less to obtain cultural legitimacy, let me correct myself, than to establish cultural values. According to *The New York Times*,[2] Harold M. Evans, the publisher of Random House's adult trade division, told an audience at the PEN American Center that "the 29 books he published that made it on to *The New York Times*'s 1993 list of Notable Books lost $680,000" and the eight books that "won awards from the American Library Association lost a total of $370,000." Evans went on to say that three of these books had advertising budgets of $71,000 to $87,000 each and that these books lost from $60,000 to $300,000 each. Innovative works of literature or criticism or scholarship that challenge the dominant cultural values of institutions such as Random House are not the most likely candidates to receive this type of support; yet without such subventions they stand little chance of being reviewed or recommended in *The New York Times*, whose reviews are closely correlated to its advertisers. The point is not that official "high" culture, just as alternative-press poetry, requires subsidies; but that a system of selection and support favors certain works over others; it is this system of selection and promotion that allows the media conglomerates to control cultural sectors that they have written off as largely unprofitable. Note, however, that the content of the selections is less important for this system of dominance than the system of selection and promotion itself, since the alternative presses can never afford to lose *as much as* these corporations.

It should be no surprise that it is neither the public nor accessibility that creates official literary product, nor that much of official "high" culture is a loss leader. Advertising and promotion of targeted "loss leaders" are evidently worth the price in influencing literary and critical taste, specifically by fostering a cultural climate in which genuinely profitable products may thrive.

Now should be the time to pull the hat out of the rabbit, the bottle out of the genie, the tree out of the paper, the riddle out of the problem. For example to extol the emerging electronic gateway as the balm for poetry, which will soothe our wounds of poor capitalization and shrink-wrapped publics of long-term outsiders, far-out insiders, subaltern-centric rhapsodes, and other statistical anomalies from the Upper West Side of Manhattan to the Castro district of San Francisco to the vacant lots behind the Galleria mall in Nowhere, USA.

I don't believe that technology creates improvement, but rather that we need to use the new technologies in order to preserve the limited cultural spaces we have created through alternative, nonprofit literary presses and

2. March 2, 1994, p. C20.

magazines. This is a particularly important time for poetry on the net be-
cause the formats and institutions we are now establishing can provide
models and precedents for small-scale, poetry-intensive activities. At the
same time, the new interactive environment suggests new possibilities for
every aspect of poetic work, from composition to visualization to display
to performance to distribution to reading, and indeed, to constructing
publics, this afternoon's putative subject. (You say subject, I say object; you
say focus, I say associate: subject, object, focus, associate, let's call the
whole thing art. But oh, if we call the whole thing art then we must part
and oh if we must part—I'd be the object and you'd be the subject or you'd
be the subject and I'd be the object: let's call the art part off.)

An enticing thing about today's Internet environment is the spirit of
innovation and engagement that prevails. A poem with a sound file elec-
tronically published by *PMC* (*Postmodern Culture*) will get many more "hits"
(user connections) than a poem published in a comparable print journal
because so many people are cruising the net looking for new material. Po-
etry enters into a performance space on the net, providing text-based con-
tent—something poetry is particularly good at!—to an audience hungry
for it. There is some general interest, from an Internet-focussed public, in
the new formats being created, including those by poets and poetry edi-
tors. The result is that for the moment the public of poetry on the net is
unusually eclectic, even open, in their specifically poetic or literary inter-
est. That is, a range of people will read and listen to poetry, or participate
in poetry-based discussion groups and bulletin boards, who would not be
interested in this genre in its print- or performance-based forms (a claim
that also could be made for performance versus print and vice versa). At
the moment, we have on the net something like a general audience for
poetry—a claim that rightly will alarm those people conscious of how
restricted physical access to cyberspace is. (Of the poets I know in New
York, less than 10 percent have e-mail accounts; while in Buffalo, in a
university-based environment, about 90 percent of the poets I know have
e-mail accounts.) But I would argue that it is the current limitation of ac-
cess and programming that gives poetry its particular edge on the net and
as the information superhighway is put in place, the public that will be
constructed by it will return poetry to its hard-core.

Poetry on the net is very small-scale: I am not talking about big numbers
so much as a certain fluidity of audience. At the University at Buffalo, we
have set up an Electronic Poetry Center. The EPC, still under construction,
provides gopher and WWW access to an extensive listing of small press
catalogs and addresses, electronic versions of print journals and archives of
electronic magazines and our Poetics listserve discussion group, recent obit-
uaries, sound files, plus alphabetically arrayed home pages for poets, with

links to all their electronically available poems and essays. A related project is *Rif/t*, an electronic poetry magazine that has 1,000 subscribers. As to the EPC, the number of hits per month has been increasing: we estimate, for 1994, something over 500 "root" connections per month and about 3,600 requests per month for all EPC subdirectories. Some of these requests may be the same user going back for more; at the same time the statistics do not account for all modes of access to the EPC, so the number of total requests is actually higher. In any case, over 500 hits in one month compares favorably to the public for an established literary magazine.[3] Luigi-Bob Drake's *Taproot* magazine is also available on line. The hard copy version of the magazine has a print run of about 2,500, of which 500 are distributed free in Cleveland, its home base. The e-mail version goes out directly to 500 subscribers and is also redistributed to an additional 1,000 e-mail accounts as part of *FactSheet5 Electric*, which in turn is available from over 20 archive and gopher sites with undetermined additional "hits". *Taproot* itself is also available via the EPC.

More startling, and more informative as to the potential for electronic distribution of "literary-niche" audience material, is the incredible success of the electronic journal *Postmodern Culture*. According to co-editor John Unsworth, in the approximately six-month period from May 18, 1994, to December 8, 1994, there were over 40,000 requests for the table of contents of all issues of the journal. In total, more than 358,000 items have been requested from the *PMC* archives during this same period.[4]

Poetry on the net is not so much a positive development as a necessary one. The Internet will become increasingly central for poetry because of the economy of scale it provides, given the high cost of printing and paper,

3. EPC root connections through the main menu are as follows: July 1994, 614; September, 367; October, 429; November, 573; January 1995, 1,079; February, 1,283. Projected total connections to all menu items are higher: January, 6,798; February, 8,083. Perhaps an additional 10 percent accessed the server through Veronica searches or direct gopher connections. [For April 1997 total requests for EPC pages numbered 67,698; for March 1998, total requests numbered approximately 200,000. Of course, a single user requests many files during one visit to the EPC, and, for technical reasons, other users may not be counted.]

4. "The WAIS-based search function for *PMC*, which operates through a WWW fill-out form, is heavily used, with more than 6,000 requests for that. The table of contents for the May 1994 issue (our most popular recent issue) has been requested over 6,000 times. Our most popular single item has been the popular culture column on Krazy Kat, with roughly 2,500 requests for the opening page. By the way, the page of information and archives on PMC-MOO has been requested almost as many times (5,700+). PMC-MOO is now the second largest virtual community on the internet, with 2,718 'citizens', over half of whom have been active on the MOO in the two weeks (prior to this tabulation). And we've had close to 900 requests for the table of contents of the *PMC* book of collected essays. I should add that none of these numbers reflect the non-WWW distribution channels; I don't have stats for gopher or ftp use, but we do have over 3,000 subscribers to the listserv distribution list for the journal's table of contents and calls for reviewers" (John Unsworth, personal communication, January 31, 1995).

the increasing expense for unreliable postal service, the shrinking of the presently tiny public support for literary publishing, and the absence of poetry-committed bookstores in most localities. In the words of Joe Hill, Don't mourn, organize (though there is plenty to mourn over). A crucial prerequisite for that organizing is understanding how this new space will affect the composition and presentation of our work, especially insofar as we respond in our work to this new electronic medium. We also need to explore the implications this emerging space has for the composition and disposition of the publics for poetry.

Unlike poetry on the net, poetry in print and live formats presents few physical limits to access and user-interface given the prevalence of hard-wired body systems for processing spoken language and broad familiarity with alphabetic technologies. Our limits are more conceptual and ideological: the very niche-based, specialized, focussed, small-scale, often non-overlapping readerships that are a fundamental and vital source of poetry's aesthetic and social value.

Many people say that the university, with its captive audience of mostly 18–24 year-olds, has become the primary site for the distribution of poetry. I don't think this is quite true, but few can fail to recognize how much of poetry's public consists of students. This reflects badly neither on poetry nor on universities, quite the contrary; rather, it reflects the appalling lack of public cultural space outside the narrows confines of the literary academy. It is bad for poetry, and for poets, to be nourished so disproportionately; for the sort of poetry I care for has its natural habitat in the streets and offices and malls and parks and fields and farms and houses and apartments and elevators and stores and alleys and parades and woods and bookstores and public libraries.

Sometimes I imagine the kind of audience contemporary poetry would have if it were on the radio on a daily basis: say a new half-hour program every night at 8. The public for this programming would be small, although larger than our current publics for poetry. At the turn of this now turning century, radio promised to revolutionize the distribution of poetry, making widely accessible, at no cost, the new acoustic riffs of the language arts. For, of all our technologies, radio has the greatest potential to create a democratic listening space. Without access to the public soundwaves, subsidiary, privately available, spoken art media (tapes, CDs) cannot flourish. The exclusion of contemporary language arts from the public air, from radio, is a stark warning about what we can expect from the upcoming merging of cable TV, radio, and the Internet.

If contemporary poetry is able to construct only a series of disconnected publics, then poetry is banished from that virtual republic that we aspire to, all the more, knowing it unattainable. For all the utopian promise of technological optimists, the answer is not in our machines but in our politics. For we see in this society a constant erosion of public space— space not privatized for maximum profit, but made available for common use. And so it seems we can only imagine the public square, the town green, a Central Park of our poetries, where, leaving the solitude or sustenance of our rooms or communes, we might jostle against one another, unexpectably mingle, confuse our borders: refigure ourselves, reconstitute our affiliations, regroup.

There is no education in the arts equivalent to having art works available in open channels—public spaces—to intrigue, befuddle, and engage those unfamiliar and familiar, but especially unfamiliar. Such initial points of public access to art must not be abolished; neither should they be privatized, through the restrictions of pay TV or high admission prices. For such sites to have a democratizing function they must be maximally accessible from a physical, technological, and financial point of view, just that what they exhibit may not be so immediately accessible in other ways. We must resist the idea that difficult art is elitist, any more than that science is elitist or that learning is elitist. Such arguments breed demagoguery not populist empowerment. By denying the value of the labor necessary to become linguistically and culturally informed, we encourage the maintenance of an uninformed, indeed, ignorant, citizenry.

If the arts are denied public support, it is not the artists or dedicated readers and viewers who will suffer, for one way or another their commitment will keep them working and they will be prepared to find art in out-of-the-way places. But for the uninitiated, the decline of public space for art can be devastating, for they will have no common place to find non-market-driven art production. Public radio and public television, despite their manifest inadequacies, are, like public arts funding through the NEA and other agencies, a fundamental point of intersection between the public and the arts. They are the town square of art. In a society that has few such points of access, any diminishment of our public spaces for culture is a catastrophe.

Don't lament, or don't lament only: construct.

The Republic of Reality

Suffice it to suppose
that across the street
a humming bird imagines
its nest as spun of
pure circumstance, or
that the corridor beside
the calendar is cloaked
in disarray, arriving
at sometime or other
aboard a bubble cast about
in air or
dumped unceremoniously
into the asymptote
that becomes your
journey's life, I
beside you, cutting in
& over flips of
imperceptible switches
just out of reach of
the laughter, larder,
larceny of inability's
raptured threnody.

Imagine you're on a log or nail
or disposable table-length
heliotrope and the man in the
corner booth buttonholes you
about the price of seats to
the game, demanding more than
could be gained in the course

of a dead-end run to
victory, the children safely
tucked in their cabanas, jumping
three or four leaps at a throw,
mimicking maniacs like it was
going out of the question, when
you fall upon a fellow with
falters and a fit for a glove:
not the machine in your
eye but the ladder in your
mind—two out of one,
five into thirteen & the punch
of it into the exterior, exteriorizing
hunch of terry cloth transversals
and cotton coasters.

Sometimes, alone at night, falling
into what lies beyond sleep,
irritably interrogating the irregular
anticipations of dent & groove,
grovelling toward that station lit
like lullabies, lurching at the
divide between instant and
instantiation, mindful of racks,
lockers, lilts, levels &
lurches; loading capfuls
of collateral musings into
jacuzzi cyclodramas, pedestrian
luggage slides, stiff brocade
souvenir place holders, armoires
with genuine polymer fluting ruggedly
coordinated against a toxocomial
profile of fully monitorable text
transmission and limited access
interface
              —the subject, cheesy
little thing under all this weight,
chewing its cud, relents,
pivoting and bobbing before
lapsing into blank.

In the picture, a man holds
a candle up to a brightly
lit window, his eyes cast
downward. Several flies hover
overhead tracing the lines
of a triangle. Two young
children approach the man, the
younger with arms outstretched
and leaning on one foot, the older
with head peering forward toward
the candle. A wooden table,
crowded with books and papers
and cups, is at the opposite
end of the room from the
window. Above the table
is a picture of a man holding
a candle to a brightly lit
window.

The bandleader takes a puff of
his cigarette then crushes it under
his heel. A delirious midget
delivers toasted almonds to the
corporate tower. Spurting with
uneven temperature, the shower
epitomized her climb from secretary
to sorcerer. The shelves
sagged under the weight of Kevin's
pet rhinoceros. Insolvent and
insoluble, the conundrums of life's
mysteries greeted the weary
passengers on the subway train
to the hidden hills beyond
the visible horizon. Going
no where fast, Sally took
another picture. No hope
was held out for the recovery of
three visually challenged mice who
had brought hope to the financially
challenged village of itinerant
homeopaths.

to be proud
to have blinders
to pull a load
to collapse
to hold hope
to linger
to long
to seem to fail
to be forgotten
to travel suddenly
to invent
to inveigle
to disappoint
to cast adrift
to stare
to be shunned
to gather dust
to tremble
to hold tight
to stray
to fill up cups
to shudder
to tense
to undergo humiliation
to skip
to stall
to make up motives
to tiptoe lightly

This line is stripped of emotion.
This line is no more than an
illustration of a European
theory. This line is bereft
of a subject. This line
has no reference apart
from its context in
this line. This line
is only about itself.
This line has no meaning:
its words are imaginary, its
sounds inaudible. This line

cares not for itself or for
anyone else—it is indifferent,
impersonal, cold, uninviting.
This line is elitist, requiring,
to understand it, years of study
in stultifying libraries, poring
over esoteric treatises on
impossible to pronounce topics.
This line refuses reality.

ENVOI

What falls on air yet's lighter
than balloon? What betrays time
yet folds into a cut? Who flutters
at the sight of song then bellows
into flight? What height is
halved by precipice, what gorge
dissolved by trill? Who telling
tales upbraids a stump when
prattle veils its want?

Stone breaks it not, nor diamonds,
yet splits with just one word: it's
used for casting devils out; still,
fools obey it first.

Notes and Acknowledgments

First publications are given for the original versions of each of the works collected. Many thanks to the editors, interviewers, and organizers who supported, and in a number of cases initiated, this work.

Preface. The epigraph is from "On Being Charged with Writing Incorrectly", which was first published in the *Barbados Gazette* and is collected in *Eighteenth Century Women Poets*, edited by Roger Londsdale (Oxford: Oxford University Press, 1990). The poem was called to my attention by Jerome McGann in his Siren song, *The Poetics of Sensibility: A Revolution in Literary Style* (Oxford: Clarendon Press, 1996).

A Defence of Poetry. *Aerial*, nos. 6/7 (1991). A reply to "Making (Non)Sense of Postmodernist Poetry" by Brian McHale, a discussion of poems by John Ashbery, J. H. Prynne, and myself published in *Language, Text, and Context*, edited by Michael Toolan (London and New York: Routledge, 1992).

The Revenge of the Poet-Critic, or The Parts Are Greater than the Sum of the Whole. Sections of this essay were first presented at "The Reinvention of the Poet-Critic", organized by Keith Tuuma at Miami University (Ohio) in 1994. Citations from Nanni Cagnone are from a special 1993 issue of *Forum Italicum*, edited by Luigi Ballerini and entitled *Shearsmen of Sorts: Italian Poetry, 1975–1993*. Different versions of this essay have appeared in *Michigan Quarterly Review* 35, no. 4 (1996) and *Onward: Contemporary Poetry and Poetics*, edited by Peter Baker (New York: Peter Lang Publishing, 1996).

Thelonious Monk and the Performance of Poetry. Response to editor Lawrence Smith's symposium on the relation of contemporary poetry to the music of Thelonious Monk. Published as "Applied Monk: Preliminary Notes", *Caliban* 4 (1988).

An Interview with Manuel Brito. Written responses to Manuel Brito's questions. There are references in the text to *Recollections of Wittgenstein*, edited by Rush Rhees (Oxford: Oxford University Press, 1984), *The Spoken Word and the Work of Interpretation* by Dennis Tedlock (Philadelphia: University of Pennsylvania Press, 1983), and three films by Henry Hills: *Plagiarism*, *Money*, and *Radio Adios* (see also Hills's *Making Money* [New York: Segue, 1986]). *A Suite of Poetic Voices*, edited by Manuel Brito (Santa Brigida, Spain: Kaddle Books, 1994).

Solidarity Is the Name We Give to What We Cannot Hold. *Political Diction* (1996).

What's Art Got to Do with It?: The Status of the Subject of the Humanities in an Age of Cultural Studies. Presented as the keynote address to Northeast Modern

Language Association meetings in Buffalo, on April 3, 1992. In charting traditions—here and in "Frame Lock"—that can be multiply traced to Montaigne; to Wilde's essay-in-dialogue, "The Critic as Artist"; to Emerson's essays, Thoreau's *Walden*, and Dickinson's "letters"; to Stein's *How to Write, Lectures in America,* and "An Elucidation"; or to Wittgenstein's *Tractatus, Zettel,* and *Philosophical Investigations,* a number of studies prove useful, of which let me single out three: Morris Croll's essential work on the anti-Ciceronian English prose of the 16th and 17th centuries, Viktor Shklovski's *Theory of Prose,* and Roland Barthes's *Writing Degree Zero* and *Barthes par lui-meme.* More recently, consider Wlad Godzich and Jeffrey Kittay's *The Emergence of Prose,* Ron Silliman's title essay in *The New Sentence,* and Ruth-Ellen Boetcher Joeres's and Elizabeth Mittman's, editors, *The Politics of the Essay* (particularly the essays by Joeres). There is also a significant new anthology of innovative prose by women: Lou Robinson's and Camille Norton's *Resurgent,* and, related to this, a feature section on "Women/Writing/Theory" in *Raddle Moon,* no. 11 (1992) and no. 13 (1994). Finally, let me just mention Evan S. Connell's diary/essay/poem *Notes from a Bottle Found on the Beach at Carmel.* "What's Art Got to Do with It" has been collected in *American Literary History Reader,* edited by Gordon Hutner (New York: Oxford University Press, 1995) and *Beauty and the Critic: Aesthetics in an Age of Cultural Studies,* edited by James Soderholm (Tuscaloosa: University of Alabama Press, 1997). It was initially published in *American Literary History* 5, no. 4 (1993).

A Test of Poetry. This poem is based on a letter from Ziquing Zhang, who translated poems from *Rough Trades* and *The Sophist* for *Selected Language Poems* (Chengdu, China: Sichuan Literature and Art Publishing House, 1993); quotations from the poems are italicized. I thank Ziquing Zhang for his early and continuing interest and support and his extraordinary commitment to cultural exchange. *Situation* 4 (1993).

The Book as Architecture. In June 1986, Alan Davies asked me this question: "When you select and balance a gathering of works to make a book, of what does that balancing (and imbalancing?) consist? What factors of the works, as you look at them, seem to recommend them to particular places within what is finally made to be 'this book'?" The discussion of architecture is indebted to a correspondence with the Detroit artist Cay Bahnmiller. *Harvard Review,* no. 1 (1992).

"Dear Mr. Fanelli". *Notus* 11 (1993).

An Interview with Hannah Möckel-Rieke. Conducted by e-mail in February 1994. *Amerikastudien/American Studies,* vol. 40 (Munich: Wilhelm Fink Verlag, 1995).

I Don't Take Voice Mail: The Object of Art in the Age of Electronic Technology. Presented (with slides) at a symposium, sponsored by the Parsons School of Design and organized by Lenore Malen, on "The Art Object in the Age of Electronic Technology", at the New School for Social Research, in New York, on April 16, 1994. I have resisted the tendency to revise this essay in the light of the often oppressively (or possibly exhilaratingly) fast changes in computer technology and the formats for using it. For example, the essay was written before the World Wide Web had become generally available in its current form. The essay is an extension of "Play It Again, Pac-Man" in *A Poetics,* and relies on some of the concepts developed there. *M/E/A/N/I/N/G* 16 (1994).

Weak Links. Preface to Hannah Weiner's *Weeks* (Madison: Xexoxial Editions, 1990).

Claire-in-the-Building. *Mirage #4/Period(ical)* (1993).

Again Eigner. Larry Eigner died in 1996 at the age of 69. I've combined some comments written at the time of his death with a brief introduction I wrote for an Eigner celebration at UC-Berkeley's University Art Gallery in June 1993, which appeared in *Private Arts* 10 (1966). The citations are from Eigner's essay on the cover of the first issue of *L=A=N=G=U=A=G=E*. "The Only World We've Got" was written as a commentary for the 1988 republication of Eigner's "Anything on Its Side" in *O One/An Anthology*, edited by Leslie Scalapino (Oakland: O Books); citations are from this poem.

Frame Lock. Presented on December 29, 1992, at the annual meeting of the Modern Language Association, in Washington, D.C., as part of a panel called "Framing the Frame: Theory and Practice". *College Literature* 21, no. 2 (1994).

"Passed by Examination": Paragraphs for Susan Howe. *The Difficulties, Susan Howe Issue*, edited by Tom Beckett (1989).

The Value of *Sulfur.* Based on a speech delivered at "An Evening with *Sulfur*" at the PEN American Center in New York on October 6, 1988. The original version was published in *Margin*, no. 11 (1990).

Gertrude and Ludwig's Bogus Adventure. Gabriele Mintz is Marjorie Perloff's original name, as she notes in the preface to *Wittgenstein's Ladder*. *Ribot* 5 (1997).

Introjective Verse. Written in response to a request from Olivier Cadiot and Pierre Alféri for a piece about "Olson and Projective Verse" for their *Revue Générale de Littérature* and published in the second issue (1996), translated and chopped into hexameter by Jean-Paul Auxemery. *Chain* 3, no. 1 (1996).

Poetics of the Americas. Written for *"An Area of Act": Race and Readings in American Poetry*, edited by Aldon Nielsen (University of Illinois Press, in press) and first published in *Modernism/Modernity* 3, no. 3 (1996). Much of the material in this essay was presented in a series of seminars at the Poetics Program at SUNY-Buffalo; I am indebted to many of the participants for their response. Thanks also to Nick Lawrence, Robert von Hallberg, and Jessica Burstein for valuable comments on the manuscript; and to Ernesto Livon Grosman for providing me an opportunity to present an early version of this essay at a symposium, "The Poetics of the Americas", at NYU in the fall of 1994. "Bans O' Killing" is quoted with Louise Bennett's permission.

Unzip Bleed. *Hambone* 12 (1995).

Stein's Identity. Stein issue, edited by Marianne DeKoven. *Modern Fiction Studies (MFS)* 42, no. 3 (1996).

Provisional Institutions: Alternative Presses and Poetic Innovation. Presented at the annual meeting of the Modern Language Association on December 29, 1993, in Toronto, at a session of the institutions of poetry, organized by Robert von Hallberg. Reprinted from *Arizona Quarterly Review* 51, no. 1 (1995), by permission of the Regents of the University of Arizona.

Pound and the Poetry of Today. Versions of the first section were posted on March 17 and 22, 1996, on the UB Poetics List, an electronic discussion group, and replies to some previous posts. The second section was originally presented at a symposium, "Ezra Pound: Past and Present", on November 2, 1985, at the Yale Center for British Art and was published in *The Yale Review* 75, no. 4 (1986). *Words nd Ends from Ez* by Jackson Mac Low is quoted with his permission.

Inappropriate Touching. *Talisman* 16 (1996).

Robin on His Own. Presented as the opening address for "The Recovery of the Public World: A Conference and Poetry Festival in Honour of Robin Blaser, His Poetry and Poetics", on June 1, 1995, at the Emily Carr Institute of Art and Design, Vancouver. *West Coast Line* 17 (1995).

Water Images of *The New Yorker.* Published as "Wet Poems" in *Harper's*, November 1989.

The Response as Such: Words in Visibility. A response to "Visualizing the Poetic Text", a double panel on the visual representation of language, organized by Marjorie Perloff; presented at the annual meeting of the Modern Language Association on December 29, 1990. Renée Riese Hubert presented a slide lecture on the use of language in Tapies and Twombly; Johanna Drucker gave a brief history of visual poetry in the twentieth century and presented her own bookworks; Ellen Esrock spoke on imaging and visualization in reader-response theory; Susan Howe discussed the graphic irreducibility of Dickinson's fascicles, in a version of an essay subsequently collected in *The Birth-mark*; Henry Sayre's topic was "Holzer in Venice". I have included some additional remarks, first published in *Modernism/Modernity* 2, no. 3 (1995), on Drucker's *Visible Word* (Chicago: University of Chicago Press, 1994), quoting from pp. 67, 95, and 97. *M/E/A/N/I/N/G* 9 (1991).

From an Ongoing Interview with Tom Beckett. Sections published in *Iowa Review* 26, no. 2 (1996), *New American Writing* 14 (1996), and *Green Mountains Review* 9, no. 2, and 10, no. 1 (1997).

Explicit Version Number Required. *Verse* 14, no. 2 (1997).

Hinge Picture. I take the title from Susan Howe's first book, *Hinge Picture. George Oppen: A Special Issue, Ironwood* 26 (1985).

Reznikoff's Nearness. *Sulfur* 32 (1993).

An Autobiographical Interview. Written in the summer of 1995 via e-mail, with some emendation for this collection. The interview was published in *Charles Bernstein: A Dossier* in *boundary* 2 23, no. 3 (1996); it first appeared, with photos, in *Contemporary Authors: Autobiography Series*, edited by Shelley Andrews, vol. 24 (1996).

Beyond Emaciation. I was delighted by the subject of lecture by J.-F. Lyotard, which I kept hearing as "beyond emaciation", just my topic, so it was with some great disappointment that, after a while, I realized the philosopher's title was "Beyond Emancipation". *RIF/T* 1, no. 1 (1993).

Riding's Reason. I am grateful to Lisa Samuels for suggesting the epigraph and for her comments on the manuscript. Published as the introduction to Laura (Riding) Jackson and Schuyler B. Jackson, *Rational Meaning: A New Foundation of Words and Supplementary*

Essays, edited by William Harmon (Charlottesville: University Press of Virginia, 1997). *College Literature* 24, no. 3 (1997).

Whose He Kidding. Contribution to the "Irony" issue of *Open Letter*, edited by Steve McCaffery (8, no. 1 [1991]).

Unrepresentative Verse. Presented at a panel on "The Difference That Poetry Makes", at the Poetry and the Public Sphere conference, Rutgers University, on April 25, 1997. The organizers asked that we respond to Adorno's remarks on the fate of poetry after Auschwitz and Auden's "Poetry makes nothing happen".

Poetry and [Male?] Sex. This essay was prompted by a question from Douglas Messerli, sent to several writers: "How do you see your poetry as being related to, or as being a product of, sexuality or sexual politics?" My discussion, in the final section, of the "semiotic" is a response to Julia Kristeva's *Revolution of Poetic Language* as filtered through the essays of Steve McCaffery; this is more explicitly framed in a version of part of this essay published as "Panoptical McCaffery" in *Open Letter* 6, no. 9 (1987). The relevant references to Kristeva are provided in "Close Listening". Thanks to Bill Luoma and Peter Middleton for useful comments on this essay. An early version of the piece was published in *Sulfur* 24 (1989).

Close Listening: *Poetry and the Performed Word*. Adapted from the introduction to *Close Listening: Poetry and the Performed Word* (New York: Oxford University Press, 1998), which I edited. Thanks to George Lakoff, Peter Middleton, Steve McCaffery, Peter Quartermain, Marjorie Perloff, Lorenzo Thomas, and Dennis Tedlock for incisive comments.

Taps. *First Offence*, no. 10 (1996), *Colorado Review* 23, no. 1 (1996).

Warning—Poetry Area: *Publics under Construction*. Presented at the Twentieth Century Literature Conference, at the University of Louisville, on February 25, 1995, at a panel called "Constructing Publics", organized by Robert von Hallberg. *Arachne* 3, no. 1 (1996).

The Republic of Reality. *Fifty: A Celebration of Sun & Moon Classics*, edited by Douglas Messerli (Los Angeles: Sun & Moon Press, 1994).